Macintosh

Programming

Techniques, 2E

Macintosh

Programming

Techniques, 2E

Dan Sydow

M&T BOOKS

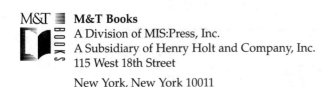

M&T Books

A Division of MIS:Press, Inc.

A Subsidiary of Henry Holt and Company, Inc.

115 West 18th Street

New York, New York 10011

© 1996 by M&T Books

Printed in the United States of America

Limits of Liability and Disclaimer of Warranty

The Author and Publisher of this book have used their best efforts in preparing the book and the programs contained in it. These efforts include the development, research, and testing of the theories and programs to determine their effectiveness.

The Author and Publisher make no warranty of any kind, expressed or implied, with regard to these programs or the documentation contained in this book. The Author and Publisher shall not be liable in any event for incidental or consequential damages in connection with, or arising out of, the furnishing, performance, or use of these programs.

All products, names and services are trademarks or registered trademarks of their respective companies.

Library of Congress Cataloging-in-Publication Data

```
Sydow, Dan Parks.
    Macintosh programming techniques / Dan Parks Sydow. -- 2nd ed.
        p.   Cm.
    ISBN 1-55851-458-9
    1. Macintosh (Computer)--Programming.   I. Title.
QA76.8.M3S9582    1996
005.265--dc20                                          95-51548
                                                           CIP
```

10 9 8 7 6 5 4 3 2 1

Associate Publisher: Paul Farrell	**Managing Editor:** Cary Sullivan
Editor: Michael Sprague	**Technical Editor:** Peter Ferranti
Copy Edit Manager: Shari Chappell	**Copy Editor:** Suzanne Ingrao
Production Editor: Maya Riddick	

DEDICATION

To Nadine
-Dan

Acknowledgments

Michael Sprague, Development Editor, M&T Books, for keeping things rolling and on schedule.

Maya Riddick, Production Editor, M&T Books, for such a fine page layout effort.

Carole McClendon, Waterside Productions, for making this book happen.

MACINTOSH PROGRAMMING TECHNIQUES, 2E

Contents

Chapter 3: QuickDraw Graphics 109

Chapter 5: Dealing with Dialog Boxes 241

Chapter 7: Text and Strings 387

Chapter 8: Power Mac Programming 435

Chapter 9: The Varying Mac 459

Appendix D: Toolbox Routine Summary 579

MACINTOSH PROGRAMMING TECHNIQUES, 2E

Why This Book is for You

If you've programmed in C, whether on a Windows, DOS, or UNIX platform, and are now about to try your hand at programming the Macintosh—this book is for you. If you've tried writing a Macintosh program in the past, but had less than desirable results, this book is also for you. This book starts out with the basics of Macintosh programming—topics such as the elements of a simple Mac application and how the use of memory differs on a Mac compared to other computers. From there you'll move on to working with windows, dialog boxes, and menus. *Macintosh Programming Techniques* doesn't make a lot of assumptions about what you already know as it teaches you the practical techniques that you will use again and again in all the Macintosh programs you'll be writing.

This book is for anyone interested in learning the techniques and concepts basic to writing programs that will run on the Macintosh and Power Macintosh computers. The example code in the book is in the C language. This book does not teach C; it is assumed that you already know either C or C++. The book doesn't, however, assume you've used either of these languages on the Macintosh.

MACINTOSH PROGRAMMING TECHNIQUES, 2E

Introduction

Chapter 1 is an introduction to the basic concepts you need to know in order to program on the Macintosh. If you haven't programmed on the Mac, you'll appreciate the definitions of Mac terminology. If you have programmed the Mac, this chapter serves as a refresher. Chapter 1, like every chapter in the book, ends with an example program.

Chapter 2 introduces you to the elementary organization of memory in the Macintosh. Concepts and terms covered here will pop up throughout the remainder of the book.

Chapter 3 covers QuickDraw—the Macintosh way of drawing. You'll see how to draw shapes and patterns, in both monochrome and color. This chapter also demonstrates how to add color to the content and title bar of a window.

Chapter 4 discusses windows. Here, basic window management techniques, such as dragging and closing a window, are covered. A large part of this chapter is devoted to the handling of multiple windows.

Chapter 5 covers dialog boxes and alerts. This chapter describes the items that appear in a dialog, including the powerful but seldom-discussed user item. Here you'll see how to work with both stationary (modal) dialogs and movable (modeless) dialogs.

Chapter 6 shows you how to manage menus. You'll see how to define menus using resources and then how to change the characteristics of menus within your source code. After reading this chapter you'll be able to enable and disable menus, change the text of menu items, and add checkmarks to menu items.

Chapter 7 discusses strings—how to store text in memory and on disk. In this chapter you'll also see how to change the characteristics of text. That is, how to change the size, font, and style of words that are drawn to a window.

Chapter 8 provides you with the details of writing source code that will properly compile and execute on the new Power Macintosh computers. Here you'll learn how to create a single program that takes advantage of the speed of the PowerPC microprocessor when run on a Power Macintosh, yet is also compatible with older Macintoshes—Macs that don't have a PowerPC chip.

Chapter 9 covers the important topic of writing programs that are compatible with the many Macintosh models and configurations now on the market. You'll learn how to write programs that will run properly on both monochrome and color Macs, and on a Macintosh that has more than one monitor.

Chapter 10 topics are focused on the Finder, or desktop, and how your program interacts with it. Here you'll learn how to allow the Finder to communicate with your program. You'll also see how to give your program a distinctive icon so that users can quickly identify it.

Each chapter ends with an example program. You start out with a simple program that uses just the basics. As you progress through the book, the example programs will become more involved.

What's on the CD

The CD that is bundled with this book has three folders on it. One folder contains the example programs from this book. To eliminate your concern as to whether the examples will work with your compiler, three versions of every example have been included. If you own Metrowerks CodeWarrior, you'll find a folder that holds the source code files, resource files, and project files for all of the programs presented in this book. The same applies to you owners of the Symantec C++ compiler. And even though Symantec is going to phase out their THINK C compiler, you'll find that this book supports readers who own this product—there's a folder on the CD with versions of all the examples in THINK C format. If you don't own a compiler yet, you can still run each of the programs—standalone versions of all nine programs, each ready for you to run, are included.

The second folder contains a handful of Macintosh utility programs that you'll find helpful in your programming endeavors. Among the programs found in this folder is a utility called Swatch, which allows you to "look inside" your own Macintosh. This small program watches your Mac as it runs. It displays and constantly updates interesting and important information about the memory used by each program.

The third folder contains a program called *In Action! Mac Techniques.* This Macintosh program serves as a tutorial that reinforces many of the techniques you'll read about. It displays over thirty animated scenes that bring to life the concepts in this book.

Also on the CD is a limited version of Symantec C++ for the Mac. It will only run on a Power Mac and doesn't contain all the libraries and functionality of the complete version. However, if you don't own a compiler, this will enable you to test-drive Symantec C++—the leading programming environment for the Macintosh.

WHAT YOU NEED

To understand this book you should be familiar with a higher-level language—preferably C or C++. While you should know one of these languages, you don't have to have ever used one of these languages to program the Mac.

All you need to run the example programs included on the disks is a Macintosh computer that has a CD-ROM drive. If you want to edit, modify, and recompile the included source code, you'll need either the THINK C or Symantec C++ compiler, or the Metrowerks CodeWarrior compiler.

The *In Action! Mac Techniques* program is also ready to run. It runs on any Macintosh that has System 6.0.7 or later, including System 7. It runs on a monochrome or color Mac. Your Macintosh needs 1 MB of memory or more to run it.

Chapter 1

Macintosh
Programming Overview

When you look at a Macintosh screen with the menus, windows, and icons that make up its graphical user interface, you discover that it's visually quite different from a PC or mainframe computer screen. The programming effort and techniques that go into achieving this effect are different as well.

If you currently program in a text-based rather than a graphically oriented system, this chapter will serve as your introduction to the differences between the two. If you program for MS Windows, you'll learn the similarities and differences between Windows and the Macintosh. And if you've programmed the Macintosh before, you'll get a refresher on Macintosh basics and perhaps gain a better understanding of the qualities unique to the Macintosh.

DEVELOPMENT SYSTEMS

On a Macintosh, there are a variety of ways of accomplishing your programming goal. Besides using a programming language, you can also create a program using an information environment or an application framework.

Information Environments

Every Macintosh comes with an Apple program called HyperCard, which runs HyperCard stacks. These are programs written expressly for HyperCard and designed to display screens of information. A stack is not a stand-alone application. In order for users to run stacks, they must have HyperCard on their Macintoshes.

Although you can create simple stacks in a purely visual manner, that is, without any programming, most of the interesting stacks are written using HyperTalk, a language designed strictly for HyperCard. HyperTalk's strength is its simplicity, but it is also its weakness. To expand its usefulness, HyperTalk has the capability for adding functions written and compiled in a true programming language such as C or Pascal.

HyperCard's competition comes in the form of an Allegiant product called SuperCard. SuperCard is very similar to HyperCard, but its language is more powerful.

Application Frameworks

An application framework is a sophisticated class library for object-oriented programming. A class library is a group of predefined classes. These classes provide the kinds of functionality needed by most programs, such as opening and closing files, printing, and working with documents. The effect is to give you a functioning program shell. You write a minimal amount of code to turn this generic shell into a complete application that meets your needs.

Metrowerks's PowerPlant, Symantec's THINK Class Library, and Apple's MacApp are application frameworks. With an application framework, you write the guts of a program. As an example, you write the code to display what goes into a window, while the prewritten framework code manages the window for you.

Programming Languages

Most programmers who create programs for the Macintosh use a conventional programming language that allows them to write source code and then compile and link that code into a stand-alone application. You can buy a Macintosh compiler for any of the major, and most of the less-than-major, programming languages. These include C++, C, Pascal, FORTRAN, and Lisp.

This book assumes you will be using a programming language, rather than one of the information environments or an application framework mentioned previously. Most of the example code provided in this book is in C, but the concepts and techniques are applicable to any higher-level language, including C++ and Pascal.

About Macintosh Programming

The Macintosh has gained its enormous popularity with users because of its ease of use—its reputation as "the computer for the rest of us." For programmers, its reputation is altogether different. While its GUI (graphical user interface) makes learning to *use* the Macintosh a simple process, it does nothing to make *programming* it easy. The "Macintosh way" presents a host of new challenges to programmers. If you are a PC or mainframe programmer, be prepared to reorient yourself—completely.

If you are an MS Windows programmer you already know many of the programming concepts that will be new to others. But don't get too relaxed—Windows programming differs from Macintosh programming in many respects, and you'll still have much to learn.

If you've programmed the Macintosh, but aren't confident or satisfied with the level you are now at, it may be because you've pieced together your Macintosh applications without a sound knowledge of basic Macintosh programming techniques.

This book covers the fundamentals of Macintosh programming through in-depth discussions of general techniques. It then backs up that theory by providing many straightforward examples. You will receive a firm foundation on which you can build the Macintosh programs you want, regardless of your choice of programming language.

BITMAPPED GRAPHICS

The Macintosh, like other systems that use a GUI, uses *bitmapped* graphics. Bitmapped means that every pixel, or display dot, shown on the screen has a corresponding bit, or bits, in memory. The corresponding memory controls the status of each pixel. For a monochrome system, the memory keeps track of whether a pixel is on or off. For a color system, the memory keeps track of the color of each pixel. By way of contrast, in a character-mapped system a program cannot control pixels on the screen; it can control only text characters. Characters are located on a character grid, usually 25 rows by 80 columns.

In a bitmapped system, each pixel is specified by a pair of coordinates that define a point, as in (20, 75). The first coordinate in the pairing describes the pixel's horizontal value; the second its vertical value. Pixel numbering begins at the upper-left corner of the screen, which corresponds to point (0, 0). Using this numbering system you can reference any pixel on the screen by listing its horizontal and vertical values.

To draw to the screen you must first specify a starting location, then perform the drawing operation. Here's an example:

```
MoveTo(30, 50);  /* move to pixel (30, 50)                    */
Line(0, 100);    /* draw a line downward, 100 pixels in length */
```

Unlike text-based systems, a bitmapped system allows you to draw text anywhere on the screen. Note the use of the word *draw* when speaking of placing text onto the screen. To the Macintosh, the distinction between displaying text and drawing a shape is slight. In either case, specific pixels are turned on to achieve the desired effect. Figure 1.1 shows both text and graphics and an enlarged view of the affected pixels. Figure 1.1 also illustrates the advantage of using bitmapped graphics—it's easy to mix text and graphics and place them anywhere on the screen.

Figure 1.1 On a Macintosh, both graphics and text are bitmapped.

EVENT-DRIVEN PROGRAMMING

Programs that don't use a graphical user interface normally run in a sequential manner. Each time you run a program of this type you execute steps in the same order. For a program that displays four screens of information, like that shown in Figure 1.2, the program's user would generally view the four screens one after another in a predefined order.

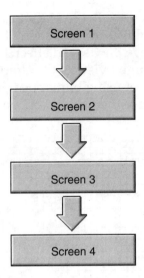

Figure 1.2 Structure of a non-Macintosh program.

The key difference between these two types of programs is something Apple refers to as an *event*. A user's action, such as the press of a key or a click of the mouse button, produces an event. When an event occurs, the Macintosh system software automatically saves information about the event in an event record. The event record consists of fields that contain information about an event. If the event was a mouse click, the event's *what* field would then hold that information. That is, this field would hold the type of event that just occurred. The event record's *where* field would hold the screen location where the mouse click occurred.

Programs that use a GUI don't follow this linear pattern, nor are they limited to full screens to display their information. Instead, they use windows. The program's user is free to view the windows in any order. For a Macintosh, the window selection would most likely be based on a menu choice. The method used to make this selection is a keyboard or, more often, a pointing device such as a mouse. Figure 1.3 shows the structure of a Macintosh program.

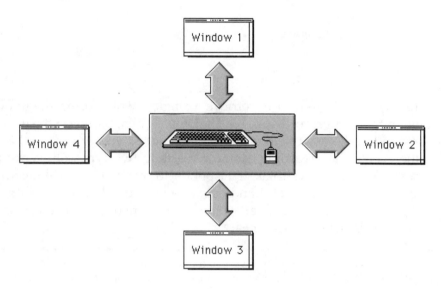

Figure 1.3 The structure of a Macintosh program.

Macintosh programs are controlled by an *event loop*. The purpose of this loop is to unceasingly retrieve and process events. As events occur they are stored in an event queue, which is serviced by the event loop. Here's a simple event loop:

```
Boolean      allDone = false;
EventRecord  theEvent;

while ( allDone == false )
{
    WaitNextEvent( everyEvent, &theEvent, 15L, nil );

    switch ( theEvent.what )
    {
        case mouseDown:
            HandleMouseDown();
            break;
```

```
        case keyDown:
            HandleKeyDown();
            break;
    }
}
```

You use `WaitNextEvent()` to retrieve a single event, storing the information in the event record variable `theEvent`. Then, based on the event
type (found in the what field of the `EventRecord`), you process, or handle, the event. The preceding example reacts to two types of events: a
mouse click and a keystroke. It responds to an event by calling the
appropriate function that handles an event of that type—either
`HandleMouseDown()` or `HandleKeyDown()`. You are responsible for writing these event-handling routines.

N O T E   If you're an MS Windows programmer, retrieving events by calling
`WaitNextEvent()` from within a loop should sound very familiar to you.
Windows programmers poll for messages by calling `GetMessage()` from
within a loop. One big difference is that on a Macintosh there is a single
event stream that all applications are aware of, while on Windows each window deals with its own designated message stream.

The accepted event-handling practice is outlined in the following steps.
Figure 1.4 illustrates these steps for a program that handles three different event types.

- Use `WaitNextEvent()` to retrieve an event and store it in an
  event record.
- Use a `switch` statement to determine the type of the event.
- Based on the event type, call a function to handle the event.
- Repeat the process.

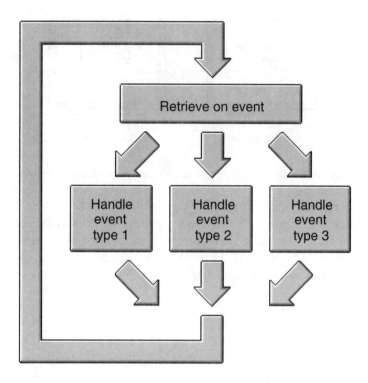

Figure 1.4 The structure of an event-driven program.

If you've programmed in the past, but not on a platform with a graphical user interface, this discussion shouldn't be entirely foreign to you. You've still written programs that have a bit of this event-driven flavor to them. You may have written a program that displayed a menu on the screen, like the first one in Figure 1.5.

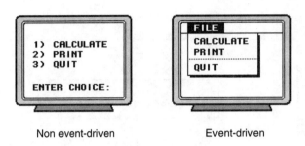

Non event-driven   Event-driven

Figure 1.5 Looping in non-event-driven and event-driven programs.

If you've written a program with output like that shown on the screen on the left side of Figure 1.5, then your program did so using a loop. At each pass through the loop, keyboard input might have been retrieved using the scanf() function. How your program then handled things depended on the value of the retrieved number. Here's an example:

```
Boolean   allDone = false;
int       theChoice;

while ( allDone == false )
{
    scanf( "%d", &theChoice );

    switch ( theChoice )
    {
        case 1:
            DoCalculations();
            break;
        case 2:
            PrintResults();
            break;
        case 3:
            allDone = true;
            break;
    }
}
```

The monitor pictured on the right side of Figure 1.5 shows how a Macintosh would display choices to the user. While the scanf() example waits for user input and then responds to it, it is not truly event- driven, it forces the user to wait at the screen until a choice is made from the limited menu. The Macintosh, on the other hand, is aware of all types of events, including keyboard input, mouse clicks, and the insertion of a disk into the computer. Most importantly, the user's actions control the type of event and the time the event will occur. This freedom and power that the Macintosh user enjoys are what make events and the event loop such an important aspect of Macintosh programming.

RESOURCES

All of the elements that make up a program's interface—such as menus, windows, dialog boxes, and icons—are defined by resources. A resource defines an element by holding descriptive information about that element. For example, a resource that defines a window will hold information about the window's size, placement on the screen, whether the window has a zoom box in its title bar, and so forth.

Resources are not part of your source code, though your source code will be aware of them, use them, and eventually become linked to them. Instead, a resource is code that is held in a file separate from the source code file. The code in the *resource file* is viewed not as words or numbers, but as the interface element that the code defines.

It is advantageous to create an element of the interface as a resource because a resource can be:

- Created and edited graphically, with no programming knowledge—even after a program has been developed and distributed.
- Copied to another program for reuse.

N O T E

For MS Windows programmers, much of this should sound familiar. Macintosh resources and Windows resources are very similar. If you've only programmed for non-Windows PCs, or mainframes, pay close attention. In the Macintosh world, an appreciation for resources is very important.

Resource Editors

To create a resource, you use a resource-editing program such as Apple's ResEdit or Mathemaesthetics' Resorcerer. You save a resource, or several resources, in a resource file. The icons for ResEdit and a ResEdit file are shown in Figure 1.6.

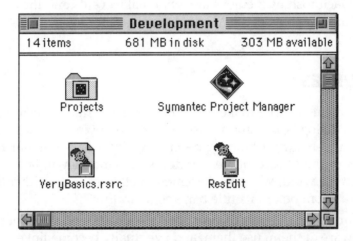

Figure 1.6 The icons of ResEdit and a ResEdit file.

Different elements of a program's interface are defined by different resource types. Each resource type has a four-character, case-sensitive name. For example, the resource type of a menu is MENU, the resource type of a window is WIND, and the resource type of a dialog box is DLOG.

A program such as ResEdit allows you to graphically create a separate resource for each part of your application's interface. Figure 1.7 shows a MENU resource being created. Instead of writing source code to define the items in a menu, you use ResEdit to create a MENU resource.

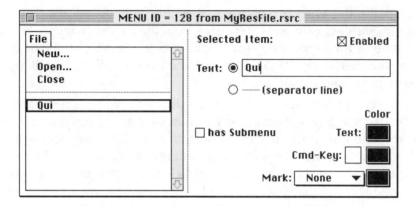

Figure 1.7 Editing a MENU resource in ResEdit.

 MS Windows programmers may be familiar with editing resources using a tool such as Borland's Resource Workshop or Microsoft's AppStudio. ResEdit is Apple's version of a resource-editing program. As in Windows, resources can be created by purely visual means or by compiling a text representation of resources. Unlike Windows, most Macintosh programmers standardize on the visual method—ResEdit or Resorcerer.

N O T E

Creating a Resource File and a Resource Using ResEdit

When you launch ResEdit, you'll encounter a dialog box that asks you to either open an existing resource file or create a new file. Click the **New** button to create a new file. After typing in a file naming and clicking the **New** button, you're ready to add a resource to the *type picker*. The type picker is the name of the main ResEdit window. This window displays an icon for each resource type in the resource file. Figure 1.8 shows a type picker for a resource file that holds only one type of resource—the WIND type.

Initially, the type picker for a new file will be empty. To add a resource, select **Create New Resource** from the Resource menu. Scroll to the name of the type of resource you wish to create, click once on the name, and then click the **OK** button. When you do, ResEdit will open a *resource picker* and a *resource editor*.

The type picker lets you know the different types of resources in a file, but it doesn't reveal how many resources of any given type are in the file. For example, a file usually holds several MENU resources—one for each menu that will appear in a program's menu bar. To see the resources of a given type, you double-click on the resource type's icon in the type picker. When you do, you'll see a *resource picker*. The resource picker lists each resource of a given type. In Figure 1.8, the WIND resource picker shows that this file holds a single WIND resource.

When you create a new resource—such as the new WIND resource created above—ResEdit opens an editor in which to edit the resource. To view or edit an existing resource, double-click on its **ID** in the resource picker. This brings up an editor. The look and actions of ResEdit editors vary with the resource being edited. In Figure 1.8 you can see the result of double-clicking on **128** in the resource picker. In that figure the resource editor is the WIND editor. From the figure, you can see that it's easy to change the size and placement of a window by typing in new values in the four editable text boxes. Changing the look of the window is accomplished by clicking on one of the icons in the row of icons at the top of the WIND resource editor.

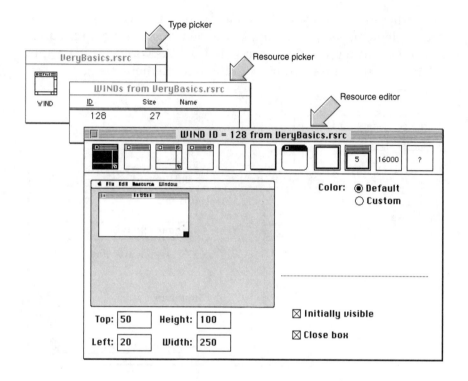

Figure 1.8 Editing a WIND resource in ResEdit.

After adding a resource or resources to a file, select **Save** from the File menu to save the file. Then either close the file or quit ResEdit.

ResEdit doesn't only make window resource editing easy—other interface elements are just as easy to define using this resource editor. In Figure 1.9 you can see a menu being defined. As you'll see in Chapter 6, the MENU resource allows your program to implement menus.

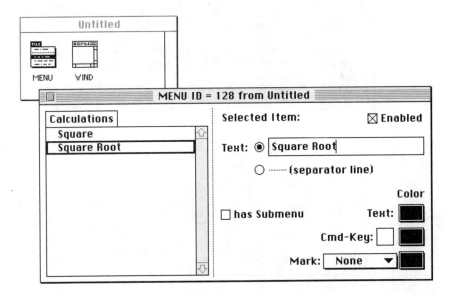

Figure 1.9 Editing a MENU resource in ResEdit.

 NOTE As mentioned, a resource file can, and usually does, hold more than one type of resource. Figure 1.9 shows a resource file with two types of resources in it. A resource file can also hold more than one resource of any given resource type. Figure 1.9 doesn't reveal how many WIND or MENU resources are in the as yet untitled resource file—it only shows that there are two *types* of resources present. To see the various resources of any given type, double-click on the resource icon in the type picker window of a resource file. For example, double-clicking on the WIND icon would display the WIND resource picker, which lists the different WIND resources in the file.

Resources, Source Code, and Applications

When you look at your Macintosh monitor, everything you see originated as a resource. Figure 1.10 illustrates the following:

- The menu bar has an MBAR resource that specifies which individual menus are in it.

- Each individual menu has its own MENU resource that defines the items in that menu.

- A window has a WIND resource that defines its size and initial position on the screen.

- A dialog box has a DLOG resource that defines its size and initial position.

- A dialog box has a second resource, the DITL, that defines items such as buttons that are to appear in the dialog box.

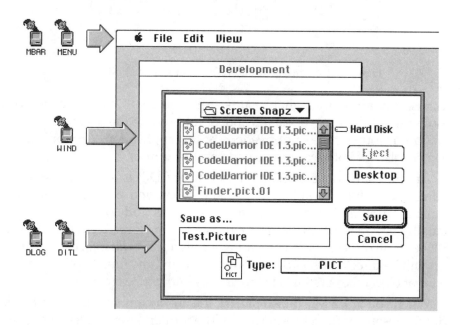

Figure 1.10 Everything that you see on your Macintosh screen
has a resource that defines it.

Once you've used a resource editor to create the resources that define the interface elements of your program, you write source code that uses these resources. Throughout this book the source code/resource connection will be mentioned—and expanded upon.

When it is time to turn your source code into a stand-alone application, your compiler compiles your source code, then joins the compiled code with the resources in your resource file by linking them together. The result is an application. This process is shown in Figure 1.11.

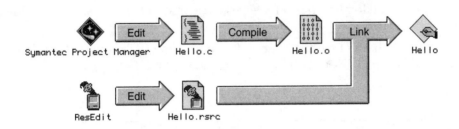

Figure 1.11 Source code and resources form an application.

Because the application that results from the combining of code with resources holds a copy of each resource that was in the resource file, the separate resource file is not needed by the application. An application then consists of both executable code and resources.

An integrated development environment (IDE) is a combination of a source code editor, compiler, and linker. When you use an IDE like the Symantec Project Manager (SPM) or Metrowerks CodeWarrior, you won't actually see a file such as the *Hello.o* file shown in Figure 1.11. A Macintosh IDE holds all object code in something it calls a *project file*. Since your attention will be directed toward the source code and the final application, the fact that object files are invisible to you should not be a concern.

When you link a Macintosh project, the linker combines the object code with the resources from a resource file. The result is a single file—the application, or program. If resources and source code are eventually joined, why do they initially exist in separate files? Because source code is created with a text editor, while resources are created with a resource editor.

Resource Types

There are more than 100 different resource types. You'll probably need to use fewer than a dozen types in your programs. The following is a list of some of the more common resource types. In your reading of this text you'll encounter each of these types—and a few others.

ALRT	Defines the look of an alert box
BNDL	Relates an icon to a program
CODE	All the instructions of a program
DITL	Contents of a dialog box
DLOG	Defines the look of a dialog box
ICN#	List of icons
PICT	Picture
SIZE	Partition size of a program
STR#	List of strings
WIND	Defines the look of a window
snd	Sound

THE TOOLBOX

With a resource editing tool such as ResEdit, creating menus, windows, and dialog boxes is easy. But a resource contains only a description of a piece of the interface—it doesn't do anything with it. For example, ResEdit easily allows you to list the items that will be in a menu. To then display that menu—to track the user's mouse movements over it and then drop it down and display the items in it—you need to write source code.

The menu scenario just described shows up in every Macintosh program. You can therefore infer that much of the code to perform that scenario should look the same in any Macintosh program. The phrase "don't reinvent the wheel" comes up a lot in programming, and Macintosh takes this phrase to its limit. Apple programmers wrote several thousand routines that handle all of the actions common to most Macintosh programs. They then graciously gave them away—free. Well, not exactly free. To get the thousands of routines, you have to buy a Macintosh computer.

Instead of creating libraries of routines, as is the common practice with languages for other computers, Apple has taken the code that makes up these routines and burned it into ROM chips that are then placed inside each Macintosh. Collectively, Apple refers to these routines as the *Macintosh User Interface Toolbox*, or Toolbox for short.

N O T E If you're a PC or mainframe programmer who has never programmed in a windowed environment, don't let the idea of these invisible routines overwhelm you. On a mainframe or PC you also use routines that you didn't write, like standard C library functions such as `strlen()` and `printf()`. You just don't have a fancy name for them like the Macintosh User Interface Toolbox!

Figure 1.12 shows how the Toolbox will be shown in the remainder of this chapter. This figure emphasizes the point that the code for Toolbox routines lies in ROM and not in your source code.

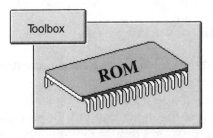

Figure 1.12 The Toolbox is in ROM.

N O T E PCs have software built into their ROMs too—the ROM BIOS services. The difference? The Macintosh Toolbox is easier to use and provides a means to display and work with graphics and a sophisticated user interface.

Resources, Source Code, and the Toolbox

Earlier it was stated that you first create a resource, then write source code that uses that resource. This, of course, implies that source code somehow communicates with resources. Toolbox routines provide this communication link. Here's a brief example:

```
WindowPtr  theWindow;
theWindow = GetNewWindow( 128, OL, (WindowPtr)-1L );
```

The routine GetNewWindow() is a Toolbox function that locates a WIND resource and loads the resource data into memory. The code that makes up the Apple-supplied function GetNewWindow() exists in ROM. When your source code makes a call to GetNewWindow(), your program is interrupted while the code in ROM is executed. In Figure 1.13 an application named *Hello* is shown as executable code (denoted here by a series of ones and zeros) and two WIND resources (denoted here by ResEdit icons). Figure 1.13 emphasizes that a call to GetNewWindow() means that the program's code accesses Toolbox code in the Macintosh ROM.

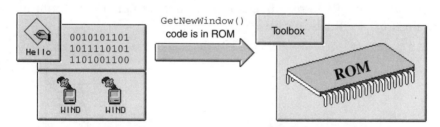

Figure 1.13 Calling a Toolbox routine from within the *Hello* program.

The GetNewWindow() code in ROM searches the program's resources for the desired WIND resource—that's shown in Figure 1.14. Notice in the above example that there are parameters passed to GetNewWindow(). The first parameter is an ID that tells the Toolbox which WIND is to be used. Because an application may hold more than one WIND resource, it's necessary to specify which WIND resource to use.

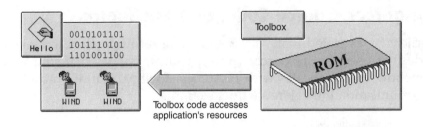

Figure 1.14 Getting resource information from the application.

NOTE

The fact that resources exist in a resource file, and then in an application, is a source of confusion to many. Recall that resources begin their life in a resource file—just as code begins its life in a source code file. When an application is generated from the CodeWarrior IDE or the Symantec Project Manager, the code from the source code file and the resources from the resource file get merged. The final stand-alone application contains both code and resources, and thus no longer needs either the source code file or the resource file in order to execute.

Once the correct WIND resource is found, its data gets loaded into memory. Figure 1.15 illustrates this.

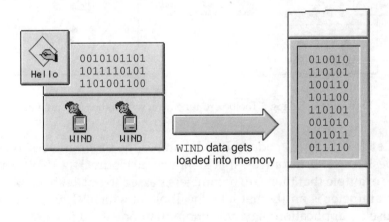

Figure 1.15 Loading WIND resource data into memory.

NOTE

If an application consists of both code and resources, shouldn't one part of a program be able to access another part without going through the aforementioned song and dance? The answer, of course, is "No"—the code must explicitly load the resource data. It all has to do with application launching and memory. When a program is launched, all of its code and all of its resources aren't loaded into memory. In particular, most of the resources remain on disk. So when a program needs to access a resource, the resource's data need to be loaded into memory.

GetNewWindow() finishes by returning a pointer to the data to the program. When the application needs to access the data, it can then do so by accessing memory via this pointer. The window pointer variable, of the Macintosh data type WindowPtr, provides the means of identifying this one particular window. When the application needs to perform operations on the window—such as moving it or drawing graphics to it—the window's pointer is used to reference the window. For example, if the program wants to hide this newly created window from the view of the user, the program will change some of the WIND data that is now in memory. This data manipulation won't be obvious, though. That's because rather than directly altering data you'll let Toolbox routines do the dirty work. Hiding a window, for example, can be done as follows:

```
HideWindow( theWindow );
```

In the above code, HideWindow() is a Toolbox routine and theWindow is a WindowPtr variable—the same window pointer returned by the call to GetNewWindow(). By simply passing a Toolbox routine the address of a window's data, you let the Toolbox do the work of locating the window data and changing the appropriate part of that data to reflect the new condition of the window. Figure 1.16 illustrates.

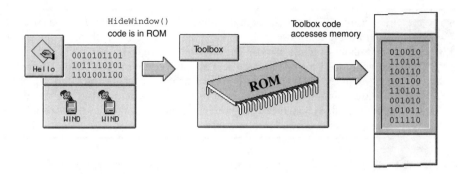

Figure 1.16 The source code, resources, and the Toolbox.

 This section uses windows to demonstrate how the Toolbox loads resource data into memory. In Chapter 4 you'll see more on this topic as it pertains to windows. Other chapters will discuss the loading of other resource types.

NOTE

Toolbox Routines and Application-Defined Routines

The GetNewWindow() routine is just one of the thousands of functions that make up the Macintosh Toolbox. This book covers many of these Toolbox functions. The example snippets and programs often make calls to Toolbox functions as well as calls to non-Toolbox functions. So that you can readily tell the difference between the two types of functions, discussions in this text will always refer to a Toolbox function as just that—a Toolbox function. Other functions will be referred to as *application-defined* routines. Application-defined means that you define these functions in your source code—they aren't supplied by Apple. Consider the following snippet:

```
void  main( void )
{
   WindowPtr  theWindow;

   ...
   HideWindow( theWindow );
```

```
PerformCalculations();
   ...
}
```

In describing the above snippet, this text might say "...the Toolbox function HideWindow( ) is called before the application-defined function PerformCalculations( ) executes.

THE OPERATING SYSTEM

Like the Toolbox, the code that makes up the Macintosh Operating System is located in ROM—that's why Figure 1.17 is so similar to Figure 1.13. The Operating System is different from the System file, which is found in the System Folder and is described in the next section.

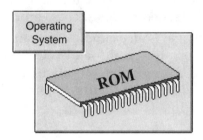

Figure 1.17 The Operating System is in ROM.

The Operating System, like the Toolbox, consists of routines that you can access by way of function calls in your source code. The difference between the routines in the Toolbox and those of the Operating System is in the level of the tasks they perform. Operating System routines deal with low-level tasks such as allocating memory and handling keystrokes and disk insertions. Toolbox routines deal with higher-level tasks. The result of a higher-level chore is generally more noticeable to the user— the display of windows and the drawing of shapes or pictures in those windows are accomplished by Toolbox routines.

You perform an Operating System task just as you do a Toolbox task—you make the appropriate function call. An example of an

Operating System call is Eject(), which physically ejects a disk from the floppy disk drive.

NOTE

PC and mainframe programmers will appreciate the simplicity of accessing the Macintosh Operating System. To perform a task, you need only know the proper Operating System routine to call; you use no direct-memory addressing using jumps or interrupts.

SYSTEM SOFTWARE

Now that you know what Toolbox routines and Operating System routines are, you should also know that you can refer to them collectively as *system software*. System software is divided into the two broad categories of the Toolbox and the Operating System. It is then further sectioned into groups of functionally related routines. These groups are called *managers*.

The Window Manager is an example of a manager. It consists of routines that allow you to create and work with windows—the GetNewWindow() and HideWindow() routines that you've seen in this chapter are part of the Window Manager. Some of the other managers are shown in Figure 1.18.

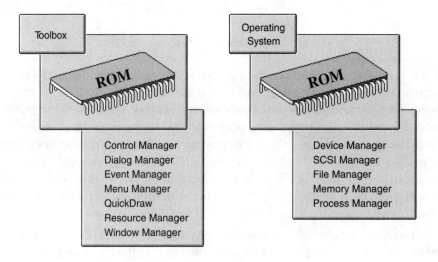

Figure 1.18 Some of the Macintosh managers.

From the names of the managers in Figure 1.18 you can see that the Toolbox managers deal with the user interface: windows, dialog boxes, and menus. The managers that comprise the Operating System, on the other hand, deal with low-level tasks such as memory management and the control of devices such as monitors. Many of the individual managers shown in Figure 1.18 will be discussed in the remainder of this book.

THE SYSTEM FILE AND FINDER

The System Folder that appears on every Macintosh contains two files of particular note: the System file and the Finder.

The System File

The System file, not to be confused with the Operating System in ROM, holds resources that are accessible by all programs. These resources allow your programs to display the standard Macintosh graphical user interface. The System file also holds the code for some Toolbox routines. Earlier it was mentioned that the Toolbox routines were housed in ROM—so the preceding statement requires some elaboration.

As years have gone by, the price of memory has dropped markedly, and computers have become more sophisticated. New models of the Macintosh have taken advantage of these two facts. Over the years, the amount of ROM in a Mac has increased, as has the number of Toolbox routines. That means that owners of newer model Macs have Toolbox routines in their ROM that aren't found in the ROM of earlier model Macintoshes. Owners of older Macs can't just replace the ROM chips in their Macs—yet they can get access to the same routines found in the new ROM chips. This is made possible by the inclusion of new Toolbox routine in the System file. If the owner of an older Mac upgrades to a newer version of the System file (say, from System 6.0.7 to System 7.5), that owner gets access to the same new Toolbox routines that are present in the ROM of newer Macs.

When the owner of the older Mac restarts his or her Mac, the routines in the System file will be loaded into RAM. That means that when a program calls a Toolbox routine, the Operating System may find the code for that routine in either ROM or RAM. Fortunately, it's not up to you, the programmer, to keep track of the whereabouts of Toolbox routines. That's a job for the Mac Operating System.

The Finder

The *Finder* is a program that, like most Macintosh programs, consists of code and resources. The Finder is loaded into memory and starts running when you turn on your computer. It is responsible for displaying the desktop pattern and the icons you see on it, such as the trash can, files, and folders. When you move, copy, and delete files the Finder is doing the work. The Finder makes use of some of the common resources in the System file to display the interface that the user sees. Figure 1.19 shows the System file and the Finder and what the Finder is responsible for doing. In this figure you can see that the Finder, made up of resources and code, interacts with the System file—also made up of resources and code. Once the Finder has the system information it needs, it displays a part of the user interface, as shown at the bottom of the figure.

NOTE

On PCs running DOS, there is no real equivalent to the Finder and to the base-level user interface it provides. Unless you consider the **C:>** prompt in DOS to be a user interface!

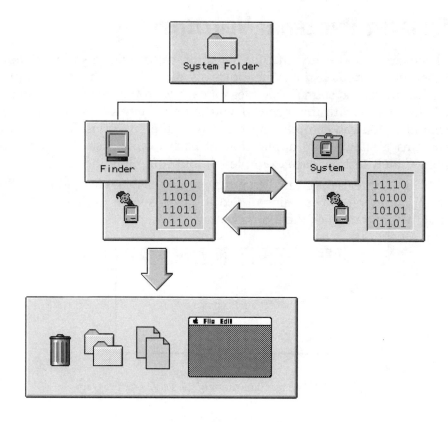

Figure 1.19 The Finder and the System file.

Chapter Program: VeryBasics

This chapter, and every chapter hereafter, closes with a short example program that demonstrates the topics discussed in the chapter. The project, resource, and source code files for each example are included on the CD that came with this book. If you own a Metrowerks or Symantec compiler, you can compile and run any of the programs. The CD also contains a stand-alone application of each example so that you can immediately test out each example without compiling the code.

This chapter's program, *VeryBasics*, simply displays a window on the screen and then draws a line of text to it—as shown in Figure 1.20. To quit the program click the mouse button.

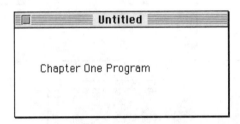

Figure 1.20 The result of running the *VeryBasics* program.

Though the *VeryBasics* program may not appear to do much, it does illustrate several of the concepts discussed in this chapter. *VeryBasics* demonstrates:

- Bitmapped graphics by drawing text to the window.
- Retrieving and processing an event using an event loop.
- Use of a resource file with a WIND resource.
- Calls to Toolbox functions.

Project Resource File: VeryBasics.rsrc

The resource file used in the creation of a full-featured Mac program consists of dozens—perhaps hundreds—of resources of a variety of types. Because the *VeryBasics* program is the most minimal of Mac programs, the resource file used in its development is much smaller. In fact, the

VeryBasics.rsrc file holds just a single resource. As shown in Figure 1.21, this file consists of a single `WIND` resource with an ID of 128.

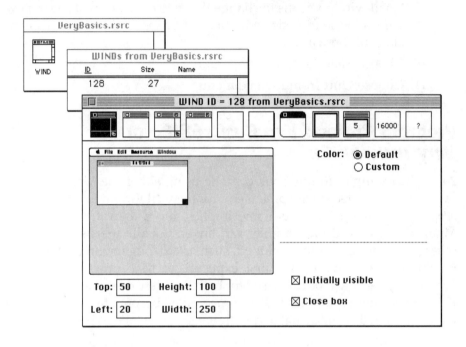

Figure 1.21 The `WIND` resource for the VeryBasics project.

The following list provides the steps for creating a new resource file and adding a `WIND` resource to it. While the *VeryBasics.rsrc* file is included on this book's CD, you may want to create your own version so that you feel comfortable with the process.

1. Launch ResEdit.
2. If an introductory dialog box opens, click on it to dismiss it.
3. Click the **New** button in the dialog box that opens.
4. Name the resource file *VeryBasics.rsrc*.
5. Click the **New** button.
6. Choose **Create New Resource** from the Resource menu.
7. Scroll to the `WIND` type, then click on it.

8. Click the **OK** button.

9. You now have a WIND resource. If you wish, click on one of the small window icons to change the type of window. Type in new values in the four size editable text boxes to change the dimensions of the window.

10. Choose **Save** from the File menu.

11. Choose **Quit** from the File menu.

Program Project: *VeryBasics68K.μ* or *VeryBasics68K.π*

All of the examples in this book compile using either the Metrowerks or Symantec integrated development environment (IDE). An *integrated development environment* is, as its name implies, more than just a compiler. Minimally, it's an editor, compiler and linker. Usually there's at least one other programming utility included, such as a debugger. Since this chapter provides you with your first exposure to Mac programming, the *VeryBasics* project will be discussed for both the Metrowerks and Symantec IDEs. Subsequent examples will assume you've become familiar with the basics of the IDE your using, and will forego the details of project files.

All the files necessary to build a *VeryBasics* application are included on this book's CD. If you'd like a little practice with your integrated development environment, follow the steps in the next sections. If you do that, you'll re-create the *VeryBasics*-related files found on the CD. If you're a CodeWarrior user, read on. If you're using the Symantec IDE, skip the next section and move on to the section titled "The Symantec Project: *VeryBasics68K.π*."

N O T E   Every Mac program starts as a *project*. A project is represented by a project window that holds the names of the files that will get linked together to form a stand-alone program. Regardless of the IDE you use, you'll want to keep the following tips in mind—they apply to both Metrowerks and Symantec project windows. You can move a file from one group to another by clicking on its name and dragging it. You can create a new group by dragging a file past, or beneath, the last group in the window. You can rename an existing group (such as Sources or Resources) by double-clicking on the group name and then typing in a new name. You can open a source code file or resource file by double-clicking on its name in the project window.

Before creating a new project, as described below, create a new folder in the main folder that holds your Symantec or Metrowerks IDE. Supply the folder with a name of your choosing, then place the *VeryBasics.rsrc* file in the folder. If you haven't already created that file, use ResEdit to do so now. Name the file *VeryBasics.rsrc* and add a single WIND resource to it—the steps for doing so precede this section. Figure 1.21 shows that resource.

N O T E

As you read the following pages you'll notice that the terms *68K* and *PPC* appear occasionally. Both the Metrowerks and Symantec IDEs let you specify the final application's *target machine*. That is, you can choose whether the resulting program should consist of code that uses the 680x0 instruction set or the PowerPC instruction set. By selecting 68K as the target, the resulting application will be one that runs on either a Mac (with one of the Motorola 680x0 microprocessors) or a Power Mac (with one of the PowerPC microprocessors). That's opposed to a PPC target, which results in an application that will run only on a Power Mac. If you're working on a 680x0-based Mac, choose 68K as your target so that you can run the program. If you're working on a PowerPC-based Mac, you can choose either 68K or PPC as your target. Chapter 8 discusses the advantages and disadvantages of both types of applications, as well as the perfect compromise program—the *fat app*.

The Metrowerks CodeWarrior Project: *VeryBasics68K.µ*

To create the VeryBasics project, launch the CodeWarrior IDE, then select **New Project** from the File menu. Use the pop-up menu at the top of the dialog box that opens to move into your *VeryBasics* folder. Then type in a name for the project. By convention, a Metrowerks project typically has a *.µ* extension. To create the *µ* character, press the *m* key while holding down the **Option** key. As you're about to see, the *VeryBasics* project will be generating 68K instruction set code—that's why the program name includes *68K* in it. Again, Chapter 8 provides the details regarding the differences between 68K and PPC programs.

Before saving the new project, choose a project stationary from the **Project Stationary** pop-up menu. When you create a project, you always need to add at least one Metrowerks library to the project. Among other purposes, libraries hold precompiled code that provide support for the Macintosh Toolbox and the Metrowerks PowerPlant application framework. All that a project stationary does is tell CodeWarrior which libraries to add to a project. This saves you the effort of determining which libraries your project needs, and the chore of then adding those libraries. In Figure 1.22 you can see that the *VeryBasics68K.μ* project is using the **Min MacOS 68K C/C++.μ** stationary. Because the *VeryBasics* program doesn't use any ANSI C functions, doesn't use the PowerPlant application framework, and isn't a PowerPC program, this stationary works fine. Because the stationary name includes *68K* in it, you know that the application that gets generated will consist of 680x0 code.

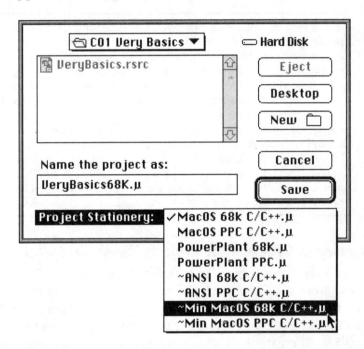

Figure 1.22 Selecting project stationary to use with the *VeryBasics* CodeWarrior project.

After clicking the **Save** button, the new project will open in a project window like the one shown in Figure 1.23. Using the selected project stationary causes CodeWarrior to add the *CPlusPlus.lib* and *MacOS.lib* libraries to the project. If you had used a different stationary, different libraries would be in the project. As denoted by the *<replace me>* names in the window, it's now up to you to add the source code file and resource file to the project.

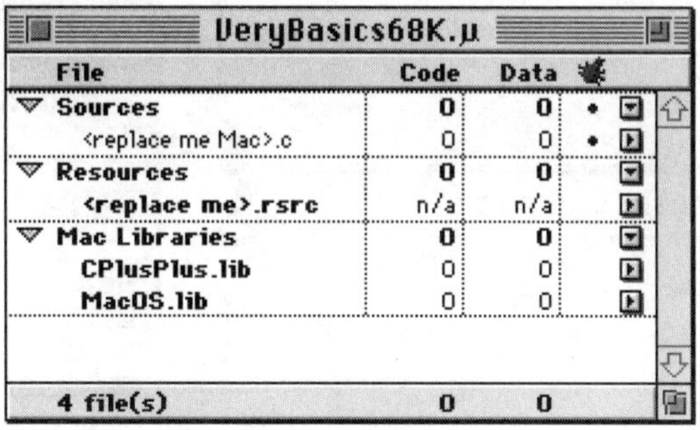

File	Code	Data	🐞	
▽ **Sources**	0	0	• ▼	⇧
\<replace me Mac\>.c	0	0	• ▶	
▽ **Resources**	0	0	▼	
\<replace me\>.rsrc	n/a	n/a	▶	
▽ **Mac Libraries**	0	0	▼	
CPlusPlus.lib	0	0	▶	
MacOS.lib	0	0	▶	
				⇩
4 file(s)	**0**	**0**		

Figure 1.23 The *VeryBasics* CodeWarrior project before the source code and resource file are added.

To make the *VeryBasics.rsrc* resource file a part of the project, choose **Add Files** from the Project menu. When you do, you'll see a dialog box like the one shown in Figure 1.24. If the project folder isn't named in the pop-up menu at the top of the dialog box, use the menu to move into that folder. Then double-click on the name of the resource file, as is being done in Figure 1.24. That moves the file from the top list to the bottom list, and tells CodeWarrior that it should be added to the project. When you click the **Done** button, the dialog box will be dismissed and the file will appear in the project window.

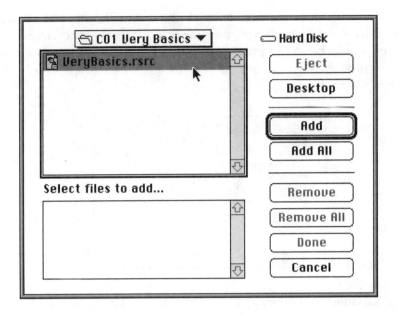

Figure 1.24 Adding a file to the *VeryBasics* CodeWarrior project.

To create a new text file to serve as the source code file, select **New** from the File menu. Select **Save As** from the same menu to name and save the file. You can give the file any name that ends with the *.c* extension. To match the following figure, use the name *VeryBasics.c*. Now choose **Add Window** from the Project menu. You won't have to go through the dialog box shown in Figure 1.24 to add the file—CodeWarrior adds it for you. Consider this menu item a shortcut for adding the frontmost window to a project.

To remove one of the *<replace me>* marker files from the project window, click on its name, then select **Remove** from the Project menu. After removing both markers, your project window should look similar to the one shown in Figure 1.25.

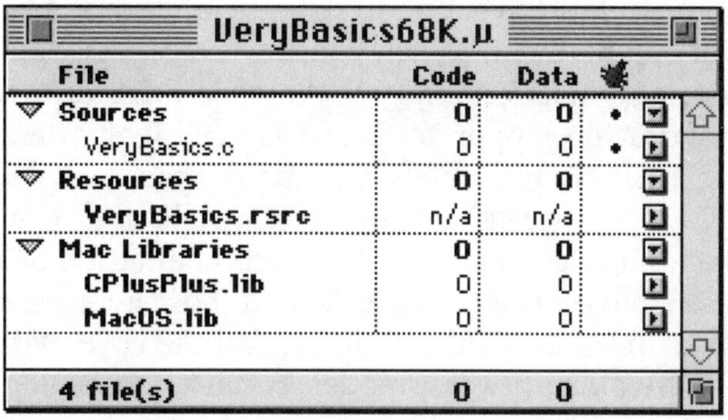

File	Code	Data	🐛	
▽ **Sources**	**0**	**0**	• ▼	⇧
VeryBasics.c	0	0	• ▶	
▽ **Resources**	**0**	**0**	▼	
VeryBasics.rsrc	n/a	n/a	▶	
▽ **Mac Libraries**	**0**	**0**	▼	
CPlusPlus.lib	0	0	▶	
MacOS.lib	0	0	▶	
				⇩
4 file(s)	**0**	**0**		🗗

VeryBasics68K.µ

Figure 1.25 The *VeryBasics* CodeWarrior project after the source code and resource file are added.

At this point the *VeryBasics.c* source code file is empty. Add the code by typing in the C code from the listing that appears later in this chapter. If you're satisfied that you now know how CodeWarrior projects work, you can save a little typing by opening the *VeryBasics.c* source code file included with this book and copy and pasting its contents into your own *VeryBasics.c* file. Finally, select **Run** from the Project menu to compile and run the program.

The Symantec Project: *VeryBasics68K.π*

To create the *VeryBasics* project, launch the Symantec IDE. When you do, you'll be faced with the dialog box shown in Figure 1.26. Use the pop-up menu at the top of the dialog box to move into your *VeryBasics* folder. Then type in a name for the project. By convention, a Symantec project has a .π extension. To create the π character, press the *p* key while holding down the **Option** key. Because the *VeryBasics* project will be generating 68K instruction set code, the program name includes *68K* in it. As mentioned, Chapter 8 provides more information about the differences between 68K and PPC programs.

Before clicking the **Save** button, choose a project model from the **Project Model** pop-up menu. When you create a project, you always need to add at least one Symantec library to the project. Libraries hold precompiled code that provide support for the Macintosh Toolbox and the THINK Class Library application framework, among other purposes. A project model can be thought of as a template that tells the Symantec Project Manager which libraries to add to a project. Letting the SPM determine which libraries a project needs, and then add those libraries to the project, saves you effort. In Figure 1.26 you can see that the *VeryBasics68K.π* project is using the **C Mac Application** model. Because the *VeryBasics* program doesn't use any ANSI C functions and doesn't use the THINK Class Library application framework, this model is a good choice.

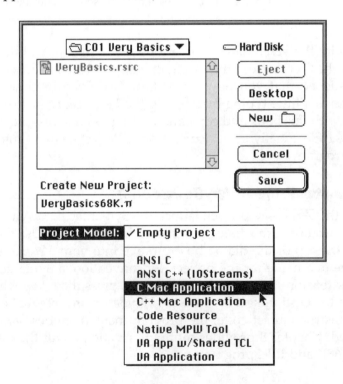

Figure 1.26 Selecting project stationary to use with the *VeryBasics* Symantec project.

After clicking the **Save** button, a new project will open. As shown in Figure 1.27, the contents of a project are displayed in a project window. Using the selected project model causes the SPM to add a folder that holds the libraries necessary to support the code you'll be writing. You can see the names of the libraries SPM selected by clicking on the **Triangle** icon to the left of the folder. Note that if you had selected a different project model, the contents of this folder would differ. As shown in the figure, the Symantec Project Manager also added a "dummy" *main.c* file that could be used to hold your code.

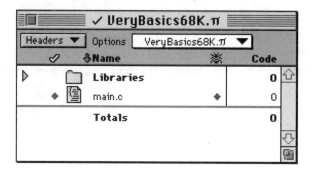

Figure 1.27 The *VeryBasics* Symantec project before the source code and resource file are added.

To add the *VeryBasics.rsrc* resource file to the project, choose **Add Files** from the Project menu. That menu selection brings up the dialog box shown in Figure 1.28. If the pop-up menu at the top of the dialog box doesn't show the name of the project folder, use the menu to move into that folder. Then double-click on the name of the resource file to move the file from the top list to the bottom list. When you click the **Done** button, the dialog box will be dismissed and the resource file will appear in the project window.

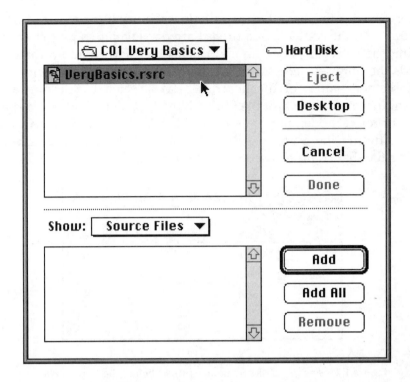

Figure 1.28 Adding a file to the *VeryBasics* Symantec project.

To create a new, empty source code file, select **New** from the File menu. Then choose **Save As** from the File menu to provide the file with a name and to save the file to disk. While you can use any name that ends with a *.c* extension, you might want to name the file *VeryBasics.c* to match the figures. Next, select **Add "VeryBasics.c"** from the Project menu. This menu item allows you to bypass the Add Files dialog box to quickly add the frontmost window to the project.

To remove the main.c file from the project window, click on its name and select **Remove "main.c"** from the Project menu. After removing this file, your project window should look like to the one shown in Figure 1.29.

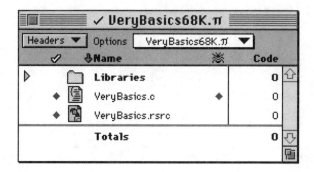

Figure 1.29 The *VeryBasics* Symantec project after the source code and resource file are added.

The *VeryBasics.c* source code file that is a part of the project is empty. Add the source code by typing in the C code from the listing that appears next. If you're comfortable using the Symantec Project Manager, you can save some typing by opening the *VeryBasics.c* source code file found on the CD that came with this book. Select all the code, then copy it and paste it into your own *VeryBasics.c* file. To compile and test run the VeryBasics code, select **Run** from the Project menu.

Program Listing: *VeryBasics.c*

Now it's time to take a look at the *VeryBasics.c* source code listing. Following the program listing is a walk though of the key elements of the source code.

```
// _____
// Function prototypes

void   InitializeToolbox( void );
void   HandleMouseDown( void );


// _____
// Global constants
```

```
#define        rTextWindow        128


//  _____
// Global variables

Boolean  gAllDone = false;



//  _____
// Program execution starts here

void  main( void )
{
    WindowPtr      theWindow;
    EventRecord    theEvent;

    InitializeToolbox();

    theWindow = GetNewWindow( rTextWindow, nil, (WindowPtr)-1L );
    ShowWindow( theWindow );
    SetPort( theWindow );

    MoveTo( 30, 50 );
    DrawString( "\pChapter One Program" );

    while ( gAllDone == false )
    {
        WaitNextEvent( everyEvent, &theEvent, 15L, nil );

        switch ( theEvent.what )
        {
            case mouseDown:
                HandleMouseDown();
                break;
        }
    }
}


//  _____
// Handle a click of the mouse button

void  HandleMouseDown( void )
```

```
{
    SysBeep( 1 );

    gAllDone = true;
}



// _____
// One-time initialization of the Macintosh Toolbox

void  InitializeToolbox( void )
{
    InitGraf( &qd.thePort );
    InitFonts();
    InitWindows();
    InitMenus();
    TEInit();
    InitDialogs( 0L );
    FlushEvents( everyEvent, 0 );
    InitCursor();
}
```

Stepping through the Code

If you're new to Mac programming, there are several lines of code in the listing that will look unfamiliar to you. That code is examined here.

Where are the #include Directives?

When you look at the C source code for programs that run on non-Macintosh platforms, the first thing you usually see are several #include directives that include header files in the program. Macintosh programs also use #includes, but you usually need to include only one header file, and that's done for you automatically.

Your C or C++ compiler gets its information about the calling convention of a Toolbox routine from a header file. Macintosh compilers come with over 100 header files—the universal interface files written by Apple. When you make a call to a Toolbox routine such as GetNewWindow(), your compiler looks to the *Windows.h* header file to find the prototype for GetNewWindow().

Your IDE—whether Symantec or Metrowerks—includes a single precompiled file in each project. This file is the result of compiling several of the most commonly used header files. If you use Symantec, your project will include one of four precompiled header files: *MacHeaders* for 68K C projects, *MacHeaders++* for 68K C++ projects, *PPC MacHeaders* for PowerPC C projects, or *PPC MacHeaders++* for PowerPC C++ projects. If you use Metrowerks, your project will include one of just two precompiled header files: *MacHeaders68K* for any 68K project or *MacHeadersPPC* for any PowerPC project. Both environments automatically include the correct precompiled header file for the type of project your working on. That means you don't have to use #include directives for the precompiled header file or for any of the universal interface files from which the header file was created.

NOTE   MS Windows programmers know that Windows programs always include one large header file—*Windows.h*. If a Windows compiler automatically included this header in all of its windows source code, it would function in the same way as a Mac IDE that includes one of the precompiled MacHeader files.

Sometimes, you will need to include some of the other Macintosh header files in a program. When you do, you simply use standard #include directives. Examples abound throughout this book. Like any other IDE, a Macintosh IDE also allows you to write your own headers and include them in a project.

Function Prototypes

Prototypes aid the compiler in determining if functions are being called properly. Though some compilers might let you slip by without them, always use them. For the Macintosh, prototypes are written in the same form as they are for any other computer whose compiler supports this construct. You do not have to include a variable name when you list the arguments, just the type of the argument. Here's the prototype of the HandleMouseDown() function used in the *VeryBasics* project:

```
void  HandleMouseDown( void );
```

NOTE
If you program on an older minicomputer or mainframe, it is possible that your C compiler does not support prototypes—a relatively recent extension to the C language. If so, consult any book that describes the ANSI standard definition of the C language.

The #define Directives

As you can tell from the listing, Macintosh programs use #define directives in the same manner as #defines are used by compilers for other computer systems. Here is the one #define *VeryBasics* uses:

```
#define       rTextWindow       128
```

The rTextWindow constant is used to define the ID of the WIND resource used in the call to GetNewWindow():

```
theWindow = GetNewWindow( rTextWindow, nil, (WindowPtr)-1L );
```

While not required, Macintosh source code usually follows the convention of preceding a constant name with a lowercase character. The character provides readers of your code with a hint of what the constant will be used for. Here's the characters used in this book. You may want to adopt this same technique in your own programs:

```
#define       mFileMenu         129     // 'm' for menu resource ID
#define       rMyWindow         128     // 'r' for other resource ID
#define       iQuit               4     // 'i' for menu item number
#define       kTaxRate         0.05     // 'k' for non-resource constant
```

Global Variables

Variable declarations take on the same format for Macintosh C as they do for other versions of C. Macintosh C, however, has some data types all its own. Many of these types that are unique to the Mac will be described at various places in this book and summarized in Appendix A. Here is the one global variable used by *VeryBasics*:

```
Boolean   gAllDone = false;
```

The gAllDone variable is used to end the program. When the user clicks the mouse button, *VeryBasics* toggles the value of gAllDone from its initialized value of false to true.

To make it readily apparent that a variable is a global variable, Mac programmers often precede a global variable name with a lowercase *g*. Again, this isn't a requirement, just a commonly used convention.

The main() **Function**

Like other C programs, Macintosh programs always begin at the main() function. And like all C programs, you don't explicitly call main(); it is automatically the first function to execute when you run a Macintosh program. In a Mac program, the return type of main() and the parameter to main() are both void.

```
void   main( void )
{
    ...
    ...
}
```

MS Windows programs use WinMain() rather than main().

N O T E

The **Application-Defined** InitializeToolbox() **Function**

The various managers must be initialized before performing calls to Toolbox routines. The initialization calls used in *VeryBasics* should be included in every Macintosh program you write, in the order given here. Since very program uses these same Toolbox function calls, for convenience you'll want to define a routine that you can copy and paste between projects. Make sure to always call such an application-defined routine at the start of your main() function.

```
void   InitializeToolbox( void )
{
    InitGraf( &qd.thePort );
    InitFonts();
    InitWindows();
```

```
    InitMenus();
    TEInit();
    InitDialogs( 0L );
    FlushEvents( everyEvent, 0 );
    InitCursor();
}
```

The Macintosh requires several new ways of orienting the process of writing a computer program. So you'll be happy to learn that when programming the Macintosh, you'll still do some things exactly as have in the past! A function for a Macintosh program is written and invoked in the same manner as a function you write for any other computer.

WARNING

A call to a Toolbox routine that exists in a manager that was not initialized will crash your program. For example, if the call to InitWindows() was omitted from a program, a subsequent call to GetNewWindow() would cause a crash.

Loading a Window

Finally, some action! A call to GetNewWindow() loads a WIND resource into memory. When you create a WIND resource in ResEdit, you have the option of specifying whether the window should be visible or hidden when this call is made. If you examine the WIND resource in the *VeryBasics.rsrc* file you'll see that the **Initially visible** check box is checked. That means that when this call is complete a window will appear on the screen. Here's the call that loads the WIND resource:

```
theWindow = GetNewWindow( rTextWindow, nil, (WindowPtr)-1L );
ShowWindow( theWindow );
```

As a precaution, you might want to follow a call to GetNewWindow() with a call to ShowWindow(). This Toolbox routine displays a hidden window. If the window is already visible, ShowWindow() has no effect.

The first parameter passed to GetNewWindow() is the ID of the WIND resource to load. The second parameter to GetNewWindow() tells the Window Manager where in memory to store this newly loaded window. Using a nil pointer here tells the Window Manager to use whatever available memory it wants. Chapter 4 shows you how to be more specific about where in memory the window should be stored.

The last parameter to `GetNewWindow()` specifies whether the new window should open in front of or behind all other open windows. This is the program's only window, so this parameter doesn't have an impact on the call. In general, you'll open a new window in front of all others. A value of -1 accomplishes this. This parameter, however, must be a pointer. Affixing an uppercase *L* to a value forces that value to occupy 4 bytes. In Macintosh programming, that's the same number of bytes used to hold a pointer. There's one more step to turning the number -1 into an acceptable parameter to `GetNewWindow()`. This third parameter can't be any type of pointer—it must be a `WindowPtr`. Preceding the value -1L with (`WindowPtr`) casts the value -1L to a `WindowPtr` type.

N O T E If you are a PC programmer or write code for a machine in which pointers and integers are not the same size, you'll notice that Macintosh programmers are much more relaxed about placing integer values such as -1L and 0L in slots meant for pointers. Since they're both 32 bits in size, it all works out.

Drawing to a Window

Every window has its own drawing environment, or *graphics port*. That's how different windows can do things like display text in fonts different from one another. Before drawing to a window, you must set the port to that window. A call to the Toolbox routine `SetPort()` accomplishes this. The parameter to `SetPort()` is a pointer to the window whose port you want to use:

```
SetPort( theWindow );
```

To move to a particular area in a window, you use the Toolbox routine `MoveTo()`. The first parameter is the horizontal location to move to, the second parameter is the vertical position. The effect of `MoveTo(30,50)` is as follows: start at the window's upper-left corner; move 30 pixels to the right; move 50 pixels down; then stay put until asked to move again or until asked to draw. You'll find more in-depth discussion of drawing to windows in Chapter 3.

The Toolbox routine `DrawString()` draws a single line of text to a window. The line of text is preceded by \p, and the entire string is placed in double quotes. The Toolbox will be looking for a string in Pascal format. Strings that are in Pascal format are not terminated with a null byte, as they are when in C format. Rather, Pascal strings begin with a byte that contains the size of the string, followed by the text bytes of the string. The "Chapter One Program" string is sent to DrawString() from a C program. The \p lets the Toolbox know this so that it can make the internal conversions necessary to display the string. You'll find a more comprehensive discussion of strings and DrawString() in Chapter 7.

NOTE

PC programmers use the \ character all the time:

```
printf("Start a new line.\n");
```

It should make sense that the escape character \ is used to signal the compiler that the letter *p* that follows does not stand for the letter in the alphabet, but rather indicates that the string that follows is in Pascal format.

The Event Loop

The event loop, the driving force of the program, appears just as discussed earlier in the chapter. The only event type *VeryBasics* handles is a click of the mouse. It handles this mouseDown event by calling an application-defined routine named HandleMouseDown():

```
while ( gAllDone == false )
{
    WaitNextEvent( everyEvent, &theEvent, 15L, nil );

    switch ( theEvent.what )
    {
        case mouseDown:
            HandleMouseDown();
            break;
    }
}
```

The Toolbox function WaitNextEvent() accepts four parameters. The first tells the Event Manager what types of events the program is interested in responding to. By passing the Apple-defined constant everyEvent, *VeryBasics* tells the Event Manager to return information about any type of event that occurs.

N O T E

The phrase *Apple-defined* will appear throughout this book. It simply refers to the fact that a constant is defined in the Apple universal header files (the same files that hold the function prototypes for all the Toolbox routines) rather than by the application in its source code.

The second parameter to WaitNextEvent() is a pointer to a variable of type EventRecord. After WaitNextEvent() retrieves the next event from the event queue, it returns descriptive information about that event in this second parameter. The Event Manager does this by placing the information in the various fields of an EventRecord data structure. Here's how Apple defines the EventRecord structure:

```
struct EventRecord
{
    MacOSEventKind          what;
    UInt32                  message;
    UInt32                  when;
    Point                   where;
    MacOSEventModifiers  modifiers;
};
```

As you can see in the *VeryBasics* event loop, the what field of the EventRecord structure is used to hold information about the type of event that was returned by WaitNextEvent(). *VeryBasics* compares the value in the what field with the Apple-defined mouseDown constant. If it's a match, the code under the mouseDown case label executes.

While *VeryBasics* compares the what field of the EventRecord variable theEvent to only one Apple-defined constant, your programs can compare this field to several others. The following is a list of event type constants that will be discussed in this book:

```
mouseDown        // mouse button was clicked
keyDown          // keyboard key was pressed
updateEvt        // window contents need to be redrawn
activateEvt      // window has been activated or deactivated
```

The Application-Defined HandleMouseDown() **Function**

When the user clicks the mouse, *VeryBasics* plays the system alert sound and then quits. The application-defined HandleMouseDown() routine takes care of these two tasks. First, a call to the Toolbox routine SysBeep() plays the system alert sound. This sound varies from Mac to Mac—it's the sound that the user has previously selected using the Sound Control Panel. Years ago, the Mac had only one system alert sound, and SysBeep() allowed you to use its parameter to specify the duration for which that sound would play. Now, the parameter to SysBeep() goes unused. Though the number you pass to SysBeep() has no effect on the way the function operates, you still need to pass a value.

```
void  HandleMouseDown( void )
{
    SysBeep( 1 );

    gAllDone = true;
}
```

Finally, the global variable gAllDone is set to true. When HandleMouseDown() completes, program execution returns to the event loop in main(). When it does, the loop's while test will fail, and the loop will end. As shown below, the body of the while statement executes only when gAllDone has a value of false. The HandleMouseDown() routine sets gAllDone to true, thus ending main() and the program.

```
    while ( gAllDone == false )
```

Chapter Summary

The Macintosh graphical user interface, or GUI, presents special challenges to programmers of the Macintosh. This book presents the techniques to overcome these challenges.

The Macintosh uses bitmapped graphics. You can turn each pixel, or display dot, on or off on the screen. On a color monitor, each pixel has more than the two states of on or off. Color systems allow a single pixel to take on hundreds, thousands, or even millions of different values. Whether a Mac uses a monochrome or color monitor, each pixel on the screen has a pair of coordinates that make up a point that defines its position on the screen.

Macintosh programs don't run in a sequential, linear manner. Instead, a Mac program responds to events—user actions such as a click of the mouse button. An event record holds descriptive information about a single event. A Macintosh program is driven by an event loop— code that repeatedly checks for and responds to these events.

All elements of a Macintosh program, such as its menu, windows, and dialog boxes, are resources. A resource is a description of one of these elements. A WIND resource, for example, holds the type, or look, of a window. It also defines the size of the window and the screen location where it will first appear. Resources can be graphically, or visually, edited using a program such as Apple's ResEdit resource editor.

Resources are simply descriptions of interface elements; they don't do anything with the elements. For that, you must write source code. So that you don't have to start from scratch, Apple provides thousands of prewritten functions to help you in working with resources. These routines are stored in the ROM and the System file of your Macintosh and are collectively referred to as the Toolbox.

The Macintosh Operating System, like the Toolbox, consists of routines you access from within your source code. The Operating System routines are low-level functions that perform tasks such as handling keystrokes, while the Toolbox routines are higher level, performing the more noticeable tasks such as displaying windows and drawing pictures.

Collectively, the Toolbox and Operating System are called system software. The system software is divided into groups of functionally related routines—managers. The Window Manager and Menu Manager are two examples.

The System file, found in the System Folder of each Macintosh, contains resources that are shared by programs. The Finder is another program found in the System Folder. It gets launched when your Macintosh starts up, and remains running for as long as your Mac is running. The Finder is responsible for displaying the desktop pattern and for performing file housekeeping like copying and deleting files.

Chapter 2

Macintosh Memory

Understanding how the Macintosh works with memory is an important and often understudied topic. A knowledge of what is going on in RAM will aid you in writing programs that behave in a predictable manner.

The Macintosh uses a set of terminology and concepts all its own. This chapter will make you familiar with the basic terms and techniques of Macintosh memory. In Chapter 9 you will discover the details of memory management and learn actual techniques you can use to avoid memory problems.

In this chapter you will learn how memory is organized into *partitions*. You'll see how each partition is composed of the same basic areas of memory. You'll also learn the techniques the Macintosh uses to make the most efficient use of memory.

MEMORY ORGANIZATION

The Macintosh Operating System divides a Mac's RAM into two main sections, or areas. The area at the low end of memory is the *system partition*; it is reserved by the Macintosh for its own use. The system partition starts at the lowest memory address, 0x00000000. The Macintosh dedicates the other area to applications that you run. The Mac will further subdivide this application area into *application partitions*. For every application you run, there is a corresponding application partition. Figure 2.1 illustrates this.

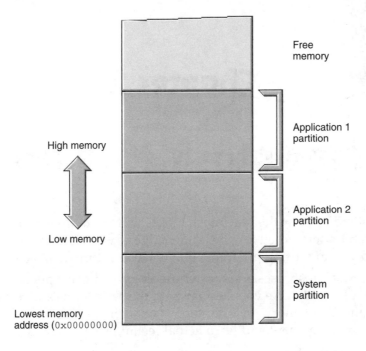

Free memory

Application 1 partition

High memory

Application 2 partition

Low memory

System partition

Lowest memory address (0x00000000)

Figure 2.1 Memory organization.

What does a RAM partition contain? That depends on whether the partition is a system partition or an application partition. Figure 2.2 shows RAM when a single 68K application is running. The individual areas in the application and system partitions are described in the following pages.

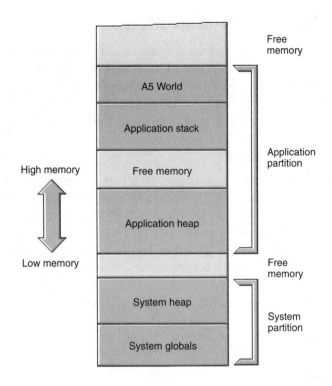

Figure 2.2 The system and application partitions.

NOTE

A native PowerPC application (a program generated by a PowerPC compiler) in memory looks very similar to the 68K application shown in Figure 2.2. The only difference is that a native application doesn't have an A5 World in its application partition. The topic of application type (68K or PowerPC) was introduced in Chapter 1 and is discussed in greater detail in Chapter 8.

System Partition Organization

The RAM of a Macintosh always contains a single system partition. This is true whether the computer is a 680x0-based Mac or a PowerPC-based Macintosh. It's also true regardless of the number of applications that are running. The system partition is made up of two sections: one that contains system global variables and one called the system heap.

System Global Variables

At the bottom of memory, starting at address 0x00000000, the Mac reserves a section of memory for system global variables. The operating system uses these variables to keep track of what is going on in the operating environment. There are also variables stored here that establish constant environment values, such as the pixel height of the menu bar. While it's possible to directly access these variables, you'll want to avoid that practice. Apple reserves the right to change the layout of this area—and has so informed programmers. If your program directly alters this memory (to, say, temporarily set the menu bar height to 0 to hide it), it may not run properly in the future.

System Heap

Above the system global variables is the system heap. Only the Operating System uses this section of memory; you will never have a need to access information contained within it. The system heap contains things such as system file resources that have been loaded into memory, the code that makes up extensions, and the code necessary to run the Finder. When you start up the Macintosh, the system heap size is set and remains fixed until the next time the computer starts. At startup, extensions (such as Apple's QuickTime) call upon a software mechanism to expand the system heap to accommodate them. That's why you have to restart your computer after you move an extension into your System folder—the system heap doesn't have room to accommodate a newly added extension.

Application Partition Organization

When a program launches, the operating system reserves a section of free RAM for that application's use. This application partition devotes itself entirely to that application for the duration of the application's execution. When you quit the application, the memory within that partition becomes free for the Macintosh to use for a different application.

As was shown in Figure 2.2, the system partition for a 68K application has an A5 World that holds application global variables, an application stack that holds application local variables, and an application heap section that contains the program's code, resources, and data objects that are created as the program executes.

A5 World

A 68K program's global variables are stored in a section of the application partition called the A5 World. The name *A5 World* comes from the fact that the operating system uses the 680x0 microprocessor's A5 register to keep track of where this memory section starts.

Variables stored in the A5 World of an application partition are accessible only to the program to which the application partition is devoted. On the other hand, variables in the system partition are accessible by both the system and any application that is executing. While the word *global* can be used in describing variables in both an application partition's A5 World and the system partition's system globals section, the difference is noteworthy. A5 World variables are global to the application residing in the application partition. That is, any function in the program in the partition can make use of an A5 World global variable. Variables in the system partition, on the other hand, are global to the entire system. Any program can make use of them. Figure 2.3 illustrates this.

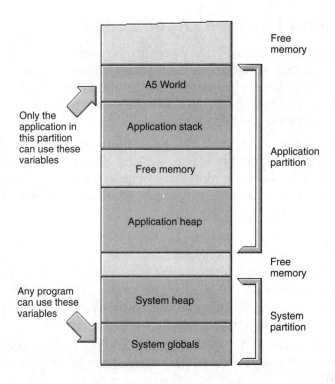

Only the application in this partition can use these variables

Any program can use these variables

Figure 2.3 Application global variables and system global variables.

A native PowerPC application doesn't use an A5 World—it groups its global variables together and stores them in a single block in the program's application heap.

N O T E

Application Stack

The *application stack* is a section of memory used for holding the local variables of the program to which the application partition is dedicated. The stack also holds parameters as they are passed to functions.

The number of global variables in any single program is fixed. Upon loading a 68K program into the application partition, the operating system can determine the exact amount of memory it should allot to the A5

World; this is why the size of the A5 World is fixed when an application is loaded. The exact number of local variables and passed parameters in a program are not as well-defined. Variables local to functions are created and destroyed dynamically as the program executes. This necessitates a stack that can grow and shrink in size.

The bottom of the stack is fixed in memory. For a 68K application, the bottom of the stack is "anchored" just under the A5 World. For a PowerPC application, the bottom of the stack is also fixed—there's no A5 World above it. As the stack adds variables, it grows *downward* in memory. As the stack removes variables, the stack recedes back *upwards*. Variables are always added and removed from the top of the stack. Figure 2.4 shows the application stack. The shaded arrow emphasizes that as the stack grows it moves toward the application heap.

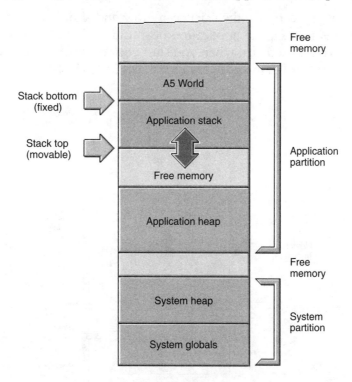

Figure 2.4 The application stack grows toward the application heap.

Application Heap

The next component of the application partition is the application heap. The *heap* holds the executable code of an application and application resources as they get loaded into memory. If a program creates data objects dynamically, then those objects get added to the heap. Unlike the stack, which stores variables in a linear manner, the heap can load, store, and unload objects anywhere in the area of memory that the system has established as the heap.

NOTE The word *object* is used in this book as a general term for the data in any one block of memory in the heap. An object could be the resource data that gets loaded when a call to GetNewWindow() is made, it could be a block of executable code, or it could be the data from an application-defined data structure.

The application heap, like the stack, can grow and shrink as it needs more space. In this respect, the application heap differs from the system heap, which takes on a fixed size when you start your computer. The application heap grows upward in memory, toward the stack; this is shown in Figure 2.5.

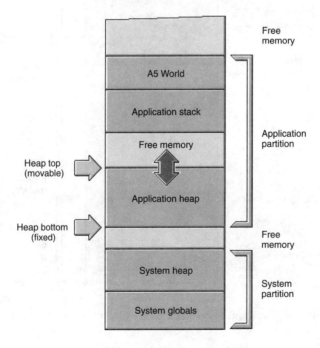

Figure 2.5 The application heap grows toward the application stack.

Now that you know that the stack can grow down toward the heap, and the heap can grow up toward the stack, a question may come to mind. What prevents the stack and heap from running into one another? The answer: sometimes they do run into each other! The Memory Manager does its best to prevent this from occurring, and you can help the manager by using some of the simple memory management techniques discussed in this chapter.

Summary of Memory Organization

Figure 2.6 summarizes several ideas and terms unique to Macintosh memory organization.

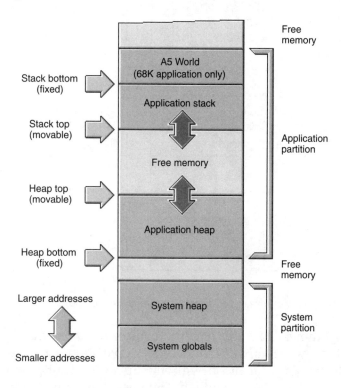

Figure 2.6 Memory organization summary.

Up to this point, the discussions on memory have centered on examples that have just a single application running, but a Macintosh allows a user to have multiple programs running at one time. Each program that runs gets its own application partition, and each partition has its own A5 World (if it's a 68K application), application stack, and application heap. Figure 2.7 shows memory when two applications are running: a native PowerPC program and a 68K program.

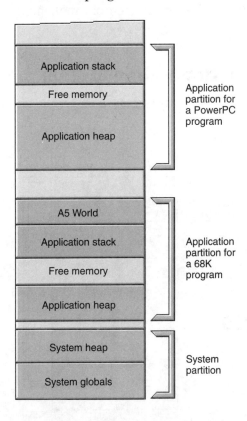

Figure 2.7 Memory organization when more than one application is running.

As a programmer, you will have no control of—nor will you be very interested in—what happens in the system partition. Any program that you create for the Macintosh will end up in an application partition when it executes. Since you'll be interested in how your program behaves in memory, you'll be interested in the memory management of application partitions. For this reason, the topics in the rest of this chapter apply only to application partitions. Of particular importance is the area of memory where your program's code and resources reside—the application heap.

NOTE Is the computer that holds the memory shown in Figure 2.7 a Mac or a Power Mac? That is, does the computer have a 680x0 microprocessor or a PowerPC processor? From Chapter 1 you know that a 680x0-based Mac can only run 68K programs, while a PowerPC-based Mac is capable of running both 68K programs and new native PPC programs. With those facts in mind, you know that the memory pictured in Figure 2.7 must be from a Power Mac.

THE APPLICATION HEAP

For a given application, certain things will remain constant each time the application is executed. When an application calls a particular function it will always pass the same number of parameters. Each time the function begins execution it will create the same number of local variables. Each time the function terminates, the program disposes these local variables. This is why an application's stack is designed to hold objects in an orderly linear manner. The same *cannot* be said for an application's heap.

As a program executes, it does so in a nonlinear manner. Running a program twice may result in several different sections of code being executed and several different resources being used. Because of this, the implementation of the heap is different from that of the stack.

Heap Fragmentation

When a program loads a resource (such as a WIND) to memory, the resource data ends up in the heap. When a program is finished with a resource, it may *release*, or dispose of, the memory that the resource data occupied. As a program runs, "pockets" of free memory will develop in the program's heap. When the program later loads another resource, it will attempt to place the resource data in one of these free pools of memory rather than simply adding the data to the top of the heap. If no one single area of this free memory is large enough to hold the entire object, the object will be placed on top of the heap, as shown in Figure 2.8.

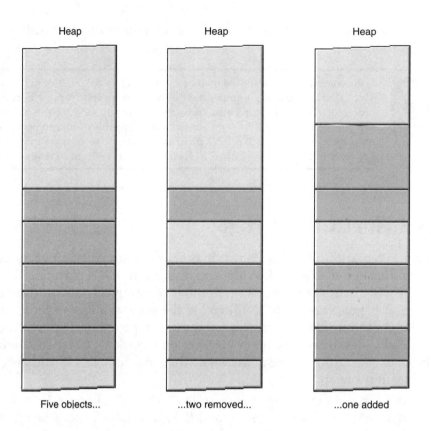

Figure 2.8 How the heap gets fragmented.

In Figure 2.8, the object that was added was not placed in free space between existing objects because the object was larger than either of the two free areas. When the Memory Manager adds an object to the heap it always places it in contiguous memory—it never divides one object between blocks of memory. This results in heap memory that is unused. When several small areas of memory are free but (due to their small individual size) they are unused, *fragmentation* is said to exist. This is shown in Figure 2.9.

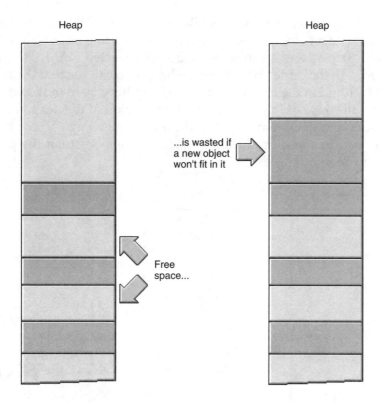

Figure 2.9 Fragmentation creates free memory blocks that may be unused.

Heap Compaction

Over time, the amount of wasted space, or fragmentation, could become so great that a program is unable to bring new objects into memory, even if there is plenty of free memory available. Obviously, this is unaccept-able. To prevent fragmentation, the Memory Manager uses a concept called compaction. *Compaction* is the act of rearranging blocks of memo-ry in an application heap in order to reduce or eliminate small islands of potentially unusable memory. Ideally, the Memory Manager would like to make the most efficient use of memory by shifting objects in the heap to fill the free spaces so they don't become wasted RAM. Figure 2.10 shows this. In the center version of the heap you can see that the two top objects pictured in the left version of the heap have been moved down to eliminate the gaps of free space. The right version of the heap has a new object added to it. Even with the addition of a new large object, the version of heap pictured on the right uses less memory than the precompaction version on the left.

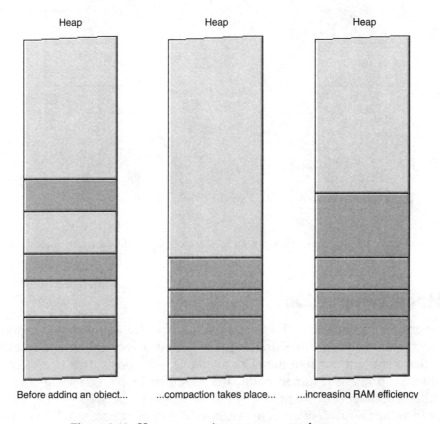

Figure 2.10 Heap compaction restores wasted memory.

During memory compaction, the Memory Manager may decide to *purge*, or remove from memory, some blocks. Only blocks that are not currently in use, and that are specifically marked as *purgeable*, can be removed.

Nonrelocatable and Relocatable Blocks

One of the attributes of a block is whether the block is marked as relocatable or nonrelocatable. Blocks that are marked as *relocatable* can be moved from one area of the heap to another by the Memory Manager. Blocks that are marked as *nonrelocatable* always stay in one place—even when memory is being compacted.

Because the Memory Manager can't move nonrelocatable blocks, you might think they could cause fragmentation, and they do. Though it is vastly preferable to use relocatable blocks, there are occasions when the Macintosh must use nonrelocatable blocks. One such situation is discussed later in this chapter.

With all this shifting of memory taking place, how do the Memory Manager and your application keep track of where things in memory will be at any given moment? For this, the Macintosh uses a technique involving master pointers. A *master pointer* is a special pointer that points to an object and stays fixed in memory, regardless of where the object to which it points moves. If the object moves in memory, the *contents* of the master pointer will change to reflect the object's new address, but the placement of the master pointer in memory will never change.

Figure 2.11 shows an object in an application's heap memory. For no particular reason (other than to provide a reference point in this and subsequent figures), the object starts at memory address 0x01234500.

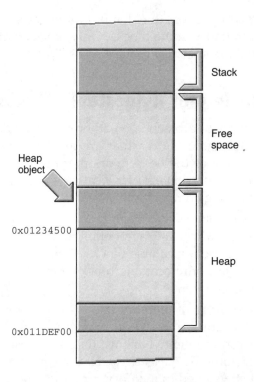

Figure 2.11 An object in heap memory.

N O T E   When an object is placed into memory, its starting address is always smaller than its ending address. Recall that when portraying Mac memory, lower memory addresses are always shown toward the bottom, so in figures such as Figure 2.11, an object appears to be "upside down" in memory. That is, the starting address of the object appears at the bottom of the object. A pointer to the object appears to be pointing to the bottom of the object, rather than to the start of the object.

Figure 2.12 shows that the lowest object in the heap pictured in Figure 2.11 is a master pointer. The master pointer is set to point to the lone object in the heap; it holds the starting address of this object, 0x01234500.

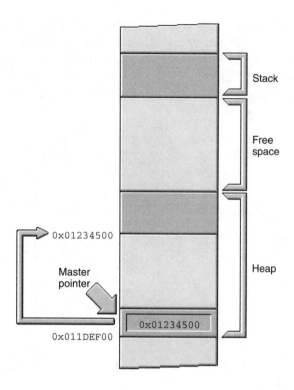

Figure 2.12 A master pointer holds the address of a heap object.

The distinction between the contents of the master pointer and the address of the master pointer can be a source of confusion. In Figure 2.12, the content of the master pointer is 0x01234500, while the address of the master pointer—where the master pointer is physically located in memory—is 0x11DEF00.

The Memory Manager uses the master pointer to keep track of a moving object. You, the programmer, still need one other device—a handle—so that your program can also keep track of this moving object. A *handle* contains the address of a master pointer. To keep tabs on a moving object in memory, you declare a handle variable in your program.

Assuming the variable is local to a routine in the program (as opposed to being declared as a global variable), it will reside on your application's stack. While the variable might be on the stack, what it points to—the master pointer—will always be in the heap. The handle variable will contain the address of this master pointer. Figure 2.13 illustrates this.

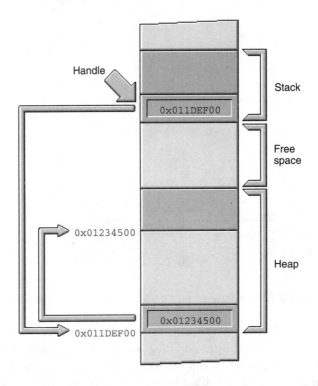

Figure 2.13 A handle holds the address of a master pointer.

If you compare Figures 2.13 and 2.12, you'll see that the addition of the handle to the stack made the stack grow downward, as expected.

N O T E

Once declared, the *content*, or value, of the handle variable will not change. In Figure 2.13, you can see that the handle has the value of the master pointer—0x011DEF00. Because the master pointer never moves, the handle's value will never change.

If the Memory Manager compacts memory, the value held in the master pointer will change. In Figure 2.14, the object in memory is moved from address 0x01234500 to address 0x01210000.

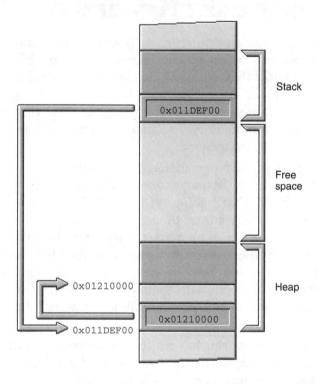

Figure 2.14 The value in the master pointer is updated after the object moves.

Note in Figure 2.14 that the object has moved and the content of the master pointer has changed to reflect this move, but the value of the handle remains the same.

If the value of the handle variable remains the same, how does your program become aware of the memory movement? The updating of the master pointer provides the answer. When your program looks to the master pointer, still located at address 0x01DEF00, it examines the contents of the master pointer to see where in memory it should look for the object. The master pointer always contains this information, so the handle variable can also track down the object.

Macintosh Memory Management

The term *memory management* refers to the allocation, movement, tracking, and removing of objects in memory. These objects are often resources. You know that menus, dialog boxes, and windows all start out as resources. As you'll see in Chapter 8, if you're generating a 68K application, your program's code itself is turned into `CODE` resources that get loaded and moved in memory. Together, these things may be referred to generically as *objects* in memory.

At the heart of memory management is the Macintosh Memory Manager. The Memory Manager does much of the behind-the-scenes work to keep track what's going on in RAM. It also provides the programmer with a set of routines to assist in memory-management tasks. Because the Macintosh uses memory-management techniques not found on most other computers, programmers new to the Macintosh often inject memory-related bugs into their programs. A thorough understanding of how the Macintosh works with memory, as described in this chapter, along with the more specific programming techniques described on the following pages, will help you reduce the number of bugs of this type.

Objects in memory can have different attributes applied to them. These *attributes*, or characteristics, are discussed in some detail throughout this chapter. For now, here's a brief overview.

A block can be relocatable. A *relocatable* block can be moved about in memory and released from memory by the Memory Manager, without any intervention by your program. The Memory Manager would do this in reaction to a scarcity of memory. A block can also be marked nonrelocatable. If a block is *nonrelocatable* it is fixed in memory; the Memory Manager will never move it or purge it on its own. It can only be released from memory by your program explicitly calling a Toolbox routine to dispose of it.

If a block is relocatable it can be either locked or unlocked. A *locked* block cannot be moved in memory. If it's *unlocked*, it can be shuffled about in memory during compaction. If it's unlocked, it can also potentially be removed from memory by the Memory Manager. The locking and unlocking of memory is often done on relocatable blocks. To guarantee that the Memory Manager doesn't move a particular block during some operation, a program can temporarily lock that block in place.

If a block is relocatable and unlocked it can be made either purgeable or unpurgeable. If it's *purgeable,* the Memory Manager can release it from memory if memory becomes scarce. If an object is important enough to remain in memory even when memory is in short supply, it can be marked as *unpurgeable.*

Although nowadays even many low-cost Macs come equipped with 8 MB of memory, memory remains a scarce resource. Why? The size of applications—including the operating system—has grown at an equal pace. So regardless of the amount of memory on the Mac your completed program is running on, your program's code or data is likely to be shuffled around in memory.

Figure 2.15 shows the different attributes that can be imposed on a block. Notice that if a block is marked as nonrelocatable it can't be unlocked or purged.

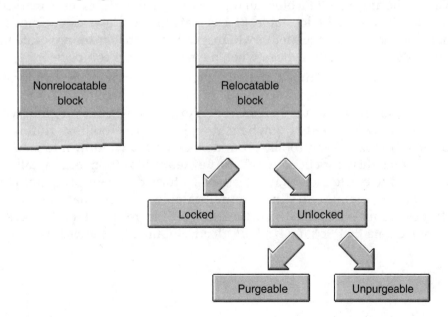

Figure 2.15 Attributes of a block in memory.

The remainder of this chapter is devoted to supplying you with the specific techniques you need to be aware of in order to write Mac programs that work with the Memory Manager.

Avoiding Heap Fragmentation

Earlier in this chapter, heap fragmentation was discussed. You know that objects get loaded into memory and then stay where they are, get moved, or are eventually purged. It's the objects that don't move, the nonrelocatable objects, that can play havoc on your program's execution. They cause roadblocks in the heap that prevent efficient use of memory. This heap fragmentation can literally kill a program; some memory-related errors will cause a program to terminate or freeze. In this section, you'll see how fragmentation can be minimized.

How Nonrelocatable Blocks Get Created

One of the attributes of a block in memory is whether the block is marked as relocatable or nonrelocatable. Blocks that are relocatable can be moved about in the heap by the Memory Manager. Blocks that are nonrelocatable always stay in one place, even when memory is being compacted.

You have only a limited amount of control when it comes to allocating nonrelocatable blocks—any call your program directly makes to the Toolbox function NewPtr() creates one. Additionally, your program will indirectly call NewPtr() when it calls some Toolbox routines. GetNewWindow()—the Toolbox routine that loads a window into memory—is one such function. A call to GetNewWindow() makes a call to NewPtr() to create the WindowPtr that is returned to your program. The WindowPtr points to the nonrelocatable block that holds a WindowRecord—the data structure that is the recipient of the WIND resource data that GetNewWindow() loads. Figure 2.16 shows this.

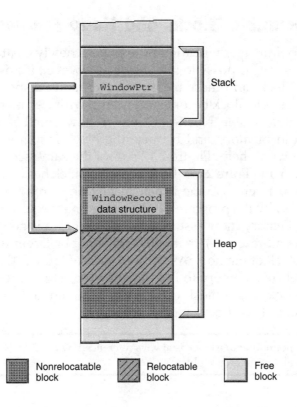

Figure 2.16 The `WindowRecord` structure is nonrelocatable and is referenced by a `WindowPtr`.

In Figure 2.16, the `WindowPtr` variable is shown on the stack. That means it's a local variable. If the program declared the `WindowPtr` variable at the global level, it would appear in the A5 World if the program was a 68K program. PowerPC applications have no A5 World, so if the program was a PowerPC application, the variable would appear somewhere in the heap.

Nonrelocatable Blocks and Heap Fragmentation

The Memory Manager will attempt to place a newly created nonrelocatable block as low as possible in the heap. However, if it is placed above relocatable blocks and those blocks are eventually disposed of (*purged*), the nonrelocatable block becomes an island, with free memory on either side. A nonrelocatable block—no matter how small it is—creates an obstruction in memory, and because the block is nonrelocatable, heap compaction won't help. Figure 2.17 shows the same section of memory as Figure 2.16. In Figure 2.17, the relocatable block has been purged from memory (you might assume it held data from a resource that was no longer needed by the program). If the program is required to load a new object into memory (now assume that the program is going to load data from a different resource), that object must not be larger than the largest *single* free block of memory. As you can see in Figure 2.17, while there is enough total free memory to hold the new object pictured on the right, there is no one single block of memory large enough to hold it. That means the object can't be loaded.

NOTE   A nonrelocatable block is always referenced by a *pointer*. A relocatable block is always referenced by a *handle*.

When a window is closed, the nonrelocatable WindowRecord block is removed from memory. That's good, but it could be too late. While the window is open, an attempt to load a large object into memory could fail. Additionally, some programs will keep one or more windows open for the entire duration of the program, eliminating the closing of the window as a solution to this dilemma.

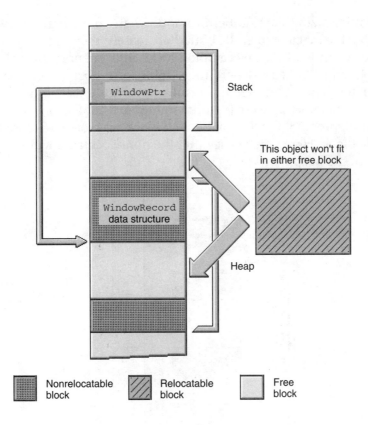

Figure 2.17 A nonrelocatable block can create an island in memory.

Nonrelocatable Block Placement in the Heap

It should be obvious by now that nonrelocatable blocks are to be avoided whenever possible. However, you don't want to go to such lengths as to try minimizing the number of windows in your programs; windows are what the Macintosh is all about. Fortunately, there is a way out of this predicament: load nonrelocatable blocks into memory first. That puts them low in the heap, where they don't form obstructive islands—no matter how long they remain in memory. Figure 2.18 shows the same objects in memory as were pictured in Figure 2.16. The only difference is that in Figure 2.18, the WindowRecord block was loaded before the relocatable block. Here you can see that the nonrelocatable window block is lower in the heap than it was in Figure 2.16.

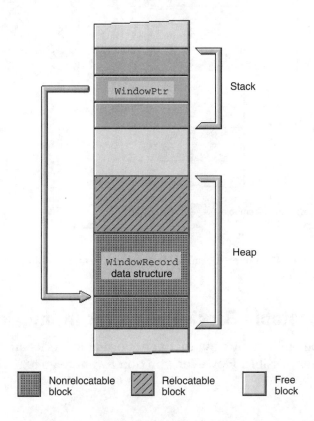

Figure 2.18 It is preferable to load a nonrelocatable block low in memory.

If the relocatable block is now purged from memory, the total amount of free space will be the same as it was back in Figure 2.17. However, because the WindowRecord block isn't left trapped in the middle of the heap, the free space is together in one block. As shown in Figure 2.19, the same object that couldn't be loaded before can be added to the heap now.

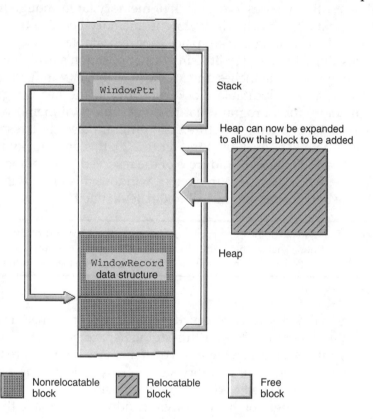

Figure 2.19 With the nonrelocatable block low in memory, the Memory Manager can make more efficient use of free space.

Reserving Memory to Reduce Fragmentation

The next best thing to avoiding a nonrelocatable block is participating in its placement. If you can control where the block goes, you can place it as low as possible in memory. As you've just read, if you do this it won't be an obstruction later as the Memory Manager attempts to load other objects into memory.

When your program first starts up, you can reserve storage for your window—even if it hasn't been opened yet. If very early in your program's execution you reserve a block of memory large enough to hold a window's data, the block will be low in memory because the Memory Manager always attempts to place nonrelocatable blocks at lower addresses. Since there's very little in your application's heap immediately after the program launches, the Memory Manager will have no problem placing a nonrelocatable block very low in the heap. Figure 2.20 shows memory for a program that reserves a block of memory the size of a `WindowRecord` data structure. The program also declares a global variable of type `Ptr`. As shown in Figure 2.20, this generic pointer variable will be used to hold the address of the reserved block of memory. At a later time, when the program opens a window, this block will be used to hold the data loaded by the call to `GetNewWindow()`.

NOTE

In Figure 2.20, the `Ptr` variable is shown in the A5 World of the application partition. That's where global variables are kept in 68K applications. If this were a PowerPC application, the variable would instead be in the heap.

What if the window you've reserved storage for isn't opened until much later in your program? Doesn't this storage space go wasted until that time? Yes, but you aren't trying to save on memory here; you're trying to avoid fragmentation. Your memory storage may be as few as a hundred bytes or so. If you created a window without using storage, the resulting fragmentation brought on by a 100-byte window could make thousands of bytes unusable.

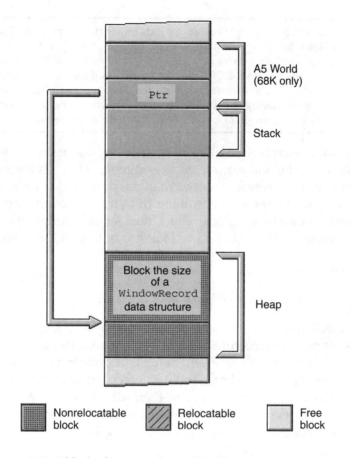

Figure 2.20 A block of memory reserved for future use and referenced by a generic Ptr variable.

NOTE Thousands of bytes? Sure. It depends on what your program is attempting to load. Imagine your application is up and running; it has 300 KB of free space—divided into two 150KB areas by a nonrelocatable block. If your program tries to load a 200KB picture resource (a resource of type PICT), it will fail. The program won't crash, but the picture won't be displayed. In case you're wondering, the situation of a 200KB picture is not unreasonable, especially if your program has color pictures in its resource file.

Your program can reserve a block of memory by using the Toolbox function NewPtr(). The one parameter passed to NewPtr() is the number of bytes of memory to reserve. Rather than passing a value here, use the C sizeof operator to obtain the number of bytes of the data structure for which the memory is being reserved. Consider an example that reserves a block of memory that will be used later to hold window data:

```
Ptr   gWindStorage;

gWindStorage = NewPtr( sizeof( WindowRecord ) );
```

In the preceding snippet of code, sizeof returns the size, in bytes, of the WindowRecord data structure. NewPtr() then allocates a nonrelocatable block of memory of this size and returns a pointer to the start of the block. If NewPtr() is called near the start of a program—such as just after Toolbox initialization takes place—then the Memory Manager will reserve the block very low in the heap, as desired. The following snippet of code provides a more comprehensive example:

```
#define    rTextWindow      128

Ptr        gWindStorage;
WindowPtr  theWindow;

InitializeToolbox();

gWindStorage = NewPtr( sizeof( WindowRecord ) );

// The program can perform any number of tasks before opening a new
// window. Not until the following line does the reserved memory
// actually get used by the application

theWindow = GetNewWindow( rTextWindow, gWindStorage, (WindowPtr)-1L );
```

As was mentioned in Chapter 1, the second parameter to GetNewWindow() tells the Window Manager where in memory to store the newly loaded window. Using a nil pointer (as has been the case up to this point) tells the Window Manager to use whatever available memory it wants. If your program instead passes a pointer as the second parameter, GetNewWindow() will store data in the block referenced by your pointer.

Let's say you're writing a program that will open a window that allows the user to draw in it. Optionally, the user can open a second window that will display a graph of some data the user has entered. With the possibility of two windows being opened, you know that your program should reserve space for two WindowRecords. Here's a code fragment that reserves memory for two windows and then opens the windows:

```
#define          rDrawWindow          128
#define          rGraphWindow         129

Ptr   gDrawWindStorage;
Ptr   gGraphWindStorage;

WindowPtr   theWindow;

InitializeToolbox();

// Reserve memory for both windows
gDrawWindStorage  = NewPtr( sizeof( WindowRecord ) );
gGraphWindStorage = NewPtr( sizeof( WindowRecord ) );

// Do stuff here...then open the first window
theWindow = GetNewWindow( rDrawWindow , gDrawWindStorage,
                    (WindowPtr)-1L );

// Do stuff here...then open the second window
theWindow = GetNewWindow( rGraphWindow , gGraphWindStorage,
                    (WindowPtr)-1L );
```

NOTE What if your program doesn't limit the user to a predefined known number of windows? One scheme that would provide at least some control over the positioning of nonrelocatable blocks would be to use the preceding techniques for known windows and then pass nil as the second parameter to GetNewWindow() to let the Window Manager handle memory assignments for other windows.

Heap Management

Setting aside window storage early in the execution of your program is a way of reserving memory for nonrelocatable blocks, but it's not the only memory-management scheme available to your applications. Your program can also reserve a small amount of memory that will help it work with relocatable blocks. Additionally, your IDE allows you to set the size of the heap to a value that is optimal for your type of program.

Allocating Master Pointer Blocks

Earlier in this chapter you saw that a master pointer is a special pointer. Like any pointer, it points to an object. But unlike a normal pointer, a master pointer can track moving objects—not just fixed ones—in memory. A WindowPtr is an example of a normal pointer; it points to a fixed nonrelocatable block of memory that holds the data of a WindowRecord data structure. A master pointer, on the other hand, points to a relocatable block.

How does a relocatable block get formed? One means of allocating a relocatable block is by calling the Toolbox function NewHandle(). NewHandle(), like NewPtr(), allocates a block of memory, the size of which is specified in the parameter to the function. The difference is that NewHandle() allocates a relocatable block and returns a handle to the memory, while NewPtr() allocates a nonrelocatable block and returns a pointer to the memory. A second way to allocate a relocatable block is through the use of a Toolbox routine that allocates such a block and returns a handle to it. For example, the GetPicture() routine that you'll see in Chapter 3 loads a picture resource into memory and returns a handle to the relocatable block of memory that holds the picture data. Just as GetNewWindow() uses NewPtr() to allocate memory, GetPicture() uses NewHandle() to allocate a new block.

When NewHandle() is called, it returns a handle. As you saw earlier in this chapter, a handle contains the address of a master pointer. The Macintosh uses master pointer blocks to hold master pointers. A *master pointer block* is a contiguous area set aside for 64 master pointers. When your program starts up, the Memory Manager creates one master pointer block for your program's use. It does this immediately so that this nonrelocatable block is placed low in your application's heap memory. Figure 2.21 shows such a block. Because the master pointers don't initially point to any data, the figure shows the contents of each as a series of question marks rather than addresses.

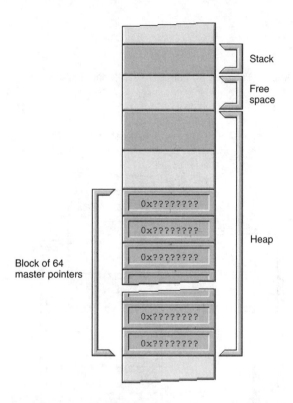

Figure 2.21 Master pointers are always present in blocks of 64.

If your program calls NewHandle() (or a Toolbox routine that calls NewHandle()), a block will be allocated in the heap and a handle returned to your program. The handle will hold the address of a master pointer, and the master pointer will hold the address of the newly allocated block. The master pointer will be one of the 64 master pointers available in the master pointer block reserved by the system for your program. The following snippet of code provides an example of how a handle variable can be declared and how NewHandle() allocates memo-

ry for a data structure. Figure 2.22 shows what memory might look like
after this snippet of code executes:

```
typedef  struct
{
    Str255  name;
    short   position;
    long    salary;

}  TeamMemberRec, *TeamMemberPtr, **TeamMemberHandle;

TeamMemberHandle  theShortStop;

theShortStop = NewHandle( sizeof( TeamMemberRec ) );
```

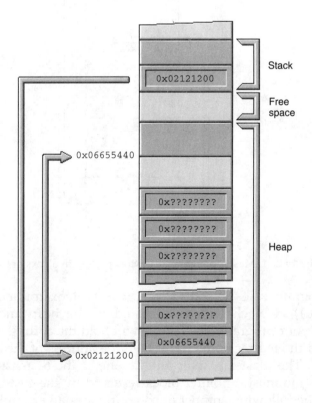

Figure 2.22 Allocating memory for an object referenced by a handle will
cause one master pointer to be used.

N O T E

In Macintosh C programming, as in programming on other platforms, a pointer declaration is made by preceding the variable name with the * operator:

```
long *theLongPtr        // pointer to a long, allocate using NewPtr()
```

A handle is declared by using the * operator twice:

```
long **theLongHandle    // handle to a long, allocate using NewHandle()
```

The definition of the data structure in the code snippet that precedes this note defines three new data types: a data structure named TeamMemberRec, TeamMember Ptr (a pointer to a data structure of type TeamMemberRec), and TeamMemberHandle (a handle to a data structure of type TeamMemberRec). Once defined, variables of any of these three types can be declared.

In Figure 2.22, the variable on the stack is the handle variable theShortStop. Like any handle, it contains the address of a master pointer. The master pointer appears at the bottom of the figure and is one of the 64 found in a master pointer block. The contents of the master pointer is the address of the block of memory allocated by the call to NewHandle().

One master pointer points to one relocatable block of memory. One master pointer block can thus point to 64 relocatable blocks. It may seem unlikely that your program would call NewHandle() more than 64 times, but it could. If your program has application-defined data structures referenced by handles (such as the TeamMemberRec data structure), it could use a number of master pointers if the program creates numerous instances of the structure. Additionally, you know that some Toolbox functions (such as GetPicture()) return handles and thus also use master pointers.

If your program uses all 64 master pointers in the master pointer block allocated to your program at application startup, the system simply allocates a second block to your program; your program doesn't need to explicitly allocate the block. There is a potential problem that arises from allowing the system to allocate the block, however. If your program has been running for a while, the new block may end up in the middle of the application's heap. Since master pointers (and thus a master pointer block) are fixed in memory, this may cause fragmentation. The solution here is similar to the one proposed for allocating memory for windows: reserve memory early so that the allocated block is low in the heap. For master pointers, a single Toolbox call does that. The MoreMasters() function not only reserves memory for a new block of master pointers, it creates the master pointers for your program's use. By calling this function a single time, your program will have 128 master pointers (the 64 from the original block and 64 from the block allocated by MoreMasters()).

When you reserve memory for windows, you do so based on the number of windows your program will open. To reserve memory for master pointers, you should base the number of master pointers on the number of relocatable blocks that your program will use, blocks created by calls to NewHandle(). How do you do this? It's not as easy as counting the number of times you use NewHandle() in your source code—you might never call it, but the Toolbox will. Some Toolbox calls result in two or three calls to NewHandle(). All this makes calculating the number of calls to NewHandle() difficult.

In determining how many times to call MoreMasters() you should keep the following in mind. A pointer always holds an address, and an address on the Macintosh always occupies 4 bytes. Thus a pointer is always 4 bytes in size, regardless of the size of the block it points to. This means that a single master pointer block, which holds 64 master pointers and an 8-byte header, is always 264 bytes in size.

From the preceding paragraph you know that a master pointer block does not occupy a lot of memory. The second thing to consider is that a nonrelocatable object, no matter how small, can cause fragmentation. Whenever possible, you want to allocate nonrelocatable objects low in memory, where they can do the least amount of damage.

From these two ideas you may accurately draw the conclusion that to avoid fragmentation, it is better to call MoreMasters() too many times than too few. Programmers generally call MoreMasters() about three or four times (though large applications may call it more than that). Including the block that the Memory Manager creates, that gives a program five master pointer blocks.

You want your master pointer blocks low in memory so you want to make the calls to MoreMasters() right away. Make the calls to MoreMasters() just before or after other initialization calls, as in this example:

```
main()
{
    InitializeToolbox();

    MoreMasters();
    MoreMasters();
    MoreMasters();

    // rest of the program...
}
```

Expanding the Heap

When your application first starts up, its application heap is set to a small size. As your program requires more memory the Memory Manager will gradually increase the size of the heap. This method of heap expansion can lead to fragmentation. A much more efficient method of enlarging the application's heap is to do so all at once at program startup; that gives the Memory Manager greater freedom in moving relocatable blocks. Conveniently, there's a Toolbox routine that does just that. MaxApplZone() should be one of the first calls your program makes. By expanding the heap all at once, future memory allocations will be carried out much more quickly. Here's how your main() routine should look, now that you know about MaxApplZone() and the MoreMasters() routine covered in the previous section:

```
main()
{
    InitializeToolbox();

    MaxApplZone();
    MoreMasters();
    MoreMasters();
    MoreMasters();

    // rest of the program...
}
```

Setting the Application Partition Size of a Program

When a user double-clicks on an application's icon in the Finder, the system sets up a memory partition for that application, then loads all or part of the program into the partition. The size of the application's partition is initially set up by the programmer, but it can be overridden by the user.

The User's Role in Setting the Partition Size

All programs come with a partition size suggested by the program's developer. The program's user can change the partition size by selecting **Get Info** from the File menu in the Finder. In any version of System 6, the user can make just a single change to the partition size. Starting with System 7, however, the user can set both the minimum partition size and a preferred size. The *minimum partition size* is the limit below which the application will not run. The *preferred partition size* is the memory size at which the developer feels the application will run effectively. If the amount of memory entered in the preferred size is not available, the system will place the application into the largest available block of memory. Allowing the user to configure the partition size lets the user base the program's partition on the amount of RAM installed in his or her Macintosh. The System 7 Get Info dialog box is shown in Figure 2.23.

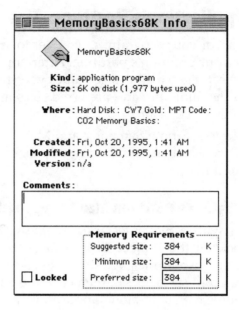

Figure 2.23 The Get Info window under System 7.

NOTE

Memory chip prices have fallen greatly in recent years, and the amount of memory in users' Macintoshes is increasing. Additionally, many users make use of virtual memory and RAM-doubling software. You may wonder if it's worth the extra effort to plan out partition size. After all, you could just do what many program developers do and assign a very large partition to your program, guaranteeing that the entire program will load in memory. That's why you shouldn't. As Macs get more memory, users are loading more of these large programs at once. While a user may have 8 MB or more of RAM, that person will typically have several programs running at once. Even with a large amount of RAM, that user might still find that he or she is just 100 KB shy of being able to load another program—maybe yours.

Setting an Application's Partition Size

You're the developer of your program, so you get to set the developer's suggested size for your program's partition. After you build an application from your project, the partition size values you specify in your project will appear as the minimum and preferred sizes in the Get Info dialog box of the Finder's File menu.

As you're about to see, both Symantec and Metrowerks make it easy for you to set the preferred and minimum heap sizes for your application before you build it.

Setting an Application's Partition Size Using the Symantec IDE

If you're working with a Symantec project, select **Options** from the Project menu. Click on the **Project Type** icon on the left side of the Options dialog box to display the page shown in Figure 2.24. Type in the minimum and preferred sizes, in KB, then click the **Save** button. When you perform a build, the stand-alone application will have these two sizes associated with it.

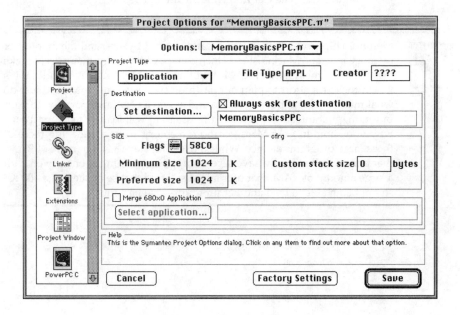

Figure 2.24 Setting your application's partition size using the Symantec IDE.

Setting an Application's Partition Size Using the Metrowerks IDE

If you're working with a Metrowerks project, select **Preferences** from the Edit menu. Click on the **68K Project** or **PPC Project** icon on the left side of the Preferences dialog box to display the panel shown in Figure 2.25. Type in the minimum and preferred sizes, in KB, then click **OK**. When you build the stand-alone application, it will have these two sizes associated with it.

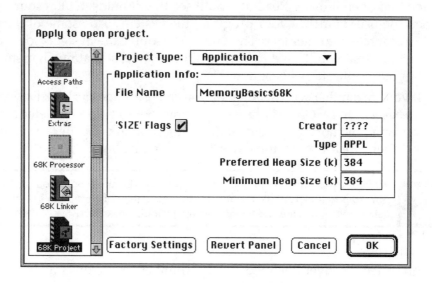

Figure 2.25 Setting your application's partition size using the Metrowerks CodeWarrior IDE.

Determining Your Application's Memory Needs

Determining the memory requirements of your program may be difficult, especially if it is a large application that relies on a lot of dynamic memory allocation. There are many factors that play a role in the amount of memory a program needs. Here are some of those factors:

- Loading of static `CODE` resources, such as `CODE 1`.
- Loading and unloading of purgeable `CODE` resources.

- Creation of objects in response to program menu commands; this can vary based on user's selections.
- Amount of global data.
- Size of the stack.

Some factors you may be able to determine, including the amount of memory the static CODE resources will occupy. If you build a 68K application and open it using ResEdit, you'll see that it holds CODE resources. When the user launches your program, the system loads some of these CODE resources into memory. The CODE 1 resource always gets loaded. This means that you'll need to always allocate at least that much memory for your application's partition.

If you are familiar with debuggers, you can use *MacsBug*, Jasik Designs *The Debugger*, or *TMON* as a heap-exploring tool to help you determine the dynamic memory requirements of your program. Debuggers aren't covered here; their use is a topic worthy of an entire book.

 If you're planning on thumbing through every Macintosh book you can find in order to find a simple formula for the calculation of a program's partition size, save your time and energy. Such a formula doesn't exist.

N O T E

If you're feeling overwhelmed by the number of factors involved in determining memory use and you're not well versed in the use of debuggers, you may be wondering if there are any "quick and dirty" methods of getting at least a rough idea of program memory use. Fortunately for you, there are.

Watching Program Memory Using the Finder

Regardless of the IDE you use, set your project's partition size as discussed earlier, then build your application. If you wish, you can start with the default sizes that your IDE suggests. Leave your IDE and return to the desktop. Go to your program's icon in the Finder and double-click on it to run your program.

Put your program through its paces. Select menu options, open dialog boxes, force the program to use the data structures you've programmed into it. In short, do everything the user will be allowed to do, and do each thing more than once.

As you're running your program, click periodically on the desktop. This will take you out of your program and into the Finder. The menu bar will change to that displayed by the Finder. Select **About This Macintosh** from the Apple menu. You'll see a window like that shown in Figure 2.26.

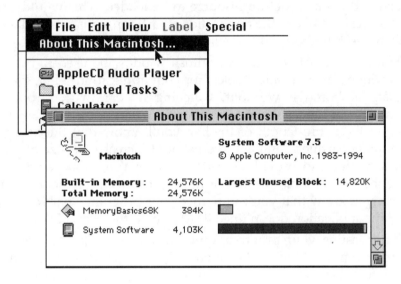

Figure 2.26 The About This Macintosh window.

The window you see when you select **About This Macintosh** shows information about memory use for each application currently running on your Macintosh. The bar that displays your program's partition and the amount of it that is currently in use, will be of most interest to you. The bar consists of two parts: the light part (which is blue on a color monitor) shows the free memory in the heap of an application's partition. The dark part (which is charcoal gray on a color monitor) shows the amount of memory in use in the heap. The overall length of the bar will remain fixed as your program runs, but the length of the dark part will fluctuate as your program runs. Figure 2.26 shows you that a small program named *MemoryBasics68K* is currently using very little of its allotted

384 KB partition, while the operating system is using most of its almost 4 MB partition.

If you continue to run your program, will the partition fill completely and crash the program? Maybe. Remember, memory allocation is dynamic in both directions—a program frees memory by purging objects from memory and consumes memory by loading objects. The next action taken by your program may cause, say, a large sound resource to be purged and a small picture resource to be loaded. This would free up some of the memory in the application's partition, causing the dark part of the bar in the About This Macintosh window to shrink.

How can the About This Macintosh window be used to determine the partition size you should select for your application? First, give your program a thorough workout, watching its bar in the About This Macintosh window as you do so. If the dark part of the bar comes close to filling the entire length of the bar, you'll know that the program is reaching its partition limit, and you should increase the size of the program's partition to provide a buffer. If after a vigorous workout you notice that the dark part of the bar never goes anywhere near the end of the bar, you know that you can reduce your program's partition size so that your application doesn't needlessly tie up the user's RAM.

After testing your program, quit and return to the desktop. Select **Get Info** from the Finder's File menu. Change the program's minimum and preferred sizes to values you think may be more appropriate. Again, run your program and test it vigorously. Check the About This Macintosh window periodically. Use this trial-and-error method until you settle on a partition size that seems right for your program.

You can see that the *MemoryBasics68K* application heap has plenty of free memory—too much, in fact. There's a good chance that the partition size for this obviously small program could be reduced from 384 KB to about 100 KB.

NOTE

Before you build your final application, take note of the partition values you've settled on. Then open the program's project and use those values in your Symantec or Metrowerks IDE. Each time you build an application from the project, the resulting program will have this optimal partition size.

NOTE

All right, hard-core hackers, you're correct; this technique isn't meant to put debugger manufacturers out of business, but it is a quick and informative way to get a feel for the fluctuations in a program's memory requirements. If the topic of partition sizes seemed theoretical before, things should seem a little more real after this first-hand experience.

Watching Program Memory Using *Swatch*

Using the **About This Macintosh** menu option is about as quick and dirty as you can get. With that method you can get a very rough idea of your program's memory use without using any programming tools. To get a much more accurate idea of what's going on in RAM, try running a nifty utility program called *Swatch*. In fact, *Swatch*, written by Joe Holt, is so handy that M&T Books has included a copy of it on the CD included with this book. *Swatch* (which stands for *System Watch*) is a very small Macintosh program (about 40K) that has just one purpose: it watches the memory usage of all applications that are running. The window that *Swatch* displays, shown in Figure 2.27, gives much more information than the window you see using the **About This Macintosh** menu item.

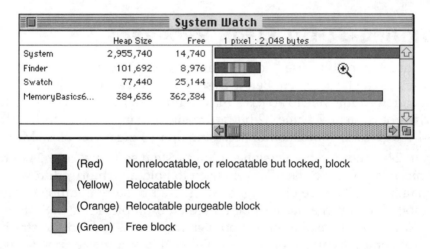

	(Red)	Nonrelocatable, or relocatable but locked, block
	(Yellow)	Relocatable block
	(Orange)	Relocatable purgeable block
	(Green)	Free block

Figure 2.27 The Swatch window as *Swatch* views the system.

Swatch shows the application heap for each running program. It shows not only how much of the heap is being used, but *how* it's being used.

Parts of the heap that are nonrelocatable or are relocatable but locked are shown in black on a monochrome system or red on a color system. Figure 2.27 shows the *Swatch* window on a Mac that has a program named *MemoryBasics68K* running. The figure also adds a key that explains the color-coding for each type of block.

Notice in Figure 2.27 that the cursor has the appearance of a magnifying glass with a plus sign in it. By clicking the mouse you can magnify the right side of the window to get a more detailed view of memory. As shown, one pixel represents 2048 bytes of RAM. A click of the mouse will make one pixel represent only 1024 bytes. You can keep clicking to get more and more detail. Holding the **Option** key while clicking the mouse button will reduce the view. *Swatch* has a few other tricks that provide more insight into the memory your program uses; they're mentioned in the text file included in the Swatch folder on the CD.

Computer memory is an abstract concept that lends itself to much confusion for both beginning and advanced programmers. *Swatch*'s ability to allow you to visualize memory helps clarify what's going on in those mysterious RAM chips of the Macintosh.

WRITING 32-BIT CLEAN PROGRAMS

The number of bits used to hold an address determines how many addresses can be accessed. Before System 7, 24-bit addressing was used. That allowed the Mac to access a maximum of 16 MB of RAM. With the arrival of System 7 came 32-bit addressing. Using 32 bits to hold an address gives the potential for accessing up to 4 gigabytes of RAM.

In 24-bit addressing versions of Mac system software, only 24 of the 32 bits of a pointer or handle were used to hold a memory address. The remaining 8 bits were either ignored or used to store additional information. The bits in a master pointer are an example. Prior to System 7, the lower 24 bits of the master pointer were used to hold the starting address of a relocatable block. The highest bit of a master pointer was used to keep track of whether the block was locked in memory. Two of the other upper 8 bits also held flags, and the remaining 5 bits went unused. Figure 2.28 provides an enlarged view of a master pointer to illustrate this.

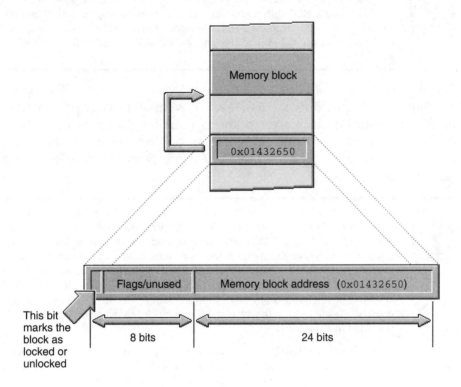

Figure 2.28 Bits of a master pointer, pre–System 7.

With the advent of System 7, Apple discontinued the use of the upper 8 bits of a pointer for anything but part of an address and encouraged developers to do the same. When the Memory Manager looks at 32 bits, it will assume that all 32 bits comprise an address. If a program stores other information in some of these bits, that information will not be recognized by the Memory Manager; they will be assumed to be part of an address. The results, of course, can be disastrous.

Programs that are written with no extraneous information in any of the 32 bits of an address are said to be *32-bit clean*, that is, they will run cleanly on a Macintosh that is using 32-bit addressing.

NOTE To allow you to run programs that aren't 32-bit clean, the Memory Control Panel lets you switch between 24-bit and 32-bit addressing in System 7. It can do this because ROMs that contain a 32-bit Memory Manager also contain, for compatibility reasons, a 24-bit Memory Manager. The downside is that with your Mac set to 24-bit addressing, only 8 MB of RAM will be accessible, even if you have more than that.

Because most users now use a version of System 7—and will soon be moving on to Copland (System 8)—you'll want all of your programs to be 32-bit clean. Bits in master pointers used for purposes other than addressing are the primary cause for an application not to be 32-bit clean. This was an acceptable practice for pre–System 7 programs, but not anymore.

IMPORTANT Don't become alarmed by all this talk of "disastrous results." If you don't try anything really tricky, your programs will most likely be 32-bit clean. Take the example in Figure 2.28. Rather than setting master pointer bits to lock a block in memory, you'll use the Toolbox routine HLock( ). The HLock( ) function won't do what's shown in Figure 2.28 (change a bit in the master pointer). Instead, it stores block information elsewhere. By using the provided Toolbox routine, you don't have to worry about the structure of a master pointer or exactly how the system locks a block (an example of HLock( ) is provided in Chapter 3).

If you don't use the Toolbox routine HLock( ) and instead you use your knowledge of what the bits in a master pointer look like (or used to look like) to try to set or clear the upper bit using direct bit manipulation, your program will no longer be considered 32-bit clean.

Master pointer bit manipulation is one source of breaking 32-bit clean standards. Another is using customized window definition functions and customized control definition functions—resources of type WDEF and CDEF. Definition functions let you create your own types of windows and controls that differ from the standard types. Both of these topics are beyond the scope of this book. If you plan to use either custom window or custom control definitions, make sure your reference sources were written with System 7 and 32-bit clean addressing in mind.

How can you be sure your program is 32-bit clean? Test it thoroughly on a Macintosh that has a version of System 7. Check the Memory

Control Panel and make sure that 32-bit addressing is turned on. If it isn't, turn it on and reboot the system. Then run your program, testing each aspect of it.

"Testing each aspect" of your program is something you'd want to do with or without the issue of 32-bit addressing, right?

IMPORTANT

CHAPTER PROGRAM: MEMORYBASICS

This chapter's example program is similar to the Chapter 1 *VeryBasics* example. *MemoryBasics* opens a window and draws a line of text to it, just as *VeryBasics* did. The window is shown in Figure 2.29. A click of the mouse button ends the program.

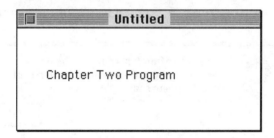

Figure 2.29 The window displayed by the *MemoryBasics* program.

After running *MemoryBasics*, you can verify that your Mac does indeed set aside a separate area in memory for the *MemoryBasics* program. Whether *MemoryBasics* (or any other program) runs successfully isn't dependent on the total amount of memory in your computer; it's dependent on the amount of memory allocated to the partition that will hold the program. From the desktop, click once on the **MemoryBasics** icon, then select **Get Info** from the File menu. Change the partition size values to a very small number, like **12** KB. Then close the Get Info window. When you do, you'll see the alert pictured in Figure 2.30. Click **OK**.

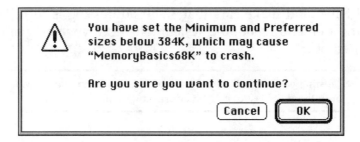

Figure 2.30 Setting a program's partition to a value below its recommended minimum size results in the display of a caution alert.

Rerun the *MemoryBasics* program. Just a moment after launching, the program will suddenly quit and return to the Finder. An alert similar to one of the two pictured in Figure 2.31 will be displayed. The rather cryptic "error of type 15" message refers to a "Segment Loader Error." You might instead see "an error of type 25," which is an "out of memory" error.

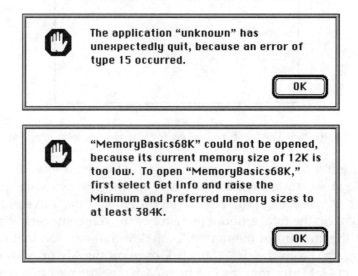

Figure 2.31 Low memory error messages.

Your Mac has at least a few megabytes of memory, most likely 8 or more. Of those megabytes, you might have several free when you run

MemoryBasics, but with all this free memory, the *MemoryBasics* program will still quit due to a shortage of memory. With possibly several megabytes of free memory at your disposal, you saw a program that needs just a little over 16 KB refuse to run. This should show you that memory partitions are indeed real.

Program Resources: MemoryBasics.rsrc

The resource file for *MemoryBasics* is identical to that of last chapter's *VeryBasics* resource file. In fact, the resource file is nothing more than a copy of the *VeryBasics* file. Opening the **MemoryBasics.rsrc** file will reveal that it holds just one `WIND` resource.

Program Listing: MemoryBasics.c

As mentioned, the source code for *MemoryBasics* is almost identical to that of *VeryBasics*.

```
//_____

void   InitializeToolbox( void );
void   HandleMouseDown( void );


//_____

#define        rTextWindow        128


//_____

Boolean   gAllDone = false;
Ptr       gWindStorage;


//_____

void   main( void )
{
   WindowPtr     theWindow;
   EventRecord   theEvent;
```

```
        MaxApplZone();
        MoreMasters();
        MoreMasters();
        MoreMasters();

        InitializeToolbox();

        gWindStorage = NewPtr( sizeof( WindowRecord ) );

        theWindow = GetNewWindow( rTextWindow, gWindStorage, (WindowPtr)-1L
        );
        if ( theWindow == nil )
            ExitToShell();

        ShowWindow( theWindow );
        SetPort( theWindow );

        MoveTo( 30, 50 );
        DrawString( "\pChapter Two Program" );

        while ( gAllDone == false )
        {
            WaitNextEvent( everyEvent, &theEvent, 15L, nil );

            switch ( theEvent.what )
            {
                case mouseDown:
                    HandleMouseDown();
                    break;
            }
        }
    }


    //_____

    void  HandleMouseDown( void )
    {
        SysBeep( 1 );

        gAllDone = true;
    }


    //_____
```

```
void  InitializeToolbox( void )
{
    InitGraf( &qd.thePort );
    InitFonts();
    InitWindows();
    InitMenus();
    TEInit();
    InitDialogs( OL );
    FlushEvents( everyEvent, 0 );
    InitCursor();
}
```

Stepping through the Code

MemoryBasics begins by calling `MaxApplZone()` to expand the application's heap to its maximum size. Without this call, *MemoryBasics* would still be allotted the heap size you specified in your IDE when you built the program. However, the program wouldn't allocate all the memory at once. Instead, it would take it on demand, as it was needed to load objects. Calling `MaxApplZone()` causes the program to grab the entire heap memory just after the program starts up. That allows for better heap management by the system—objects can be relocated more freely when the entire heap is available.

NOTE

To get the same results as described in the following discussion, work with the 68K version of *MemoryBasics*. The PowerPC version gets loaded into memory differently from the 68K version. Chapter 8 provides more details.

You can verify that `MaxApplZone()` does what it claims by running *MemoryBasics* twice. First, run the *Swatch* utility. Then run *MemoryBasics*. Click once on the *Swatch* window and take note of the heap size for the *MemoryBasics* program. The top window in Figure 2.32 shows the heap for a version of *MemoryBasics* that has an application partition size of 384 KB. Click the mouse button to end the program. Next, comment out the call to `MaxApplZone()` in the *MemoryBasics.c* source code file:

```
//  MaxApplZone();
```

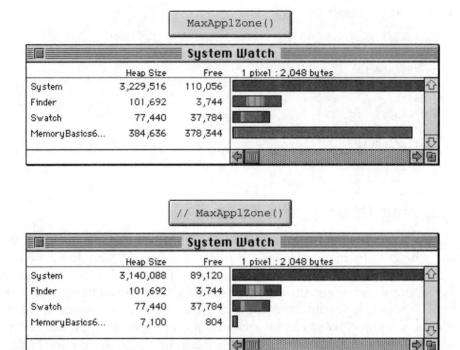

Figure 2.32 *Swatch* reveals that a call to MaxApplZone() does expand the heap to its maximum size.

Now rerun the program. Again, click on the *Swatch* window and note the size of the *MemoryBasic* heap. As shown in the bottom window of Figure 2.32, the heap size will be nowhere near the partition size that was set in the IDE.

After calling MaxApplZone(), the program calls MoreMasters() three times. While the very short and simple *MemoryBasics* program certainly won't need more than the 64 master pointers the system provides any program, it's good programming to call MoreMasters() a few times shortly after program startup.

Before opening the program's one window, *MemoryBasics* reserves enough memory to hold one WindowRecord. That reserved memory is then used in the subsequent call to GetNewWindow().

MemoryBasics uses one memory-checking trick not discussed in the text. After calling a Toolbox routine that loads a resource, it's always a good idea to verify that the request was granted. You can do this by checking the value of the pointer or handle that the Toolbox returns to your program. In the case of the loading of a WIND resource, check the value of the returned WindowPtr. If the load failed, the system will give the returned pointer a value of nil (0x00000000). If the load succeeded, the pointer will hold a valid address—a value other than nil. If a load fails, you can safely exit your program by calling the Toolbox routine ExitToShell(). In Chapter 7 you'll see how you can provide the user with a descriptive error message before exiting.

The remaining *MemoryBasics* code is the same as that used by the *VeryBasics* program. If you have any questions about the rest of the code, refer back to Chapter 1.

Chapter Summary

The Macintosh Operating System divides RAM into two main sections, or partitions. It reserves one partition, the system partition, for its own use. The other partition is dedicated to applications that you run. This second partition is further subdivided into application partitions. There is one application partition for every application that's running.

The application partition of a 68K program is composed of three main areas: the A5 World, the application stack, and the application heap. The A5 World is used to store a program's global variables. The application stack is used to hold a program's local variables. Finally, the application heap is used to hold the bulk of a program: its resources, including the program's code resources. The application partition of a PowerPC program is composed of just the application stack and heap—there is no A5 World. Information normally held in the A5 World can be found in the heap or has been eliminated.

The Memory Manager is the set of system routines that allocate the blocks, or sections, of memory. A block of memory can hold many different things, such as program code or other resources. This book generically refers to these "things" as objects.

Each block of memory has attributes, or characteristics, that can be set. Whether a block is relocatable, or movable in memory, is one such attribute. A relocatable block can be temporarily locked in memory. Because a nonrelocatable block is always fixed in memory, it doesn't have a locked/unlocked attribute. A relocatable block can also be marked as purgeable, which means that the system can remove it from the heap if the space it occupies is needed. Because a nonrelocatable block must be explicitly removed from memory by the program, and not by the system, it doesn't have a purgeable/unpurgeable attribute.

The section of memory called the application heap is the area of most interest to a Macintosh programmer. Because some memory blocks can be moved about in the heap, the heap can become fragmented—areas of memory develop that are too small to fit an object. One technique that the Memory Manager performs periodically on its own is compaction; that is, blocks are rearranged to eliminate small pockets of wasted space that lie between them. Chapter 3 covers programming techniques you can use to help the Memory Manager minimize fragmentation.

Because blocks of memory that are purgeable can be shifted about in memory, a special memory-management technique is necessary to keep track of blocks. A master pointer is a special pointer that holds the address of a single object. Though the object it points to can be moved, the master pointer itself never moves. Instead, when the block the master pointer points to is moved, the contents of the master pointer are simply updated to reflect the object's new location.

The programs you write will have to keep track of where objects reside in memory. A handle is a variable that allows a program to keep track of an object that moves about in memory. Once declared, the value of a handle doesn't change because a handle holds the address of a master pointer, which itself is a nonmoving object.

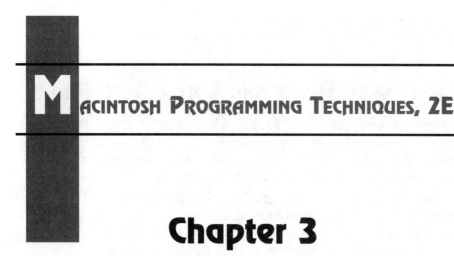

Chapter 3

QuickDraw Graphics

What would be the point of programming on a Macintosh if you couldn't draw? Drawing is fun, creative, and gives you a chance to express yourself—something you can't say about some other areas of programming. If you have a color system, as most people now do, you can really let loose. This chapter will show you how.

Here you'll learn just what QuickDraw and Color QuickDraw are, and how they work. You'll also look at graphics ports—the data structures that allow drawing styles to change from one window to the next.

In this chapter you'll see how to draw lines and shapes. You'll then add a little flair to your shapes by filling them with patterns, including color patterns that you define. Next, you'll read about pictures and how to display them. You'll also see how to combine two techniques to achieve some very interesting graphical results—this chapter shows you how to turn a picture, or part of a picture, into a small pattern that can be repeatedly stamped across a window.

Lastly, you'll learn how to change the look of the cursor. In your study of the cursor, you'll also pick up a hint and warning pertaining to avoiding the pitfalls that accompany the Memory Manager's practice of moving objects in memory.

About QuickDraw and Color QuickDraw

Everything you see on a Macintosh screen is there because of QuickDraw. QuickDraw is a group of Toolbox routines and is the single largest group of Toolbox functions. QuickDraw consists of more functions than any of the managers mentioned in Chapter 1.

Some things are obviously graphical, like the screen results of a paint program. But even windows, menus, and icons are all graphical images that have to be drawn. QuickDraw does this drawing. If any drawing has to be done, the managers rely on QuickDraw to do it.

While your program constantly makes indirect use of QuickDraw via managers such as the Window Manager and Menu Manager, it will also directly use it by calling any of the hundreds of QuickDraw Toolbox functions.

NOTE

If you're used to programming in a non-GUI environment, you might have written a few drawing routines of your own. Don't try bypassing QuickDraw by using or modifying any of your own routines. QuickDraw is fast, refined, and simple to use—you won't one-up it.

Initializing QuickDraw

QuickDraw has its own set of variables and data structures that need initialization. You've seen the following call in previous example programs in this book:

```
InitGraf( &qd.thePort );
```

Your program must call this function to initialize QuickDraw before any QuickDraw operations take place. Make this call right off the bat.

Speaking of initializations, you may recall that several other calls are included along with InitGraf(). They initialize other parts of the Toolbox, such as the Font Manager and the Window Manager. Note that the order in which these calls take place is extremely important and should remain the same as has been shown. Here's another look at the call to InitGraf() and its place in the initialization of the Toolbox:

```
void   InitializeToolbox( void )
{
    InitGraf( &qd.thePort );
    InitFonts();
    InitWindows();
    InitMenus();
    TEInit();
    InitDialogs( 0L );
    FlushEvents( everyEvent, 0 );
    InitCursor();
}
```

Pixels and the Coordinate System

Chapter 1 introduced the pixel and the coordinate system. Remember from that discussion that the Macintosh uses bitmapped graphics; every pixel on the screen has one or more bits in memory that keep track of the state of that pixel. For a monochrome Mac the state is on or off. For a color system, the state is the color of the pixel.

You can refer to each pixel by a pair of coordinates, which define a point. This coordinate system starts at point (0, 0) in the upper-left corner of the screen and moves positively to the right and downward. Figure 3.1 shows two views of the upper-left corner of a Macintosh screen. The top view is close to actual size, while the bottom view is an enlarged look at the section pictured in the top view. Both views illustrate where two pixels can be found. The first is the origin of the coordinate system—the point (0, 0). The second pixel that's referenced is found 18 pixels in from the left of the screen and 7 pixels down from the top— it's the point defined by the coordinate pair (18, 7).

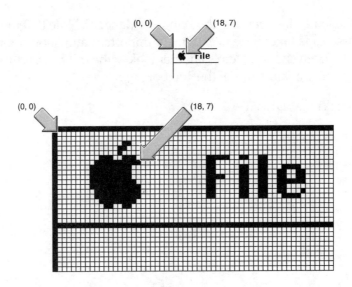

Figure 3.1 The coordinate system.

The screen isn't the only part of the Macintosh that has a coordinate system. As you'll see in the next section, every window on the screen has its own system.

GRAPHICS PORTS

When two windows are open on the screen, each is capable of displaying different styles of text. This is possible because each window has its own set of properties independent of all other windows.

The GrafPort and GrafPtr

Associated with a window is a *graphics port*. The port is the *drawing environment* of the window. It describes the window's type and style of text, the thickness of drawn lines, and numerous other aspects of the graphics that are displayed in the window.

With more than one window open on the screen you'll have to tell QuickDraw in which window or, more precisely, in which graphics port it should perform drawing operations. Issuing a call to the Toolbox function SetPort() does this. SetPort() requires a pointer to the graphics port you wish to make the current port. A GrafPort is the structure that holds all this port information. A GrafPtr is a pointer to a GrafPort.

In previous chapters you've seen SetPort() in action in code that looks like this:

```
WindowPtr   theWindow;

SetPort( theWindow );
MoveTo( 30, 50 );
DrawString( "\pChapter One Program" );
```

You may wonder how it was possible to pass SetPort() a variable of type WindowPtr when you now know that SetPort() requires a GrafPtr as its parameter. Figure 3.2 hints at the answer. This figure shows two sections of memory, each with a pointer pointing to an object. On the right, a GrafPtr points to a GrafPort. On the left, a WindowPtr points to a WindowRecord structure. Within the WindowRecord data structure, the very first member is a GrafPort. So the first thing that both a GrafPtr and a WindowPtr point to is a GrafPort—which is good enough for SetPort(). Consider Figure 3.2 a brief introduction to the WindowRecord—you'll learn all the sordid details about this data structure in the next chapter.

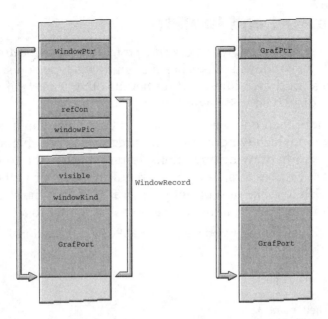

Figure 3.2 The `WindowPtr` and `GrafPtr` both point to a `GrafPort`.

NOTE

While a graphics port is usually thought of as holding the drawing environment for a window, it is actually a more general entity. For example, the look of the desktop is defined by a graphics port. Additionally, your printer serves as a graphics port during printing—printing involves sending QuickDraw drawing commands not to the port of a window, but to the printer port. Printing is a topic covered in the M&T book *More Mac Programming Techniques*.

Color Windows and the CGrafPort

The Macintosh was originally a monochrome-only machine. As such, the `GrafPort`—the data structure that holds all the information about a window's graphics port—doesn't hold any information about color. For several years now the Mac has supported color, and for the last few years all Macs other than portables have been color machines. To support color windows, Apple defined a new type of graphics port—the color graphics port. Information about a color graphics port is held in a `CGrafPort` data structure.

To create a window that is to be used to hold black and white graphics, you call the Toolbox function GetNewWindow(). To create a window that can hold color graphics, you call the Toolbox function GetNewCWindow(). Both routines ask for the same number and type of parameters, and both return a WindowPtr. Here's a call to each.

```
#define    rMonochromeWindow      128
#define    rColorWindow           129

WindowPtr  theMonoWindow;
WindowPtr  theColorWindow;

theMonoWindow  = GetNewWindow( rMonochromeWindow, nil, (WindowPtr)-1L );
theColorWindow = GetNewCWindow( rColorWindow, nil, (WindowPtr)-1L );
```

A few pages back you read about graphics ports and the GrafPort type—every window has one. Standard windows have a GrafPort. Color windows have a CGrafPort. Most of the differences will be transparent to you. Drawing operations in either type of port are similar, as you'll see later in this chapter.

Whether or not the user of your program has a color system is important. Users with older systems have the original QuickDraw in their machines, not the newer Color QuickDraw. Toolbox routines you'll be calling to display color will fail on older machines—something you certainly want to avoid. Color QuickDraw is a part of System 7. As the Mac approaches System 8 (Copland), you'll need to make the programming decision as to whether or not to support System 6 users. You'll find that most professionally developed applications now require System 7.0 or later. This book makes the assumption that you'll do the same.

The Toolbox routine Gestalt() checks the machine a program is running on for a variety of things, including the presence of Color QuickDraw. Gestalt() is covered in great depth in Chapter 9. Here you need only know how to use it—you won't need all the details on how it works. Near the start of your program, call Gestalt() with the two parameters shown below.

```
OSErr  theError;
long   theResponse;

theError = Gestalt( gestaltQuickdrawVersion, &theResponse );
```

The Gestalt() function checks for a number of system parameters. The rather ungainly Apple-defined constant gestaltQuickdrawVersion will tell the versatile Gestalt() function that on this occasion it should check for the version of QuickDraw that is present on the user's Macintosh. Gestalt() will dig that information out of the Mac your program is running on and relay it to your program in the variable named theResponse. It will also notify your program if it somehow failed its mission; that's what the variable theError is for.

Immediately after the call to Gestalt(), check the result. A response value equal to the Apple-defined constant gestaltOriginalQD means the system has the original black and white version of QuickDraw. Any other value means that there's one of several versions of Color QuickDraw present. If Gestalt() has set theResponse to a value of gestaltOriginalQD, then the user's Mac doesn't support color. If that's the case, you'll want your color program to exit:

```
if ( theResponse == gestaltOriginalQD )
    ExitToShell();
```

You'll see this color-checking code in the example program at the end of this chapter. And remember, you'll find a more thorough explanation of the Gestalt() function when you arrive at Chapter 9.

The Graphics Pen

A graphics port holds the graphical information about a window. When you draw to a window, QuickDraw uses the information held in that window's graphics port. By adjusting the settings of a port's *graphics pen* you can change many of the port's drawing properties. The graphics pen is an invisible drawing tool that exists as a convenience for making changes to the properties of lines drawn in a window.

You saw the pen in use in the example program of Chapter 1 with the call to the Toolbox routine MoveTo(). MoveTo() moves the pen—without drawing—to the pixel coordinates you specify. The reference point for moving is the current window's upper-left corner. The companion function to MoveTo() is Move(). Move() uses the pen's current position as a reference—not the window's corner. Figure 3.3 shows where the pen would end up after a call to MoveTo(150, 100). Figure 3.3 also shows that each port, including the desktop port, has its own coordinate system.

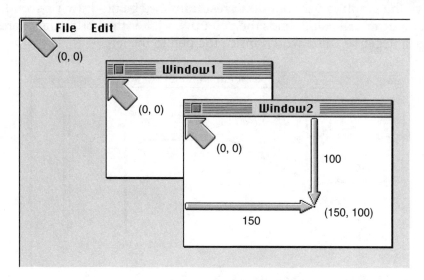

Figure 3.3 Result of MoveTo(150,100) in a window's port.

You just saw that you can move the graphics pen. You can also change its characteristics. Call PenSize() to change the size of the pen's tip. The first parameter to PenSize() controls the pen's pixel width, the second parameter controls the pen's pixel height.

Changing the pen size will affect the thickness of lines drawn with all subsequent calls to LineTo(). The first parameter to LineTo() gives the horizontal length of a line, and the second parameter gives the vertical length. The reference point for the line is the window's upper-left corner. The companion to LineTo() is Line(), which uses the current location of the pen as its reference. Here's a code fragment using all five of these calls.

```
PenSize( 3, 3 );
MoveTo( 100, 100 );
Line( 90, -50 );
Move( 100, 0 );
LineTo( 290, 140 );
```

Figure 3.4 shows the two lines that result from executing the above code. Take note of two things in this figure. First, calls to Move() and MoveTo() move the graphics pen, but don't result in lines being drawn. Second, a negative vertical value sends the pen upward. For the horizontal coordinate, a negative value would move the pen to the left.

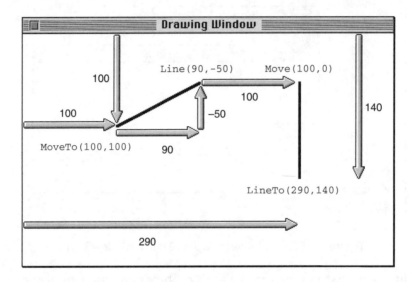

Figure 3.4 The results of moving and line drawing.

DEFENSIVE DRAWING

Every window has its own port, which makes it possible for a user to select different graphics settings in each window. It's not up to the user to keep track of all this; it's up to you, the programmer. Fortunately, the Toolbox contains a few routines that make this task painless.

Changing Ports

When you issue a command to QuickDraw, it will faithfully execute that command. The results of the command will always end up in the current port. If you have more than one window on the screen, you must tell

QuickDraw which port should be considered the current port. The Toolbox function SetPort() is your means of doing this. Before you begin drawing to a window, call SetPort(). After calling SetPort(), all subsequent drawing will take place in the window specified in the parameter to SetPort(). To draw to a different window, again call SetPort():

```
WindowPtr   theWindow1;
WindowPtr   theWindow2;

SetPort( theWindow1 );
// all subsequent drawing takes place in theWindow1

SetPort( theWindow2 );
// all subsequent drawing takes place in theWindow2

SetPort( theWindow1 );
// all subsequent drawing again takes place in theWindow1
```

When drawing, the best strategy is to first make a call to the Toolbox routine GetPort() to get a GrafPtr to the current port. Only then do you call SetPort(). The call to GetPort() will capture, or preserve, the port that was current before you set the port. When your drawing is complete, return things to their previous state by setting the port to the previously current port. Here's the format.

```
void   DrawSomething( WindowPtr theWindow )
{
    GrafPtr   theSavePort;

    GetPort( &theSavePort );
    SetPort( theWindow );

    // perform drawing here

    SetPort( theSavePort );
}
```

Notice that the GetPort() routine accepts a pointer to a GrafPtr as its parameter, while SetPort() accepts a GrafPtr. Also, recall that because the first field of the data structure that a WindowPtr points to is a GrafPort. A WindowPtr variable can be used in place of a GrafPtr variable as the parameter to SetPort().

N O T E

Apple states that the misuse of SetPort() is one of the most common sources of errors in programming the Macintosh. Don't ignore Apple! Even if your application uses only one window you should still adhere to this strategy of preserving the current port before drawing. If in the future you add multiple-window support to your program, you'll be assured that your program's drawing routines will draw to the proper window.

Changing Characteristics of a Port

One of the reasons the Macintosh gained its reputation as a computer that is easy to use is because the Mac gives control to the user. Program users don't have to be programmers to change the look of text or to draw into windows. Macintosh applications let users make changes easily to a window's environment, or graphics port, through menu choices or dialog box selections.

When a user makes an effort to set graphics characteristics for a desired effect, that user will find it disconcerting if the characteristics change on their own. If you're going to change the state of the graphics pen, you'll want to first save the present state of the pen with the Toolbox function GetPenState(). Pass GetPenState() a variable of type PenState. You can then change properties of the pen with calls to routines like PenSize(). When done, return the pen to its previous condition with a call to SetPenState(). Here's a code fragment that does that:

```
PenState  theSaveState;

GetPenState( &theSaveState );

// change pen characteristics

SetPenState( &theSaveState );
```

When would a program allow both the user and the program itself to change the state of the pen? Figure 3.5 shows one possibility. In this hypothetical paint program, the user clicked on a line thickness of four to change the pen size. When the user drew a circle, it was drawn with the selected pen size. The program has a feature that automatically adds a crosshair to a circle—and always using a pen size of 1 pixel by 1 pixel.

After the crosshair is drawn the program should return the pen to the state the user last selected—a size of four pixels.

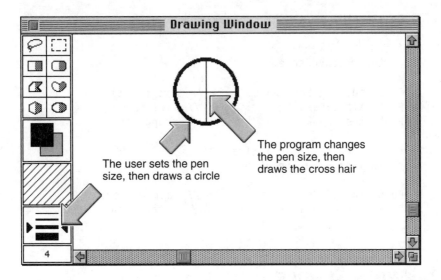

Figure 3.5 Both the user and program can control the pen.

The following is a summarization of the defensive drawing tactics covered in this section:

- Save the state of the graphics pen with `GetPenState()`.
- Save the current port with `GetPort()`.
- Make the port you're about to use the active port with `SetPort()`.
- Make any desired pen changes.
- Draw any desired shapes.
- Reset the port to the previously active port with `SetPort()`.
- Reset the state of the pen with `SetPenState()`.

The following snippet is another version of the application-defined `DrawSomething()` function. You'll want to pattern all your routines that change the pen or draw to a window on this one. Keep in mind that the calls to these routines will add very little to the size of your final application—and may save you hours in trying to find the cause of bugs later.

```
void   DrawSomething( WindowPtr theWindow )
{
    GrafPtr    theSavePort;
    PenState   theSaveState;

    GetPenState( &theSaveState );      // save pen state
    GetPort( &theSavePort );           // save port
    SetPort( theWindow );              // change port

    // change pen characteristics
    // perform drawing operations

    SetPort( theSavePort );            // restore port
    SetPenState( &theSaveState );      // restore pen state
}
```

DRAWING SHAPES

The rectangle is the basis of many of the shapes QuickDraw creates. In Macintosh programming, the information about a rectangle is stored in a variable of the data type Rect. A Rect is a structure with four members— right, left, top, and bottom. Use the Toolbox routine SetRect() to set the pixel coordinates of a rectangle. Pass SetRect() a pointer to a Rect variable along with the pixel boundaries you want the rectangle to have. The order of the boundaries is important. Here's an example that sets the upper-left corner of a rectangle at coordinates (75, 40) and gives the rectangle a width of 100 pixels and a height of 50 pixels.

```
#define       kRectLeft       75
#define       kRectTop        40
#define       kRectRight      175
#define       kRectBottom     90

SetRect( &the_rect, kRectLeft, kRectTop, kRectRight, kRectBottom );
```

The upper-left corner of the window is the reference point for the rectangle's boundaries. Figure 3.6 shows where the rectangle would be located for the above example. The figure uses a dashed line to show the rectangle because SetRect() only sets up a rectangle—it doesn't actually display one.

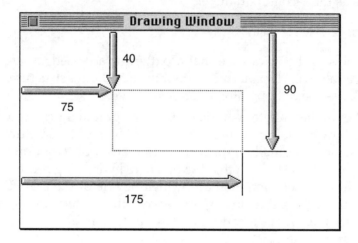

Figure 3.6 SetRect() sets a rectangle's boundaries.

Once you've set the boundaries for a rectangle you can perform several different drawing operations on the rectangle, as discussed in the next section.

Working with Rectangles

With the coordinates of a rectangle established through a call to SetRect(), you can frame it with the Toolbox function FrameRect():

```
Rect  theRect;
```

```
FrameRect( &theRect );
```

If you'd like to fill the inside of a rectangle with a pattern, you can use the Toolbox function FillRect(). Pass FillRect() a pointer to the rectangle to fill and a pointer to the pattern to use for the fill. There are five standard patterns of the C data type Pattern available for your use: white, ltGray, gray, dkGray, and black. Each of these patterns exists as a field in a data structure named QDGlobals. To hold these patterns—and a few other items—the system defines a QDGlobals variable named qd. The fact that qd is a system global variable means that it is available for use by any program—without that program having to declare it. Keeping in mind that C is case-sensitive, use a pointer to one of these patterns as the second parameter:

```
FillRect( &theRect, &qd.ltGray );
```

In the above call you can see that a pattern is accessed through the qd global variable. Each pattern is a field in the qd data structure variable, so you'll use the dot operator, as shown above.

Earlier in this chapter you read about the graphics pen. You saw that it could draw black lines using Line() and LineTo(). Lines drawn with these functions normally appear in solid black, but they don't have to. You can change the pattern that the pen uses in drawing routines by calling the Toolbox function PenPat(). Include one of the predefined patterns as the sole parameter. Again, access the pattern through the qd global variable. Here's a call that draws a diagonal line in a dark gray pattern rather than black.

```
PenPat( &qd.dkGray );
MoveTo( 20, 30 );
Line( 100, 100 );
```

Once you change the pen pattern, the change stays in effect until the next call to PenPat(). If the pen pattern is set to your liking, you can call FillRect()'s companion Toolbox routine PaintRect(). The only difference between the two is that PaintRect() uses the current pen pattern to fill the rectangle, while FillRect() requires that you pass a pattern as a parameter.

```
Rect   theRect;

SetRect( &theRect, 20, 20, 120, 120 );
PenPat( &qd.gray );
PaintRect( &theRect );
SetRect( &theRect, 50, 50, 150, 150 );
FillRect( &theRect, black );
```

Figure 3.7 shows the result of the above code. Note that the call to PaintRect() uses the current pen pattern gray, as set by the call to PenPat(). FillRect() ignores the current pen pattern and uses the passed pattern of black. The next section discusses patterns in greater detail.

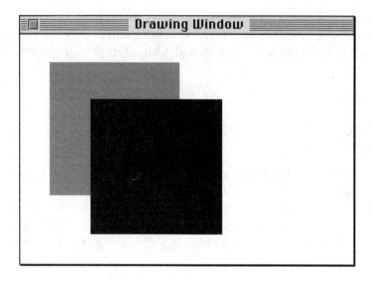

Figure 3.7 The result of calling PaintRect() and FillRect().

You can invert a rectangle using the Toolbox function InvertRect(). This routine doesn't add a pattern to a rectangle like PaintRect() or FillRect(). Instead, it inverts each pixel that falls within the boundaries of the rectangle. If the window happens to be all white at the time of the call, the rectangle will be all black.

```
InvertRect( &theRect )
```

When you're finished displaying a rectangle you can remove it with a call to the Toolbox routine EraseRect(). This function wipes out the entire rectangle and replaces it with the background color, which is usually white.

```
EraseRect( &theRect )
```

Working with Ovals

Now that you know all about rectangles, ovals will be a breeze. An oval begins with a call to SetRect(). Why set a rectangle to draw an oval? QuickDraw will not display the rectangle; it will only use it as a guide in which to inscribe the oval when you call the Toolbox function

FrameOval(). Look at the following code, then check out the results in Figure 3.8. Take note that the dashed rectangle in Figure 3.8 is there only to give a feel for what bounds the oval; QuickDraw will not actually display it.

```
Rect    theRect;

SetRect( &theRect, 50, 50, 200, 150 );
FrameOval( &theRect );
```

All the operations that work on rectangles also work on ovals—there's an oval-drawing Toolbox routine that corresponds to each of the rectangle-drawing functions. You frame an oval with FrameOval(). Add pattern to an oval using PaintOval() and FillOval(). You can invert an oval using InvertOval() and erase it with EraseOval(). Here's a call to each:

```
Rect    theRect;

SetRect( &theRect, 60, 80, 200, 235 );
FillOval( &theRect, &qd.dkGray );

PenPat( &qd.black );

SetRect( &theRect, 150, 180, 300, 330 );
PaintOval( &theRect );

SetRect( &theRect, 100, 100, 160, 185 );
InvertOval( &theRect );

SetRect( &theRect, 200, 200, 250, 250 );
EraseOval( &theRect );
```

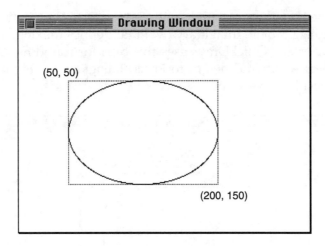

Figure 3.8 An oval is inscribed in the boundaries set by `SetRect()`.

Working with Round Rectangles

The Macintosh has an interesting shape called the *round rectangle,* which is a rectangle with rounded-off edges. If you think back to the definition of an oval, you'll have a pretty good clue of how the Macintosh defines the round rectangle.

```
short   theRndWidth  = 100;
short   theRndHeight =  50;
Rect    theRect;

SetRect( &theRect, 40, 60, 240, 160 );
FrameRoundRect( &theRect, theRndWidth, theRndHeight );
```

First, set the boundary rectangle with `SetRect()`. Then define the pixel width and height of an imaginary oval that defines the degree of rounding of the corners. QuickDraw uses this oval for rounding each corner. Pass the oval width and height to `FrameRoundRect()`. Figure 3.9 illustrates the result of executing above code snippet.

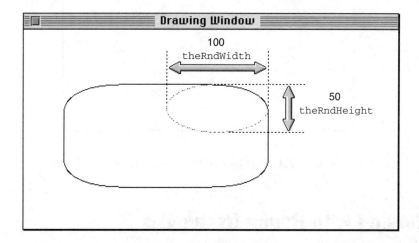

Figure 3.9 An oval defines the corners of a round rectangle.

Don't be surprised to learn that round rectangles can have the same operations performed on them as rectangles and ovals. Frame a round rectangle with `FrameRoundRect()`. Apply a pattern to a round rectangle using `PaintRoundRect()` or `FillRoundRect()`. Invert a round rectangle using `InvertRoundRect()`. Finally, erase a round rectangle using `EraseRoundRect()`. Once again, here is a call to each:

```
short   theRndWidth  = 40;
short   theRndHeight = 75;
Rect    theRect;

SetRect( &theRect, 10, 10, 200, 200 );
FillRoundRect( &theRect, theRndWidth, theRndHeight, &qd.dkGray );

PenPat( &qd.ltGray );

SetRect( &theRect, 30, 200, 100, 250 );
```

```
PaintRoundRect( &theRect, theRndWidth, theRndHeight );

SetRect( &theRect, 50, 45, 255, 320 );
InvertRoundRect( &theRect, theRndWidth, theRndHeight );

SetRect( &theRect, 200, 100, 250, 250 );
EraseRoundRect( &theRect, theRndWidth, theRndHeight );
```

PATTERNS

The five standard patterns are handy to have around, but you'll find occasion to develop your own, especially if you want a pattern that includes color. That's easy to do with the aid of the PAT and ppat resource types. You'll use ResEdit (or Resorcerer) to first create and edit your own pattern. Then you'll add a little C or C++ source code to your program to bring the pattern resource into memory and use it in drawing.

NOTE

Remember, every resource type has a four-character name. For the PAT type, there is a space after the letter 'T'.

The PAT Resource

The PAT resource is used to create a black and white pattern, while the ppat resource is used for color patterns. In this section and the next, you'll see how to work with the PAT resource. After that, it's on to color.

If you've created a WIND resource with ResEdit, you're proficiency with that resource editor is great enough to create a pattern resource by simply looking at the following steps:

1. Choose **Create New Resource** from the Resource menu.
2. In the Select New Type dialog box that opens, double-click on PAT in the list of resource types.
3. A pattern editor will open. There, click the small pencil tool on individual pixels in the enlarged view of the pattern on the left side of the window.

In the PAT editor you'll edit an 8-pixel-by-8-pixel square—that's always the size of a pattern resource. Later, when your program uses this pattern, QuickDraw will lay copies of that square end-to-end and side-by-side to fill whatever area you specify. ResEdit's PAT editor gives you an idea of how your pattern will look when it's used to fill an area. In Figure 3.10, only one pixel has been turned on in the pattern. But the right side of the editor shows quite a few pixels on. That's because the right side of the editor provides an actual size view of how a rectangle 64 pixels across by 64 pixels in height would look when filled with the pattern being worked on in the editor.

Figure 3.11 shows a completed PAT resource. In the next section you'll call on this resource to fill the lines and shapes that you display with QuickDraw calls.

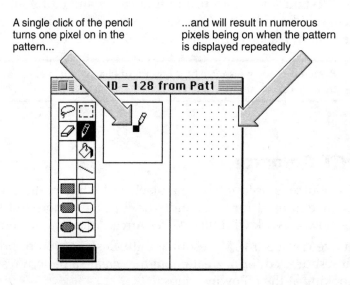

Figure 3.10 ResEdit's pattern editor in use.

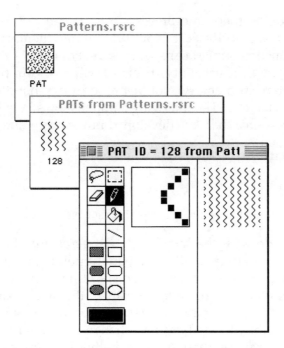

Figure 3.11 A completed PAT in the pattern editor.

The PAT Source Code

By now you should be able to see the pattern for using resources—no pun intended. First, you use a resource editor to create the appropriate resource. Then you use a Toolbox call to load that resource into memory. The Toolbox supplies your program with a handle to the memory that holds the resource. That gives you something to work with—you then use this handle in calls to other Toolbox routines.

Patterns follow this same process. You created a PAT resource in a resource editor such as ResEdit. Now, bring it into memory with a call to the Toolbox function GetPattern(). Pass GetPattern() the resource ID of the PAT to load. In return, GetPattern() will give your program a handle to the pattern in memory. Not just an ordinary handle, of course—you'll get a PatHandle. The following snippet shows how this is done to load the PAT resource that was developed in the preceding section:

```
#define      rPatternZigZagLine        128

PatHandle   thePenPatHand;

thePenPatHand = GetPattern( rPatternZigZagLine );
```

What can you do with the handle? By dereferencing the handle twice you move from a pattern handle to a pattern pointer, then to a Pattern. Note the capital 'P' in Pattern. When speaking of patterns in general, use lowercase. When referring specifically to the Macintosh C data type, use Pattern. You can pass a Pattern, or a doubly dereferenced PatHandle variable, to PenPat() to change the current pattern of the pen. Then, any drawing that you do, whether it be lines or shapes, will make use of your new pattern. Here's a comprehensive example. Figure 3.12 follows and shows the result.

```
#define      rPatternZigZagLine        128

PatHandle   thePenPatHand;
Rect        theRect;

thePenPatHand = GetPattern( rPatternZigZagLine );
PenPat( **thePenPatHand );

PenSize( 10, 10 );
MoveTo( 20, 20 );
Line( 300, 0 );

SetRect( &theRect, 20, 50, 150, 100 );
PaintRect( &theRect );
```

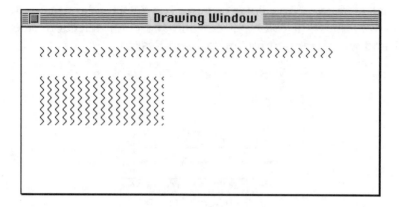

Figure 3.12 Drawing routines using a PAT resource.

Creating a PAT resource is simple and fun. Using the resource in your source code is just as easy. Since the number of patterns you can develop is huge, the PAT resource can really open the door for you to express your own creativity.

The ppat Color Pattern Resource

The monochrome representation of a pattern is the 8-pixel-by-8-pixel square with a C data type of Pattern. For color, the size is the same, but each pixel can take on any of the available colors, not just black or white. The C data type for a color pattern is PixPat—a pixel pattern. There's also a color pattern resource, the ppat.

The color ppat is analogous to the monochrome PAT. If you know how to use ResEdit's pattern editor, and you now do, then you already know how to make a ppat resource. Using ResEdit, select **Create New Resource** from the Resource menu. Scroll to the ppat name and double-click on it. The editor that opens will look similar to the PAT editor. One important difference is that the ppat editor has a pop-up menu that displays a palette that allows you to select any of the available colors for use in the pattern. You can use as many different colors as you want in a single ppat resource. For a color pattern you select colors for each pixel. Figure 3.13 shows a color pattern and the color selection palette—in black and white print, unfortunately—in ResEdit.

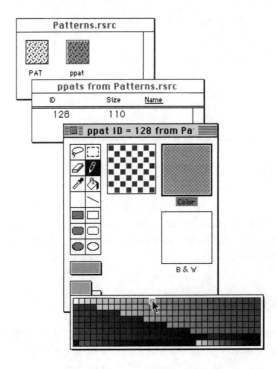

Figure 3.13 A ppat resource in ResEdit's color pattern editor.

The number of colors that appear in the palette depends on the number of colors your Mac is capable of displaying, and the color level setting you currently have your Mac set to via the Monitors control panel.

N O T E

The ppat Color Pattern Source Code

Similar to GetPattern(), the call that brings a PAT into memory, GetPixPat() is the call that loads a ppat into memory. As the following snippet shows, `GetPixPat()` returns yet another handle type, a `PixPatHandle`:

```
#define        rPixPatPurple        128

PixPatHandle  thePixPatHand;

thePixPatHand = GetPixPat( rPixPatPurple );
```

To change the current setting of the pen to your new color pattern, use the color version of `PenPat()`: the Toolbox function `PenPixPat()`. This routine conveniently takes a `PixPatHandle` as its parameter, so there's no dereferencing involved to get to the color pattern. You have the handle from the call to `GetPixPat()`, now use it in `PenPixPat()`, shown as follows:

```
#define        rPixPatPurple        128

PixPatHandle  thePixPatHand;
Rect           theRect;

thePixPatHand = GetPixPat( rPixPatPurple );
PenPixPat( thePixPatHand );

PenSize( 10, 10 );
MoveTo( 20, 20 );
Line( 300, 0 );

SetRect( &theRect, 20, 50, 150, 100 );
PaintRect( &theRect );
```

If the preceding example looks familiar, it should; the last five lines are the same as those of the monochrome pattern example a few pages back. Once the pen pattern is set, whether it be with a call to `PenPat()` or a call to `PenPixPat()`, line drawing and shape painting takes place with the same calls. Shape filling is just a little different, as you'll soon see.

Figure 3.14 shows the results you could expect from the preceding example, assuming the ppat pattern shown in Figure 3.13 is used. Again, the actual pattern displayed in the window will of course contain whatever colors were used for the ppat resource.

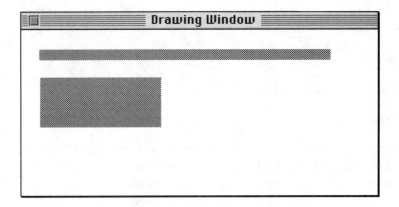

Figure 3.14 Drawing routines use the **ppat** resource.

Now that you know about color patterns, the rest of color drawing is a snap. Everything you know from the "old" monochrome QuickDraw applies. Once you set the pen pattern using PenPixPat(), lines and painted shapes will use this new pattern. For instance, the preceding example used Line() and PaintRect().

A QuickDraw fill routine (such as FillRect()) requires that you specify the pattern to use; it ignores the current pen pattern. With color you're working with a PixPatHandle and not a Pattern. Because of this the fill routines for color QuickDraw are somewhat different. Each of the monochrome Toolbox routines has a companion routine for color. Here's a call to each:

```
#define          rPixPatPurple          128

PixPatHandle    thePixPatHand;
Rect            theRect;

thePixPatHand = GetPixPat( rPixPatPurple );

SetRect( &theRect, 20, 150, 200, 250 );
FillCRect( &theRect, thePixPatHand );
FillCOval( &theRect, thePixPatHand );
FillCRoundRect( &theRect, thePixPatHand );
```

Inverting shapes in monochrome is simple because black is defined as the opposite of white. For color, things aren't quite so simple. Just what is the opposite of light chartreuse, anyway? It is possible to invert all or part of a color shape by calling `InvertRect()`, but you should avoid an inversion attempt such as this because of its unpredictable nature.

Toolbox routines originally intended for monochrome systems will work in color windows. The reverse is not always true. A call to `FillRect(&theRect, &qd.ltGray)` will draw a light gray rectangle in a color window. A call to `FillCRect(&theRect, thePixPatHand)` will not draw anything if color QuickDraw is not present.

N O T E

PICTURES AND ANIMATION

The `PICT` resource is the Macintosh way of storing a graphical image for use by a program. A program can display pictures in its windows and dialog boxes. You can also use pictures to easily add simple animation to your programs.

The PICT Resource

If you have a drawing or painting application, you can create a `PICT` resource. MacDraw, Canvas, and PixelPaint are just a few examples of programs you can use. After you draw a picture, find a piece of clip art you like, or open a digitized image, just select it from within your paint program and copy it. Then run your resource editor. Once you're in your resource editor, open your project's resource file and paste the picture into it. A resource editor such as ResEdit will automatically save the pasted picture as a `PICT` resource.

Figure 3.15 shows a simple picture in a drawing program. If you follow the preceding procedure for transferring the picture to ResEdit, your resource file will have a new resource type in it—a `PICT`, as shown in Figure 3.16.

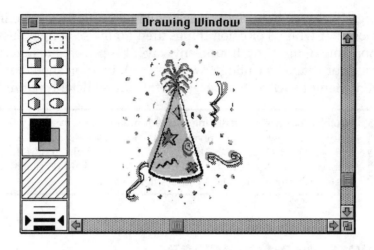

Figure 3.15 A picture in a Macintosh paint program.

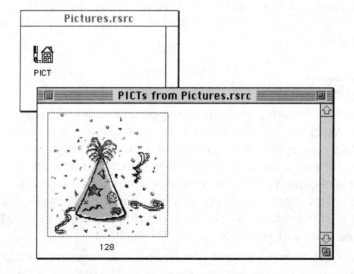

Figure 3.16 A single PICT in a resource file viewed from ResEdit.

Double-clicking on the PICT icon in a resource file will open a window that displays all of the PICT resources in the resource file. The example shown in Figure 3.16 has just one PICT, an example presented later in this chapter has more. No matter how big the picture resource is, ResEdit will display it in a small rectangle like that of Figure 3.16. ResEdit will scale the picture as best it can. This shrunken version is for display only. If you double-click on the scaled picture, you'll see it at its actual size.

Displaying a PICT in a Program

Now that you have a picture safely tucked away into a resource file, you can display it in a program.

You know all about handles from Chapter 2. Programs on the Macintosh have a special handle for working with pictures—the PicHandle. To load a PICT resource into memory, you make a call to the Toolbox routine GetPicture(). This routine returns a PicHandle for use by your program. Here's an example:

```
#define     rPartyHatPicture      128

PicHandle   thePicture;

thePicture = GetPicture( rPartyHatPicture );
```

GetPicture() brings a PICT into memory; it doesn't display the picture. To do that you make a call to the Toolbox routine DrawPicture(), which requires two parameters: a handle to a picture, and a rectangle in which to display the picture.

You can display a picture in a rectangle of any size. DrawPicture() will scale the original picture to fit the rectangle. But if you want to display the picture in its original, actual size, you'll need to determine that size.

A PicHandle is a handle to a data structure called a Picture. One of the members of this structure is the picFrame, which is a Rect that surrounds the picture. The picFrame member holds the boundaries of the picture. To access the picFrame, you dereference the PicHandle. The following snippet adds to the previous code fragment to show how this is done.

```
#define     rPartyHatPicture      128

PicHandle   thePicture;
Rect        theRect;
```

```
thePicture = GetPicture( rPartyHatPicture );
theRect = (**thePicture).picFrame;
```

Now you have the rectangle that bounds the original picture. Your real interest is in the picture's size. You want to set up a rectangle of the proper size to display the picture anywhere in a dialog box or window. The picFrame rectangle might not have left and top coordinates of 0, so you can't just assume that the right and bottom coordinates reveal the picture's size. Instead, subtract the value of the left coordinate from the value of the right coordinate to determine the picture's width. Determine the height from the bottom and top coordinates of picFrame. Here's an example that uses the rectangle variable theRect—the rectangle that holds the coordinates of picFrame:

```
short   theWidth;
short   theHeight;

theWidth  = theRect.right  - theRect.left;
theHeight = theRect.bottom - theRect.top;
```

With the picture's width and height known, set up a new rectangle to be used to display the picture anywhere within a window. Select a top-left coordinate for the picture, then use the picture's width and height. The following snippet defines a rectangle with a top-left coordinate of (60, 30). Figure 3.17 shows where the party hat picture would appear in a window if it were to be drawn to this rectangle.

```
#define      kPictureLeft      60
#define      kPictureTop       30

SetRect( &theRect, kPictureLeft, kPictureTop, kPictureLeft +
         theWidth, kPictureTop + theHeight );
```

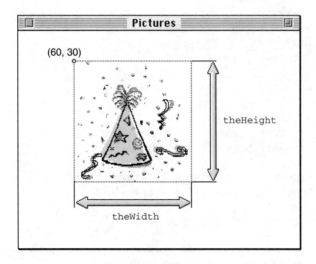

Figure 3.17 Defining the placement of a picture in a window.

Now you know how to get the original rectangle that holds the picture boundaries and how to set up your own display rectangle using SetRect(). Finally, display the picture in your rectangle using DrawPicture(). Here's a complete example:

```
#define      rPictureWindow      128
#define      rPartyHatPicture    128
#define      kPictureLeft         80
#define      kPictureTop          50

WindowPtr   theWindow;
PicHandle   thePicture;
Rect        theRect;
short       theWidth;
short       theHeight;
```

```
theWindow = GetNewWindow( rPictureWindow, nil, (WindowPtr)-1L );
if ( theWindow == nil )
    ExitToShell();
SetPort( theWindow );

thePicture = GetPicture( rPartyHatPicture );

theRect = (**thePicture).picFrame;
theWidth  = theRect.right  - theRect.left;
theHeight = theRect.bottom - theRect.top;

SetRect( &theRect, kPictureLeft, kPictureTop, kPictureLeft +
            theWidth, kPictureTop + theHeight );

DrawPicture( thePicture, &theRect );
```

NOTE Many of this book's short snippets that include code for opening a window don't include code for reserving memory for the window—they just pass `nil` as the second parameter to `GetNewWindow()` to let the Memory Manager take care of the allocation. For your own full-featured application, consider using the memory-reserving technique described in Chapter 2.

The above example loads the PICT resource with an ID of 128 into memory using `GetPicture()`. It then dereferences the `PicHandle` that `GetPicture()` returned in order to access the `picFrame` member of the `Picture` data structure in which the PICT data was stored. The width and height of the original picture are determined from the `picFrame`. A rectangle is then set up to display the picture. This rectangle starts 60 pixels in from the left of a window and 30 pixels down from the top. The width and height of the rectangle are the same as those of the original PICT. Finally, the picture is displayed in the window with a call to `DrawPicture()`.

Now you know exactly how to create a picture, save it as a PICT resource, and display it in the window of a program. With just a little more work, you can use several PICT resources to really add a little flair to your applications—especially in the form of animation.

Using PICT Resources to Create Animation

You can create animated effects in your programs by loading and displaying a series of PICT resources one after another. To do this you first create a series of pictures and save them as PICT resources. You then write a routine that includes a loop. Within the loop body you bring a PICT into memory and display it in a window. If each pass through the loop displays a different picture, and does so *over* the previous picture to obscure the old picture, the effect of animation is achieved.

Creating a Series of PICT Resources

Figure 3.18 shows a screen shot of a document from a Macintosh paint program. In this figure the author shows off his drawing expertise by drawing four characters, each in a different pose. Actually, only the leftmost character was drawn. The other three characters are copies of the first, each rotated using the paint program's free rotate feature to shift the character to a slightly different pose.

Figure 3.18 Scenes for an animation, drawn in a paint program.

Each of the characters in Figure 3.18 has a frame surrounding it for one reason only, so that each will be the same size when copied individually to the Scrapbook. When copying a single character, the selection is made just within, and not including, the border. After copying all four pictures to the Scrapbook, ResEdit can be launched and each of the pictures can in turn be pasted into the resource file for the current project. After doing so, double-clicking on the resource file's PICT icon opens a window that displays the four PICT resources, as shown in Figure 3.19.

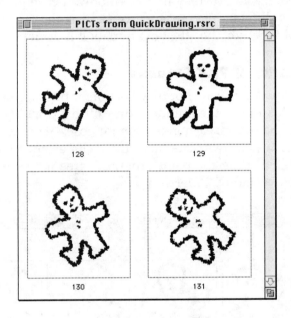

Figure 3.19 A resource file after pasting four PICT resources into it.

After taking note of the resource ID of each PICT, quit ResEdit and run your development environment. It's time to write some code.

Animation Source Code

Earlier in this chapter you learned how to display a PICT in a window by getting a PicHandle to it using the Toolbox function GetPicture() and then showing the picture using another Toolbox routine: DrawPicture(). You'll use this same technique to create animation.

As an example of simple animation, consider the application-defined AnimatePictureResource() routine. This function contains a loop that cycles through the four PICT resources created in the last section. Recall that those `PICT`s had resource IDs of 128, 129, 130, and 131, respectively. Drawing these four pictures gives the illusion that the character is dancing. Examine the function, then read the discussion of it that follows.

```
#define         rFirstDancerPicture       128
#define         kDancerDelay                7
#define         kDancerLeft                70
#define         kDancerTop                 20

void   AnimatePictureResource( WindowPtr theWindow )
{
    PicHandle      thePicture;
    short          thePictID;
    Rect           theRect;
    short          theWidth;
    short          theHeight;
    short          i, count;
    long           theTicks;

    thePicture = GetPicture( rFirstDancerPicture );

    theRect = (**thePicture).picFrame;
    theWidth  = theRect.right  - theRect.left;
    theHeight = theRect.bottom - theRect.top;
    SetRect( &theRect, kDancerLeft, kDancerTop, kDancerLeft +
             theWidth, kDancerTop + theHeight );

    count = 0;
    for ( i = 1; i <= 50; i++ )
    {
        ++count;
        switch ( count )
        {
            case 1:
                thePictID = rFirstDancerPicture;
                break;
            case 2:
                thePictID = rFirstDancerPicture + 1;
                break;
            case 3:
            case 5:
                thePictID = rFirstDancerPicture + 2;
                break;
            case 4:
                thePictID = rFirstDancerPicture + 3;
```

```
            break;
        case 6:
            thePictID = rFirstDancerPicture + 1;
            count = 0;
            break;
    }

    thePicture = GetPicture( thePictID );
    DrawPicture( thePicture, &theRect );

    Delay( kDancerDelay, &theTicks );
    }

    SetRect( &theRect, 0, 0, 1000, 1000 );
    FillRect( &theRect, &qd.white );
}
```

Much of AnimatePictureResource() should look familiar to you. It uses GetPicture() to get a handle to one of the PICT resources for the purpose of determining its pixel dimensions. This size is used to display each of the four pictures, thus the importance of making them all the same size in your drawing program.

The heart of AnimatePictureResource() is the for loop. The loop body executes 50 times, though you can of course choose to make it execute as few or as many times as you want. Within the loop body, the variable count keeps track of which of the four pictures is to be displayed during the current pass. One way to display the four pictures would be to draw them in order, that is, PICT 128, PICT 129, PICT 130, then PICT 131. After the last picture was displayed, the sequence could repeat itself, again starting at PICT 128. Continually cycling through the four PICT resources in order would be a simple task, but would result in animation that looks jerky after showing the fourth picture and then jumping back to the first. AnimatePictureResource() uses a slightly different approach. After displaying the fourth PICT, the routine "backtracks" by displaying the third, then second, and finally the first picture. It's similar to the motion of a pendulum. Figure 3.20 elaborates on this plan.

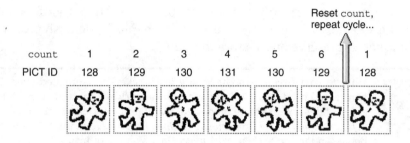

Figure 3.20 Animation: Cycling through the PICT resources.

After using variable count to determine which PICT to use, the function gets a handle to the correct PICT and then displays the picture—right on top of the previous picture. That way the AnimatePictureResource() doesn't have to bother erasing the previous picture.

After drawing one picture, and before displaying the next, AnimatePictureResource() pauses for a very short period. Some Macintosh computers, especially PowerPC-based ones, can run through this loop very quickly. Too quickly—the little man would be really dancing up a storm. By using the Toolbox function Delay(), a pause of about one-tenth of a second is added between the display of pictures to slow things down.

The Delay() function requires two parameters. The first is the length of the delay. Give the desired delay in sixtieths-of-a-second increments—that's how the Macintosh keeps track of time. Thus a value of 1 results in a delay of one-sixtieth of a second, while a value of 120 results in a two-second delay. You'll usually ignore the second parameter to Delay(). This is a pointer to a variable of type long. When the Delay() routine has finished, the Toolbox will have filled this variable with the time, in sixtieths of a second, since the system was started; that is, since the Macintosh was turned on.

The QuickDrawing example program found near the end of this chapter provides an example of animation using pictures. That program uses a version of the application-defined function AnimatePictureResource()

that is almost identical to the one described here. The only difference is that the QuickDrawing version uses this chapter's defensive drawing techniques to preserve and restore the port.

N O T E Want to create really smooth, really fast, flicker-free animated effects? For that, you'll need to use offscreen graphics worlds. That topic is beyond the scope of this text. If you're interested, you'll find information about GWorlds in *Graphics and Sound Programming Techniques for the Mac*, published by M&T Books, and in the *Imaging With QuickDraw* volume of Inside Macintosh.

Pictures as Patterns

In this chapter you've seen how to use ResEdit to create a ppat resource that holds a color pattern of your own. A second way to create a ppat resource is to start with a picture and convert it to a pattern. Doing this enables you to easily create patterns that are *far* more sophisticated than anything you could create using ResEdit's simple pattern editor. Once the picture has been converted to a ppat resource, you can use it as you would any other color pattern: draw a shape and fill it with a few, several, or dozens of the now-miniaturized pictures.

Converting a Picture to a ppat Resource Using Pict2ppat

On the book's CD you'll find a copy of the utility program Pict2ppat—a shareware utility by John J. Calande III that converts any picture to a ppat color pattern resource. To create a ppat resource using this program, begin by finding a picture of interest. Make sure the picture is saved in a PICT or PICT2 file, then launch Pict2ppat.

N O T E Got a picture that you like, but it's not in the form of a PICT or PICT2 file? Convert it. For example, if you have a GIF file, your GIF-reading software should have a **Save As** menu item in its File menu that allows you to save the GIF file in a different format, such as a PICT. As a last resort, you can open the picture of interest and perform a screen dump. Most screen capture utilities save the screen image to a PICT file that can be opened by Pict2ppat.

To import your picture into Pict2ppat, click on the **Get PICT** button. Use the standard open file dialog box to navigate to the folder that holds your picture file and then open that file. When you do, Pict2ppat will display it on the right side of the Pict2ppat window. Figure 3.21 shows Pict2ppat after opening a file that holds a picture of a robot. Incidentally, this robot file, named *Robot.PICT*, can be found in this chapter's folder of example programs.

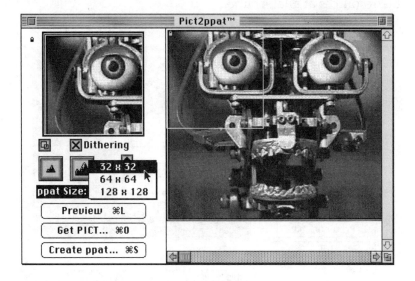

Figure 3.21 Pict2ppat with a PICT imported.

In Figure 3.21 you can see that Pict2ppat has a pop-up menu that allows you to specify the pixel dimensions of the pattern you're about to create. Earlier you edited 8-pixel by 8-pixel patterns in ResEdit. Here, you can create much larger patterns—up to 128 pixels square.

Next, take notice of the outline of a square that covers part of the picture displayed in Pict2ppat. This outlined square shows which part of the opened picture will be turned into a pattern. You can click and drag on the square to move it about the picture. You can also move it in small increments by clicking on any of the four **Arrow** buttons on the left side of the window. To save more or less of the picture as a pattern, click on either of the two "mountain" buttons.

When you're satisfied that you've selected the part of your picture that should become a pattern, click the **Create ppat** button. When you do, you'll be prompted for a ppat name, as shown in Figure 3.22. What you're naming here isn't a file, but the ppat resource itself. Pict2ppat always saves newly created ppat resources in a file named *'ppat' File*. Because this file can hold numerous ppat resources, you'll want to save each with a name so that you'll be able to identify them when you work with the resources at a later time.

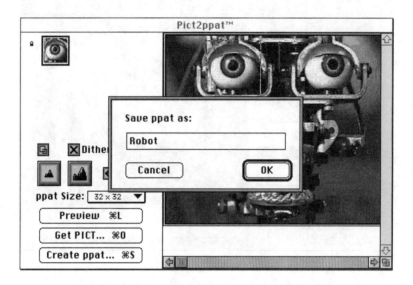

Figure 3.22 Naming a new ppat resource in Pict2ppat.

After naming the ppat, you'll quit Pict2ppat. At this time you have a new ppat resource, but it won't be of much use to you until it's in the resource file used by your current project. Launch your resource editor and open the file named *'ppat' File*—you'll find it in the same folder that holds the Pict2ppat application. Now, while still in the resource editor, also open the resource file for your project. Click once on the **ppat** icon in the file named *'ppat' File*, then select **Copy** from the Edit menu. Now click on your project's resource file, then select **Paste** from the Edit menu. (See Figure 3.23.) This chapter's QuickDrawing example program uses three ppat resources—two of them created in ResEdit, one created by

Pict2ppat. In Figure 3.23 the one ppat created in Pict2ppat is being copied from the *'ppat' File* to the *QuickDrawing.rsrc* file.

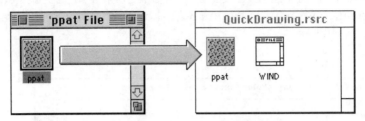

Click on the ppat icon and **Copy**...   ...then **Paste** into your project's resource file

Figure 3.23 Copying a ppat resource from the Pict2ppat file and pasting it to a project's resource file.

Double-clicking on the **ppat** icon in the resource file will reveal a list of all of the patterns in the file. For example, double-clicking on the ppat icon in the *QuickDrawing.rsrc* file now shows that there are three ppat resources in the file. In Figure 3.24 you can see that the ppat copied from the *'ppat' File* has a name (the name entered while creating the ppat in the Pict2ppat program) and an ID. The ID is a number randomly selected by Pict2ppat.

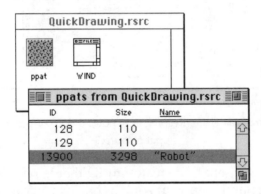

Figure 3.24 A project resource file with three ppat resources in it.

If you're using ResEdit and you double-click on the name of a ppat resource that was generated by Pict2ppat, you may see an alert that displays an error message that says the resource is corrupted. The resource, in fact, isn't corrupted; it just can't be edited in ResEdit's `ppat` editor. It can, however, still be used by any of your programs. If you use Resorcerer as your resource editor, you can open a Pict2ppat-generated `ppat` resource for editing. Figure 3.25 shows what the Resorcerer `ppat` editor looks like.

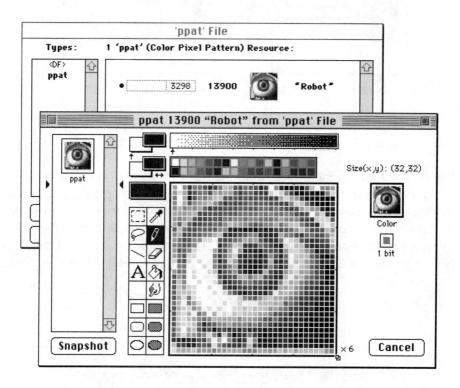

Figure 3.25 Using Resorcerer to edit a *Pict2ppat*-generated ppat resource.

Pict2ppat gives each `ppat` it creates an ID that is randomly generated. You can use this number in your source code or you can assign the `ppat` a different ID, perhaps one that better matches a resource-numbering scheme you use. To change the ID, select **Get Resource Info** from ResEdit's Resource menu. Figure 3.26 shows the ID of the *Robot* ppat being changed from the value Pict2ppat assigned it to a value of 130.

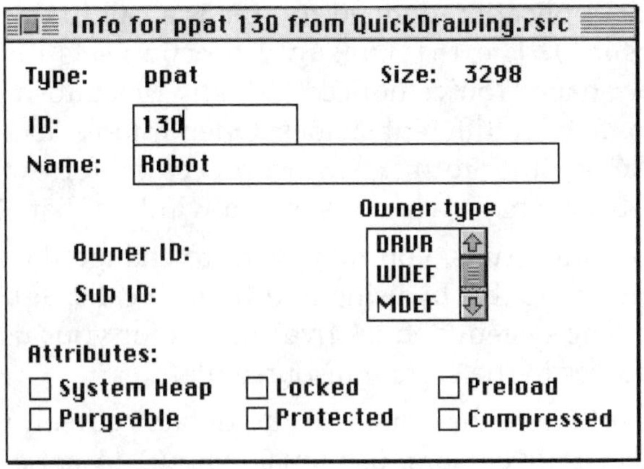

Figure 3.26 Renumbering a ppat resource in ResEdit.

A ppat resource that's created from a picture is used in the same way as a ppat resource that is created from within ResEdit's ppat editor. First, call GetPixPat() to load the resource data to memory and receive a handle to that memory. Then establish the boundaries of a shape that is to be filled with the pattern. Finally, call a FillCxxx() routine such as FillCRect() or FillCOval() to fill the shape. The following snippet fills a rectangle that is 140 by 140 pixels with the robot pattern.

```
#define        rPixPatRobot              130

PixPatHandle   theRobotPixPatHand;
Rect           theRect;

theRobotPixPatHand = GetPixPat( rPixPatRobot );

SetRect( &theRect, 140, 40, 280, 180 );
FillCRect( &theRect, theRobotPixPatHand );
```

THE CURSOR

In this book you've seen the Toolbox initialization calls packaged into one application-defined function named InitializeToolbox(). The last call in that application-defined routine is a call to the Toolbox function InitCursor(). The InitCursor() function sets the cursor to the familiar arrow shape. You've noticed in many Macintosh programs that the cursor can take on different shapes. Often it looks like an arrow, but it can also take on other forms. A word processor, for example, sets the cursor to an I-beam shape when it's over a window that allows editing.

As your program runs, you may want to change the appearance of the cursor. You can do that by using two Toolbox calls: GetCursor() and SetCursor(). The system defines five cursors for your use, and they're stored as resources in the system resource file.

InitCursor() sets the cursor to the default cursor, the arrow. For any of the other four cursors, use GetCursor() to get a handle to the desired one. You supply the resource ID of the CURS resource you want to display. You don't have to know the CURS IDs—the four system cursor resources can be referenced using Apple-defined constants: iBeamCursor, crossCursor, plusCursor, and watchCursor.

On a Macintosh, handles can be of the generic Handle type or a type specific to the object being worked with. For example, you've seen that a call to GetPicture() returns a PicHandle. A call to GetCursor() loads the data that makes up a CURS resource and returns a CurHandle to your program. After getting a CurHandle, call SetCursor() to actually make the cursor change shape. When passing the cursor handle to SetCursor(), dereference it once—SetCursor() is expecting a pointer to a cursor, and you've got a handle to one.

Here's an example that lets the user know a short wait is in order. It sets the cursor to the watch, does some task that takes some time, then sets the cursor back to the arrow.

```
CursHandle  theWatchCursor;

theWatchCursor = GetCursor( watchCursor );

HLock( (Handle)theWatchCursor );
   SetCursor( *theWatchCursor );
```

```
HUnlock( (Handle)theWatchCursor );

// do some time-consuming stuff

InitCursor();
```

Yes, you're right, something new was indeed slipped into that code snippet. The call to `SetCursor()` is sandwiched between calls to two Toolbox functions: `HLock()` and `HUnlock()`. The `HLock()` function marks a relocatable block as nonrelocatable. `HUnlock()` sets the block back to its normal condition of relocatable.

What makes the call to `SetCursor()` so different from other Toolbox calls—so different that calls to this pair of previously unseen Toolbox routines is necessary? The difference is that this is the first time you've seen a dereferenced handle being used as a parameter to a Toolbox routine. In Chapter 2, you learned about memory compaction. Memory compaction can take place during the execution of some Toolbox routines. If it does, and that routine is working with a dereferenced handle, the results can be unpredictable.

Recall that a handle holds the address of a master pointer. The master pointer won't ever move, but what it points to may. In a call to `SetCursor()`, an address is passed—the address held in the master pointer. Imagine that memory compaction takes place in the middle of the call to `SetCursor()`. `SetCursor()` was passed the address of the object—the cursor. If the block that this address points to moves, `SetCursor()` will not find the cursor, and that's a big problem.

The preceding scenario is re-created in Figure 3.27. The handle holds the address of a master pointer: 0x02233440 in the figure. Dereferencing a handle one time yields the contents of what it points to: the contents of the master pointer, or 0x03456700. So that's what is being passed when `*theWatchCursor` is used as a parameter: the address of the cursor data, 0x03456700. Just to complete this dereferencing story, if the cursor handle was dereferenced a second time you'd have the contents of address 0x03456700, the object itself—the cursor.

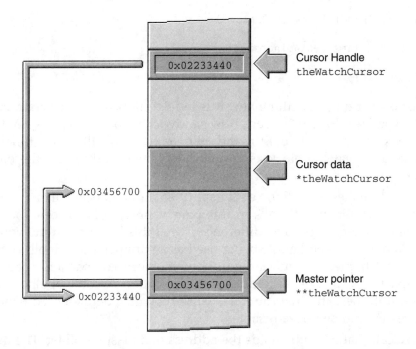

Figure 3.27 Cursor data in memory.

Now, what happens if *theWatchCursor (the address 0x03456700) is passed to SetCursor(), and memory gets compacted in the middle of the call? The relocatable block that holds the cursor might get moved. If it does, the master pointer that holds the blocks starting address will be properly updated. But the SetCursor() Toolbox function doesn't have knowledge of, or access to, the master pointer. Instead, it has only the block's original address: 0x03456700. As SetCursor() works with the data at this address, the Memory Manager could move the cursor block. If that happens, SetCursor() will be accessing no data (free memory) or incorrect data (if a different block has taken the place of the original cursor block).

Nesting code between calls to HLock() and HUnlock() prevents the above situation from occurring. The relocatable block used as the parameter to HLock() will not move, even if the heap gets compacted. The advantage to this technique should be apparent: The Toolbox call working with a dereferenced handle will work successfully. The downside is that while a relocatable block is locked, it can cause memory fragmentation. That's why a locked block should be unlocked immediately after its use is complete.

Memory compaction takes place only at select times. Not all Toolbox calls are affected. In this book, any Toolbox routines that might be affected will be called from within the safety of HLock() and HUnlock(). The Inside Macintosh series of books lists the routines that may be affected by compaction. If you don't have this information, feel free to play it safe and call HLock() every time you pass a dereferenced handle. As long as you are certain to call HUnlock() when the call is complete, you can't go wrong.

CHAPTER PROGRAM: QUICKDRAWING

QuickDrawing, this chapter's example program, uses the same format as the preceding examples in that it simply puts a single window on the screen and then does its stuff. In this case, the "stuff" is drawing.

When you run QuickDrawing you'll first see a short, animated sequence that involves the dancing man PICT resources shown earlier in this chapter. See Figure 3.28.)

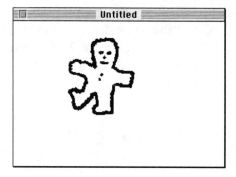

Figure 3.28 The QuickDrawing program begins with an animated sequence.

When the animation stops, QuickDrawing demonstrates how the look of the cursor can be changed. The program comes to a halt for a few seconds and, as it does so, displays the watch cursor. Soon after that the program draws a fat line and four rectangles to the window. Each of these shapes uses a ppat resource, as shown in Figure 3.29. To end the program, click the mouse button.

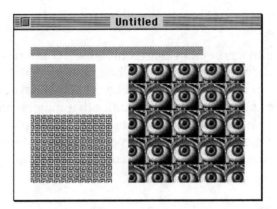

Figure 3.29 After the animation, QuickDrawing displays
pattern-filled shapes.

Program Resources: QuickDrawing.rsrc

QuickDrawing uses resources of three types: PICT, ppat, and WIND.
Figure 3.30 shows the project's resource file. The four PICT resources are
the same ones described earlier in this chapter. The first ppat resource is
a light purple pattern, and the second is a red curl. The third ppat was
created using the Pict2ppat utility. Figure 3.29 shows how each pattern
looks in use. The WIND resource is typical of the window resources
you've seen in the first two chapters.

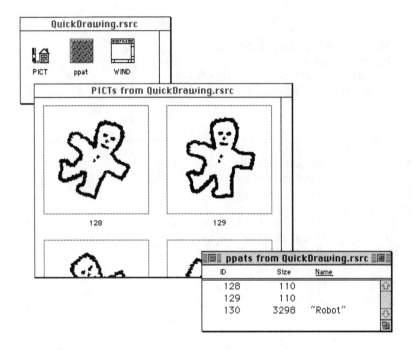

Figure 3.30 The resource file used by the QuickDrawing project.

Program Listing: ResourceUser.c

The following is the source code listing, in full, for the QuickDrawing program.

```
//_____

void   InitializeToolbox( void );
void   HandleMouseDown( void );
void   DrawWithPixPatResources( WindowPtr );
void   AnimatePictureResource( WindowPtr );


//_____

#define        rDrawingWindow          128
#define        rPixPatPurple           128
#define        rPixPatRedCurls         129
#define        rPixPatRobot            130
#define        rFirstDancerPicture     128
#define        kProgramDelay           180
#define        kDancerDelay            7
#define        kDancerLeft             70
#define        kDancerTop              20


//_____

Boolean   gAllDone = false;
Ptr       gWindStorage;


//_____

void   main( void )
{
    WindowPtr      theWindow;
    EventRecord    theEvent;
    long           theResponse;
    CursHandle     theWatchCursor;
    long           theLong;

    MaxApplZone();
    MoreMasters();
    MoreMasters();
    MoreMasters();

    InitializeToolbox();
```

```
    Gestalt( gestaltQuickdrawVersion, &theResponse );
    if ( theResponse == gestaltOriginalQD )
        ExitToShell();

    gWindStorage = NewPtr( sizeof( WindowRecord ) );
    theWindow = GetNewCWindow( rDrawingWindow, gWindStorage,
                                (WindowPtr)-1L );
    if ( theWindow == nil )
        ExitToShell();
    ShowWindow( theWindow );

    AnimatePictureResource( theWindow );

    theWatchCursor = GetCursor( watchCursor );
    HLock( (Handle)theWatchCursor );
        SetCursor( *theWatchCursor );
    HUnlock( (Handle)theWatchCursor );
    Delay( kProgramDelay, &theLong );
    InitCursor();

    DrawWithPixPatResources( theWindow );

    while ( gAllDone == false )
    {
        WaitNextEvent( everyEvent, &theEvent, 15L, nil );

        switch ( theEvent.what )
        {
            case mouseDown:
                HandleMouseDown();
                break;
        }
    }
}


//_____

void  HandleMouseDown( void )
{
    SysBeep( 1 );

    gAllDone = true;
}
```

```
//_____

void  AnimatePictureResource( WindowPtr theWindow )
{
    GrafPtr     theSavePort;
    PenState    theSaveState;
    PicHandle   thePicture;
    short       thePictID;
    Rect        theRect;
    short       theWidth;
    short       theHeight;
    short       i, count;
    long        theTicks;

    GetPenState( &theSaveState );
    GetPort( &theSavePort );
    SetPort( theWindow );

    thePicture = GetPicture( rFirstDancerPicture );

    theRect = (**thePicture).picFrame;
    theWidth  = theRect.right  - theRect.left;
    theHeight = theRect.bottom - theRect.top;
    SetRect( &theRect, kDancerLeft, kDancerTop, kDancerLeft +
             theWidth, kDancerTop + theHeight );

    count = 0;
    for ( i = 1; i <= 50; i++ )
    {
        ++count;
        switch ( count )
        {
            case 1:
                thePictID = rFirstDancerPicture;
                break;
            case 2:
                thePictID = rFirstDancerPicture + 1;
                break;
            case 3:
            case 5:
                thePictID = rFirstDancerPicture + 2;
                break;
            case 4:
                thePictID = rFirstDancerPicture + 3;
                break;
```

```
            case 6:
                thePictID = rFirstDancerPicture + 1;
                count = 0;
                break;
        }

        thePicture = GetPicture( thePictID );
        DrawPicture( thePicture, &theRect );

        Delay( kDancerDelay, &theTicks );
    }

    SetRect( &theRect, 0, 0, 1000, 1000 );
    FillRect( &theRect, &qd.white );

    SetPort( theSavePort );
    SetPenState( &theSaveState );
}


//_____

void  DrawWithPixPatResources( WindowPtr theWindow )
{
    GrafPtr        theSavePort;
    PenState       theSaveState;
    PixPatHandle   thePenPixPatHand;
    PixPatHandle   theFillPixPatHand;
    PixPatHandle   theRobotPixPatHand;
    Rect           theRect;

    GetPenState( &theSaveState );
    GetPort( &theSavePort );
    SetPort( theWindow );

    thePenPixPatHand   = GetPixPat( rPixPatPurple );
    theFillPixPatHand  = GetPixPat( rPixPatRedCurls );
    theRobotPixPatHand = GetPixPat( rPixPatRobot );

    PenPixPat( thePenPixPatHand );

    PenSize( 10, 10 );
    MoveTo( 20, 20 );
    Line( 200, 0 );
```

```
    SetRect( &theRect, 20, 40, 100, 80 );
    PaintRect( &theRect );

    SetRect( &theRect, 20, 100, 120, 180 );
    FillCRect( &theRect, theFillPixPatHand );

    SetRect( &theRect, 140, 40, 280, 180 );
    FillCRect( &theRect, theRobotPixPatHand );

    SetPort( theSavePort );
    SetPenState( &theSaveState );
}



//_____

void  InitializeToolbox( void )
{
    InitGraf( &qd.thePort );
    InitFonts();
    InitWindows();
    InitMenus();
    TEInit();
    InitDialogs( OL );
    FlushEvents( everyEvent, 0 );
    InitCursor();
}
```

Stepping through the Code

Stepping through QuickDrawing will be a breeze. All of its code was
developed in this chapter, and there are no surprises.

The define Directives

To minimize the scattering of numbers throughout the source code listing, *QuickDrawing.c* uses several #define directives. The IDs of the first
PICT, the WIND, and the three ppat resources each get their own
#define. The length of the pause between the display of frames in the
animation (7/60ths of a second) is established by the kDancerDelay constant. The length of the pause in the program after animation has completed (3 seconds) is governed by the kProgramDelay constant. Finally,

the placement of the pictures used in the animation is controlled by the kDancerLeft and kDancerTop constants.

```
#define        rDrawingWindow          128
#define        rPixPatPurple           128
#define        rPixPatRedCurls         129
#define        rPixPatRobot            130
#define        rFirstDancerPicture     128
#define        kProgramDelay           180
#define        kDancerDelay              7
#define        kDancerLeft              70
#define        kDancerTop               20
```

Global Variables

The gAllDone Boolean variable is used to signal the end of the program. Because this technique, and this variable, is used in each program in this book, this will be the last mention of it. The same applies to gWindStorage—the variable used to point to a section of memory reserved for a window.

The main() Function

QuickDrawing first calls the Toolbox functions MaxApplZone() and MoreMasters() to perform a couple of simple memory management techniques, as described in Chapter 2. Next, the usual Toolbox initializations are handled by the application-defined InitializeToolbox() function. You'll see these same lines of code in each of the remaining examples, so, again, no further mention will be made of this code.

QuickDrawing next makes a check to verify that the user's Mac has Color QuickDraw. If not, the program calls the Toolbox function ExitToShell() to quit. If Color QuickDraw is present, as is most likely the case, the QuickDrawing program reserves memory for a window and then opens a new window. Note that because the program will be displaying color patterns, it's a color window that gets loaded and opened. A call to GetNewCWindow() takes care of that. The program makes a quick check to ensure that the window was loaded successfully, then calls ShowWindow() to make sure that the window is visible.

To display the dancing man, QuickDrawing uses an application-defined routine named AnimatePictureResource(). You'll find a complete explanation of this routine earlier in this chapter. Next, the program demonstrates how to change the look of the cursor using the Toolbox functions `GetCursor()` and `SetCursor()`.

To draw pattern-filled shapes, the application-defined `DrawWithPixPatResources()` function is called. This routine calls the Toolbox function `GetPixPat()` three times—one time for each pattern. Each call loads one of the ppat resources and returns a handle to the ppat data in memory. These three patterns are then used in the drawing of a line and the filling of three rectangles.

NOTE   QuickDrawing uses a separate handle for each of the three patterns. That's a good plan if the patterns are going to be used several times, and not in a consecutive order. Since QuickDrawing uses one pattern, then another, and then the third, without re-using any of the previous patterns, the same handle could be re-used. Here's an example of a second approach, one that would work just as well:

```
PixPatHandle   thePixPatHand;

thePixPatHand = GetPixPat( rPixPatPurple );
// set pen pattern, draw a line and a painted shape

thePixPatHand = GetPixPat( rPixPatRedCurls );
// fill a shape

thePixPatHand = GetPixPat( rPixPatRobot );
// fill a shape
```

CHAPTER SUMMARY

QuickDraw is a group of Toolbox routines—the single largest group of Toolbox functions. Besides drawing the shapes and pictures you see displayed in windows, QuickDraw draws the window itself. In fact, QuickDraw is responsible for drawing everything on the Macintosh screen. QuickDraw, and other parts of the Toolbox, have to be initialized before use.

Every window has its own graphics port or environment. A graphics port defines what lines and text will look like. When you give each window its own graphics port, you allow different windows to display different styles of text and draw shapes of different patterns. You can change a graphics feature within a port by making a change to the port's graphics pen. The pen is invisible; it exists as a reference that aids you in manipulating graphics features.

You use Toolbox routines to tell QuickDraw what to draw. Because each window has its own graphics port, you must make sure that QuickDraw knows which window it should draw to in response to the commands you give it. Before you draw to a window, you'll give QuickDraw this information in the form of a call to SetPort().

The primary shape that QuickDraw works with is the Rect, the C data type that represents a rectangle. By defining the boundaries of a rectangle, you give QuickDraw the information it needs to draw rectangles, ovals, and round rectangles (rectangles with rounded corners). The Toolbox contains a host of shape-drawing routines that allows you to frame, fill, invert, and erase these different types of shapes.

You can add flair to your shapes by using patterns. The C data type Pattern allows you to choose from several defined patterns. You can also define your own monochrome patterns using PAT resources. Many Macintosh users now have color systems, and you can support these users by using Color QuickDraw. The color version of QuickDraw allows you to draw shapes in color, create color patterns using the ppat resource type, and add color to the frame or content of windows.

Chapter 4

Working with Windows

Windows are what originally set the Macintosh apart from most other computers. To display information, a Macintosh program needs at least one window. In this chapter, you'll learn about window-handling techniques.

This chapter's discussion begins with events—a topic you've been introduced to in previous chapters. Nothing happens to or with a window until an event occurs. A click of the mouse button is usually what a window responds to, so the focus will be on events involving the mouse.

Devising a system to handle events that involve one window is relatively straightforward. However, when more than a single window is on the screen, window-handling techniques become more complex. This chapter provides a strong background on the basic techniques of working with a window. It also covers the more difficult topic of working with multiple windows.

As do the previous chapters, this chapter finishes with a sample program that demonstrates the techniques highlighted in the chapter.

WINDOWS PRIMER

Before reading the details of window handling, take a look at a concise summary of just what a window is.

The WIND Resource

A window starts as a WIND resource, created using a resource editor such as ResEdit or Resorcerer. Chapter 1 covered the WIND, so this chapter will simply show the WIND editing window, shown here in Figure 4.1.

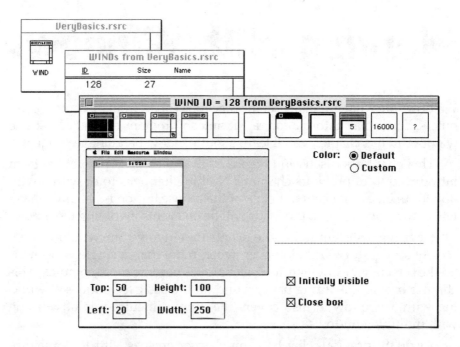

Figure 4.1 A WIND resource viewed in ResEdit.

Loading a WIND

You've already seen the Toolbox routine GetNewWindow() in action several times. It loads a window into memory and returns a pointer to the memory that holds the window information. Here's a call to GetNewWindow():

```
#define     rGraphicsWindow      128

WindowPtr   theWindow;

theWindow = GetNewWindow( rGraphicsWindow, nil, (WindowPtr)-1L );
```

The first parameter passed to GetNewWindow( ) is the resource ID of the WIND resource to use. The second parameter is a pointer that tells the Memory Manager where in memory to place the window. Passing a nil pointer here tells the Window Manager to allocate the memory for you. A value of nil is the convention used by Macintosh programmers to serve as the nil pointer. The third parameter signals the Window Manager to place the new window behind all others (0) or in front of all others (-1). The Toolbox is looking for a WindowPtr here, so you'll have to cast the value (as done by placing the data type WindowPtr in parentheses) so that the compiler does not produce an error message.

The WindowRecord, WindowPtr and WindowPeek

Every window is, in a sense, a world unto itself. Each window can have its individual properties, such as the size and font of the text it will display and whether the window is visible at this moment. The data structure WindowRecord holds this information. Here's the structure:

```
struct WindowRecord
{
    GrafPort        port;
    short           windowKind;
    Boolean         visible;
    Boolean         hilited;
    Boolean         goAwayFlag;
    Boolean         spareFlag;
    RgnHandle       strucRgn;
    RgnHandle       contRgn;
    RgnHandle       updateRgn;
    Handle          windowDefProc;
    Handle          dataHandle;
    StringHandle    titleHandle;
    short           titleWidth;
    ControlHandle   controlList;
```

```
    struct        WindowRecord *nextWindow;
    PicHandle     windowPic;
    long          refCon;
};
```

The heart of the WindowRecord is the very first member, the port member: GrafPort. Recall from Chapter 3 that a GrafPort holds all the information about a graphics port, which is a drawing environment.

You won't need to memorize the exact makeup of the WindowRecord structure. Instead, you'll work with variables of type WindowPtr. A WindowPtr points to the GrafPort of a WindowRecord. Once you have a WindowPtr, you can do just about anything you want to a window through Toolbox calls. You call the Toolbox routine name and include the pointer to the window you want to work with as follows:

```
#define    rGraphicsWindow    128

WindowPtr  theWindow;

theWindow = GetNewWindow( rGraphicsWindow, nil, (WindowPtr)-1L );

SetPort( theWindow );     // make the new window's port current

ShowWindow( theWindow ); // show the window on the screen
```

In addition to a WindowPtr, there is also a Macintosh C type called a WindowPeek. Both the WindowPtr and WindowPeek point to the start of a WindowRecord—the port field. A variable of type WindowPtr, however, can access only the port field of the WindowRecord, while a variable of type WindowPeek can access the entire WindowRecord structure. Figure 4.2 illustrates this.

From Figure 4.2 it appears that the WindowPeek is more powerful, because it allows access to all of the members of a WindowRecord, not just the port. That is, in fact, true. But there are many instances where you won't need to access any of the members other than the port. In those cases, it's best to use the WindowPtr—that minimizes the chance of inadvertently altering values in other fields of the WindowRecord. You'll also use a WindowPtr because many Toolbox routines expect a WindowPtr as one of the parameters, and won't except a WindowPeek.

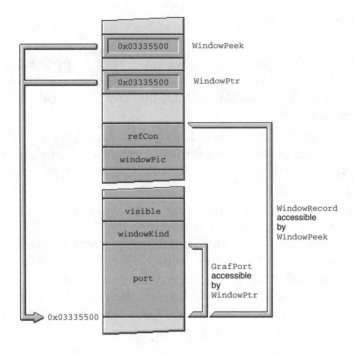

Figure 4.2 A `WindowPtr` and `WindowPeek`.

Just when *should* you use a `WindowPeek`? You'll find out in the highlight of this chapter, the section that deals with working with multiple windows.

EVENT HANDLING

Chapter 1 pointed out that the event loop is a distinguishing feature of programs written for the Macintosh and other GUI systems. A Macintosh program calls `WaitNextEvent()` to retrieve an event, then processes that event. How it does that is dependent on the type of event retrieved. Below is the `main()` function for a typical trivial Mac program.

```
void  main( void )
{
    InitializeToolbox();
```

```
    EventLoop();
}
```

The previous chapters covered the application-defined `InitializeToolbox()` routine. There, `InitializeToolbox()` called the eight Toolbox initialization routines that you should call at the start of every program.

Once the application-defined `EventLoop()` routine is called, the program will not return to main() until it is ready to terminate. It is from within `EventLoop()` that the program's continuous process of event handling takes place.

The general approach to handling a single event is to determine the type of the event, then branch to a routine that handles that particular event type. First, determine the general type of event, such as the updating of a window or a click of the mouse button. For a click of the mouse button, further determine the location of the cursor when the mouse button was pressed: the cursor could be over the menu bar, or over a window's close box, and so forth. Figure 4.3 shows this branching technique, emphasizing an event that involves the mouse.

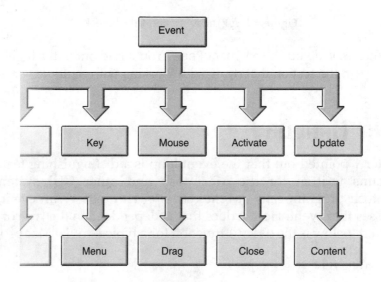

Figure 4.3 An event leads to branching.

Figure 4.3 shows only a few of the event types—you can assume that there are several more types off to the left. The same is true of the locations at which a mouse event could occur. Keeping Figure 4.3 in mind, take a look at what an EventLoop() routine might look like.

```
void  EventLoop( void )
{
   EventRecord  theEvent;

   while ( gAllDone == false )
   {
      WaitNextEvent( everyEvent, &theEvent, 15L, nil );

      switch ( theEvent.what )
      {
         case mouseDown:
            HandleMouseDown( theEvent );
            break;

         case keyDown:
            HandleKeyDown( theEvent );
            break;

         case updateEvt:
            HandleUpdate( theEvent);
            break;

         case activateEvt:
            HandleActivate( theEvent );
            break;
      }
   }
}
```

The EventLoop() routine begins by calling WaitNextEvent() to retrieve an event. After that, a switch statement is used to branch off to a routine written to handle just one type of event. In this example, events of type keyDown, mouseDown, updateEvt, and activateEvt are handled. These are Apple-defined constants, and there are a few more than appear in the example. Here's the complete list:

```
nullEvent     =  0
mouseDown     =  1
mouseUp       =  2
keyDown       =  3
keyUp         =  4
autoKey       =  5
updateEvt     =  6
diskEvt       =  7
activateEvt   =  8
osEvt         = 15
```

You write the routines to handle an event. Some will be relatively short and straightforward. Others, such as the handling of a mouse click, will be more involved. That's because a mouse click can occur on different objects on the screen. An example follows of the handling of a mouse click.

```c
void  HandleMouseDown( EventRecord theEvent )
{
    WindowPtr   theWindow;
    short       thePart;

    thePart = FindWindow( theEvent.where, &theWindow );

    switch ( thePart )
    {
        case inMenuBar:
            // handle click in the menu bar
            break;

        case inDrag:
            // handle click in a window drag bar
            break;

        case inGoAway:
            // handle click in a window close box
            break;

        case inContent:
            // handle click in a window's content area
            break;
    }
}
```

The first thing HandleMouseDown() does is to call FindWindow(). This Toolbox routine determines where the cursor is on the screen when the mouse button is pressed. If it is over a window, `FindWindow()` will return a pointer to that particular window.

`HandleMouseDown()` then handles the event depending on the screen location, (or part of the screen) where the cursor is located. The routine uses a `switch` statement to reach the code used to handle a mouse click on a specific screen part. In the preceding snippet, comments are shown rather than the event-handling code. The source code is described later in this chapter, and at other appropriate places in this book. The *part codes*, such as `inMenuBar`, are Apple-defined constants. Here's the entire list:

```
inDesk       =  0
inMenuBar    =  1
inSysWindow  =  2
inContent    =  3
inDrag       =  4
inGrow       =  5
inGoAway     =  6
inZoomIn     =  7
inZoomOut    =  8
```

Figure 4.4 serves to summarize event handling. As you study the figure, keep in mind that it shows only a few of the possible event types and only a few of the screen parts.

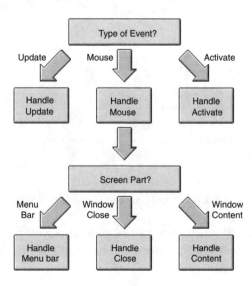

Figure 4.4 A summary of the handling of an event.

WINDOWS AND EVENTS

In case you forgot, this chapter is about windows. The previous discussion of events was a prerequisite to any serious explanation of windows. The previous section outlined how the processing of an event takes place but left some blanks, mainly some comments in place of source code. Many of those blanks deal with the handling of windows, so now is the time to fill them in.

In this chapter, you'll look at three types of events that relate to windows: mouse down, window activate, and window update events. When a mouse down event occurs you'll want to look at things a little more closely; you'll want to know where the cursor was a the time the mouse down events occurred. For instance, the use could be clicking the mouse button while the cursor is over a window's drag bar, close box, or content region. Figure 4.5 illustrates the events types that will be covered in this chapter. The figure also highlights the three window parts that will be discussed here.

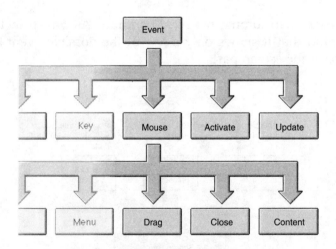

Figure 4.5 Events and part codes relating to windows.

By covering the handling of these particular events, you'll have a sound background for the finale of this chapter—the handling of multiple windows.

Mouse Down Events

When a click of the mouse button occurs in a window, your program should determine whether the click occurred in the window's drag bar, close box, or content region. Your program will then react accordingly.

Handling a Mouse Click in a Drag Bar

Handling a mouse click in a window's drag bar is easy, thanks to the Toolbox routine `DragWindow()`. You need just one line in `HandleMouseDown()`:

```
DragWindow( theWindow, theEvent.where, &gDragRect );
```

You'll add this line under the `inDrag` part code case label. Here's that line in the context of `HandleMouseDown()`:

```
void  HandleMouseDown( EventRecord theEvent )
{
   WindowPtr   theWindow;
   short       thePart;

   thePart = FindWindow( theEvent.where, &theWindow );

   switch ( thePart )
   {
      // handle clicks in other parts here

      case inDrag:
         DragWindow( theWindow, theEvent.where, &gDragRect );
         break;

      // handle clicks in other parts here
   }
}
```

Once called, the `DragWindow()` routine takes control until the mouse button is released. While the user holds down the mouse button and moves the mouse, `DragWindow()` moves the window to follow the motion of the mouse.

The first parameter in `DragWindow()` is a pointer to the window to drag. Use the `WindowPtr` variable that was filled in by the call to the Toolbox function `FindWindow()`.

The second parameter is the point coordinate at which the cursor was located when the user clicked the mouse button.

The user can move a window about the screen by clicking the mouse button and holding it down while over the window's drag bar. To prevent the user from dragging the window off the edge of a screen and entirely hiding it, you create a boundary rectangle that defines the drag limits. This rectangle is passed as the third parameter in `DragWindow()`.

Apple provides you with a system global variable named qd—you were introduced to it in Chapter 3. One of the fields of this variable of the data structure type `QDGlobals` is `screenBits`. This field, which is itself a data structure, holds a map of the user's screen. The `bounds` field of this structure is of type `Rect`, and holds the coordinates of the user's desktop. Regardless of the size of the user's monitor, its coordinates will be found in the `bounds` field.

To define a rectangle that establishes the dragging limits for windows, declare a global `Rect` variable. In this chapter, that variable is called `gDragRect`. Initialize this rectangle by setting it to the same size as the `qd.screenBits.bounds` rectangle. Next, inset this rectangle a few pixels. The inset value represents the amount of a window, in pixels, that must always remain on the screen no matter how far off the edge of the screen the user drags a window. The application-defined `SetWindowDragBoundaries()` routine bundles this short bit of code into a simple utility function that can be used in any program.

```
#define     kDragEdge      10

Rect   gDragRect;

void   SetWindowDragBoundaries( void )
{
    gDragRect = qd.screenBits.bounds;
    gDragRect.left += kDragEdge;
    gDragRect.right -= kDragEdge;
    gDragRect.bottom -= kDragEdge;
}
```

This `qd.screenBits.bounds` method assumes that your program is running on a system with only one monitor. Chapter 8 discusses a technique for establishing a boundary rectangle for dual-monitor systems.

N O T E

Once created, you'll be able to use this drag boundary rectangle anytime, thus the reasoning for making `gDragRect` a global variable.

Handling a Mouse Click in a Close Box

Should the user click the mouse button while the cursor is over a window's close box (also called the go away box), the Toolbox routine `TrackGoAway()` should be called to then follow the movement of the mouse. If the user releases the button while the cursor is over the close box of a window, the routine returns a value of `true`, and your program should then close the window.

A couple of simple housekeeping calls are all that's needed to close the window. Here's a fragment that demonstrates `TrackGoAway()`:

```
if ( TrackGoAway( theWindow, theEvent.where ) )
{
   HideWindow( theWindow );
   DisposeWindow( theWindow );
}
```

The first parameter in `TrackGoAway()` is a pointer to the window in question. The second parameter is the point at which the mouse click took place. As mentioned, `TrackGoAway()` returns a Boolean value that represents whether or not the cursor was over the close box.

While the call to `HideWindow()` is not strictly necessary, it is recommended. If a window has controls (such as scroll bars), then the housekeeping becomes more involved than shown here. You'll want the window hidden so that clean up goes on behind the scenes. `DisposeWindow()` closes a window and frees up the memory used by the window's `WindowRecord` data structure.

Here's `TrackGoAway()` in the context you'll use it in your `HandleMouseDown()` routine.

```
void  HandleMouseDown( EventRecord theEvent )
{
    WindowPtr   theWindow;
    short       thePart;

    thePart = FindWindow( theEvent.where, &theWindow );

    switch ( thePart )
    {
        // handle clicks in other parts here

        case inGoAway:
            if ( TrackGoAway( theWindow, theEvent.where ) )
            {
                HideWindow( theWindow );
                DisposeWindow( theWindow );
            }
            break;

        // handle clicks in other parts here
    }
}
```

Handling a Mouse Click in a Content Region

If many cases, a mouse button click in the content area of a window requires that you simply make the window active—if it isn't already so. The Toolbox routine FrontWindow() returns a pointer to the frontmost window. You can compare this pointer to the pointer to the clicked-on window—the pointer to that was returned by the FindWindow() call that was made at the top of the HandleMouseDown() function. If different, make a call to the **Toolbox** function SelectWindow(). This routine takes care of selecting a window by bringing it to the front and by providing the proper highlighting to the clicked-on window and to the window that was formerly the front window.

```
if ( theWindow != FrontWindow() )
    SelectWindow( theWindow );
else
{
    /* handle the needs, if any, of a click in */
    /* the contents of an active window         */
}
```

What if your program uses a window that does more than simply display information? Then you must write your program so that it is prepared to do more than just highlight a window. What else should it do? You'll see when you get to the end of the chapter. There you'll find a concrete programming example along with the theory.

Here's the code as you'd see it within the `HandleMouseDown()` routine:

```
void  HandleMouseDown( EventRecord theEvent )
{
    WindowPtr   theWindow;
    short       thePart;

    thePart = FindWindow( theEvent.where, &theWindow );

    switch ( thePart )
    {
        // handle clicks in other parts here

        case inContent:
            if ( theWindow != FrontWindow() )
                SelectWindow( theWindow );
            else
            {
                /* handle the needs, if any, of a click in */
                /* the contents of an active window        */
            }
            break;

        // handle clicks in other parts here
    }
}
```

Handling Mouse Clicks in the Menu Bar

The version of `HandleMouseDown()` presented in this chapter includes a case label with the part code `inMenuBar`. If your program includes menus and menu-handling capabilities, this is where menu-handling would take place. You'll find the code for managing menus in Chapter 6.

Now that you know how to handle a mouse click involving each of the most commonly watched for part codes, it's time to look at a near-complete version of the application-defined `HandleMouseDown()` routine. Note that the code for the `inContent` case will be completed in this chapter's Multiple-Window Techniques section. That section also discusses dealing with window activate and update events.

```
void  HandleMouseDown( EventRecord theEvent )
{
    WindowPtr   theWindow;
    short       thePart;

    thePart = FindWindow( theEvent.where, &theWindow );

    switch ( thePart )
    {
        case inMenuBar:
            break;

        case inDrag:
            DragWindow( theWindow, theEvent.where, &gDragRect );
            break;

        case inGoAway:
            if ( TrackGoAway( theWindow, theEvent.where ) )
            {
                HideWindow( theWindow );
                DisposeWindow( theWindow );
            }
            break;

        case inContent:
            if ( theWindow != FrontWindow() )
                SelectWindow( theWindow );
            else
            {
                /* handle the needs, if any, of a click in */
                /* the contents of an active window        */
            }
            break;
    }
}
```

SINGLE-WINDOW TECHNIQUES

The EventLoop() routine is the hub from which your program branches off to handle a particular event. So far, the focus has been on a mouse down event. For window handling you should be aware of two other event types: activates and updates.

Activate Events

Any Macintosh program has one and only one window *active* at any given time. The active, or *current*, window is the window that responds to user actions such as keystrokes or a click of the mouse. If there is more than one window on the screen, the active window is frontmost. The drag bar of the active window has a highlighted appearance that sets it apart from other windows.

An activate event is represented by the Apple-defined `activateEvt` part code. For a program with more than one window, a click on a deactivated window will generate two activate events: one to signify the deactivation of the frontmost window and one to signify the activation of the clicked-on window. The Window Manager handles the changing highlight conditions of window frames; you will be responsible for handling changes to the content of a window.

For a program that creates only one window, it is not uncommon to omit code that handles an activate event. That's because only one activate event will occur in a program of this type. When the window is first created, `GetNewWindow()` will generate an activate event.

You'll find more information about activate events in this chapter's pages that deal with the handling of multiple windows.

Updating a Window

When a covered, or obscured, window becomes exposed, its contents will need updating; that is, you need to redraw what is in the window. A window that needs updating will trigger the occurrence of an update event. An update event is represented by the Apple-defined `updateEvt` part code. To handle such an event, begin by branching from the application-defined `EventLoop()` function to another application-defined routine; one that handles an update. Here, this routine is aptly named `HandleUpdate()`:

```
void  EventLoop( void )
{
    EventRecord  theEvent;

    while ( gAllDone == false )
    {
        WaitNextEvent( everyEvent, &theEvent, 15L, nil );

        switch ( theEvent.what )
        {
            // handle other event types here

            case updateEvt:
                HandleUpdate( theEvent);
                break;
        }
    }
}
```

Here's a typical HandleUpdate() routine that updates a window in a program that displays a single window.

```
void  HandleUpdate( EventRecord theEvent )
{
    WindowPtr  theWindow;

    theWindow = ( WindowPtr )theEvent.message;

    BeginUpdate( theWindow );
        DrawSomething( theWindow );
    EndUpdate( theWindow );
}
```

Because it's best to use techniques that apply to all sorts of programs, HandleUpdate() should be written in a manner that you can use, with some modification, in a program that has more than one window. Instead of assuming that a particular window will be updated, HandleUpdate() gets a pointer to the window to update from the mes-sage field of the event record. The Event Manager conveniently places a pointer to the window that needs updating in the message member. As you can see from the listing for HandleUpdate(), a window update involves these steps:

- A call to `BeginUpdate()`
- The drawing of the window contents
- A call to `EndUpdate()`

Mac programs that allow a window to be resized include one other step. Before drawing the window's contents, the contents are erased. If a window is enlarged, that's a necessary step in order to clear away the old scroll bars and grow box. If you see example code that includes a line that looks similar to the one below, you'll now know what's going on—the window's entire graphics port is being erased:

N O T E

```
EraseRect( theWindow->portRect )
```

You're at this point in your code because there's an update event in the event queue. The Mac knew a window had become exposed and placed the event there. What the Macintosh doesn't know on its own is when the update event has been handled by your code. The calls to the Toolbox routines `BeginUpdate()` and `EndUpdate()` tell the Mac just that, and let the computer know it should remove the update event from the queue.

Note the indented code between the calls to `BeginUpdate()` and `EndUpdate()`. This isn't required—it's this book's convention, intended to clarify the logic of the `HandleUpdate()` routine.

N O T E

The Window Manager at all times keeps track of the portion of a window that is exposed, or visible. It keeps this area in the `visRgn` member of the window's `WindowRecord` data structure. A call to `BeginUpdate()` causes the Window Manager to save this value, and then to temporarily set the visible region to that area of the window that was obscured. When you draw the contents of the window, QuickDraw will be limited to drawing in only this temporarily visible region. The result is that QuickDraw doesn't update the entire window—only the part that was formerly obscured (see Figure 4.6).

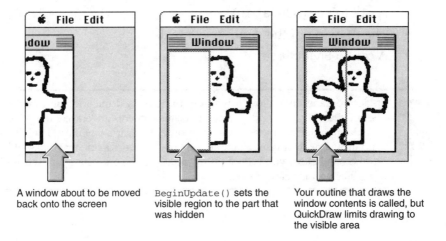

| A window about to be moved back onto the screen | BeginUpdate() sets the visible region to the part that was hidden | Your routine that draws the window contents is called, but QuickDraw limits drawing to the visible area |

Figure 4.6 Updating a window.

N O T E   What about setting the port before updating? A common mistake in window updating is forgetting to set the port. If there is more than one window on the screen, QuickDraw will draw to the window whose port is current, regardless of whether that window needs the updating or not. HandleUpdate() doesn't set the port, because it doesn't actually do any drawing—it calls the application-defined function DrawSomething() to take care of the task. So you can bet that DrawSomething() *does* make a call to SetPort().

Now, on to that rather vaguely named routine DrawSomething(). What does this routine draw? The contents of the entire window. In short, everything your program drew to the window in the first place. Why redraw everything when only a portion of it may need updating? Remember, the call to BeginUpdate() will tell QuickDraw what part of the window to draw to. When done, the call to EndUpdate() resets the window's visible region to its actual area, not to just the newly exposed area. So while your draw routine contains the code to draw an entire window's worth of content, QuickDraw will be smart enough to perform only the drawing that needs to be done to satisfy the update.

What your DrawSomething() routine will look like is entirely dependent on your application. In Figure 4.6, you can see that the content of the window is simply a picture—the display of a PICT resource. Chapter 3 covered PICT resources and displaying pictures in a window. For the window shown in Figure 4.6 the code for DrawSomething() might look like this:

```
#define          rWildManPicture        128

void  DrawSomething( WindowPtr theWindow )
{
    PicHandle   thePicture;
    Rect        theRect;
    short       theWidth;
    short       theHeight;
    GrafPtr     theSavePort;

    GetPort( &theSavePort );
    SetPort( theWindow );

    thePicture = GetPicture( rWildManPicture );

    theRect = (**thePicture).picFrame;
    theWidth  = theRect.right  - theRect.left;
    theHeight = theRect.bottom - theRect.top;
    SetRect( &theRect, 10, 10, 10 + theWidth, 10 + theHeight );

    DrawPicture( thePicture, &theRect );

    SetPort( theSavePort );
}
```

NOTE As this example demonstrates, you update a window by actually going through all of the work of redrawing the contents of the window. If you haven't programmed a Mac, you may have assumed you somehow get a "snapshot" of the contents of a window, then simply display that picture whenever appropriate.

Window updating is an important topic. An improper window update is immediately noticeable to the user in the form of a blank white area in a window or the appearance of graphics in the wrong part of the window (or even in the wrong window). For those reasons, well take a look at another example.

Displaying a picture is easy; it's an operation that is unchanging. But what if some or all of a window's contents depend on information the user supplied? Consider this example: Your program calls two application-defined routines—one that asks the user to enter the four coordinates of a rectangle, the other to then draw the rectangle. Later in the program, the user moves the window partially off screen, then back on. An update event is generated, and your DrawSomething() routine is called. Did you save those four values to some global variable, such as a Rect? Of course you did. If you hadn't, there would be no way to reproduce the rectangle now. Below is a code fragment to clarify this example.

```
Rect      gDisplayRect;            // global - hold the rectangle
Boolean   gRectIsDrawn = false;    // global - used in updating

void   GetRectDataFromUser( void )
{
    short   left, right, top, bottom;

    // Display dialog box here. It's used to read in rectangle
    // coordinate values and save to variables l, r, t, and b.
    // (Chapter 5 describes how to do this!)

    SetRect( gDisplayRect, left, right, top, bottom );
}


void   DrawUsersRectangle( WindowPtr theWindow )
{
    // local variables and save and set port calls here

    FillRect( &gDisplayRect, &qd.ltGray );
    FrameRect( &gDisplayRect );

    gRectIsDrawn = true;

    // restore port here
}
```

After DrawUsersRectangle() draws the rectangle, the function sets the global flag gRectIsDrawn to true. When it comes time to update the window, DrawSomething() will check to see if gRectIsDrawn is true. If it is, the rectangle gets redrawn. And the rectangle coordinates to use? They were saved in the global Rect variable gDisplayRect in the GetRectDataFromUser() function.

```
void  DrawSomething( WindowPtr theWindow )
{
   if ( gRectIsDrawn == true )
      DrawUsersRectangle( theWindow );

   // draw anything else that should appear in the window here
}
```

From this example, you can see that your updating routine might get quite involved and may contain decision-making logic, like the check of the gRectIsDrawn flag in the preceding example.

Simple Window Techniques

Before finishing this chapter with an example program that works with multiple windows, a quick look at some simple window techniques is in order. The following are all techniques that you can use in any program that has a window, or more than one window. All of the simple window manipulations described in the following sections revolve around using the correct Toolbox call to perform the task at hand.

Moving a Window

When you create a WIND window resource in ResEdit, you have the option of specifying whether a call to GetNewWindow() displays the window when it loads the WIND into memory. If your program will be moving the window upon opening, it is best to mark the WIND resource as invisible (see Figure 4.7). Then, after you load the window you can, unbeknownst to the user, move the window to wherever you want on the screen and show it.

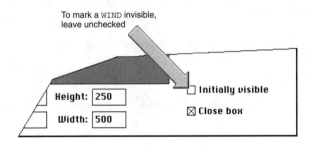

Figure 4.7 Using ResEdit to mark a WIND as invisible.

To move a window—even one that is invisible—use the `MoveWindow()` Toolbox routine. Pass a pointer to the window you want to move, the pixel coordinates of the screen location to move the window to, and a `Boolean` value that tells whether to activate (highlight) the window. Here's an example:

```
#define    kLeftOffset    20    // 20 pixels from left of screen
#define    kTopOffset     50    // 50 pixels from top of screen

WindowPtr  theWindow;
Boolean    activateWind = true;

MoveWindow( theWindow, kLeftOffset, kTopOffset, activateWind );
```

Showing and Hiding a Window

Earlier you learned that you can make a window invisible, or hidden, by using the Toolbox function `HideWindow()`. You can make the same window visible again with a call to another Toolbox routine: `ShowWindow()`. Here's an example:

```
WindowPtr  theWindow;

HideWindow( theWindow );
ShowWindow( theWindow );
```

Changing a Window's Title

When you load a window with a call to `GetNewWindow()`, the window's title will be "Untitled"—not a very polished look for your slick application. To give a window a title more befitting its purpose, use the Toolbox function `SetWTitle()`.

```
#define    kGraphicsWindowTitle    "\pGraphics Window"

WindowPtr  theWindow;

SetWTitle( theWindow, kGraphicsWindowTitle );
```

MULTIPLE-WINDOW TECHNIQUES

A program that is capable of putting more than one window on the screen has a special set of needs that you must meet. There is a new twist to window updating: the contents of one window might not be the same as those of another window. This means that you don't have the luxury of simply calling on one generic update routine to handle any and all updates.

You'll need to devise a strategy that allows your program to distinguish between different types of windows. In this section, you'll do just that. Imagine that you want to create a program that puts two types of windows on the screen. One window will be a control window with two buttons: one for drawing a shape, and one for erasing the shape. The second type of window will be a drawing window that displays the drawn shape. Additionally, the program will be capable of opening more than one drawing window.

From the program description, you may have surmised that there are a few extra challenges presented by a program capable of working with multiple windows; challenges that you did not have to worry about when you planned out a program that would make use of just one window. For the described program, here they are:

- An update event must be handled in two different ways, depending on which type of window needs updating.
- Once it has been determined that the update event corresponds to a drawing window, you must then determine which drawing window the event applies to.
- The user must be allowed to choose which of the drawing windows a click in the control window corresponds to.

These points make it clear that some planning is in order. That plan starts by examining a method that allows the addition of window information to the window's existing `WindowRecord` structure.

Expanding the WindowRecord

You know from earlier in this chapter that a WindowPtr points to a window. More specifically, it points to the port member of a WindowRecord that holds the information about the window. You also know that you can use a WindowPeek to gain access to the entire WindowRecord; not just the port. The following figure, Figure 4.8, appeared at the start of this chapter. It appears again to drive home the difference between a WindowPtr and a WindowPeek.

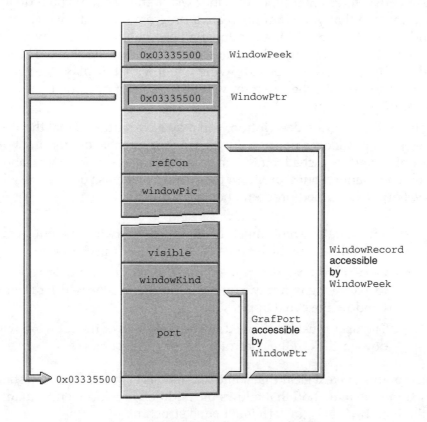

Figure 4.8 A WindowPtr and WindowPeek.

When you call GetNewWindow(), the Window Manager selects a block of memory and puts the window information—based on the WIND resource—in that memory. This information needs to be stored in a known, consistent order so that it can be retrieved by the Window Manager as your program works with the window. The WindowRecord provides that order. After placing the WIND data in memory in the format of a WindowRecord, the Window Manager provides your program with a pointer to the first member of the WindowRecord—the GrafPort. That allows your program to work with the window's graphics port. To work directly with other fields of the WindowRecord your program can declare a WindowPeek, then use typecasting on the WindowPtr to access the window's entire WindowRecord. Here's an example.

```
#define      rDrawWindow          129

WindowPtr    theWindow;
WindowPeek   theWindPeek;

theWindow = GetNewWindow( rDrawWindow, nil, (WindowPtr)-1L );

theWindPeek = (WindowPeek)theWindow;
```

This is the standard way to call GetNewWindow(), and to create a WindowPeek variable. There's another method you can use to create your own version of a WindowPeek that enables you to store, and access, *extra* information along with a WindowRecord.

This method involves creating your own data type by way of the C typedef keyword. Here's one example:

```
typedef   struct
{
   WindowRecord    theWindRecord;
   short           theWindType;
   Boolean         isDrawnIn;

}  MyWindRecord, *MyWindPeek;
```

This definition creates a structure that has three members. The first member is of type WindowRecord—the same window record structure you've been working with all along. The remaining two members give additional information about a window—information specific to your program. The field theWindType will be used to specify the type of a window, while the isDrawnIn field will let the program know whether the window currently has a drawing in it. Like any structure, you can have as many or as few members as you want—whatever makes sense for the windows used by your application.

The typedef names this new data type MyWindRecord. It also creates a type that is a pointer to the structure—MyWindPeek. You know that a variable of the Macintosh C type WindowPeek points to an entire WindowRecord. What will a variable of MyWindPeek type point to? A MyWindRecord. That means a variable of type MyWindPeek can be used to access everything in a WindowRecord *and* some extra information. Figure 4.9 illustrates the difference between a variable of type WindowPeek and a variable of the application-defined type MyWindPeek.

Note in Figure 4.9 that both a WindowPeek pointer and a MyWindPeek pointer begin by pointing to the start of a WindowRecord. What's at the start of a WindowRecord—the very first member of the WindowRecord? The port member, which is the window's graphics port. Making the first member of the MyWindRecord data type a WindowRecord was not an accident. When loaded in memory, you'll want the start of your application-defined MyWindRecord window structure to be in the same format as Apple's WindowRecord window structure—so its important that the first field of MyWindRecord be of type WindowRecord. This allows you to use a variable of MyWindPeek anywhere that you would normally use a WindowPtr or WindowPeek.

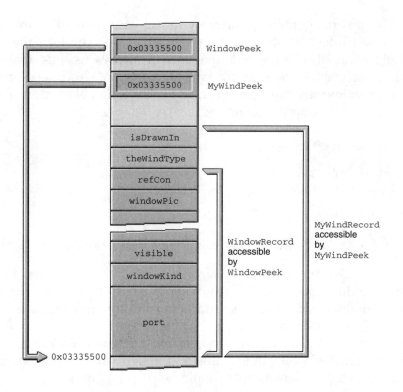

Figure 4.9 The difference between WindowPeek and MyWindPeek.

You've seen that the GetNewWindow() function offers you the option of allowing the Window Manager to assign the memory storage for a window (by passing nil as the second parameter) or of selecting the storage area yourself (by passing a pointer to an area in memory as the second parameter). When opening a window to have its data stored in an application-defined structure, your program *must* allocate the memory.

Consider this the golden opportunity to use your own structure rather than the Macintosh `WindowRecord`. When left alone to perform the memory allocation, the Window Manager will always assume that only enough memory is needed for a `WindowRecord`. Your application-defined window structure, however, requires additional memory. Here's your chance to set up that memory.

```
#define        rDrawWindow          129

WindowPtr   theWindow;
Ptr          theStorage;

theStorage = NewPtr( sizeof( MyWindRecord ) );

theWindow = GetNewWindow( rDrawWindow, theStorage, (WindowPtr)-1L );
```

Now you know how to define your own window structure and how to open a window that uses that structure. The only thing left to know is how to go about accessing the additional information that a window contains. First declare a variable to be of type `MyWindPeek`. Then set it to point, or peek, at a window by typecasting the window's pointer. With that accomplished you can examine and assign values to the structure members. A code fragment that should help you follows.

```
#define        rDrawWindow          129

WindowPtr    theWindow;
Ptr           theStorage;
MyWindPeek    theWindPeek;

theStorage  = NewPtr( sizeof( MyWindRecord ) );
theWindow   = GetNewWindow( rDrawWindow, theStorage, (WindowPtr)-1L );
theWindPeek = (MyWindPeek)theWindow;

// theWindPeek was just set to peek at this newly created
// window. Assigning a value to a member of the structure
// that theWindPeek points to only effects this one window.

theWindPeek->isDrawnIn = false;   // nothing drawn in new window yet

// Later in the program you can check to see if the window
// has been drawn to by checking it's personal isDrawnIn member.
// First, make sure the variable theWindPeek is pointing to the
```

```
// window to examine. Then check the isDrawnIn member.

theWindPeek  = (MyWindPeek)theWindow;

if ( theWindPeek->isDrawnIn == true )      // examine a member
   // do something here
```

The above code "reuses" theWindPeek. It first assigns it to point to a newly created window in order to write some information (the value false) to one of the fields of the new window (the isDrawnIn field). Later, the program again uses theWindPeek in an assignment statement. This second assignment to theWindPeek is made so that one of the fields of the window can be read from (the isDrawnIn field). You can assume that between these two usages of theWindPeek, that drawing may or may not have occurred in this window.

The method just described will be the backbone of the example program at the end of this chapter. It also can be a technique you use in any of your own multiple-window programs.

NOTE This technique is one way to manage multiple-window types in an application. Another approach is to store a value in the refCon field of the WindowRecord. The refCon field is a holder for any user-defined 32-bit value. Consult the *Macintosh Toolbox Essentials* volume of the *Inside Macintosh* series of books if this approach interests you.

Activates and Multiple Windows

Clicking the mouse on a window obscured by another window triggers the occurrence of an activate event. The clicked-on window appears to be brought to the forefront by a change in the highlighting of the window's title bar and frame. For single-window programs, activate events usually aren't significant. For multiple-window programs, they may be.

You can use an activate event to keep track of the most recently clicked on, or active, window. In the drawing window example that's been introduced, you could use a global WindowPtr variable for this purpose. When the user clicks on the **control window** and clicks the **Drawing** button, action will take place in whichever window global variable gCurrentDrawWindow is pointing to. With that in mind, look at one way to handle an activate event.

```
#define        kControlWindowType     1
#define        kDrawWindowType        2

WindowPtr   gCurrentDrawWindow;

void   HandleActivate( void )
{
    WindowPtr    theWindow;      // Window that was activated
    MyWindPeek   theWindPeek;    // Access to the window fields
    short        theType;

    theWindow = (WindowPtr)theEvent.message;

    theWindPeek = (MyWindPeek)theWindow;   // cast theWindow to
                                           // a MyWindPeek
    theType = theWindPeek->theWindType;

    if ( theType == kDrawWindowType )
        gCurrentDrawWindow = theWindow;
}
```

As it does for updates, the Event Manager places a pointer to the window that is being activated in the message element of the EventRecord. After your program has a pointer to this window, it should typecast it to a variable of MyWindPeek type so that the theWindType field of the MyWindRecord structure can be accessed. If the window that is activated is a drawing window, set the global gCurrentDrawWindow variable to point to it. That way you always know which drawing window was the most recently activated. Figure 4.10 summarizes the program flow from the start of the event to the pointer that's set to point to the activated window. The light arrows in the figure serve as a reminder that EventLoop() handles events of types other than activateEvt.

 NOTE   When your program opens a window with GetNewWindow(), it should initialize the application-specific field information in the window's data structure. For this example, that means that the call to GetNewWindow() that is used to open a drawing window would be followed by code like this:

```
theWindow   = GetNewWindow( rDrawWindow, theStorage, (WindowPtr)-1L );
theWindPeek = (MyWindPeek)theWindow;

theWindPeek->theWindType = kDrawWindowType;
theWindPeek->isDrawnIn = false;
```

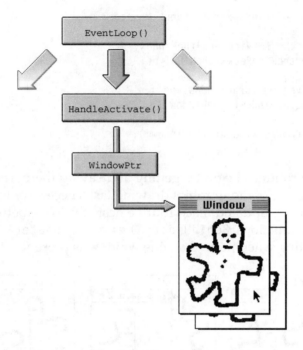

Figure 4.10 Using an activate event to keep track of the
current drawing window.

Updates and Multiple Windows

All of the window updating information you read for single-window
programs applies to programs with more than one window. If you have
different types of windows, as in the drawing example, you'll want to
have separate routines to update each. HandleUpdate() then becomes a
branching point:

```
#define      kControlWindowType      1
#define      kDrawWindowType         2

void  HandleUpdate( EventRecord theEvent )
{
   WindowPtr    theWindow;      // Window to update
   MyWindPeek   theWindPeek;    // Access to the window type
   short        theType;
```

```
theWindow  = (WindowPtr)theEvent.message;

theWindPeek = (MyWindPeek)theWindow;
theType = theWindPeek->theWindType;

if ( theType == kDrawWindowType )
    UpdateDrawWindow( theWindow );
else
    UpdateControlWindow( theWindow );
}
```

Both update routines begin by getting and saving the ports. They then perform all the text and graphics drawing tasks necessary for a window of the type being updated. Each routine nests this code between calls to the **Toolbox** functions BeginUpdate() and EndUpdate(). Figure 4.11 shows updating when more than one window is present.

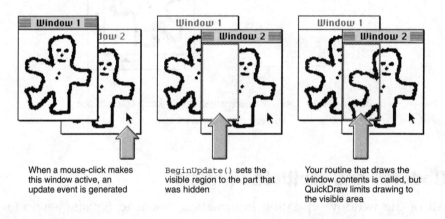

When a mouse-click makes this window active, an update event is generated

BeginUpdate() sets the visible region to the part that was hidden

Your routine that draws the window contents is called, but QuickDraw limits drawing to the visible area

Figure 4.11 Updating a window in a multiple-window program.

Chapter Program: MultiWindows

As a working example of the multiple-window techniques just discussed, this chapter presents MultiWindows. As its name suggests, this program is capable of displaying multiple windows. MultiWindows will put two types of windows on the screen: a control window and a drawing window. Additionally, the program will open more than one drawing window. Figure 4.12 is a screen shot of the windows you'll see when you run MultiWindows.

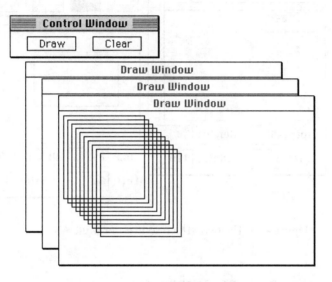

Figure 4.12 MultiWindows program in action.

MultiWindows allows the user to draw a pattern or erase an existing pattern in any one of the three drawing windows. The last drawing window selected will be the window where the action takes place.

Program Resources: MultiWindows.rsrc

The MultiWindows program has just two resources, both of type WIND. The WIND with ID 128 will be used for the control window, while WIND 129 will serve as the template for each of the drawing windows. Figure 4.13 shows the two resources.

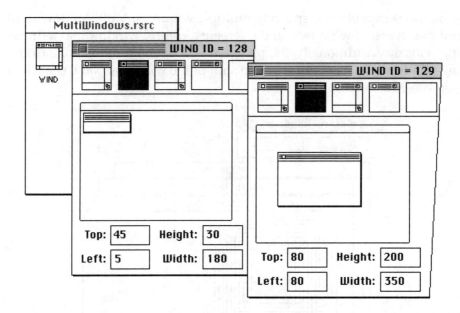

Figure 4.13 The two WIND resources for MultiWindows.

Program Listing: MultiWindows.c

Here is the source code listing for MultiWindows, in its entirety. A walk-through of the program follows.

```
//_____
//

void        InitializeToolbox( void );
void        InitializeVariables( void );
void        SetWindowDragBoundaries( void );
void        EventLoop( void );
void        HandleMouseDown( EventRecord );
void        HandleUpdate( EventRecord );
void        HandleActivate( EventRecord );
void        OpenControlWindow( void );
void        OpenDrawWindow( void );
void        HandleControlWindow( WindowPtr, Point );
void        UpdateControlWindow( WindowPtr );
void        UpdateDrawWindow( WindowPtr );
```

```
void      DrawSomething( WindowPtr );
void      CloseOneWindow( WindowPtr );
void      SetWindowType( WindowPtr, short );
short     DetermineWindowType( WindowPtr );
void      SetDrawnInFlag( WindowPtr, Boolean );
Boolean   DetermineDrawnInFlag( WindowPtr );
```

//_____

```
#define        rControlWindow              128
#define        rDrawWindow                 129
#define        kControlWindowType          1
#define        kDrawWindowType             2
#define        kMaxWindows                 4
#define        kWindowLeft                 30
#define        kWindowTop                  100
#define        kWindowOffset               20
#define        kDragEdge                   10
#define        kControlWindowTitle         "\pControl Window"
#define        kDrawWindowTitle            "\pDraw Window"
#define        kDrawButtonTitle            "\pDraw"
#define        kClearButtonTitle           "\pClear"
```

//_____

```
typedef   struct
{
    WindowRecord      theWindRecord;
    short             theWindType;
    Boolean           isDrawnIn;

}   MyWindRecord, *MyWindPeek;
```

//_____

```
Boolean     gAllDone = false;
Ptr         gWindStorage;
WindowPtr   gCurrentDrawWindow;
short       gWindowType;
Rect        gDrawRect;
Rect        gClearRect;
short       gNumDrawWindsOpen;
Rect        gDragRect;
```

```
//_____

void  main( void )
{
    MaxApplZone();
    MoreMasters();
    MoreMasters();
    MoreMasters();

    InitializeToolbox();
    InitializeVariables();
    SetWindowDragBoundaries();

    OpenControlWindow();
    OpenDrawWindow();
    OpenDrawWindow();
    OpenDrawWindow();

    EventLoop();
}


//_____

void  InitializeVariables( void )
{
    gWindStorage = NewPtr( kMaxWindows * ( sizeof ( MyWindRecord ) ) );

    gNumDrawWindsOpen = 0;

    SetRect( &gDrawRect, 20, 6, 80, 23 );
    SetRect( &gClearRect, 100, 6, 160, 23 );
}


//_____

void  SetWindowDragBoundaries( void )
{
    gDragRect = qd.screenBits.bounds;
    gDragRect.left += kDragEdge;
    gDragRect.right -= kDragEdge;
    gDragRect.bottom -= kDragEdge;
}
```

```
//_____

void  OpenControlWindow( void )
{
    WindowPtr   theWindow;
    Ptr         theWindStorage;

    theWindStorage = gWindStorage;
    theWindow = GetNewWindow( rControlWindow, theWindStorage,
    (WindowPtr)-1L );

    if ( theWindow == nil )
        ExitToShell();

    SetDrawnInFlag( theWindow, false );
    SetWindowType( theWindow, kControlWindowType );

    SetWTitle( theWindow, kControlWindowTitle );
    ShowWindow( theWindow );
}


//_____

void  OpenDrawWindow( void )
{
    WindowPtr   theWindow;
    Ptr         theWindStorage;
    short       theLeft, theTop;
    long        theAddressOffset;

    theAddressOffset = ( 1 + gNumDrawWindsOpen ) * ( sizeof(
    MyWindRecord ) );
    theWindStorage = gWindStorage + theAddressOffset;

    theWindow = GetNewWindow( rDrawWindow, theWindStorage, (WindowPtr)-1L
    );

    if ( theWindow == nil )
        ExitToShell();

    SetDrawnInFlag( theWindow, false );
    SetWindowType( theWindow, kDrawWindowType );
```

```
    SetWTitle( theWindow, kDrawWindowTitle );
    theLeft = kWindowLeft + ( gNumDrawWindsOpen * kWindowOffset );
    theTop  = kWindowTop  + ( gNumDrawWindsOpen * kWindowOffset );
    MoveWindow( theWindow, theLeft, theTop, true );
    ShowWindow( theWindow );

    gNumDrawWindsOpen++;
}


//_____

void  EventLoop( void )
{
    EventRecord  theEvent;

    while ( gAllDone == false )
    {
        WaitNextEvent( everyEvent, &theEvent, 15L, nil );

        switch ( theEvent.what )
        {
            case mouseDown:
                HandleMouseDown( theEvent );
                break;

            case updateEvt:
                HandleUpdate( theEvent);
                break;

            case activateEvt:
                HandleActivate( theEvent );
                break;
        }
    }
}


//_____

void  HandleActivate( EventRecord theEvent )
{
    WindowPtr  theWindow;

    theWindow = ( WindowPtr )theEvent.message;
```

```
   gWindowType = DetermineWindowType( theWindow );

   if ( gWindowType == kDrawWindowType )
      gCurrentDrawWindow = theWindow;
}
```

```
//_____

void   HandleUpdate( EventRecord theEvent )
{
   WindowPtr   theWindow;

   theWindow = ( WindowPtr )theEvent.message;
   gWindowType = DetermineWindowType( theWindow );

   if ( gWindowType == kDrawWindowType )
      UpdateDrawWindow( theWindow );
   else
      UpdateControlWindow( theWindow );
}
```

```
//_____

void   UpdateControlWindow( WindowPtr theWindow )
{
   GrafPtr   theSavePort;

   GetPort( &theSavePort );
   SetPort( theWindow );
   BeginUpdate( theWindow );
      FrameRect( &gDrawRect );
      MoveTo( gDrawRect.left + 15, gDrawRect.bottom - 4 );
      DrawString( kDrawButtonTitle );
      FrameRect( &gClearRect);
      MoveTo( gClearRect.left + 15, gClearRect.bottom - 4 );
      DrawString( kClearButtonTitle );
   EndUpdate( theWindow );
   SetPort( theSavePort );
}
```

```
//_____
```

```
void  UpdateDrawWindow( WindowPtr theWindow )
{
    GrafPtr  theSavePort;

    GetPort( &theSavePort );
    SetPort( theWindow );
    BeginUpdate( theWindow );
        if ( DetermineDrawnInFlag( theWindow ) )
            DrawSomething( theWindow );
    EndUpdate( theWindow );

    SetPort( theSavePort );
}


//_____


void  DrawSomething( WindowPtr theWindow )
{
    GrafPtr  theSavePort;
    Rect     theRect;
    short    i;

    GetPort( &theSavePort );
    SetPort( theWindow );

    for ( i = 1; i <= 10; i++ )
    {
        SetRect( &theRect, i*5, i*5, i*5+100, i*5+100 );
        FrameRect( &theRect );
    }

    SetPort( theSavePort );
}


//_____


void  HandleMouseDown( EventRecord theEvent )
{
    WindowPtr  theWindow;
    short      thePart;

    thePart = FindWindow( theEvent.where, &theWindow );
```

```
    switch ( thePart )
    {
        case inMenuBar:
            break;

        case inDrag:
            DragWindow( theWindow, theEvent.where, &gDragRect );
            break;

        case inGoAway:
            if ( TrackGoAway( theWindow, theEvent.where ) )
                CloseOneWindow( theWindow );
            break;

        case inContent:
            if ( theWindow != FrontWindow() )
                SelectWindow( theWindow );
            else
            {
                gWindowType = DetermineWindowType( theWindow );
                if ( gWindowType == kControlWindowType )
                    HandleControlWindow( theWindow, theEvent.where );
            }
            break;
    }
}


//_____

void  HandleControlWindow( WindowPtr theWindow, Point thePoint )
{
    GrafPtr   theSavePort;

    SetPort( theWindow );
    GlobalToLocal( &thePoint );

    if ( PtInRect( thePoint, &gDrawRect ) )
    {
        InvertRect( &gDrawRect );
        if ( DetermineDrawnInFlag( gCurrentDrawWindow ) == false )
        {
            DrawSomething( gCurrentDrawWindow );
            SetDrawnInFlag( gCurrentDrawWindow, true );
        }
```

```
        InvertRect( &gDrawRect );
    }
    if ( PtInRect( thePoint, &gClearRect ) )
    {
        InvertRect( &gClearRect );
        if ( DetermineDrawnInFlag( gCurrentDrawWindow ) == true )
        {
            GetPort( &theSavePort );
            SetPort( gCurrentDrawWindow );
            EraseRect( &gCurrentDrawWindow->portRect );
            SetDrawnInFlag( gCurrentDrawWindow, false );
            SetPort( theSavePort );
        }
        InvertRect( &gClearRect );
    }
}


//_____

void  SetWindowType( WindowPtr theWindow, short theType )
{
    MyWindPeek   theWindPeek;

    theWindPeek = (MyWindPeek)theWindow;
    theWindPeek->theWindType = theType;
}


//_____

short  DetermineWindowType( WindowPtr theWindow )
{
    MyWindPeek   theWindPeek;

    theWindPeek = (MyWindPeek)theWindow;
    return ( theWindPeek->theWindType );
}


//_____

void  SetDrawnInFlag( WindowPtr theWindow, Boolean theDrawnFlag )
{
```

```
   MyWindPeek  theWindPeek;

   theWindPeek = (MyWindPeek)theWindow;
   theWindPeek->isDrawnIn = theDrawnFlag;
}
```

```
//_____

Boolean  DetermineDrawnInFlag( WindowPtr theWindow )
{
   MyWindPeek  theWindPeek;

   theWindPeek  = (MyWindPeek)theWindow;
   return ( theWindPeek->isDrawnIn );
}
```

```
//_____

void  CloseOneWindow( WindowPtr theWindow )
{
   HideWindow( theWindow );
   CloseWindow( theWindow );
   DisposePtr( ( Ptr )theWindow );
   gAllDone = true;
   gNumDrawWindsOpen—;
}
```

```
//_____

void  InitializeToolbox( void )
{
   InitGraf( &qd.thePort );
   InitFonts();
   InitWindows();
   InitMenus();
   TEInit();
   InitDialogs( 0L );
   FlushEvents( everyEvent, 0 );
   InitCursor();
}
```

Stepping Through the Code

Now, a walkthrough of the MultiWindows code, with emphasis on the new material.

The define Directives

MultiWindows opens two types of windows, each defined by a WIND resource template. Their resource IDs are defined in the source code by the constants rControlWindow and rDrawWindow. To distinguish between the two window types, MultiWindows calls one a kControlWindowType and the other a kDrawWindowType. The constant kMaxWindows exists to tell the program the maximum number of windows that will be open. The titles to the two window types and the two buttons are kept in the constants kControlWindowTitle, kDrawWindowTitle, kDrawButtonTitle, and kClearButtonTitle. After loading a drawing window, and before displaying it, the program moves the window on the screen to stagger it from other open drawing windows. The constants kWindowLeft, kWindowTop, and kWindowOffset help there. The constant kDragEdge defines a pixel buffer that prevents a window from going completely off screen.

```
#define        rControlWindow              128
#define        rDrawWindow                 129
#define        kControlWindowType            1
#define        kDrawWindowType               2
#define        kMaxWindows                   4
#define        kWindowLeft                  30
#define        kWindowTop                  100
#define        kWindowOffset                20
#define        kDragEdge                    10
#define        kControlWindowTitle         "\pControl Window"
#define        kDrawWindowTitle            "\pDraw Window"
#define        kDrawButtonTitle            "\pDraw"
#define        kClearButtonTitle           "\pClear"
```

NOTE

You could use rControlWindow and rDrawWindow as both WIND resource IDs and window type references—that would eliminate the need for the kControlWindowType and kDrawWindowType constants. If you decide to add new window types to the program, however, you'll find it works better to use a separate set of constants for the WIND IDs and the window types. That's because it might make sense to use the same WIND for different window types. For example, the MultiWindows program could have a drawing window, text window, and pie chart window that all used WIND 128.

Global Data Types

This chapter devoted several pages to the description of a strategy that would allow a program to be able to distinguish one type of window from another. The MyWindRecord struct and the MyWindPeek that point to it are defined here exactly as they were earlier in this chapter.

```
typedef   struct
{
    WindowRecord    theWindRecord;
    short           theWindType;
    Boolean         isDrawnIn;

}  MyWindRecord, *MyWindPeek;
```

Global Variables

As with all chapter examples, MultiWindows looks to the global variable gAllDone to know when to quit. The program sets up rectangle gDragRect to prevent a window from disappearing off the screen. The program uses gCurrentDrawWindow to keep track of the drawing window that was clicked on last. Variable gNumDrawWindsOpen is used to stagger the drawing windows as they open, as well as in the determination of where in memory a new drawing window should be stored. The control window has two rectangles that serve as buttons. The gDrawRect and gClearRect variables hold the boundaries of these rectangles.

```
Boolean    gAllDone = false;
Ptr        gWindStorage;
WindowPtr  gCurrentDrawWindow;
short      gWindowType;
Rect       gDrawRect;
Rect       gClearRect;
short      gNumDrawWindsOpen;
Rect       gDragRect;
```

The main() Function

Like most good main() functions, this one is short and simple. First, it calls the usual memory-related Toolbox functions. Then three application-defined initialization routines are invoked. You're already quite familiar with InitializeToolbox(). The SetWindowDragRectangle() was developed in this chapter. The InitializeVariables() routine groups together a few miscellaneous one-time assignments. While it's a very short routine, InitializeVariables() deserves a closer examination, which it gets just after the remainder of main() is covered.

MultiWindows opens four windows—one control window and three drawing windows. The best way to display the windows is to put the control window on the screen, then to let the user select as many drawing windows as desired from a File menu. Menus aren't discussed until Chapter 6, so MultiWindows simply calls the application-defined OpenDrawWindow() function three times to simulate three menu selections. The main() function ends with a call to the ever-faithful EventLoop()—the function that holds the while loop that drives the program.

```
void  main( void )
{
    MaxApplZone();
    MoreMasters();
    MoreMasters();
    MoreMasters();

    InitializeToolbox();
    InitializeVariables();
    SetWindowDragBoundaries();

    OpenControlWindow();
    OpenDrawWindow();
```

```
    OpenDrawWindow();
    OpenDrawWindow();

    EventLoop();
}
```

Global Variable Initializations

InitializeVariables() sets the global variable gNumDrawWindsOpen to 0. As each drawing window is opened, this variable will be incremented. The two global Rect variables, gDrawRect and gClearRect, are given their coordinates in InitializeVariables(). Later in the program, these two rectangles will be used when drawing the two buttons in the control window.

```
void  InitializeVariables( void )
{
    gWindStorage = NewPtr( kMaxWindows * ( sizeof( MyWindRecord ) ) );

    gNumDrawWindsOpen = 0;

    SetRect( &gDrawRect, 20, 6, 80, 23 );
    SetRect( &gClearRect, 100, 6, 160, 23 );
}
```

The first assignment in InitializeVariables() requires the most explanation—it might not be immediately apparent as to what's taking place here:

```
    gWindStorage = NewPtr( kMaxWindows * ( sizeof( MyWindRecord ) ) );
```

In Chapter 2, you saw that to avoiding memory fragmentation is ensured by to reserving a block of nonrelocatable memory at application startup. When the program is to open a window, the block of memory that is to hold that window's record should be allocated from this block. In this chapter, you saw an example that did just that for a window that used the application-defined MyWindRecord structure rather than Apple's WindowRecord structure:

```
#define     rDrawWindow     129

WindowPtr  theWindow;
```

```
Ptr          theStorage;

theStorage = NewPtr( sizeof( MyWindRecord ) );

theWindow = GetNewWindow( rDrawWindow, theStorage, (WindowPtr)-1L );
```

While the above approach works for opening a single window, it isn't sufficient for opening multiple windows. For that, your program should reserve a block larger than a single MyWindRecord—it should reserve a block large enough to hold all of the windows that will eventually be opened by the program. For the MultiWindows program, that means the block should be large enough to hold four MyWindRecord structures—one for the control window and one for each of the three drawing windows. That's exactly what the first line in InitializeVariables() does. Keeping in mind that the constant kMaxWindows is defined to have a value of 4, and that gWindStorage is a global Ptr variable, take another look at the memory allocation:

```
gWindStorage = NewPtr( kMaxWindows * ( sizeof( MyWindRecord ) ) );
```

In Figure 4.14, the MultiWindows program has been run from the CodeWarrior development environment, with its debugger on and a breakpoint set on the statement that allocates the block of memory. After stepping once to execute this statement, memory might look something like that pictured to the right of the debugger window.

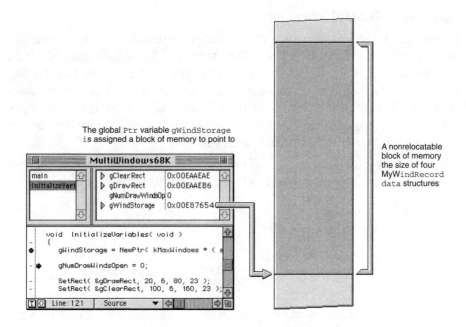

Figure 4.14 Reserving a block of memory, as seen from
the CodeWarrior debugger.

The global `Ptr` variable `gWindStorage` points to the start of the newly
allocated block. As you'll soon see, when a window is to be opened,
MultiWindows will use this pointer in setting up the memory area for
the new window.

Opening a Control Window

When MultiWindows opens a new window it reserves memory the size of MyWindRecord rather than the size of the Macintosh C type WindowRecord. This allows it to store the type of the window and a flag that tells whether the window has a drawing in it. The application-defined function OpenControlWindow() does all of that. It also changes the title that appears in the window's title bar from "Untitled" to the more descriptive title "Control Window."

First, take a look at how OpenControlWindow() reserves memory for the control window, and then loads that window to memory:

```
WindowPtr   theWindow;
Ptr         theWindStorage;

theWindStorage = gWindStorage;
theWindow = GetNewWindow( rControlWindow, theWindStorage,
                          (WindowPtr)-1L );
```

The memory location OpenControlWindow() chooses for the control window is that area pointed to by gWindStorage. Notice that NewPtr() isn't called here. As you saw just before, NewPtr() *was* called in InitializeVariables() to allocate the one block of memory that is large enough to accommodate four MyWindRecord data structures. Passing the address of this block to GetNewWindow() tells the Window Manager to place the control window at the start of this block, as shown in Figure 4.15.

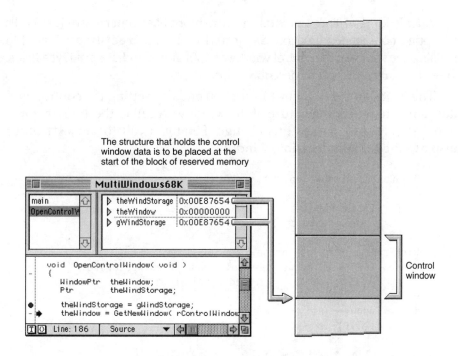

Figure 4.15 Placing the control window data structure at
the start of the reserved memory block.

As you'll see, the first drawing window that opens will get loaded just
above the control window in the reserved block of memory.

After loading WIND resource data into memory, OpenControlWindow() calls the application-defined functions SetDrawnInFlag() and SetWindowType() to initialize the values of the control window's isDrawnIn and theWindType fields. These two functions will be described a little later.

The OpenControlWindow() function ends by setting the control window's title to reflect the nature of the window. A call to the Toolbox function SetWTitle() makes this change. Finally, a call to ShowWindow() displays the initially invisible window.

```
void   OpenControlWindow( void )
{
    WindowPtr    theWindow;
    Ptr          theWindStorage;

    theWindStorage = gWindStorage;
    theWindow = GetNewWindow( rControlWindow, theWindStorage,
                                (WindowPtr)-1L );

    if ( theWindow == nil )
        ExitToShell();

    SetDrawnInFlag( theWindow, false );
    SetWindowType( theWindow, kControlWindowType );

    SetWTitle( theWindow, kControlWindowTitle );
    ShowWindow( theWindow );
}
```

Opening a Drawing Window

Opening a drawing window involves all of the same steps as opening a control window, and a few more. First, the determination of where in memory the window should reside requires an extra step:

```
WindowPtr   theWindow;
Ptr         theWindStorage;
long        theAddressOffset;

theAddressOffset = ( 1 + gNumDrawWindsOpen ) *
                      ( sizeof( MyWindRecord ) );
theWindStorage = gWindStorage + theAddressOffset;

theWindow = GetNewWindow( rDrawWindow, theWindStorage,
                      (WindowPtr)-1L );
```

The control window was opened first, so it was placed at the start of the memory reserve. Recall that the starting address for the control window was set to match the pointer value gWindStorage, which happened to be 0x00E87654 in this running of the program. Refer back to Figure 4.15 if you need to confirm that. The first drawing window should be placed in the memory reserve just after the control window. The first line of OpenDrawWindow( ) calculates the offset from the start of the reserve:

```
theAddressOffset = ( 1 + gNumDrawWindsOpen ) *
                      ( sizeof( MyWindRecord ) );
```

The offset is the number of open windows, times the memory used by one window. Because the control window was opened first, you know there is at least one window open. The global variable gNumDrawWindsOpen holds the number of drawing windows that are open. Because this is the first time OpenDrawWindow( ) is being called, gNumDrawWindsOpen still has its initial value of 0. That means the offset will be 1 times the size of MyWindRecord. Now add that offset to the base address of the memory reserve to define the starting address for the first drawing window. Figure 4.16 illustrates this.

```
theWindStorage = gWindStorage + theAddressOffset;
```

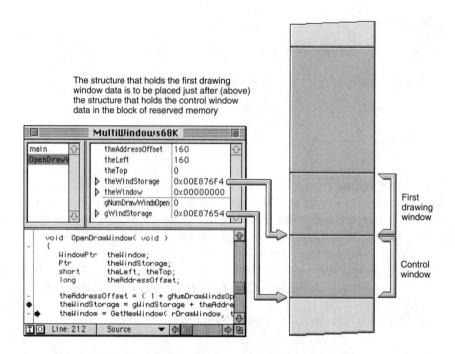

Figure 4.16 Placing the first drawing window data structure just after the control window in the reserved memory block.

Figure 4.16 shows that the starting address for the control window is 0x00E87654 and the starting address for the drawing window is 0x00E876F4. While it *isn't* likely that the Metrowerks compiler made a mistake, it *is* possible that the author did, so you might want to confirm that the memory allocation plan is sound! Here's how. Begin by running MultiWindows from your development environment, with its debugger turned on.

To see if the reserved memory is being used as planned, determine the size of the MyWindRecord data structure. Your development environment can easily do that for you. If you use CodeWarrior, select **Show Expressions** from the Window menu, then choose **New Expression** from the Data menu. Now type in the expression you want the debugger to calculate. The top of Figure 4.17 shows that typing in "sizeof(MyWindRecord)" and then pressing the **Return** key results in a display of the number 160—the size of any MyWindRecord. If you use a Symantec IDE, just type the expression in the debugger's Data window and press return. As shown in the bottom of Figure 4.17, the value 160 will be displayed.

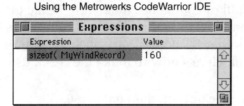

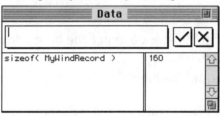

Figure 4.17 Evaluating an expression in both the Metrowerks and Symantec debuggers.

N O T E

At the time of this writing, the Apple-defined data type `WindowRecord` has a size of 156 bytes—you can verify this by doing a `sizeof(WindowRecord)` in your debugger. This is as you'd expect. Both of the fields that are added to the `WindowRecord` field to make up the `MyWindRecord` structure are two bytes (a `short` occupies two bytes, as does a `Boolean`), so the total size of `MyWindRecord` is 160 bytes. Note that "at the time of this writing" a `WindowRecord` occupies 156 bytes. Apple reserves the right to change the size of its data structures—that's something that may be necessary when a new operating system such as Copland (System 8) is being developed. The possibility of a data structure being redefined is the reason `NewPtr()` and `NewHandle()` should always be passed the value returned by `sizeof()` rather than a hard-coded numerical value such as 160.

Knowing the base address of the reserved memory and the size of a `MyWindRecord` structure is all you need to determine if the drawing window ended up in the anticipated area of memory. Since the first drawing window is expected to follow the control window in memory, adding the size of the control window to the base address should result in the starting address of the drawing window. Of course, since addresses are expressed as hexadecimal numbers, your addition should be in hexadecimal. For this, you'll of course use the handy PCalc utility, developed by James Thomson and found on the CD that accompanies this book—right? Figure 4.18 shows that PCalc is a very slick version of a programmable scientific calculator. Here's how to make the check using PCalc:

1. Press the **Dec** button, then enter **160**.
2. Press the **Hex** button to convert 160 decimal to a hexadecimal value.
3. Press the **plus (+)** key.
4. While still in Hex mode, enter the base address. For this example, that's E87654.
5. Press the **equal (=)** key.

Figure 4.18 shows the result of the addition. Compare this value, $0x0E876F4$ with the address shown for `theWindStorage` in the debugger window of Figure 4.15. Unsurprisingly, its a match. The drawing window does indeed follow the control window in memory, so the memory allocation scheme used by MultiWindows works.

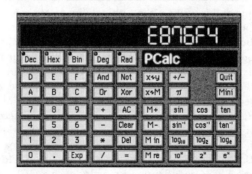

Figure 4.18 The PCalc calculator utility.

Egads—that seems like an awful lot of work just to toss a window into memory! Sure it is, but you don't *have* to go through all of that effort. This painstaking walkthrough exists only to enhance your understanding of Macintosh memory. Once you have a grasp of how memory is reserved and how data structures are stored in memory, you won't need to expend a large amount of time on such matters.

Each time OpenDrawWindow() is called, the starting address for the new window that is about to be opened is recalculated. Each new window will be given a slice of the reserved block—just above the last window to be opened.

Notice that MultiWindows' memory management scheme is tailored to this one program. For instance, it assumes that the program will always open a control window first—that's why the first drawing window is placed 160 bytes from the start of the memory reserve. MultiWindows also assumes there'll be up to four windows open at one time—that's why it starts by reserving a block of nonrelocatable memory the size of four MyWindRecord structures.

What if the MultiWindows program were to allow more windows to be opened at one time—say, up to six windows? One solution would be to simply change the value of kMaxWindows from 4 to 6. Then the appropriate sized block would be reserved. What if the program were to allow *any* number of windows to be opened at one time, such as one, two, three, or thirty? How large a block should MultiWindows then reserve? One simple solution would be to reserve a block that would accommodate *most* users. That might be the size of ten MyWindRecord structures—one for the control window and one for nine drawing windows. If gNumDrawWindsOpen ever exceeded nine, then GetNewWindow() could be called with a value of nil as the second parameter. That would tell the Window Manager to take care of the memory allocation. The pertinent snippet is shown here:

```
if ( gNumDrawWindsOpen < 10 )
{
    theAddressOffset = ( 1 + gNumDrawWindsOpen ) *
```

```
                            ( sizeof( MyWindRecord ) );
    theWindStorage = gWindStorage + theAddressOffset;
}
else
{
    theWindStorage = nil;
}
theWindow = GetNewWindow( rDrawWindow, theWindStorage, (WindowPtr)-1L );
```

While the preceding approach may result in something you'd rather avoid—allocation of nonrelocatable blocks that may not be low in memory—it can be considered a happy medium: under most circumstances, all of the windows will end up low in memory in the reserved block. Only in the unusual event where the user opens ten or more windows will memory be allocated outside the reserved block.

N O T E   MultiWindows doesn't allow for the closing and reopening of windows. What if it did? Then the memory management scheme would work as written. As long as gNumDrawWindsOpen was incremented at the opening of each new window, and decremented at the closing of each open window, then the value calculated for theAddressOffset in OpenDrawWindow() would be correct.

OpenDrawWindow() finishes up by setting the window's title, then prettying things up a little by offsetting the window from any other newly opened drawing windows. It uses the number of open windows in the calculation of the location for the new window. The more windows that are open, the greater the offset will be.

```
void  OpenDrawWindow( void )
{
    WindowPtr   theWindow;
    Ptr         theWindStorage;
    short       theLeft, theTop;
    long        theAddressOffset;

    theAddressOffset = ( 1 + gNumDrawWindsOpen ) *
                    ( sizeof( MyWindRecord ) );
    theWindStorage = gWindStorage + theAddressOffset;

    theWindow = GetNewWindow( rDrawWindow, theWindStorage, (WindowPtr)-1L );

    if ( theWindow == nil )
        ExitToShell();
```

```
SetDrawnInFlag( theWindow, false );
SetWindowType( theWindow, kDrawWindowType );

SetWTitle( theWindow, kDrawWindowTitle );
theLeft = kWindowLeft + ( gNumDrawWindsOpen * kWindowOffset );
theTop  = kWindowTop  + ( gNumDrawWindsOpen * kWindowOffset );
MoveWindow( theWindow, theLeft, theTop, true );
ShowWindow( theWindow );

gNumDrawWindsOpen++;
}
```

Marking and Examining a Window

This chapter's Multiple-Window Techniques section worked out a strategy for adding information to a window so that it can contain more data than a WindowRecord alone. MultiWindows makes full use of this technique. When the program creates a window, the application-defined function SetWindowType() is called. This routine receives a pointer to the new window and then marks the window as one of the program's two types, depending on the passed-in type value. To access the theWindType, the WindowPtr variable is cast to a MyWindPeek variable. Figure 4.19 shows what happens with this typecasting.

```
void  SetWindowType( WindowPtr theWindow, short theType )
{
   MyWindPeek  theWindPeek;

   theWindPeek = ( MyWindPeek )theWindow;
   theWindPeek->theWindType = theType;
}
```

All of the windows that open in MultiWindows use the application-defined MyWindRecord data structure rather than a standard WindowRecord data structure. If a program used both structures, be aware that the typecasting of a WindowPtr variable to a MyWindPeek variable must occur only with a WindowPtr variable that you are sure points to a MyWindRecord structure. Otherwise, theWindPeek->theWindType will access unrelated memory that lies beyond the end of the WindowRecord structure!

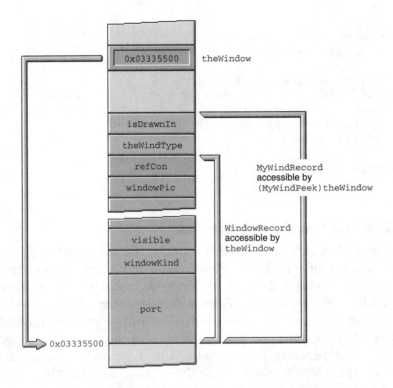

Figure 4.19 Typecasting a `WindowPtr` to a `MyWindPeek`.

If you understand `SetWindowType()`, you'll understand the next three routines. Instead of *setting* a window's type, `DetermineWindowType()` *returns* the a window's type. It does this by examining the `theWindType` `field` of the window structure referenced by the passed-in `WindowPtr` variable. `DetermineWindowType()` returns the window type so that the program can make decisions based on the this information.

```
short  DetermineWindowType( WindowPtr theWindow )
{
   MyWindPeek  theWindPeek;

   theWindPeek = (MyWindPeek)theWindow;
   return ( theWindPeek->theWindType );
}
```

The `SetDrawnInFlag()` and `DetermineDrawnInFlag()` work in the same way as the preceding two routines.

```
void  SetDrawnInFlag( WindowPtr theWindow, Boolean theDrawnFlag )
{
   MyWindPeek  theWindPeek;

   theWindPeek = (MyWindPeek)theWindow;
   theWindPeek->isDrawnIn = theDrawnFlag;
}


Boolean  DetermineDrawnInFlag( WindowPtr theWindow )
{
   MyWindPeek  theWindPeek;

   theWindPeek  = (MyWindPeek)theWindow;
   return ( theWindPeek->isDrawnIn );
}
```

Event Handling

To handle events, MultiWindows uses the `EventLoop()` routine that you're already familiar with. The program responds to three types of events: `mouseDown`, `updateEvt`, and `activateEvt`.

```
void  EventLoop( void )
{
   EventRecord  theEvent;

   while ( gAllDone == false )
   {
      WaitNextEvent( everyEvent, &theEvent, 15L, nil );

      switch ( theEvent.what )
      {
         case mouseDown:
            HandleMouseDown( theEvent );
            break;

         case updateEvt:
            HandleUpdate( theEvent);
```

```
                break;

            case activateEvt:
                HandleActivate( theEvent );
                break;
        }
    }
}
```

There is only one task that `HandleActivate()` is responsible for handling: setting `gCurrentDrawWindow` to point to the activated window—provided, of course, the window is a drawing window.

```
void   HandleActivate( EventRecord theEvent )
{
    WindowPtr   theWindow;

    theWindow = ( WindowPtr )theEvent.message;
    gWindowType = DetermineWindowType( theWindow );

    if ( gWindowType == kDrawWindowType )
        gCurrentDrawWindow = theWindow;
}
```

Because more than one drawing window will be open, the program should keep track of which one is active. The question might arise as to why the global window pointer `gCurrentDrawWindow` isn't set to point to the window that opens in `OpenDrawWindow()`. If a window just opened, it surely must be the active, or current, window—right? Right. But there's no need to make note of that in `OpenDrawWindow()`. The opening of a new window triggers an activate event. A mouse click on an obscured draw window will also trigger an activate event. So both a click on a window and the opening of a new window will lead the program to `HandleActivate()`. If `gCurrentDrawWindow` is updated in `HandleActivate()`, the program is assured of keeping that variable pointing at the right window no matter how the window gets activated.

If the event is an update event, MultiWindows determines the type of window the update is for. It then branches to the correct routine for further processing.

```
void  HandleUpdate( EventRecord theEvent )
{
    WindowPtr  theWindow;

    theWindow = ( WindowPtr )theEvent.message;
    gWindowType = DetermineWindowType( theWindow );

    if ( gWindowType == kDrawWindowType )
        UpdateDrawWindow( theWindow );
    else
        UpdateControlWindow( theWindow );
}
```

The control window is updated by redrawing the two rectangles that serve as its buttons. Since drawing is taking place, SetPort() is called to make the control window's port current.

```
void  UpdateControlWindow( WindowPtr theWindow )
{
    GrafPtr  theSavePort;

    GetPort( &theSavePort );
    SetPort( theWindow );
    BeginUpdate( theWindow );
        FrameRect( &gDrawRect );
        MoveTo( gDrawRect.left + 15, gDrawRect.bottom - 4 );
        DrawString( kDrawButtonTitle );
        FrameRect( &gClearRect);
        MoveTo( gClearRect.left + 15, gClearRect.bottom - 4 );
        DrawString( kClearButtonTitle );
    EndUpdate( theWindow );
    SetPort( theSavePort );
}
```

Speaking of drawing buttons, did you notice that MultiWindows didn't explicitly draw them when the control window was opened back in OpenControlWindow()? Yet, the buttons were drawn at that time. That's because GetNewWindow() highlights the new window, then generates both an activate and update event. HandleActivate() doesn't do anything related to the control window, but HandleUpdate() calls UpdateControlWindow(), which then draws and labels the rectangles. Figure 4.20 illustrates this.

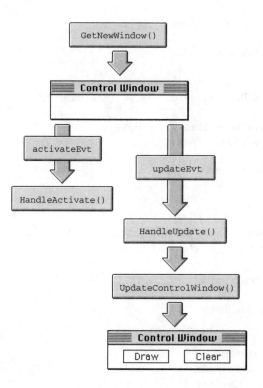

Figure 4.20 GetNewWindow() triggers two events.

When a new drawing window is opened, or an existing window is activated or moved from off screen to on screen, an update event occurs and UpdateDrawWindow() is called. This routine checks the isDrawnIn field of the window that needs updating to see if a drawing is present. If a drawing is present, DrawSomething() is called to redraw the graphics. Because drawing might take place, the port is set and calls BeginUpdate() and EndUpdate() and update are made.

```
void  UpdateDrawWindow( WindowPtr theWindow )
{
    GrafPtr  theSavePort;

    GetPort( &theSavePort );
    SetPort( theWindow );
    BeginUpdate( theWindow );
        if ( DetermineDrawnInFlag( theWindow ) )
```

```
        DrawSomething( theWindow );
    EndUpdate( theWindow );

    SetPort( theSavePort );
}
```

Earlier in this chapter, you saw a routine named DrawSomething() used to load a PICT resource and to display it to a window. Here, DrawSomething() uses a loop to frame ten overlapping rectangles. You'll be able to come up with something much more interesting for your own program, but for this book's examples, simplicity rules.

```
void  DrawSomething( WindowPtr theWindow )
{
    GrafPtr    theSavePort;
    Rect       theRect;
    short      i;

    GetPort( &theSavePort );
    SetPort( theWindow );

    for ( i = 1; i <= 10; i++ )
    {
        SetRect( &theRect, i*5, i*5, i*5+100, i*5+100 );
        FrameRect( &theRect );
    }

    SetPort( theSavePort );
}
```

A click of the mouse is the third and final type of event MultiWindows handles. Because there are no menus, the program ignores a click in the menu bar. Calls to the appropriate Toolbox routines are made to handle a mouse click in the various parts of a window. A mouse click in the content of a window warrants more discussion. If the window was not active before the click, SelectWindow() is called and the event is then considered to be handled. If the window is already active, a check is made to see if the window is the control window. If so, it needs to be determined if the cursor was over one of the two control window rectangles at the time of the mouse button click. The where field of theEvent holds the screen pixel coordinates of the cursor at the moment the mouse button was pressed, so this value is passed onto the application-defined HandleControlWindow() routine for further processing.

```
void  HandleMouseDown( EventRecord theEvent )
{
    WindowPtr  theWindow;
    short      thePart;

    thePart = FindWindow( theEvent.where, &theWindow );

    switch ( thePart )
    {
        case inMenuBar:
            break;

        case inDrag:
            DragWindow( theWindow, theEvent.where, &gDragRect );
            break;

        case inGoAway:
            if ( TrackGoAway( theWindow, theEvent.where ) )
                CloseOneWindow( theWindow );
            break;

        case inContent:
            if ( theWindow != FrontWindow() )
                SelectWindow( theWindow );
            else
            {
                gWindowType = DetermineWindowType( theWindow );
                if ( gWindowType == kControlWindowType )
                    HandleControlWindow( theWindow, theEvent.where );
            }
            break;
    }
}
```

HandleControlWindow() uses a Toolbox routine called GlobalToLocal() to determine if the cursor was over either of the control window's two rectangles. The Point value passed into HandleControlWindow(), theEvent.where, is in global, or screen, coordinates. Drawing in a window takes place in local, or window coordinates. Figure 4.21 should clarify this idea.

The Toolbox routine PtInRect() returns a value of true if the passed-in Point variable lies in the passed-in rectangle. If the mouse click is in the drawing rectangle, the rectangle is inverted to let the user know the click was registered. After that, the window's isDrawnIn field is examined. If the last drawing window to be active already has a drawing in it, the program won't want to bother drawing it again. If there isn't already a drawing in the window, a call to DrawSomething() needs to be made to do the drawing. Then the window's isDrawnIn field is set to mark the window as having a drawing in it—vital information needed during window updating. When complete, the Draw rectangle is inverted back to its original state.

A mouse button click in the **Clear** button is handled in a manner similar to a click in the **Draw** button.

```
void  HandleControlWindow( WindowPtr theWindow, Point thePoint )
{
    GrafPtr  theSavePort;

    SetPort( theWindow );
    GlobalToLocal( &thePoint );

    if ( PtInRect( thePoint, &gDrawRect ) )
    {
        InvertRect( &gDrawRect );
        if ( DetermineDrawnInFlag( gCurrentDrawWindow ) == false )
        {
            DrawSomething( gCurrentDrawWindow );
            SetDrawnInFlag( gCurrentDrawWindow, true );
        }
        InvertRect( &gDrawRect );
    }
    if ( PtInRect( thePoint, &gClearRect ) )
    {
        InvertRect( &gClearRect );
        if ( DetermineDrawnInFlag( gCurrentDrawWindow ) == true )
        {
            GetPort( &theSavePort );
            SetPort( gCurrentDrawWindow );
            EraseRect( &gCurrentDrawWindow->portRect );
            SetDrawnInFlag( gCurrentDrawWindow, false );
            SetPort( theSavePort );
        }
        InvertRect( &gClearRect );
    }
}
```

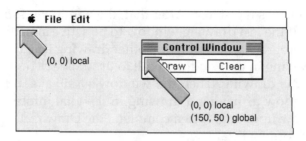

Figure 4.21 Global and local pixel coordinates.

Since MultiWindows has no menu bar, the program uses a click in a window's Go Away box as the signal to end the program—a click on any window's close box closes that window and then sets gAllDone to true. In a real world application, you'd omit the gAllDone line and instead set gAllDone to true when the user selects **Quit** from the program's File menu.

Notice that to close the window, two Toolbox routines are called: CloseWindow() and DisposePtr(). Earlier in this chapter you saw a window closed by simply calling a different Toolbox routine— DisposeWindow(). When your program supplies the window storage for GetNewWindow(), as MultiWindows does, call CloseWindow() and DisposePtr(). If you let the Mac handle window storage, as you do when you pass nil as the second parameter, just call DisposeWindow().

```
void  CloseOneWindow( WindowPtr theWindow )
{
    HideWindow( theWindow );
    CloseWindow( theWindow );
    DisposePtr( ( Ptr )theWindow );
    gAllDone = true;
    gNumDrawWindsOpen—;
}
```

CHAPTER SUMMARY

The WIND resource type defines the look of a window. A call to GetNewWindow() loads a WIND resource into memory, ready to be displayed on the screen with a call to ShowWindow().

The descriptive information about a window is read in from the WIND resource and, along with additional information that can be set within source code, is stored to a WindowRecord. Rather than access the fields of the WindowRecord directly, you use Toolbox routines. These Toolbox routines accept a WindowPtr, a pointer to the WindowRecord, rather than the WindowRecord itself.

Most window-related information that a programmer needs to access is available through use of the WindowPtr, which points to a window's graphics port. For those few times when you need to access other information, you'll use a WindowPeek. A WindowPeek points to the entire WindowRecord, rather than just to the graphics port.

Much of the work involved in handling a window occurs when a user presses the mouse button, causing a mouse down event. When your program receives a mouse down event you'll handle it according to the location on the window where the event took place. To drag a window, you'll call DragWindow(). To close a window, you can first hide it with a call to HideWindow(), then dispose of it with DisposeWindow(). In response to a click in the content of the window, you can call SelectWindow() to bring the window to the front of the screen.

When a covered window becomes exposed, you call the Toolbox routines BeginUpdate() and EndUpdate(). In between the calls, you take care of any of the drawing that needs to be done for the particular window that needs updating.

Some applications make use of windows that perform different functions. One window may accept input from the user, while another displays some graphical output. For a multiple-window application, you have to use a technique that lets your application distinguish between these different windows. Failure to do so will cause window-updating problems.

One strategy for handling multiple windows is to expand the WindowRecord. To do this you create your own data structure that contains an entire WindowRecord and any additional information you want associated with a window. The primary new information will be a variable that holds the type of the window.

Chapter 5

Dealing with Dialog Boxes

The primary method of relaying information to a Macintosh program is through a dialog box. Allowing a user to adjust program settings is a typical use of a dialog box. A Macintosh program issues warnings to the user in the form of an *alert*, the simplest of dialog boxes.

In this chapter, you'll learn how to create alerts using the ALRT and DITL resources. This will be the foundation for creating dialog box resources as well. Dialog boxes use the DLOG and DITL resource types.

Here you'll see the similarities between windows and dialog boxes. You will learn that dialog boxes are little more than embellished windows. This chapter will cover both the fixed modal dialog box and the movable modeless dialog box.

Finally, the example program will demonstrate all the dialog box techniques covered in this chapter, along with a method for handling the case of both a window and a dialog box coexisting on the screen.

ALERTS

When a program's user makes a mistake, or is about to embark on a path the program's creator feels is dangerous, the user meets with an alert. An alert provides a warning. It can strictly prohibit the impending action from taking place, or it may provide a warning and then give the user the chance to back out or carry on. Figure 5.1 shows an alert.

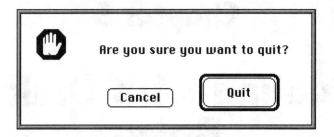

Figure 5.1 A typical alert.

An alert typically contains text and one or two push buttons, such as the **Cancel** and **Quit** buttons in Figure 5.1. You'll need two resource types for an alert: the ALRT and the DITL. Both these resource types are described in the next few pages.

Alert Resources: ALRT and DITL

The ALRT resource defines the size and screen placement of an alert, just as the WIND resource defines the same for a window. Whereas you specify the type of window to display for a WIND, you don't for an ALRT. An alert always has the appearance of the one pictured in Figure 5.1.

An ALRT requires that you give the ID of yet another resource—a DITL that corresponds to the ALRT. The ALRT defines the size and placement of the alert; the DITL defines the contents of the alert. The *contents* of an alert consists of such things as the buttons and text that are to appear in the alert. Figure 5.2 shows an ALRT resource, viewed from within ResEdit. As can be seen in the title bar of the alert editor, the ALRT resource has an ID of 129. As shown in Figure 5.2, the ID of the DITL resource used by the ALRT resource is also 129.

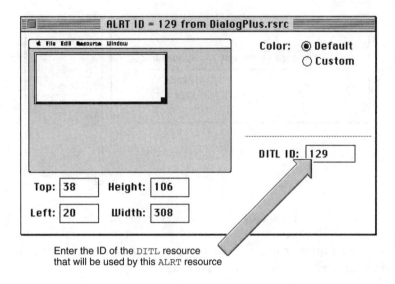

Enter the ID of the DITL resource
that will be used by this ALRT resource

Figure 5.2 The ALRT editor in ResEdit.

The DITL that corresponds to an ALRT doesn't *have* to have the same ID as the ALRT, but because it makes sense to do so, programmers usually give it the same ID.

N O T E

You create the ALRT using the **Create New Resource** command from ResEdit's Resource menu. After sizing the alert in the alert editor and entering a DITL ID, you create the DITL. Once again you'll use the **Create New Resource** command.

Figure 5.3 shows a typical DITL resource. The DITL (for dialog box item list) lists the items in an alert *or* a dialog box. The various items, such as buttons and checkboxes, appear in the floating palette in Figure 5.3. You create an item by clicking on its picture in the floating palette and then, with the mouse button still held down, dragging the mouse over to the window. Releasing the mouse button places the item in the window. Figure 5.3 shows a DITL with three items: a static text item and two buttons. Alerts are meant to be simple; they don't have provisions for working with checkboxes and radio buttons. For those items you'll use a dialog box instead of an alert.

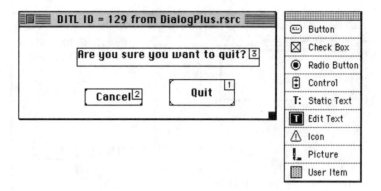

Figure 5.3 The DITL editor in ResEdit.

To change the name or location of an item, double-click on it. That opens a window that allows you to do just that.

Each item in a DITL has an identifying number. When you select the **Show Item Numbers** option from the DITL menu, ResEdit displays the item number for each item—see Figure 5.3.

In an alert, the button that is item 1 has special significance. When a program displays an alert, that button will appear with an outline—just as the **Quit** button does in Figure 5.1. That tells the user that pressing the keyboard's **Return** key will select that button, just as would clicking the mouse button while the cursor was over it.

ResEdit numbers items in the order you create them. If you aren't satisfied with the numbering of items in a DITL use ResEdit's **Renumber Items** option from the DITL menu to make changes.

With the ALRT and DITL complete, you're ready to write the code that brings the alert to the screen.

Alert Source Code

To load an ALRT resource into memory and display the alert on the screen, use the Toolbox routine Alert(). There are two ways to use Alert(). The first is for an alert that does not give the user an option, like the alert on the left in Figure 5.4. The second use of Alert() is for an alert that presents the user with more than one choice, such as **Cancel** and **Quit**. That type of alert is on the right in Figure 5.4.

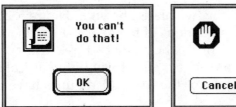 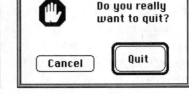

Figure 5.4 An alert without an option, and one with options.

The following snippet provides an example of one of the two ways you can use the Alert() function. The first parameter to Alert() is the resource ID of the ALRT resource that is to be used when posting the alert. The second parameter specifies a pointer to an optional filter function. Filter functions are discussed later in this chapter. Here, a nil pointer will be passed to tell the Toolbox to handle all event processing:

```
#define      rNoWayAlert      128

Alert( rNoWayAlert, nil );
```

By definition, the return type of a call to Alert() is of type short. As shown in the preceding code snippet, your code can ignore the return value. A second way to call Alert() is to keep track of the returned value. Because the returned value indicates which button the user clicked, you'll want to use this next method of calling Alert() when your program's alert has more than a single button:

```
#define      rQuitOrCancelAlert      129
#define      kQuitButton               1
#define      kCancelButton             2

short   theAlertItem;

theAlertItem = Alert( rQuitOrCancelAlert, nil );

if ( theAlertItem == kQuitButton )
```

```
ExitToShell();

// else go on with code as if nothing happened
```

You may have noticed that the two alerts shown in Figure 5.4 have different icons. There are four variations of the Alert() routine. The first, Alert(), displays no icon. The other three, NoteAlert(), CautionAlert(), and StopAlert(), all display different icons. Figure 5.5 shows these icons. All four of the Alert() routines have the same two parameters.

    Alert()   NoteAlert()   CautionAlert()   StopAlert()

Figure 5.5 Variations of Alert() and the icons they display.

DIALOG BOXES

A dialog box is similar to both an alert and a window. A dialog box is like an alert in that it has items in it, but it has a much greater variety of items. A dialog box requires a DITL resource, just as an alert does. A dialog box can take the appearance of a window and, like a window, can be movable. You can think of an alert as a stripped-down dialog box, and a dialog box as a souped-up window.

This chapter discusses the two basic varieties of dialog box: *modal* and *modeless*. A modal dialog box is fixed on the screen—it can't be moved. No action unrelated to the dialog box can take place until the dialog box is dismissed. A modeless dialog box can be moved. Its behavior is similar to a window in that it can contain a title bar that allows the user to drag the dialog box. Figure 5.6 shows an example of both types of dialog boxes.

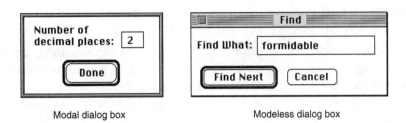

Figure 5.6 Modal and modeless dialog boxes.

DIALOG BOX RESOURCES

A dialog box can contain several types of items. Figure 5.7 shows the Search dialog box from Microsoft Word, a typical dialog box with several item types. A brief description of the item types follows.

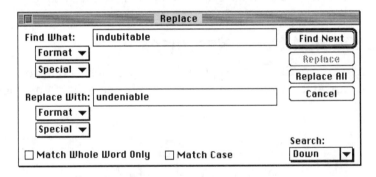

Figure 5.7 A typical dialog box.

Dialog Item Types

Almost every dialog box contains at least one *button* (sometimes called a push button) in the form of an **OK** or **Cancel** button. When you click on a button, an action will happen immediately, such as the dismissal of the dialog box with a click on a button labeled **Done**.

A *checkbox* (or check box) is used to set options. A click on a checkbox toggles that box to its opposite state. When you check or uncheck a box, the action should not occur immediately. Rather, the action occurs later, such as when the dialog box is dismissed.

Radio buttons also set options. But while a checkbox can be an independent entity, radio buttons are always found in groupings of two or more. When the mouse button is clicked while the cursor is over a radio button, that button is turned on and the button that was previously on in the grouping is turned off.

An *editable text item* is your means of supplying text to the computer. Text is typed into the framed rectangle that makes up the item. Dialog box text that cannot be edited, such as instructions to the user, is composed of *static text items*.

The graphics that appear in a dialog box can be made up of icons, pictures, or user items. An *icon* is always 32x32 pixels in size. Pictures and user items can be any size. A *picture* is defined by a PICT resource, while a *user item* is a free-form type that can be made up of a picture, an icon, or a drawing defined by calls to QuickDraw routines.

The DLOG and DITL Resources

The process of creating a dialog box is very similar to that for an alert. Instead of an ALRT resource, however, you'll use a DLOG, as shown in Figure 5.8.

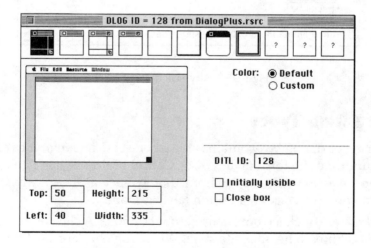

Figure 5.8 The DLOG editor in ResEdit.

Like the WIND editor, the DLOG editor in ResEdit lets you choose the look of the dialog box by selecting from a row of icons. As you did for the ALRT resource, you also specify a DITL that will hold items for a DLOG. Figure 5.9 shows a DITL with the same ID, 128, as that used for the DLOG.

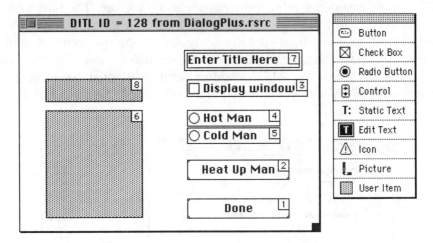

Figure 5.9 The DITL editor in ResEdit.

When you read about alerts, you learned how to add items to the DITL by dragging them from the palette and dropping them into the DITL window. The DITL for a dialog box is the same resource type as the DITL for an alert, so you already know how to create the DITL for a dialog box.

Buttons, radio buttons, checkboxes, and editable text boxes are all items that the user clicks the mouse button on or types into. Besides displaying dialog box items with which the user interacts, you might also want to add graphics to a dialog box. ResEdit allows you to do this in a few different ways.

If you have a graphic image that you want to display in a dialog box, and that image is to remain static, use an icon or a picture. A static graphic image does not move (as the dancing man did in Chapter 3) while the dialog box is on the screen. An example might be a company logo that appears in the corner of a dialog box.

In Chapter 3, you saw how to create a PICT resource. If the image is bigger than 32-pixels square, you can draw it in a paint program and then copy it to the resource file; ResEdit will save it as a PICT resource. If your image is small, you might want to just draw it in ResEdit's icon editor rather than in your paint program. This editor is shown just ahead.

If you'd like to include an icon or a picture in a dialog box, simply include the proper item in the dialog box's DITL. Figure 5.10 shows a DITL with three items: a button, an icon, and a picture. The button item you've seen before. The picture and icon were added in the same way that the button was added—by dragging and dropping from the palette. The results aren't too impressive. Why? Because for every picture you add, you must have a PICT resource, and you must have an ICON resource for every icon you add. You haven't added them yet, but you're about to.

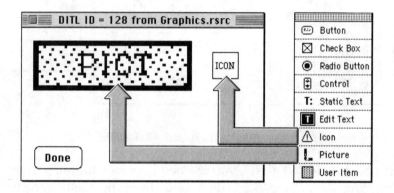

Figure 5.10 Adding a picture and an icon to a DITL.

Adding a Picture to a DITL

The picture item lets you specify the ID of the PICT resource to use. You can double-click on the picture item to edit this information. Figure 5.11 shows that this picture item will be looking for a PICT with an ID of 128.

```
┌─────────────────────────────────────────────────────┐
│▣▤▤▤▤▤▤▤ Edit DITL item #2 from Graphics.rsrc ▤▤▤▤▤▤▤│
│                                                       │
│             Resource ID: │128       │                 │
│      ┌──────────────────────┐                         │
│      │ Picture        ▼     │                         │
│      └──────────────────────┘                         │
│                                                       │
│   ☐ Enabled        Top: │15      │  Height: │60     │ │
│                                                       │
│                   Left: │15      │   Width: │190    │ │
└─────────────────────────────────────────────────────┘
```

Figure 5.11 Information window for a picture item.

NOTE

Notice the checkbox labeled **Enabled** in Figure 5.11. When you create certain items like buttons, checkboxes, and radio buttons, this checkbox will be checked. ResEdit does it for you. If an item is marked as enabled, your program will recognize mouse button clicks on the item. If an item is not enabled, mouse clicks by the user on the item will be ignored. Pictures usually aren't enabled. You can enable a picture—or any item—if you want your program to respond to clicks on that item.

From Chapter 3, you know how to create a picture and save it as a PICT resource. Optionally, you can copy an existing PICT from any other resource file and paste it into the resource file your working with. Next, use the palette that appears with the DITL editor to add a picture item to your DITL resource. Once added, double-click on the **picture item** and, in the window that opens, enter the ID of the PICT resource to use. In Figure 5.12, you see the familiar dancing man picture—one of the four PICT resources from the dancing man series back in Chapter 3 was pasted into a resource file named **Graphics.rsrc**. A look at the DITL shows that the rectangle that was the picture item now displays the dancing man picture. Notice that in Figure 5.12 the picture seems distorted. In the window that allows you to enter the PICT ID (the window that appears when you double-click on the **picture** item), you can also enter the boundaries for the picture. The PICT you specify will be sized to fit that area. You can double-click on the DITL **picture** item and change the boundaries any time. The Information window was shown in Figure 5.11.

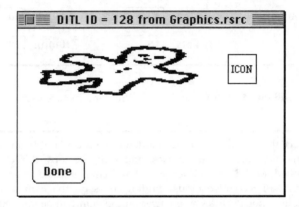

Figure 5.12 A DITL with a picture item in it.

Adding an Icon to a DITL

When you add a picture item to a DITL, you need to also supply a PICT resource to display in that item. A similar situation exists with icons. As shown in Figure 5.12, using the DITL editor palette to add an icon item isn't enough to display an icon—you also need to supply an ICON resource. To do that, first double-click an **icon** item to set the resource ID of the ICON resource to display—just as you did for the picture. Then select **Create New Resource** from the Resource menu. Select the ICON type, then click the **OK** button. When you do that, ResEdit will open an icon editor like the one pictured in Figure 5.13. In that figure an icon has been created for the Acme Fence Company.

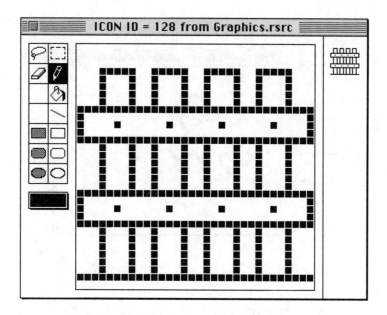

Figure 5.13 ResEdit's ICON editor in use.

N O T E

There's also an icon resource type named ICN#. And just what is the difference between an ICN# and an ICON? The ICN# holds a series of related icons, while the ICON resource holds just a single icon. If you want to create several versions of an icon, such as color, black and white, and small icons, use the ICN# resource to create and hold this family of related icons. Chapter 10 provides an example of using the ICN# resource to create a number of versions of an application's icon to be displayed on the desktop.

Figure 5.14 shows both the ICON and PICT resources that were discussed in this chapter. Since the ICON has an ID of 128, it should now appear in the DITL, where the icon item has an ID of 128. Figure 5.15 shows that this indeed is the case.

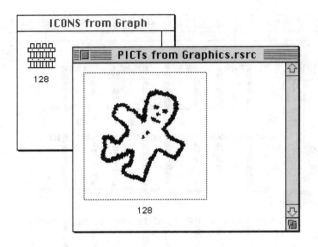

Figure 5.14 An ICON and a PICT resource in ResEdit.

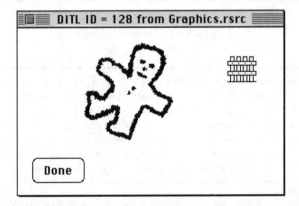

Figure 5.15 The DITL with button, picture, and icon items.

You've now seen two methods for adding graphics to a DITL. There's a third way: the *user item*. When you select the **user** item from the ResEdit palette and drag and drop it into the DITL window, a mysterious gray box appears. The only feature you can change in a user item is its size; the box will always remain gray. Where do the graphics come from? Your source code will determine that. Through your source code you'll be able to display a picture or icon or use QuickDraw commands to draw graphics or text. User items are a very powerful and useful programming tool, and something you'll find omitted from most Macintosh programming books. This situation is remedied later in the chapter.

WORKING WITH DIALOG ITEMS

To load a DLOG resource into memory and display the dialog box on the screen, you'll use a call to GetNewDialog(). But before working with a dialog box, you'll learn to work with dialog box items. Once your program opens a dialog box, you'll need to know all the information covered in the next four sections.

Once a dialog box is on the screen, the user is free to enter text in editable text boxes or click in checkboxes, radio buttons, and buttons. It's up to you to write the code that responds to these user actions. Resources are a great help in designing and implementing a program's interface, but it's still up to you, the programmer, to write the code that makes things work. You didn't think everything would be as easy as creating resources, did you?

Getting Dialog Box Item Information

Chapter 2 introduced you to handles. You've had occasion to use them since then; for example, in Chapter 3 you used a PicHandle to draw to a window a picture based on a PICT resource. A handle is your program's link to an object in memory—an object that the Memory Manager may shift, or relocate, in memory. Handles play a very important part in dealing with dialog boxes. When a dialog box is on the screen, you'll want to examine, and perhaps set, the state of some of the items in it. Before you can work with any dialog box item, you need to get a handle to that item.

GetDialogItem() is a Toolbox call you'll become very familiar with. You tell GetDialogItem() what dialog box you're working with, and which item in that dialog box you're interested in. In return, GetDialogItem() gives you three pieces of information about the item: the type of item, the rectangle that surrounds, or bounds, the item, and a handle to the item. In most instances your only concern will be with the item's handle. Here's a call to GetDialogItem():

```
#define      kDoneButton           1
#define      kAutoSaveCheckBox     2
#define      kPasswordEditBox      3

DialogPtr    theDialog;
short        theType;
Handle       theHandle;
Rect         theRect;

GetDialogItem( theDialog, kPasswordEditBox, &theType,
               &theHandle, &theRect );
```

After the above call to GetDialogItem() is complete, your program can use theHandle to obtain the text that the user typed in the dialog box's editable text box or to overwrite the text in the editable text box with new text. You'll now see just how to do that.

Working with Edit Text Items

If you want to store the string that the user types in an edit text box item, call the Toolbox routine GetDialogItemText(). Before calling this function, make a call to GetDialogItem() to get a handle to the item. Use that handle as the first parameter to GetDialogItemText(). The second parameter should be a Str255 variable. It is in this variable that GetDialogItemText() will place the string that is currently in the editable text box item. Here's a snippet that gets the text from an editable text box and then writes the string to the upper-left corner of the dialog box.

```
DialogPtr    theDialog;
short        theType;
Handle       theHandle;
Rect         theRect;
Str255       theString;

GetDialogItem( theDialog, kPasswordEditBox, &theType,
               &theHandle, &theRect );
GetDialogItemText( theHandle, theString );

SetPort( theDialog );
MoveTo( 15, 15 );
DrawString( theString );
```

GetDialogItemText() always retrieves an edit text item value as a
Str255 type, even if the user has typed in a number. If you want to convert this string to a number, use StringToNum():

```
Str255   theString;
long     theLong;

GetDialogItem( theDialog, kPasswordEditBox, &theType,
               &theHandle, &theRect );
GetDialogItemText( theHandle, theString );

StringToNum( theString, &theLong );
```

If you want to *replace* the text that's in an editable text box, call
SetDialogItemText():

```
GetDialogItem( theDialog, kPasswordEditBox, &theType,
               &theHandle, &theRect );
SetDialogItemText( theHandle, "\Welcome!" );
```

The following example uses all the Toolbox routines just covered. The
code retrieves the text from an editable text box, converts it to a number,
then changes the text in the same editable text box to a new string—a
string based on the entered number. Here goes:

```
#define     kPasswordEditBox      3
#define     kOutOfRangeString     "\pMust be between 0 and 100."
#define     kValidNumberString    "\pValid number entered."

DialogPtr   theDialog;
short       theType;
Handle      theHandle;
Rect        theRect;
Str255      theString;

GetDialogItem( theDialog, kPasswordEditBox, &theType,
               &theHandle, &theRect );
GetDialogItemText( theHandle, theString );

StringToNum( theString, &theLong );

if ( ( theLong < 0 ) || ( theLong > 100 ) )
   SetDialogItemText( theHandle, kOutOfRangeString );
else
   SetDialogItemText( theHandle, kValidNumberString );
```

Working with Checkbox Items

Some dialog box items have a state associated with them, such as on or off. The Macintosh gives these two states values: on is considered to have a value of 1, while off is 0. Items that have a value are called *control* items. Other dialog items such as icons, pictures, and edit text boxes don't have values associated with them.

A checkbox is a control item. When the user clicks the mouse button on a checkbox, you call the Toolbox function GetControlValue() to get the control value. Whatever its value, zero or one, you set it to its opposite value using another Toolbox function: SetControlValue(). Here's an example that does just that:

```
#define      kAutoSaveCheckBox      2
#define      kControlOn             1
#define      kControlOff            0

DialogPtr   theDialog;
short       theType;
Handle      theHandle;
Rect        theRect;
short       theOldValue;

GetDialogItem( theDialog, kAutoSaveCheckBox, &theType,
               &theHandle, &theRect );

theOldValue = GetControlValue( (ControlHandle)theHandle );

if ( theOldValue == kControlOn )
   SetControlValue( (ControlHandle)theHandle, kControlOff );
else
   SetControlValue( (ControlHandle)theHandle, kControlOn );
```

Take special notice that both GetControlValue() and SetControlValue() accept only the Macintosh data type ControlHandle as a parameter; they do not accept a generic Handle type. You must always typecast the handle you get from GetDialogItem(), as done previously.

Working with Radio Button Items

If you understood checkboxes, you're halfway home to working with radio buttons. Checkboxes work independently, and you might have just one in a dialog box. Radio buttons are dependent on one another and work in groups; you must have at least two. When the user clicks on one button in a group, the button that was on previous to the click turns off, and the newly clicked button goes on.

Because of this interdependency, you'll always want to keep track of the radio button that is currently on. Do this by creating a global variable that holds the dialog box item number of the radio button item that's on. When the user clicks on a radio button, you'll turn what is now the old button off and the new button on. Use SetControlValue() to change the radio button values.

The following is an example that assumes there exists a group of three radio buttons. When the snippet starts out the radio button labeled **Maximum Volume** is on. The snippet turns off that radio button and turns on a button labeled **Midpoint Volume**. The third button, labeled **Minimum Volume**, is off at the start and finish of the snippet. As you examine the code, keep in mind that the values of the first three constants (4, 5, and 6) refer to the dialog box item numbers of the three radio buttons, not to any kind of volume settings.

```
#define      kMinVolRadioButton      4
#define      kMidVolRadioButton      5
#define      kMaxVolRadioButton      6
#define      kControlOn              1
#define      kControlOff             0

short   gOldButtonNum = kMaxVolRadioButton;

DialogPtr   theDialog;
short       theType;
Handle      theHandle;
Rect        theRect;

GetDialogItem( theDialog, gOldButtonNum, &theType,
               &theHandle, &theRect );
```

```
SetControlValue( (ControlHandle)theHandle, kControlOff );

GetDialogItem( theDialog, kMidVolRadioButton, &theType,
               &theHandle, &theRect );

SetControlValue( (ControlHandle)theHandle, kControlOn );

gOldButtonNum = kMidVolRadioButton;
```

Notice that the last thing the code does is update the global variable gOldButtonNum to hold the dialog box item number of the radio button that was just turned on. Next time around, it will be considered the "old" button.

MODAL DIALOG BOXES

A modal dialog box controls the screen, and no action can take place outside the dialog box. In certain cases this disadvantage may cause you to use a modeless dialog box instead; they're discussed later in this chapter. If you're simply gathering information to use later—perhaps requesting that the user set some preferences for your program—then a modal dialog box will do just fine. Because a modal dialog box owns the screen, you don't have to worry about the user interacting with other screen elements such as menus, windows, or other dialog boxes. That makes the source code for handling a modal dialog box less complex than the code you write for a modeless dialog box.

The DialogRecord Data Structure

A dialog box, modal or modeless, is based on the DialogRecord data structure. Earlier it was stated that a dialog box had similarities to a window. That was a bit of an understatement. The first member in a DialogRecord is a WindowRecord, which means that a dialog box is actually a window, with a little embellishment. As shown below, Apple defines the DialogRecord using the same window-structure technique described in Chapter 4. Recall that in that chapter, the first member in an application-defined window structure was a WindowRecord. Additional members could be of any data type and were used to hold information related to the new type of window. The DialogRecord begins with a WindowRecord field, which is followed by a member called items that is a handle to the items in the dialog box. That's basically the difference between a window and a dialog box: a dialog box has items, a window doesn't.

```
struct  DialogRecord
{
    WindowRecord   window;
    Handle         items;
    TEHandle       textH;
    short          editField;
    short          editOpen;
    short          aDefItem;
};
```

You use a DialogPtr to reference a dialog box. Because the first member in a DialogRecord is a WindowRecord, the first thing a DialogPtr points to is a GrafPort—just as a WindowPtr does. Figure 5.16 illustrates this. This setup allows you to use a DialogPtr as a parameter to Toolbox routines that require a WindowPtr or GrafPtr. This can be confusing. If you're satisfied that this works, skip the following technical note.

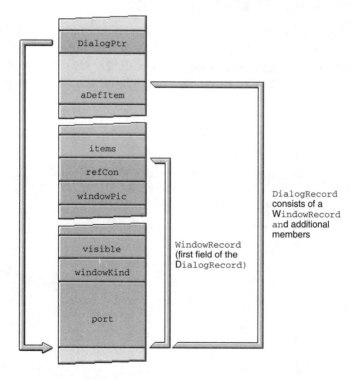

Figure 5.16 A DialogPtr points to a GrafPort, just as a WindowPtr does.

NOTE

Doesn't the idea of being able to use a `GrafPtr`, a `WindowPtr`, and a `DialogPtr` interchangeably almost seem like cheating? If you look at the type definitions of each, you'll see why this works:

```
typedef   GrafPort   *GrafPtr;
typedef   GrafPtr    WindowPtr;
typedef   WindowPtr  DialogPtr;
```

NOTE

All three types are really pointers to a `GrafPort`. Their names are different as a convenience to programmers.

A `WindowRecord` contains a `GrafPort` and other members. A `DialogRecord` contains a `WindowRecord` and other members. It therefore seems as if a `GrafPort`, `WindowRecord`, and `DialogRecord` should be different sizes; they are. But the first member of each type is the `GrafPort`, so that's what each of the three pointer types points to.

Modal Dialog Box Source Code

You load the data from a `DLOG` resource with a call to the Toolbox function `GetNewDialog()`. If the `DLOG` resource has its visible flag set, the dialog box will then appear on screen. A call to the Toolbox routine `ShowWindow()` will display the dialog box even if the visible flag isn't set:

```
#define   rDataInputDialog    128

DialogPtr theDialog;

theDialog = GetNewDialog( rDataInputDialog, nil, (WindowPtr)-1L );
```

Since a modal dialog box controls the screen, you know that it will be dismissed before the program continues. Whatever memory it occupies while it exists will soon be returned to the pool of free memory. Thus, there is no need to reserve your own memory—let it land in memory wherever the Memory Manager puts it. In general, it won't cause fragmentation because it won't be around to block things.

NOTE The preceding text mentions that you can use ShowWindow() to display a loaded, but hidden, dialog box. Recall that a DialogPtr is defined to be the same as a WindowPtr (it just is able to access extra information beyond the data of a WindowRecord). That means that any Toolbox routine that requires a WindowPtr as a parameter will work equally as well with a DialogPtr. The ShowWindow() routine is one such function. Just ahead you'll see another window-related Toolbox routine being used with a dialog box—the FindWindow() function.

After creating the dialog box, your program should enter a loop. The loop repeats itself until the user dismisses the dialog box; that's how the modal dialog controls the screen. At the heart of the loop is a call to the Toolbox function ModalDialog().

The powerful ModalDialog() routine takes control and determines if a mouse click by the user occurs on an enabled item in the dialog box. If an enabled item is clicked on, ModalDialog() returns the resource item number of the item to your program. Run that number through a switch statement to process the mouse click; that is, base your handling of the mouse click on the item the user clicked on. Figure 5.17 shows this journey from the click of the mouse to ModalDialog().

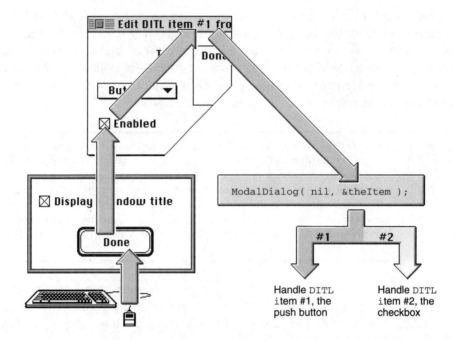

Figure 5.17 From user action to ModalDialog().

A modal dialog box remains on screen as long as the ModalDialog() loop is executing. The loop ends when the loop test condition fails. The usual time for this to occur is when the user clicks the dialog box's **Cancel**, **OK**, or **Done** button, as shown in the following application-defined HandleModalDialog() routine.

```
#define      kDisplayTitleDialog        128
#define      kDoneButton                  1
#define      kPrintScoresCheckBox         2

HandleModalDialog()
{
    DialogPtr   theDialog;
    short       theItem;
    Boolean     dialogDone = false;

    theDialog = GetNewDialog( kDisplayTitleDialog, nil, (WindowPtr)-1L );
    ShowWindow( theDialog );
```

```
   while ( dialogDone == false )
   {
       ModalDialog( nil, &theItem );

       switch ( theItem )
       {
           case kDoneButton:
               dialogDone = true;
               break;

           case kPrintScoresCheckBox:
               SetCheckBox( theDialog, theItem );
               break;
       }
   }

   DisposeDialog( theDialog );
}
```

If the user clicks on the **checkbox** item, an application-defined routine named SetCheckBox() is called. This function uses the code developed previously in this chapter's "Working with Checkbox Items" section. This chapter's example program demonstrates how to make use of such a routine. When the user clicks the **Done** button, dialogDone is set to true. When the loop again reaches the top, the while test will fail, the loop will end, and the dialog box will be dismissed by a call to the Toolbox routine DisposeDialog().

This chapter's example program makes use of the more powerful modeless dialog box. For a working example of a modal dialog box, see the program presented near the end of Chapter 6.

MODELESS DIALOG BOXES

To display a modeless dialog box on the screen, you use the same routine as that for a modal dialog box—GetNewDialog(). For a modal dialog box, you didn't specify where in memory the dialog box would go, because it wasn't going to be hanging around in memory anyway. For a modeless dialog box that might be around for the duration of your program's execution, consider the use of the Toolbox routine NewPtr() to set the storage. This process is identical to creating a new window. Refer to Chapter 4 if you need a review.

```
#define        rControlDialog        130

DialogPtr  theDialog;
Ptr        theStorage;

theStorage = NewPtr( sizeof( DialogRecord ) );
theDialog = GetNewDialog( rControlDialog, theStorage, (WindowPtr)-1L );
```

Once a modeless dialog box is on the screen, it needs special handling considerations. In the previous chapter, you saw an application-defined routine named `EventLoop()`. In Chapter 4, you saw that the `EventLoop()` routine held a loop which had the purpose of getting an event at each pass through. Here's that routine, slightly modified:

```
void  EventLoop( void )
{
    EventRecord   theEvent;
    Boolean       isEventDialog;

    while ( gAllDone == false )
    {
        WaitNextEvent( everyEvent, &theEvent, 15L, nil );

        isEventDialog = HandleDialogEvent( theEvent );

        if ( isEventDialog == false )
        {
            switch ( theEvent.what )
            {
                case mouseDown:
                    HandleMouseDown( theEvent );
                    break;

                case updateEvt:
                    HandleUpdate( theEvent);
                    break;
            }
        }
    }
}
```

This version of EventLoop() makes use of a Boolean variable called isEventDialog. If a modeless dialog box is on the screen, EventLoop() wants to know about it. The Toolbox provides a few routines specifically designed to handle an event that takes place in a dialog box. They're used in the application-defined HandleDialogEvent() routine, which is described just ahead.

If the HandleDialogEvent() function determines that an event is dialog related, it handles the event and returns a value of true to EventLoop(). If that's the case, then EventLoop() is satisfied that the event has been processed, and doesn't execute its switch statement. If, on the other hand, HandleDialogEvent() doesn't handle the event, a value of false is returned to EventLoop(). If that happens, EventLoop() knows it must go ahead and handle the event—and does so in its switch statement.

The workings of HandleDialogEvent() have been glossed over so that you'd see the overall technique for handling an event in a program that uses a modeless dialog box. Now, it's time to closely examine this routine.

```
Boolean  HandleDialogEvent( EventRecord theEvent )
{
   Boolean     isEventDialog = false;
   DialogPtr   theDialog;
   short       theItem;

   if ( FrontWindow() != nil )
   {
      if ( IsDialogEvent( &theEvent )  )
      {
         if ( DialogSelect( &theEvent, &theDialog, &theItem ) )
         {
            switch ( theItem )
            {
               case kDialogDoneButton:
                  gAllDone = true;
                  break;

               // case section to handle each enabled
               // item in the dialog box

            }
         }
      }
```

```
            isEventDialog = true;
        }
    }

    return ( isEventDialog );
}
```

The first thing HandleDialogEvent() does is call the Toolbox routine FrontWindow(), which returns a pointer to the frontmost window on the screen. If no windows—or dialog boxes—are on the screen, the routine will return a value of nil. This check verifies that the screen is not empty. If the screen is empty, HandleDialogEvent() can immediately exit, returning a value of false to signal that the event wasn't handled by the routine.

Next, IsDialogEvent() is called. This Toolbox routine determines if, at the time of the current event, the frontmost window is a dialog box. If a dialog box *isn't* in the forefront, you know the event is related to something other than a dialog box. If that's the case, IsDialogEvent() returns a value of false, and HandleDialogEvent() ends without handling the event. If the event *does* involve a dialog box, IsDialogEvent() checks to see if the event involves the dialog box content region. For example, if the event was a mouse down event, and the cursor was over the dialog box title bar, then IsDialogEvent() again returns false. Your EventLoop() function has code for dealing with mouse clicks in a window's title bar, and you can use the same code for a mouse click in the title bar of a dialog box. To summarize, in order for IsDialogEvent() to return a value of true, a dialog box must be the frontmost window, and the event must involve the content area of that dialog box. Any other event results in IsDialogEvent() returning a value of false, and the end of the HandleDialogEvent() function.

The Toolbox function DialogSelect() is called next. If HandleDialogEvent() has made it this far, then it has been established that the event is dialog related. Now it's time to handle the event. If the event was a mouse click on an enabled dialog box item (such as a button or checkbox), DialogSelect() fills its third parameter with the item number of the clicked-on item and then returns a value of true. HandleDialogEvent() examines this returned value to see if in fact an item was clicked on. If one was, it's up to HandleDialogEvent() to process the mouse click. You can see from the listing for HandleDialogEvent() that it is from within the switch statement that item handling takes place.

DialogSelect() is a powerful routine that can take care of more situations than mouse clicks in dialog box items. This function will do all of the work for you if a dialog box needs updating or activating, or if a user types in an editable text box. Because the handling of these types of events don't involve a click on a dialog box item, DialogSelect() will return a value of false after it completes its work. This tells HandleDialogEvent() to skip the switch statement code that follows the call to DialogSelect().

If DialogSelect() is called, it either handles the event itself or returns the item number of a clicked-on item and lets your code handle the event. In any case, if DialogSelect() gets called by HandleDialogEvent(), the event can be considered handled. That's why the Boolean variable isEventDialog is set to true anytime DialogSelect() gets invoked. This value of true gets returned to EventLoop(), where the event is considered handled. Figure 5.18 summarizes how things work in HandleDialogEvent().

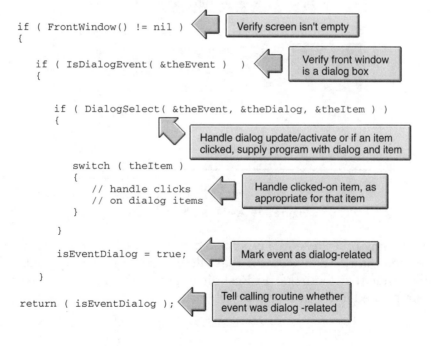

Figure 5.18 Handling a dialog-related event.

Using User Items

There may be a time when you want to include an item in a dialog box as your program executes, but not beforehand. That makes placing the item in the DITL impossible. For example, your program might display one of two pictures, depending on the action the user takes. You could include a picture item in your DITL, but which PICT resource ID would you specify? A problem like this can be overcome using a resource type called a *user item*.

The User Item Resource

The user item is a dialog box item type tailor-made for situations like the above. When you add a user item to a DITL it appears as a gray box. One such item appears on the left of the DITL in Figure 5.19.

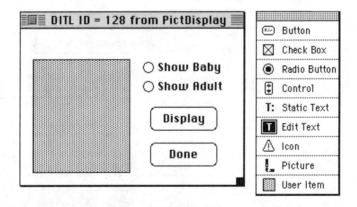

Figure 5.19 A DITL with a user item.

As with any other resource type, you can double-click on a user item to open the information window that allows you to move and resize the item. After that, your job in ResEdit is done. The rest of the work is accomplished in the source code.

The User Item Source Code

Earlier you saw that the Toolbox routine DialogSelect() performs the very helpful task of updating a dialog box. When a partially obscured dialog box is exposed, DialogSelect() will redraw buttons, checkboxes, icons, and pictures: all the items that are the contents of the dialog box. All this is done without any work on your part, which is very helpful indeed. The Dialog Manager knows exactly how to redraw these items without any help from your program because you defined these items in the DITL resource, just as they are to appear in the dialog box. The Dialog Manager uses these definitions when it first displays a dialog box and again when it has to update, or refresh, a dialog box.

The Dialog Manager can't update a user item on its own, as it can other item types. The DITL definition of a user item is incomplete; it just shows the display rectangle that will hold the item. Figure 5.20 shows an example of a dialog box that uses the DITL from Figure 5.19. An alert is obscuring part of the dialog box. Figure 5.20 takes the liberty of showing you what appears under the alert. A real alert would, of course, hide everything behind it. When the alert is dismissed, the area of the dialog box under the alert will need updating.

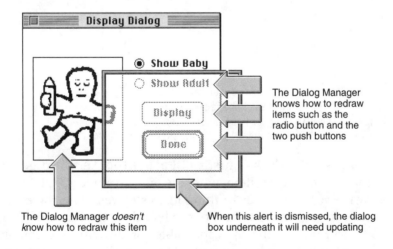

The Dialog Manager knows how to redraw items such as the radio button and the two push buttons

The Dialog Manager *doesn't* know how to redraw this item

When this alert is dismissed, the dialog box underneath it will need updating

Figure 5.20 Dialog box items will need updating by the Dialog Manager.

You provide the Dialog Manager the help it needs to update a user item by writing a function that tells this manager just what to draw in the display rectangle of the user item. You write this function, but you never call it directly. That's right: your source code never makes a call to the user item routine. Instead, your code performs a one-time initialization that associates the function with the user item. You bond the two together so that whenever an update occurs the Dialog Manager will call your function, on its own.

You know that the Toolbox routine GetDialogItem() is used to get information about an item: its type, its display rectangle, or a handle to it. The snippets you've seen so far have all been using GetDialogItem() to get a handle to an item. There's a companion routine to GetDialogItem(), called SetDialogItem(), and it's used—as you may have guessed—to set, or change, information about an item.

If your program has a dialog box that makes use of a user item, you use SetDialogItem() to override the item's handle and replace it with a drawing procedure that tells the Dialog Manager just what to draw in the rectangle making up the user item. Here's an example:

```
#define        kPictureUserItem      3

DialogPtr  theDialog;
short      theType;
Handle     theHandle;
Rect       theRect;

GetDialogItem( theDialog, kPictureUserItem, &theType,
               &theHandle, &theRect );
SetDialogItem( theDialog, kPictureUserItem, theType,
               (Handle)DoUserItem, &theRect );
```

What the above code does is first call GetDialogItem() to get all the information about a user item with the item number 3. It then calls SetDialogItem() to reset everything just as it was, with the exception of the handle to the item. In place of the handle is the name of an application-defined function that is responsible for drawing the contents of the user item—whatever the contents. The preceding code snippet uses a function named DoUserItem(), but this routine can have any name you want. By the name given to the constant that holds the user item's number, kPictureUserItem, you can assume that in the preceding snippet this user item will hold a picture. If the program is capable of displaying one of two pictures, then the DoUserItem() routine would be capable of loading and drawing pictures.

In the call to SetDialogItem(), omit the parentheses that normally follow a function name. You aren't calling the function here; you're passing the Dialog Manager the address of the function. Just as the name of an array signifies the memory address of the start of the array, to SetDialogItem() so does the name of a function signify the address of the start of the function. Finally, because SetDialogItem() is looking for a handle as the fourth parameter, you must typecast DoUserItem to a handle.

NOTE

If you're generating PowerPC code, whether it be from a Symantec or Metrowerks compiler, the user item code you'll use has a couple of small—but very important—differences. Those differences are described in the chapter that deals with PowerPC programming, Chapter 8. If you're going to test out how user items work, create a 68K project for now. You'll notice that the book's CD holds only a 68K version of the project for this chapter's example program, DialogPlus. Chapter 8 presents the PowerPC version of the project for this same program.

The DoUserItem() function is one that you write. Its purpose is to define what the Dialog Manager should draw in the user item. The Dialog Manager will be expecting DoUserItem() to have the following form:

```
pascal void  DoUserItem( DialogPtr theDialog, short theItem)
```

User items appeared when Pascal was the native language of the Macintosh. The Dialog Manager is expecting to see a Pascal function here, and you're supplying a C function. Macintosh C provides a pascal keyword; use it here and the Dialog Manager will be happy. The DoUserItem() routine can have any name, but it must have two arguments: the first of type DialogPtr, the second of type short. That's a requirement you *must* follow.

Keeping Figure 5.20 in mind, take a look at how a user item function might be used. From Figure 5.20 you can assume that the user clicks on one of the two radio buttons, then the **Display** button. One of two pictures—that of a baby or an adult—will then be drawn into the rectangle that bounds the user item. The click on a **radio** button sets a global variable gCurrentPict to the PICT resource ID of the proper picture, then an application-defined drawing routine named `DrawBabyOrAdultPicture()` is called. This function requires that the picture display rectangle be passed to it. Determining that rectangle is a simple enough task to perform: just call the Toolbox function `GetDialogItem()`, passing the item number of the user item. Note that at this point, the user item routine hasn't been called. Here's a look at what the drawing routine might look like:

```
#define      rBabyPicture       128
#define      rAdultPicture      129

short  gCurrentPict;

void  DrawBabyOrManPicture( DialogPtr theDialog, Rect theRect )
{
    GrafPtr      theSavePort;
    PicHandle    thePicture;

    GetPort( &theSavePort );
    SetPort( theDialog );

    if ( gCurrentPict == rBabyPicture )
       thePicture = GetPicture( rBabyPicture );
     else
       thePicture = GetPicture( rAdultPicture );

    DrawPicture( thePicture, &theRect );

    SetPort( theSavePort );
}
```

There's nothing special about the code that makes up `DrawBabyOrAdultPicture()` or the code that invokes this routine. The new code comes in the form of the user item routine—an example of which is shown here:

```
pascal void  DoUserItem( DialogPtr theDialog, short theItem)
{
    short    theType;
    Handle   theHandle;
    Rect     theRect;

    GetDialogItem( theDialog, theItem, &theType,
                  &theHandle, &theRect );
```

```
      DrawBabyOrAdultPicture( theDialog, theRect );
}
```

`DoUserItem()` begins by calling `GetDialogItem()` to get the display rec-tangle `theRect` that bounds the user item. Next, the application-defined picture-drawing routine is called. Here's a summary of how the user item routine fits into the given example. The user item in the dialog box `DITL` defines the rectangle in which drawing will take place. Should you ever want to change this drawing area, just change the `DITL` resource and rebuild your program—your source code can remain untouched. The `DrawBabyOrAdultPicture()` is used to draw a picture into the user item. This type of routine could also be used without a user item function; it's simply a standard application-defined drawing routine. `DrawBabyOrAdultPicture()` is called by the program whenever the user selects a new picture to draw via the radio buttons and the **Display** but-ton. The application-defined `DoUserItem()` function is called not by your program, but by the system. If the user drags the dialog box off screen, then back on, or if the dialog box becomes obscured by a window or alert, the dialog box needs to be updated. Should that be necessary, it is the sys-tem that will call `DoUserItem()`. The system will pass `DoUserItem()` the pointer to the dialog box that needs updating, as well as the item number of the user item that needs to be redrawn. In the example, `DoUserItem()` calls `DrawBabyOrAdultPicture()` to handle the drawing.

Earlier you saw that the Toolbox function `SetDialogItem()` was the device that binds the user item function to the user item itself. You only have to perform this task once, right after opening the dialog box in which the user item appears. Here goes:

```
#define      rDisplayDialog       128
#define      kPictureUserItem       3
#define      rBabyPicture         128
#define      rAdultPicture        129

DialogPtr  theDialog;
short      theType;
Handle     theHandle;
Rect       theRect;
Ptr        theStorage;

theStorage = NewPtr( sizeof( DialogRecord ) );
theDialog = GetNewDialog( rDisplayDialog, theStorage, (WindowPtr)-1L );
```

```
if ( theDialog == nil )
   ExitToShell();

GetDialogItem( theDialog, kPictureUserItem, &theType,
               &theHandle, &theRect );
SetDialogItem( theDialog, kPictureUserItem, theType,
               (Handle)DoUserItem, &theRect );

gCurrentPict = rAdultPicture
```

At this point, DITL item number 3, kPictureUserItem, is bound to the DoUserItem() function—SetDialogItem() took care of that. The call to GetDialogItem() that precedes the call to SetDialogItem() is necessary so that the proper values for theType and theRect could be passed to SetDialogItem(). If your program didn't have those values at the time of the call to SetDialogItem(), "garbage" would be passed in as the third and fifth parameters.

To start things off, assign gCurrentPict one of the two PICT IDs. When the dialog box needs updating—as it will when it is opened—the Dialog Manager will successfully draw the user item when it calls DoUserItem().

NOTE That a function defined by your program never gets called by your program can be a confusing idea. Keep in mind that your code will never directly make a call to DoUserItem(). Rather amazing, isn't it? You can write a function, then leave it to the Mac to call it when it wants to!

The previous example was for a dialog box that contained a single user item. Your program is free to use any number of user items in a dialog box—the DialogPlus program that appears later in this chapter and on the book's CD demonstrates a modeless dialog box that has two user items.

What if you want to have more than one user item? Now that you know what to do for one, working with more than one will be simple. Honest. Figure 5.21 adds a second user item to the DITL that you're already familiar with.

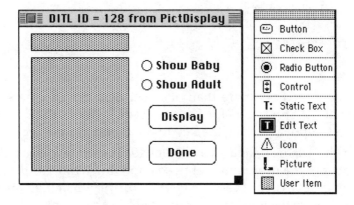

Figure 5.21 A DITL with two user items.

If your program does in fact have a dialog box with more than one user item, you can still get by with writing a single user item drawing function. Here's an example that would work for a dialog box that has two user items:

```
#define        kPictureUserItem        3
#define        kTitleUserItem          4

pascal void  DoUserItem( DialogPtr theDialog, short theItem)
{
    short    theType;
    Handle   theHandle;
    Rect     theRect;

    GetDialogItem( theDialog, theItem, &theType,
                    &theHandle, &theRect );

    switch ( theItem )
    {
        case kPictureUserItem:
            DrawBabyOrAdultPicture( theDialog, theRect );
            break;
```

```
        case kTitleUserItem:
            DrawTitle( theDialog, theRect );
            break;
    }
}
```

You may now see how more than one user item can use the same routine. Look at the arguments for DoUserItem(). One is the item number of the item to update. That's the key to the function's power.

When the Dialog Manager calls DoUserItem() it passes along the item number of the user item that needs updating. You use that number when calling GetDialogItem() to get the display rectangle of the user item. You also use the item number in a switch statement. In the switch, the code appropriate for this one item is executed. Neat, huh? But there's still more to come. In the above example, if the user item to be updated is DITL item number 4, then an application-defined function named DrawTitle() gets called. This function could be a routine that makes a call to DrawString() to draw a title above the picture. The text of the title could be based on which picture is currently being displayed, as revealed by the global variable gCurrentPicture.

What if an alert or window is covering the dialog box, and, once uncovered, the dialog box needs both user items updated? The Dialog Manager will figure this out and will call your DoUserItem() routine twice. On the first call it will pass the item number of one of the user items, and on the second call it will pass the remaining item number. If you weren't amazed before, you've got to be now!

If you could see each line of code executed during this updating, then you'd see that the DoUserItem() routine will get called twice. If you use the debugger when you run the DialogPlus example that appears later in this chapter, and if you place a break point at a line in DoUserItem(), then you can verify that this does in fact happen.

You know that when a dialog box containing a user item is first opened you use GetDialogItem() and SetDialogItem() to associate the user item with the user item function. If you have more than one user item, do this for each item. If your program defines only one user item routine, as this last example did, you associate each user item with this same routine.

```
#define      rDisplayDialog      128
#define      kPictureUserItem      3
#define      kTitleUserItem      6
#define      rBabyPicture      128
#define      rAdultPicture      129

DialogPtr    theDialog;
short        theType;
Handle       theHandle;
Rect         theRect;
Ptr          theStorage;

theStorage = NewPtr( sizeof( DialogRecord ) );
theDialog = GetNewDialog( rDisplayDialog, theStorage, (WindowPtr)-1L );
if ( theDialog == nil )
   ExitToShell();

GetDialogItem( theDialog, kPictureUserItem, &theType,
               &theHandle, &theRect );
SetDialogItem( theDialog, kPictureUserItem, theType,
               (Handle)DoUserItem, &theRect );

GetDialogItem( theDialog, kTitleUserItem, &theType,
               &theHandle, &theRect );
SetDialogItem( theDialog, kTitleUserItem, theType,
               (Handle)DoUserItem, &theRect );

gCurrentPict = rAdultPicture
```

User items are considered mysterious entities by many programmers new to the Macintosh—and by many who aren't. And because of the way the Dialog Manager gets involved with your code, user items really are a little mystical. However, as you can see from the preceding examples, when it comes to writing the code to handle them, they aren't all that tricky.

CHAPTER PROGRAM: DIALOGPLUS

DialogPlus is this chapter's example program. When you run the program, you'll come face to face with a modeless dialog box and the inescapable dancing man. The dialog box contains an editable text box, a checkbox, two radio buttons, and two push buttons. By no coincidence, this program demonstrates the use of all the items with which a user commonly interacts. A screen shot of DialogPlus in action is shown in Figure 5.22.

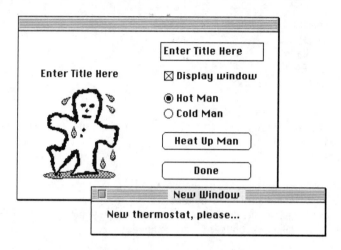

Figure 5.22 A look at the DialogPlus program.

Clicking on a **radio** button lets the program know which of two pictures the program should display when the **Heat Up Man** push button is pressed. As a bonus, a click of a **radio** button also changes the title displayed in the **Heat Up Man** button—a simple little trick that never fails to amaze onlookers.

Clicking on the **Heat Up Man** push button causes several things to happen. The program retrieves the user-entered text from the editable text box and displays it in the smaller of the two user items, the one that appears above the picture. The program also displays the proper picture in the second user item.

If the user clicks on the **Heat Up Man** push button, and if the checkbox is checked, then a window will open. The window serves two purposes. First, it provides an example of a program that supports the display of both a dialog box and a window at the same time—a very real-world kind of thing. Second, by moving the window on and off the dialog box, the Dialog Manager is forced to update things in the dialog box, including the two user items.

To give a practical example of using an alert, DialogPlus throws up a stop alert when the **Done** push button is clicked on. This alert gives the user the option of canceling and returning to the program or quitting.

Program Resources: DialogPlus.rsrc

DialogPlus contains a couple of resources you've seen before, the WIND and the PICT, and a few that you're seeing for the first time in an example program: an ALRT, a DLOG, and two DITLs.

You're familiar with the WIND resource type, so it's not shown in a figure. You've also seen plenty of PICT resources, but since the two here are new, they're shown in Figure 5.23.

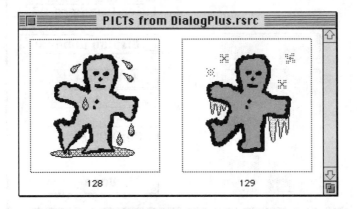

Figure 5.23 The two PICT resources from DialogPlus.

DialogPlus uses the alert shown in figures at the start of this chapter. The ALRT has an ID of 129, and so does the DITL associated with it. Figure 5.24 shows the DITL. The DITL in the figure is displayed with ResEdit's **Show Item Numbers** menu item selected from the DITL menu.

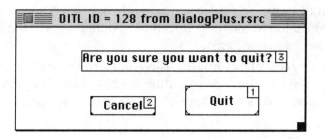

Figure 5.24 The DITL used by the ALRT.

DialogPlus has one DLOG, with an ID of 128, that makes use of DITL 128. Figure 5.25 shows that DITL.

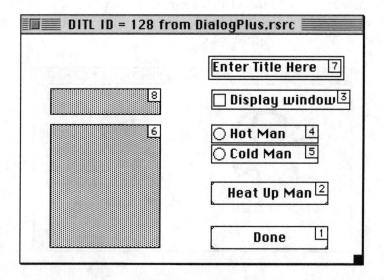

Figure 5.25 The DITL used by the DLOG.

Both an ALRT and a DLOG use the same type of resource to hold their contents—a DITL. Figure 5.26 shows the relationship of these three types, as used in DialogPlus.

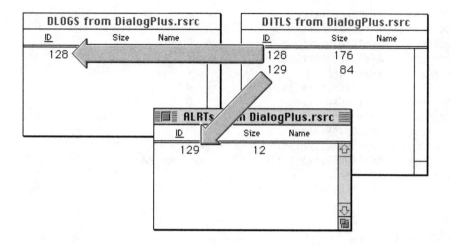

Figure 5.26 `DITL` 128 is used by `DLOG` 128, while `DITL` 129 is used by `ALRT` 129.

 Again, the ID of a `DITL` resource doesn't have to match the ID of the `ALRT` or `DLOG` resource that uses it. It just makes sense to set things up that way. For example, if the `ALRT` in Figure 5.26 had an ID of 500, it could still use `DITL` 129, **N O T E** provided the `ALRT` specified that 129 was the ID of the `DITL` to use.

Program Listing: DialogPlus.c

The complete source code listing for the DialogPlus program appears next. Following it is a discussion of the listing's key points.

```
//_____

#define     rTemperatureWindow          128
#define     rQuitAlert                  129
#define     kAlertDoneButton              1
#define     rTemperatureDialog          128
#define     kDialogDoneButton             1
```

```
#define     kClimateButton           2
#define     kShowWindCheckbox        3
#define     kHotRadioButton          4
#define     kColdRadioButton         5
#define     kManUserItem             6
#define     kTitleEditTextBox        7
#define     kTitleUserItem           8
#define     rManHotPicture           128
#define     rManColdPicture          129
#define     kHotManButtonTitle       "\pHeat Up Man"
#define     kColdManButtonTitle      "\pCool Down Man"
#define     kControlOn               1
#define     kControlOff              0
```

//_____

```
Boolean     gAllDone = false;
Ptr         gDlogStorage;
Ptr         gWindStorage;
short       gCurrentPict;
short       gOldButtonNum;
WindowPtr   gTemperatureWindow;
```

//_____

```
void  main( void )
{
    MaxApplZone();
    MoreMasters();
    MoreMasters();
    MoreMasters();

    InitializeToolbox();
    InitializeVariables();

    OpenTemperatureDialog();
    OpenTemperatureWindow();

    EventLoop();
}
```

```
//_____

void  InitializeVariables( void )
{
   gDlogStorage = NewPtr( sizeof( DialogRecord ) );
   gWindStorage = NewPtr( sizeof( WindowRecord ) );
}


//_____

void  EventLoop( void )
{
   EventRecord   theEvent;
   Boolean       isEventDialog;

   while ( gAllDone == false )
   {
      WaitNextEvent( everyEvent, &theEvent, 15L, nil );

      isEventDialog = HandleDialogEvent( theEvent );

      if ( isEventDialog == false )
      {
         switch ( theEvent.what )
         {
            case mouseDown:
               HandleMouseDown( theEvent );
               break;

            case updateEvt:
               HandleUpdate( theEvent);
               break;
         }
      }
   }
}


//_____
```

```
void  SetCheckBox( DialogPtr theDialog, short theItem )
{
    short    theType;
    Handle   theHandle;
    Rect     theRect;
    short    theOldValue;

    GetDialogItem( theDialog, theItem, &theType, &theHandle, &theRect );

    theOldValue = GetControlValue( (ControlHandle)theHandle );

    if ( theOldValue == kControlOn )
        SetControlValue( (ControlHandle)theHandle, kControlOff );
    else
        SetControlValue( (ControlHandle)theHandle, kControlOn );
}


//_____

void SetRadioButtons( DialogPtr theDialog, short theNewButtonNum )
{
    short    theType;
    Handle   theHandle;
    Rect     theRect;

    GetDialogItem( theDialog, gOldButtonNum, &theType,
                    &theHandle, &theRect );

    SetControlValue( (ControlHandle)theHandle, kControlOff );

    GetDialogItem( theDialog, theNewButtonNum, &theType,
                    &theHandle, &theRect );

    SetControlValue( (ControlHandle)theHandle, kControlOn );

    gOldButtonNum = theNewButtonNum ;
}


//_____

void  OpenTemperatureWindow( void )
{
    gTemperatureWindow = GetNewWindow( rTemperatureWindow,
```

```
                                        gWindStorage, (WindowPtr)-1L );
    if ( gTemperatureWindow == nil )
        ExitToShell();

    HideWindow( gTemperatureWindow );
}


//_____

void  OpenTemperatureDialog( void )
{
    short       theType;
    Handle      theHandle;
    Rect        theRect;
    DialogPtr   theDialog;

    theDialog = GetNewDialog( rTemperatureDialog,
                              gDlogStorage, (WindowPtr)-1L );
    if ( theDialog == nil )
        ExitToShell();

    GetDialogItem( theDialog, kManUserItem, &theType,
                   &theHandle, &theRect );
    SetDialogItem( theDialog, kManUserItem, theType,
                   (Handle)DoUserItem, &theRect );

    GetDialogItem( theDialog, kTitleUserItem, &theType,
                   &theHandle, &theRect );
    SetDialogItem( theDialog, kTitleUserItem, theType,
                   (Handle)DoUserItem, &theRect );

    gCurrentPict  = rManHotPicture;
    gOldButtonNum = kHotRadioButton;

    GetDialogItem( theDialog, gOldButtonNum, &theType,
                   &theHandle, &theRect);
    SetControlValue( (ControlHandle)theHandle, kControlOn );

    ShowWindow( theDialog );
}


//_____
```

```
pascal void  DoUserItem( DialogPtr theDialog, short theItem)
{
    short   theType;
    Handle  theHandle;
    Rect    theRect;

    GetDialogItem( theDialog, theItem, &theType,
                   &theHandle, &theRect );

    switch ( theItem )
    {
        case kManUserItem:
            ChangeMan( theDialog, theRect );
            break;

        case kTitleUserItem:
            DrawTitle( theDialog, theRect );
            break;
    }
}


//_____


void  ChangeMan( DialogPtr theDialog, Rect theRect )
{
    GrafPtr    theSavePort;
    PicHandle  thePicture;

    GetPort( &theSavePort );
    SetPort( theDialog );

    if ( gCurrentPict == rManHotPicture )
        thePicture = GetPicture( rManHotPicture );
      else
        thePicture = GetPicture( rManColdPicture );

    DrawPicture( thePicture, &theRect );

    SetPort( theSavePort );
}


//_____
```

```
void  DrawTitle( DialogPtr theDialog, Rect theUserRect )
{
    short     theType;
    Handle    theHandle;
    Rect      theRect;
    GrafPtr   theSavePort;
    Str255    theString;

    GetPort( &theSavePort );
    SetPort( theDialog );

    FillRect( &theUserRect, &qd.white );

    GetDialogItem( theDialog, kTitleEditTextBox, &theType,
                   &theHandle, &theRect );
    GetDialogItemText( theHandle, theString );

    MoveTo( theUserRect.left,theUserRect.bottom - 3 );
    DrawString( theString );

    SetPort( theSavePort );
}


//_____

Boolean  HandleDialogEvent( EventRecord theEvent )
{
    Boolean    isEventDialog = false;
    DialogPtr  theDialog;
    short      theItem;
    short      theAlertItem;

    if ( FrontWindow() != nil )
    {
        if ( IsDialogEvent( &theEvent )  )
        {
            if ( DialogSelect( &theEvent, &theDialog, &theItem ) )
            {
                switch ( theItem )
                {
                    case kDialogDoneButton:
                        theAlertItem = StopAlert( rQuitAlert, nil );
                        if ( theAlertItem == kAlertDoneButton )
```

```
                             gAllDone = true;
                         break;

                  case kShowWindCheckbox:
                      SetCheckBox( theDialog, theItem );
                      break;

                  case kHotRadioButton:
                  case kColdRadioButton:
                    SetRadioButtons( theDialog, theItem );
                    SetClimateButton( theDialog );
                    break;

                  case kClimateButton:
                      DoClimateButton( theDialog );
                      break;
             }
         }

         isEventDialog = true;
      }
   }

   return ( isEventDialog );
}


//_____


void   SetClimateButton( DialogPtr theDialog )
{
   short   theType;
   Handle  theHandle;
   Rect    theRect;

   GetDialogItem( theDialog, kClimateButton, &theType,
                  &theHandle, &theRect );

   if ( gOldButtonNum == kHotRadioButton )
      SetControlTitle( (ControlHandle)theHandle, kHotManButtonTitle );
   else
      SetControlTitle( (ControlHandle)theHandle, kColdManButtonTitle );
}
```

```
//_____

void  DoClimateButton( DialogPtr theDialog )
{
    short    theType;
    Handle   theHandle;
    Rect     theRect;
    short    theControlValue;

    GetDialogItem( theDialog, kShowWindCheckbox, &theType,
                   &theHandle, &theRect );

    theControlValue = GetControlValue ( (ControlHandle)theHandle );
    if ( theControlValue == kControlOn )
       ShowWindow( gTemperatureWindow );
    else
       HideWindow( gTemperatureWindow );

    if ( gOldButtonNum == kHotRadioButton )
       gCurrentPict = rManHotPicture;
    else
       gCurrentPict = rManColdPicture;

    GetDialogItem( theDialog, kManUserItem, &theType,
                   &theHandle, &theRect );
    ChangeMan( theDialog, theRect );

    GetDialogItem( theDialog, kTitleUserItem, &theType,
                   &theHandle, &theRect );
    DrawTitle( theDialog, theRect );
}


//_____

void  HandleUpdate( EventRecord theEvent )
{
    WindowPtr  theWindow;
    GrafPtr    theSavePort;

    theWindow = (WindowPtr)theEvent.message;

    GetPort( &theSavePort );
    SetPort( theWindow );
```

```
    TextFont( systemFont );
    TextSize( 12 );

    BeginUpdate( theWindow );
        MoveTo( 20, 20 );
        DrawString("\pNew thermostat, please...");
    EndUpdate( theWindow );

    SetPort( theSavePort );
}


//_____

void  HandleMouseDown( EventRecord theEvent )
{
    WindowPtr   theWindow;
    short       thePart;

    thePart = FindWindow( theEvent.where, &theWindow );

    switch ( thePart )
    {
        case inMenuBar:
            break;

        case inDrag:
            DragWindow( theWindow, theEvent.where, &qd.screenBits.bounds );
            break;

        case inGoAway:
            if ( TrackGoAway( theWindow, theEvent.where ) )
                CloseOneWindow( theWindow );
            break;

        case inContent:
            if ( theWindow != FrontWindow() )
                SelectWindow( theWindow );
            break;
    }
}


//_____
```

```
void  CloseOneWindow( WindowPtr theWindow )
{
   HideWindow( theWindow );
   CloseWindow( theWindow );
   DisposePtr( ( Ptr )theWindow );
   gAllDone = true;
   theWindow = nil;
}



//_____

void  InitializeToolbox( void )
{
   InitGraf( &qd.thePort );
   InitFonts();
   InitWindows();
   InitMenus();
   TEInit();
   InitDialogs( 0L );
   FlushEvents( everyEvent, 0 );
   InitCursor();
}
```

Stepping through the Code

As always, this chapter ends with a walkthrough of the example program. The coverage of the DialogPlus code will pause the longest at information pertinent to this chapter.

The define Directives

DialogPlus can display a window with ID of rTemperatureWindow, an alert with ID rQuitAlert, and the modeless dialog box that has a resource ID of rTemperatureDialog.

The alert has a **Quit** button that has a DITL item number of kAlertDoneButton. The dialog box has several items, each referred to in the code by a define: kDialogDoneButton, kClimateButton, kShowWindCheckbox, kHotRadioButton, kColdRadioButton, kManUserItem, kTitleEditTextBox, and kTitleUserItem.

The dialog box can display one of two PICT resources: rManHotPicture or rManColdPicture. The text of the push button that displays the appropriate picture changes, depending on the radio button selected. The push button title will be one of two strings, as defined by the constants kHotManButtonTitle and kColdManButtonTitle.

When a control such as a radio button is on, it has a value of kControlOn. When it's off, it has the value of kControlOff.

```
#define    rTemperatureWindow        128
#define    rQuitAlert                129
#define    kAlertDoneButton            1
#define    rTemperatureDialog        128
#define    kDialogDoneButton           1
#define    kClimateButton              2
#define    kShowWindCheckbox           3
#define    kHotRadioButton             4
#define    kColdRadioButton            5
#define    kManUserItem                6
#define    kTitleEditTextBox           7
#define    kTitleUserItem              8
#define    rManHotPicture            128
#define    rManColdPicture           129
#define    kHotManButtonTitle     "\pHeat Up Man"
#define    kColdManButtonTitle    "\pCool Down Man"
#define    kControlOn                  1
#define    kControlOff                 0
```

The Global Variables

Like the other programs in this book, DialogPlus uses gAllDone to denote the ending of the program's execution. DialogPlus reserves memory for both the dialog box and the window at the start of the program—gDlogStorage and gWindStorage are the pointers that keep track of these two blocks of nonrelocatable memory positioned low in the heap. The short variable gCurrentPict keeps track of which of two pictures is currently displayed in the dialog box. There's always one radio button on, and its item number is held in the variable gOldButtonNum. The program can have only one window open. The WindowPtr variable gTemperatureWindow is used to keep track of the window.

```
Boolean     gAllDone = false;
Ptr         gDlogStorage;
Ptr         gWindStorage;
short       gCurrentPict;
short       gOldButtonNum;
WindowPtr   gTemperatureWindow;
```

The main() Function

The main() function performs the standard memory and Toolbox initializations, then sets up memory that will hold the window and dialog box data. After that, both the dialog box and window are opened. Then it's on to the main event loop.

```
void  main( void )
{
    MaxApplZone();
    MoreMasters();
    MoreMasters();
    MoreMasters();

    InitializeToolbox();
    InitializeVariables();

    OpenTemperatureDialog();
    OpenTemperatureWindow();

    EventLoop();
}
```

Handling Checkboxes and Radio Buttons

This chapter showed you how to handle a mouse click in a checkbox. DialogPlus takes the example code shown earlier in this chapter, surrounds it with a pair of braces, and calls it SetCheckBox(). If you pass in the resource DITL item number of the clicked-on item and a pointer to the dialog box the item is in, as done here, you can use and re-use this routine in all your programs—without modification.

```
void  SetCheckBox( DialogPtr theDialog, short theItem )
{
```

```
    short    theType;
    Handle   theHandle;
    Rect     theRect;
    short    theOldValue;

    GetDialogItem( theDialog, theItem, &theType, &theHandle, &theRect );

    theOldValue = GetControlValue( (ControlHandle)theHandle );

    if ( theOldValue == kControlOn )
        SetControlValue( (ControlHandle)theHandle, kControlOff );
    else
        SetControlValue( (ControlHandle)theHandle, kControlOn );
}
```

Like SetCheckBox(), the radio button routine SetRadioButtons() is a rehash of the code snippet shown in this chapter. It too asks for the item number of the clicked-on item and a pointer to the dialog box that item appears in. The routine then turns off the old button before turning on the newly clicked one.

```
void SetRadioButtons( DialogPtr theDialog, short theNewButtonNum )
{
    short    theType;
    Handle   theHandle;
    Rect     theRect;

    GetDialogItem( theDialog, gOldButtonNum, &theType,
                    &theHandle, &theRect );

    SetControlValue( (ControlHandle)theHandle, kControlOff );

    GetDialogItem( theDialog, theNewButtonNum, &theType,
                    &theHandle, &theRect );

    SetControlValue( (ControlHandle)theHandle, kControlOn );

    gOldButtonNum = theNewButtonNum ;
}
```

Opening a Window and a Modeless Dialog Box

DialogPlus allows just one window to be opened. The user can open and close that same window as often as desired. Since that's the case, the program can use a simple trick to give the illusion of the window opening and closing. At the start of the program the window is opened and a global `WindowPtr` variable is set to point to it. Then, the window is hidden through a call to the Toolbox routine `HideWindow()`. The window stays open for the duration of the program. If the user elects to "open" the window, a call to the Toolbox function `ShowWindow()` is all that's needed. When the user want's to "close" the window, a call to `HideWindow()` is made.

```
void  OpenTemperatureWindow( void )
{
    gTemperatureWindow = GetNewWindow( rTemperatureWindow,
                                      gWindStorage, (WindowPtr)-1L );
    if ( gTemperatureWindow == nil )
        ExitToShell();

    HideWindow( gTemperatureWindow );
}
```

The dialog box that opens in DialogPlus has two user items in it. So `OpenTemperatureDialog()` calls `SetDialogItem()` twice to tell the Dialog Manager to be on the watch for a routine called `DoUserItem()` when it's update time.

The dialog box is going to display one of two pictures, so `OpenTemperatureDialog()` assigns gCurrentPict the `PICT` ID of one of them here. The program must turn on one of the two radio buttons when the dialog box opens; the Dialog Manager doesn't do that on its own. Since DialogPlus begins with the display of the hot picture, the corresponding radio button should initially be turned on.

```
void  OpenTemperatureDialog( void )
{
    short      theType;
    Handle     theHandle;
    Rect       theRect;
    DialogPtr  theDialog;

    theDialog = GetNewDialog( rTemperatureDialog,
                              gDlogStorage, (WindowPtr)-1L );
    if ( theDialog == nil )
        ExitToShell();
```

```
GetDialogItem( theDialog, kManUserItem, &theType,
                &theHandle, &theRect );
SetDialogItem( theDialog, kManUserItem, theType,
                (Handle)DoUserItem, &theRect );

GetDialogItem( theDialog, kTitleUserItem, &theType,
                &theHandle, &theRect );
SetDialogItem( theDialog, kTitleUserItem, theType,
                (Handle)DoUserItem, &theRect );

gCurrentPict  = rManHotPicture;
gOldButtonNum = kHotRadioButton;

GetDialogItem( theDialog, gOldButtonNum, &theType,
                &theHandle, &theRect);
SetControlValue( (ControlHandle)theHandle, kControlOn );

ShowWindow( theDialog );
}
```

Drawing User Items

The DoUserItem( ) routine that appears in DialogPlus has the same format
as the one shown in this chapter. Instead of drawing right here within the
function, DoUserItem( ) delegates drawing tasks to either ChangeMan( ) or
DrawTitle( ). Which of these two application-defined routines gets called
depends on which of the two user items is being updated.

```
pascal void  DoUserItem( DialogPtr theDialog, short theItem)
{
    short   theType;
    Handle  theHandle;
    Rect    theRect;

    GetDialogItem( theDialog, theItem, &theType,
                    &theHandle, &theRect );

    switch ( theItem )
    {
        case kManUserItem:
            ChangeMan( theDialog, theRect );
            break;

        case kTitleUserItem:
```

```
         DrawTitle( theDialog, theRect );
         break;
   }
}
```

If the user item that displays the picture needs updating, the program calls ChangeMan(). This routine looks at gCurrentPict to see which PICT to load and display. Notice that the user item's display rectangle is passed to ChangeMan() so that the routine knows where to draw the picture.

```
void  ChangeMan( DialogPtr theDialog, Rect theRect )
{
   GrafPtr     theSavePort;
   PicHandle   thePicture;

   GetPort( &theSavePort );
   SetPort( theDialog );

   if ( gCurrentPict == rManHotPicture )
      thePicture = GetPicture( rManHotPicture );
    else
      thePicture = GetPicture( rManColdPicture );

   DrawPicture( thePicture, &theRect );

   SetPort( theSavePort );
}
```

If the smaller of the two user items is to be updated, DrawTitle() does the work. Before drawing a string in the user item, DrawTitle() clears out the old title by calling the Toolbox function FillRect() to white out the user item. Then DrawTitle() calls GetDialogItem() to get a handle to the editable text box to use in a call to GetDialogItemText(). With the contents of the editable text box retrieved, it's a simple matter to move the graphics pen into the user item box and draw the string.

```
void  DrawTitle( DialogPtr theDialog, Rect theUserRect )
{
   short     theType;
   Handle    theHandle;
   Rect      theRect;
   GrafPtr   theSavePort;
```

```
Str255    theString;

GetPort( &theSavePort );
SetPort( theDialog );

FillRect( &theUserRect, &qd.white );

GetDialogItem( theDialog, kTitleEditTextBox, &theType,
               &theHandle, &theRect );
GetDialogItemText( theHandle, theString );

MoveTo( theUserRect.left, theUserRect.bottom - 3 );
DrawString( theString );

SetPort( theSavePort );
}
```

Event Handling

Before processing an event, `EventLoop()` calls `HandleDialogEvent()` to give that routine the opportunity to handle it. If `HandleDialogEvent()` doesn't handle the event, then one of the following is true about the event:

1. The event wasn't dialog related; handle the event in the `switch` section of `EventLoop()` as done in the past.

2. The event was in the dialog box title bar, not its content region. A dialog box title bar is the same as a window title bar, so you can again use the old window code found in the application-defined `HandleMouseDown()` routine that is called from the `switch` section of `EventLoop()` to drag the dialog box. As the age-old saying goes, "A title bar is a title bar...."

```
void  EventLoop( void )
{
    EventRecord  theEvent;
    Boolean      isEventDialog;

    while ( gAllDone == false )
    {
        WaitNextEvent( everyEvent, &theEvent, 15L, nil );
```

```
isEventDialog = HandleDialogEvent( theEvent );

if ( isEventDialog == false )
{
    switch ( theEvent.what )
    {
        case mouseDown:
            HandleMouseDown( theEvent );
            break;

        case updateEvt:
            HandleUpdate( theEvent);
            break;
    }
}
}
```

`HandleDialogEvent()` only handles an event if it's dialog related. Because the user items aren't enabled in the `DITL`, the Dialog Manager ignores mouse clicks on them. Figure 5.27 shows how a mouse button click on each dialog box item is handled.

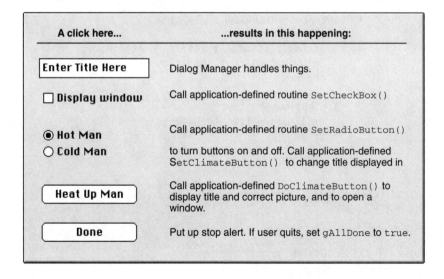

Figure 5.27 How items are handled in DialogPlus.

```
Boolean  HandleDialogEvent( EventRecord theEvent )
{
    Boolean    isEventDialog = false;
    DialogPtr  theDialog;
    short      theItem;
    short      theAlertItem;

    if ( FrontWindow() != nil )
    {
        if ( IsDialogEvent( &theEvent )  )
        {
            if ( DialogSelect( &theEvent, &theDialog, &theItem ) )
            {
                switch ( theItem )
                {
                    case kDialogDoneButton:
                        theAlertItem = StopAlert( rQuitAlert, nil );
                        if ( theAlertItem == kAlertDoneButton )
                            gAllDone = true;
                        break;

                    case kShowWindCheckbox:
                        SetCheckBox( theDialog, theItem );
                        break;

                    case kHotRadioButton:
                    case kColdRadioButton:
                        SetRadioButtons( theDialog, theItem );
                        SetClimateButton( theDialog );
                        break;

                    case kClimateButton:
                        DoClimateButton( theDialog );
                        break;
                }
            }

            isEventDialog = true;
        }
    }

    return ( isEventDialog );
}
```

A click on either **radio** button is treated in the same way. First, a call is made to the application-defined SetRadioButtons() function. After the buttons are set, a call is made to the application-defined routine SetClimateButton(). This function changes the title displayed in the push button. This is accomplished by a call to the Toolbox function SetControlTitle(). Here the button title is set to match the current radio button setting—information held in the global variable gOldButtonNum.

```
void  SetClimateButton( DialogPtr theDialog )
{
    short    theType;
    Handle   theHandle;
    Rect     theRect;

    GetDialogItem( theDialog, kClimateButton, &theType,
                   &theHandle, &theRect );

    if ( gOldButtonNum == kHotRadioButton )
        SetControlTitle( (ControlHandle)theHandle, kHotManButtonTitle );
    else
        SetControlTitle( (ControlHandle)theHandle, kColdManButtonTitle );
}
```

Clicking on the **Climate** radio button performs a few actions, all taken care of in the application-defined DoClimateButton() routine. First there is a call to GetDialogItem() to get a handle to the checkbox item. Then a call to GetControlValue() is made to find the value of the checkbox. Remember: you must typecast the generic handle returned by GetDialogItem() into a ControlHandle, as done here. If the checkbox is on, a call to the Toolbox function ShowWindow() results in the display of the previously opened and hidden window.

Next, DoClimateButton() determines which radio button is on so that gCurrentPict can be set to hold the PICT resource ID of the proper picture—the picture that is about to be displayed. To do the actual picture drawing, DoClimateButton() calls the application-defined ChangeMan() routine, passing along the display rectangle of the user item that will hold the picture. This is the same ChangeMan() routine called by DoUserItem() during dialog box updating.

The routine ends with a call to `DrawTitle()`. This function displays a title in the second user item rectangle.

```
void  DoClimateButton( DialogPtr theDialog )
{
    short    theType;
    Handle   theHandle;
    Rect     theRect;
    short    theControlValue;

    GetDialogItem( theDialog, kShowWindCheckbox, &theType,
                   &theHandle, &theRect );

    theControlValue = GetControlValue ( (ControlHandle)theHandle );
    if ( theControlValue == kControlOn )
        ShowWindow( gTemperatureWindow );
    else
        HideWindow( gTemperatureWindow );

    if ( gOldButtonNum == kHotRadioButton )
        gCurrentPict = rManHotPicture;
    else
        gCurrentPict = rManColdPicture;

    GetDialogItem( theDialog, kManUserItem, &theType,
                   &theHandle, &theRect );
    ChangeMan( theDialog, theRect );

    GetDialogItem( theDialog, kTitleUserItem, &theType,
                   &theHandle, &theRect );
    DrawTitle( theDialog, theRect );
}
```

If `HandleDialogEvent()` doesn't handle the current event, it returns a value of `false` to `EventLoop()`. The `switch` statement at the bottom of `EventLoop()` is then entered. If the event is an update event, and `HandleDialogEvent()` didn't handle it, it must be window related. There's only one window that can be on the screen, so there's no decision making to perform here; just write to the window.

```
void  HandleUpdate( EventRecord theEvent )
{
    WindowPtr   theWindow;
    GrafPtr     theSavePort;
```

```
    theWindow = (WindowPtr)theEvent.message;

    GetPort( &theSavePort );
    SetPort( theWindow );

    TextFont( systemFont );
    TextSize( 12 );

    BeginUpdate( theWindow );
        MoveTo( 20, 20 );
        DrawString("\pNew thermostat, please...");
    EndUpdate( theWindow );

    SetPort( theSavePort );
}
```

HandleDialogEvent() doesn't handle a mouse down event in a title bar, whether it's a window or dialog box. An event of that type takes the program to HandleMouseDown(). This routine, written almost exactly as it was for windows back in Chapter 4, works here for the window or dialog box.

CHAPTER SUMMARY

When a user makes a mistake, or is about to do something that could result in a loss of data, a Macintosh program will display an alert. The size and screen location of an alert is defined by an ALRT resource. The items in the alert, such as an informative message and a **Cancel** or **OK** button, are defined in a DITL resource. The Toolbox routine Alert() displays an alert, using the ID of the passed-in ALRT resource ID.

Dialog boxes can be modal—fixed on the screen; or they can be modeless—movable. The style, size, and screen location of both types are defined by the DLOG resource type. Like an ALRT, a DLOG has a related DITL that defines the items that are to appear in the dialog box.

The Toolbox routine ModalDialog() does much of the work in handling a modal dialog box. It tracks the user's mouse movements and reports back to the program when a user clicks on an item in the dialog box.

Modeless dialog boxes require more work on the programmer's part. The Toolbox routine IsDialogEvent() determines if a dialog box was the frontmost window when an event occurred. If so, the Toolbox routine `DialogSelect()` is called to handle updates or activates to the dialog box. `DialogSelect()` also tracks the user's actions to determine if he or she clicked on an item in the dialog box.

Dialog boxes can contain several types of items: push buttons, radio buttons, checkboxes, and editable text boxes are the most common. Pictures and icons can also be used as items. The user item is a less used, but very powerful, item type. This item type allows an item to change as a program executes.

Chapter 6

More About Windows

Windows and menus are what originally set Macintosh programs apart from those designed for other computers. Menus allow an application to be nonlinear; that is, it doesn't follow a set sequence of events. Thanks to menus, a user is free to perform different actions each time he or she runs a program.

In this chapter you'll learn about the two resource types used to create menus. The MENU is the template for a single menu. The MBAR resource is a collection of MENU resources used to form a single menu bar.

Here you'll learn that once you get a handle to a menu, you can make several changes to the characteristics of a menu and its menu items. You'll disable and enable a menu, change the text and style of text for a menu item, and place a check mark by an item.

About Menus

Every application has its own *menu bar* running along the top of the screen. Your program will define the individual menu names in the menu bar—the *menus*. It will also define all the *menu items*—the individual items that appear in each menu.

As conditions in a program change, the action of a menu item may not be applicable. At those times you'll want to *disable* that menu item. Disabling the item dims it and makes it impossible to select. Later, when the action of that menu item is usable, you can *enable* it to again make it selectable.

You can use *separator lines* in a menu to logically group menu items. Though technically an item, a separator line is never selectable. It serves only to visually divide a menu into sections.

For a commonly used menu command you can define a *keyboard equivalent*, or *Command equivalent*. Rather than making the selection from the menu, the keyboard equivalent allows the user to carry out the menu option by using the command key in conjunction with some other key.

Figure 6.1 shows a menu bar that contains the three *standard menus* found in almost all Macintosh programs: the Apple, File, and Edit menus.

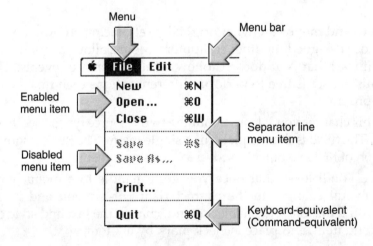

Figure 6.1 A typical Macintosh menu.

Menu Resources

You'll rely on two resource types to define the menu and menu items for your program. The MENU resource defines a single menu and the items in it. The MBAR resource groups the individual MENU resources together into a single menu bar.

The MENU **Resource**

For each menu that your program will have in its menu bar, you'll create a MENU resource. Let's step through that process now.

As is the case for any new resource, select **Create New Resource** from ResEdit's Resource menu. Then double-click on MENU in the Select New Type dialog box. You'll then see a window like the one shown in Figure 6.2.

You'll want one of your MENU resources to represent the Apple menu—the one that holds the items the user keeps in the Apple Menu Items folder in the System Folder. To do this click, on the ▪ (Apple menu) radio button, as shown in Figure 6.2.

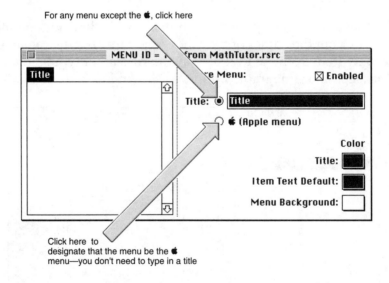

Figure 6.2 ResEdit's MENU editor.

To add menu items to a MENU, whether the Apple menu or another menu, choose **Create New Item** from the Resource menu. Then type the menu item name. Figure 6.3 illustrates typing in the **About** item that is typically the first menu item in the Apple menu.

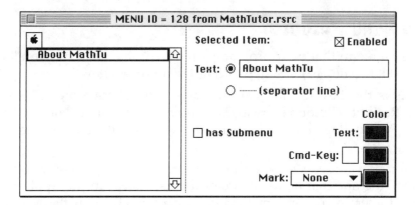

Figure 6.3 Typing in a menu item name.

To add a separator line between menu items, as is done to separate the **About** item from the names of the other Apple menu items, again select **Create New Item** from the Resource menu. Instead of typing in a name, click the (**separator line**) radio button, as shown in Figure 6.4.

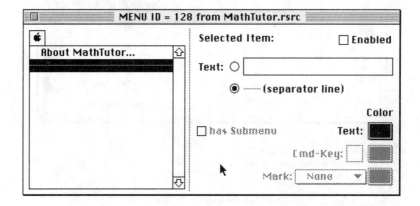

Figure 6.4. Adding a separator line in a menu.

Figure 6.4 represents a completed MENU. An application's Apple menu contains other items, but you don't add them here. That's because they vary from computer to computer. Your program will add the items only after the user launches it__that way it can add the items that are particular to the user's Mac. As you'll see later in this chapter, a call to a single Toolbox function allows your program to do this.

You need a MENU resource for each menu your program displays. Figure 6.5 shows a second menu—the traditional File menu. Apple recommends that all programs contain the Apple, File, and Edit menus. They contain items that are necessary in most programs, and they give users a sense of familiarity when your program starts up.

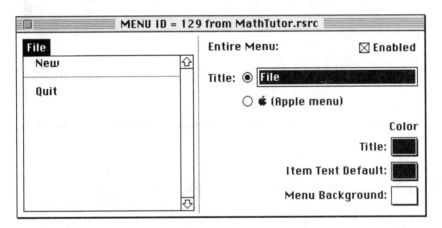

Figure 6.5 A File menu MENU resource.

The MBAR **Resource**

You've defined each of your program's menus with MENU resources. Now its time to package them together using an MBAR resource. The MBAR defines which MENU resources will appear in your program's menu bar and in what order.

Why would you have to specify which MENU resources to use in the menu bar? Why would you define a MENU that *wouldn't* be there? A program can have more than one menu bar. Depending on certain conditions during the running of the program, that program could switch menu bars as the program runs. This book won't cover applications that make use of multiple menu bars.

ResEdit makes creating an MBAR resource easy. Select **Create New Resource** from the Resource menu. You'll see an MBAR editor like that shown in Figure 6.6.

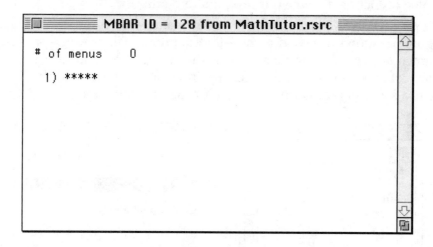

Figure 6.6 The MBAR editor in ResEdit.

The first MENU that you add will end up being the leftmost menu in a program's menu bar—so the first MENU listed in the MBAR should be the Apple menu. Click on the number 1 in the MBAR editor, then select **Insert New Field** from the Resource menu. Enter the ID of the Apple MENU in the box that appears. Since the Apple MENU created earlier had an ID of 128, that's what is entered in Figure 6.7. After you've entered the resource ID of each MENU, the MBAR is complete.

In case you haven't noticed, ResEdit usually gives the first resource of any resource type an ID of 128. That's because for some resource types, Apple reserves resource IDs in the 0 to 127 range for its own use.

N O T E

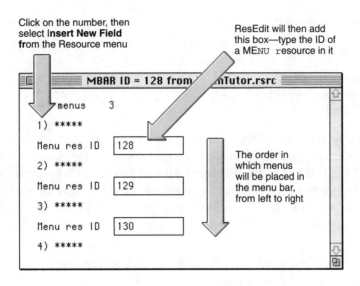

Figure 6.7 Adding MENU resources to an MBAR.

MENU SOURCE CODE

The interface between the Menu Manager and you, the programmer, is a particularly good one. There are only a few Toolbox commands you need to become familiar with in order to work with menus.

Setting up the Menu Bar

When your program starts up, one of the first things it should do is set up the menu bar; the user will be expecting it to be there immediately. Calling the Toolbox function GetNewMBar() does this for you. Pass this routine the ID of an MBAR resource and it will create a *menu list*. which contains a handle to each individual menu—each MENU resource. Here's a call that uses an MBAR with an ID of 128:

```
#define      rMenuBar      128

Handle  theMenuBar;

theMenuBar = GetNewMBar( rMenuBar );
if ( theMenuBar == nil )
   ExitToShell();
```

It's unlikely that the Menu Manager will fail in its attempt to load your menu resources, but it's a good idea to ensure that the menu bar has been set up. Check the handle returned by `GetNewMBar()` to verify that it's not empty. A missing menu bar, while a rarity, is one of those severe errors that spells immediate doom to a program. The user will have no way of quitting, so you'll want to do that for him with a call to `ExitToShell()`.

With the menu list established, call the Toolbox function `SetMenuBar()` to install the individual menus within the menu bar.

```
SetMenuBar( theMenuBar );
DisposeHandle( theMenuBar );
```

After setting the menu bar, you no longer need the handle to it; dispose of it with a call to the Toolbox function `DisposeHandle()`.

This chapter later discusses several different menu item properties you can change, such as dimming an item to disable it. Any time you work with a menu item you'll need a handle—a MenuHandle—to the menu that item is in. Given the resource ID of a `MENU` (not an `MBAR`), the Toolbox function `GetMenuHandle()` returns a `MenuHandle` to that menu.

While you're setting up the menu bar you can get a `MenuHandle` to some or all of the individual menus. If you save each as a global variable, they'll be available any time your program needs to work with a menu or menu item. The following snippet returns a handle to the Apple menu. In this snippet `mAppleMenu` is the resource ID of the `MENU` that represents the Apple menu.

```
#define      mAppleMenu      128

MenuHandle  gAppleMenu;

gAppleMenu = GetMenuHandle( mAppleMenu );
```

If your program has an Apple menu, and it should, you'll need to make a call to the Toolbox function `AppendResMenu()`. The contents of the Apple menu vary from computer to computer, so this menu needs some special treatment.

In System 6, desk accessories were stored as resources of type `DRVR` in the system resource file. On pre-System 7 Macs, these resources get placed into the Apple menu. For System 7, desk accessories and anything else the user wants in the Apple menu are stored in the Apple Menu Items folder in the System Folder. The contents of this folder, collectively called *desktop objects*, will have to be added to the Apple menu.

NOTE

DRVR stands for *driver*. A driver is the middleman in charge of the transfer of data between a program and a device. A printer is an example of a device.

Whether your program is running on System 7 or an earlier system, a call to `AppendResMenu()` will fill the Apple menu.

```
AppendResMenu( gAppleMenu, 'DRVR' );
```

With the menus all loaded there's one last thing you must do—display the menu. A call to the `DrawMenuBar()` Toolbox routine accomplishes this:

```
DrawMenuBar();
```

The following application-defined routine groups the menu set up calls into one nice neat function—suitable for use in just about any of your programs. The `SetUpMenuBar()` routine makes three calls to `GetMenuHandle()`—one call for each of the three standard menus included in just about every program: the Apple, File, and Edit menus. If your program will include additional menus, and you want your program to be able to change characteristics of items in those menus, add a global `MenuHandle` variable and a call to `GetMenuHandle()` for each new menu.

```
void  SetUpMenuBar( void )
{
   Handle      theMenuBar;
   MenuHandle  theSubmenu;
```

```
   theMenuBar = GetNewMBar( rMenuBar );
   if ( theMenuBar == nil )
      ExitToShell();

   SetMenuBar( theMenuBar );
   DisposeHandle( theMenuBar );

   gAppleMenu = GetMHandle( mAppleMenu );
   gFileMenu  = GetMHandle( mFileMenu );
   gEditMenu  = GetMHandle( mEditMenu );

   AppendResMenu( gAppleMenu, 'DRVR' );

   DrawMenuBar();
}
```

Handling a Click in a Menu

A mouse click, whether in a menu bar or not, is an event. It will be cap-
tured as a mouseDown event in your program's EventLoop() function.
From there it will be passed on to a routine that handles strictly mouse
down events. Here's a refresher:

```
void   EventLoop( void )
{
   // get most recent event from event queue

   switch ( theEvent.what )
   {
      case mouseDown:
         HandleMouseDown( theEvent );
         break;

      // handle other event types
   }
}
```

In the past HandleMouseDown() has been used to deal with mouse clicks
in various parts of a window. HandleMouseDown() will still handle all
those tasks, but now it will additionally take care of a mouse click in the
menu bar. Here's the new HandleMouseDown():

```
void  HandleMouseDown( EventRecord theEvent )
{
    WindowPtr   theWindow;
    short       thePart;
    long        theMenuChoice;

    thePart = FindWindow( theEvent.where, &theWindow );

    switch ( thePart )
    {
        case inMenuBar:
            theMenuChoice = MenuSelect( theEvent.where );
            HandleMenuChoice( theMenuChoice );
            break;

        // other case sections to handle inDrag, inGoAway, etc.
    }
}
```

MenuSelect() is the Toolbox routine that monitors menu selections. This routine will save you a great deal of programming effort. In fact, it's a Toolbox routine so powerful that you'll want to kiss an Apple Toolbox developer for creating it for you! When the user clicks the mouse button in the menu bar, MenuSelect() takes control until the user releases the button. Here's a summary of what MenuSelect() does:

- It tracks the cursor as the mouse is dragged, dropping down menus as the cursor travels across the menu bar.
- It highlights menu items as the user moves the cursor up and down over a dropped menu.
- It flashes a menu item a few times when the user finally makes a selection.
- It determines the menu item number and the ID of the MENU resource for a menu selection the user makes. It returns this information to your program for processing.

Take a good look at a call to MenuSelect(). MenuSelect() returns both the ID of the MENU resource that holds the selected menu item and the item number itself. Yet MenuSelect() only returns one value—a variable of type long. How can this be so?

```
long  theMenuChoice;

theMenuChoice = MenuSelect( theEvent.where );
```

`MenuSelect()` can do this feat by treating the long variable as two separate variables. It stores both the `MENU` ID and the menu item number within the same variable. A simple means of extracting these two values is discussed ahead.

With the display of the menu complete, and the menu selection returned to your program, call an application-defined routine to take care of the menu selection. This snippet defines such a function:

```
void  HandleMenuChoice( long theMenuChoice )
{
    short   theMenu;
    short   theMenuItem;

    if ( theMenuChoice != 0 )
    {
        theMenu = HiWord( theMenuChoice );
        theMenuItem = LoWord( theMenuChoice );

        switch ( theMenu )
        {
            case mAppleMenu:
                HandleAppleChoice( theMenuItem );
                break;

            case mFileMenu:
                HandleFileChoice( theMenuItem );
                break;

            case mEditMenu:
                HandleEditChoice( theMenuItem );
                break;
        }

        HiliteMenu( 0 );
    }
}
```

If the user scans the menu bar and then backs out of his or her decision to make a menu selection, MenuSelect() will return a value of 0. HandleMenuChoice() checks to see if this is the case. If not, it's time to extract those two pieces of information tucked inside variable the MenuChoice.

MenuSelect() stores both the MENU ID and the menu item number in one long variable. It places the MENU ID in the upper 16 bits of the 32-bit long variable and the menu item number in the lower 16 bits. Since the Toolbox performs a little trick like this, it also conveniently provides a couple of routines for extracting the two pieces of information from the one variable: HiWord() and LoWord(). Figure 6.8 shows this.

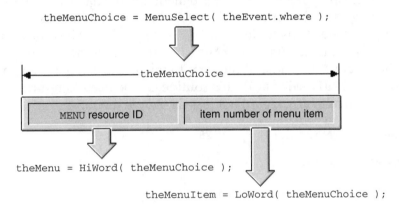

Figure 6.8 Extracting the menu and menu item from one variable.

Once you know which menu was clicked in, all you need do is branch to a routine written to handle mouse clicks in that particular menu. So that the application-defined routine knows what action to take, pass the item number of the selected menu item. The routine HandleMenuChoice() works for a program that has just the three standard menus: Apple, File, and Edit.

When a menu item is selected, MenuSelect() inverts the menu name in the menu bar. After the menu item selection is handled, your code must call HiliteMenu() to again invert the menu name back to its original state.

Handling a Click in the Apple Menu

How the selection of a particular menu item is handled depends on the item selected. Your program may have a menu item that does things no other program does. But some menu choices are standard fare and are always handled in much the same way. The items in the Apple menu fall into this category.

The first menu item in the Apple menu is usually the **About** item. Selecting this item puts up an alert that displays some information about the program's copyright. You learned how to display an alert in the previous chapter.

The remaining items in the Apple menu are the names of desk accessories, programs, documents, folders, and aliases that the user places in the Apple Menu Items folder of his or her Mac. Regardless of what the item is, a call to OpenDeskAcc() will get things going. Pass OpenDeskAcc() the name of the item to open. You can get the name by calling GetMenuItemText(). This routine can be used to return the text of a menu item in any menu, not just the Apple menu.

```
#define        rAboutAlert         128

MenuHandle  gAppleMenu;

void  HandleAppleChoice( short theItem )
{
    Str255   theItemName;
    short    theReference;

    switch ( theItem )
    {
        case iShowAboutApple :
            Alert( rAboutAlert, nil );
            break;

        default :
            GetMenuItemText( gAppleMenu, theItem, theItemName );
            theReference = OpenDeskAcc( theItemName );
            break;
    }
}
```

Handling a Click in Other Menus

The format of `HandleAppleChoice()` is the standard format for all your application-defined menu-handling routines will have. Pass the item number of the selected menu item to the routine, then use a switch statement to get to the code written for that particular item. This chapter's example program provides several examples.

This section finishes with Figure 6.9—a figure that recaps how a click of the mouse gets transformed into a menu selection. This figure shows the path that's traversed when a selection is made from a program's Edit menu.

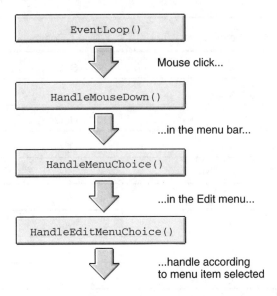

Figure 6.9 The path from mouse down to menu selection.

KEYBOARD EQUIVALENTS

To make things easy for users you'll want to provide them with *keyboard equivalents* to the most common menu selections. A keyboard equivalent, also referred to as a keyboard alias or Command-key equivalent, allows the user to bypass the menu bar and make a menu selection from the keyboard. Pressing the **Command** key in conjunction with one or more other keys does the same thing as using the menu.

Consistency between Macintosh applications is essential to the Apple philosophy of keeping the Mac user-friendly. To this end Apple has reserved some of the keyboard equivalents for common commands found in many Macintosh programs. You can use any of these reserved combinations in your own programs, but you should use them only for the commands shown in Table 6.1.

Table 6.1 Keyboard Equivalents Reserved by Apple

Keyboard Equivalent	Menu Command
⌘ – A	Select All
⌘ – C	Copy
⌘ – N	New
⌘ – O	Open...
⌘ – P	Print...
⌘ – Q	Quit
⌘ – S	Save
⌘ – V	Paste
⌘ – W	Close
⌘ – X	Cut
⌘ – Z	Undo

You can use ResEdit to add a keyboard equivalent to any menu item. That discussion is next.

The MENU **Resource**

To add a keyboard equivalent to a menu item, use ResEdit to edit the MENU resource in which the menu item appears. Click on the menu item name, then enter the character that will be used along with the **Command** key. Figure 6.10 shows the addition of a keyboard equivalent to the **Quit** command in the File menu.

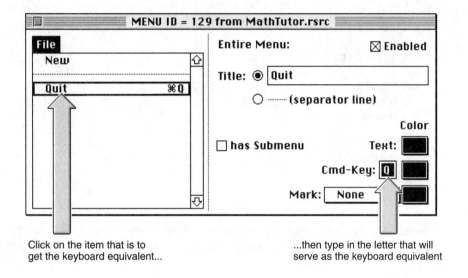

Click on the item that is to get the keyboard equivalent...

...then type in the letter that will serve as the keyboard equivalent

Figure 6.10 Adding a keyboard equivalent to a MENU.

N O T E

By convention, the character that is typed along with the **Command** key is displayed in uppercase in a program's menu even though the user won't be using the **Shift** key. Take the **Quit** menu item keyboard equivalent, **Command-Q**, for example. The user types the **Command** key and the letter 'q'. The user doesn't use the **Shift** key to type an uppercase 'Q'. When you type a character in the **Cmd-Key** editable text box in ResEdit, type it in uppercase, as shown in Figure 6.10.

Handling a Keystroke

If you want to include keyboard equivalents in your application, you have to make your program aware of keystrokes. That's something you haven't worried about up to this point. To do this, add a case section for a keyDown event in your EventLoop() routine.

```
void  EventLoop( void )
{
  // get next event here

  switch ( theEvent.what )
  {
     case keyDown:
        HandleKeyDown( theEvent );
        break;

     case mouseDown:
        HandleMouseDown( theEvent );
        break;
  }
}
```

Of course, that's only part of the work. Now you have to write the HandleKeyDown() routine. As shown below, this is a short and simple routine.

```
void  HandleKeyDown( EventRecord theEvent )
{
   short   theChar;
   long    theMenuChoice;

   theChar = theEvent.message & charCodeMask;

   if ( ( theEvent.modifiers & cmdKey ) != 0 )
   {
      if ( theEvent.what != autoKey )
      {
         theMenuChoice = MenuKey( theChar );
         HandleMenuChoice( theMenuChoice );
      }
   }
}
```

When an event involving the keyboard occurs, the `message` element of the event's `EventRecord` holds the key that was pressed. The `message` field consists of 32 bits that hold more information than just that, though. To access only the portion that contains the character the user typed you'll need to use the constant `charCodeMask` in conjunction with the bitwise & operator.

At this point you are only interested in a keystroke performed in conjunction with the **Command** key. The `modifiers` field of the event holds this information. As you did for the character, though, you have to use the & operator on the field to extract only the information you need. If the result is non-zero, the **Command** key was down.

One last check: was the key pressed and held down? That's called an auto key, and that's *not* a keyboard equivalent. If the keystroke survives the battery of tests, then you know that the user held down the **Command** key while pressing a character. That *is* a keyboard equivalent. At this point, call the Toolbox routine `MenuKey()`.

`MenuKey()` accepts a typed character and returns a long integer—just as `MenuSelect()` does for an item selected from the menu via the mouse. The `long` contains both the ID of the menu and the ID of the menu item that the **Command** key combination represents. With that information you can then call `HandleMenuChoice()` to handle things just as if a menu selection had been made.

HIERARCHICAL MENUS

To offer the user additional menu choices you can use a hierarchical menu, which is a menu that has a submenu associated with it. Figure 6.11 illustrates an example of a menu with a submenu attached to it.

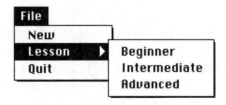

Figure 6.11 A hierarchical menu.

Adding a hierarchical menu requires a few minimal additions to both your resources and source code.

The MENU Resource

You designate a submenu for a menu item by checking the **has Submenu** checkbox in ResEdit. The submenu itself will be defined by a MENU resource—just as "normal" menu. List the resource ID of that MENU in the editable text box labeled **ID**. Figure 6.12 takes the File MENU resource developed earlier and changes the second item from a separator line to an item named **Lesson**. It also designates that this menu item be a hierarchical menu.

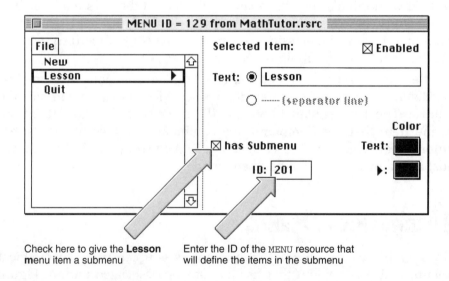

Check here to give the **Lesson** menu item a submenu

Enter the ID of the MENU resource that will define the items in the submenu

Figure 6.12 Adding a submenu to a menu item.

Next, create a new MENU resource. This one will contain the items that appear in the submenu. You create it and edit it as you would any other MENU. *Don't*, however, add its ID to the MBAR resource. Figure 6.13 shows an example of a submenu. When used in conjunction with one another, the MENU resources shown in Figure 6.12 and 6.13 will produce the hierarchical menu shown back in Figure 6.11.

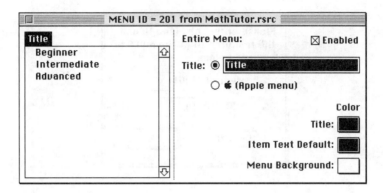

Figure 6.13 A MENU resource to be used as a submenu.

When you create the new MENU by selecting **Create New Resource** from ResEdit's Resource menu, ResEdit will most likely will not give the new MENU the same ID you specified in the original MENU—201 in Figure 6.12. Changing the MENU ID is a two step process. First, click once on the MENU resource in ResEdit's pictorial list of menus. Then select **Get Resource Info** from ResEdit's Resource menu and change the ID in the information window, as shown in Figure 6.14. Next, select **Edit Menu & MDEF ID** from the MENU menu and change the Menu ID there as well. Figure 6.15 shows this.

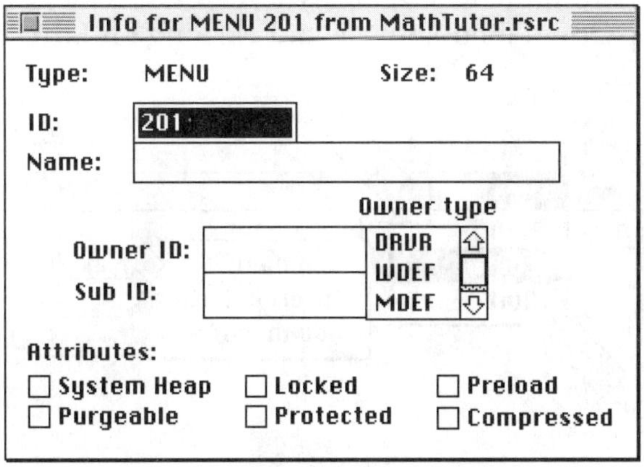

Figure 6.14 Changing a MENU ID in ResEdit's Get Resource Info window.

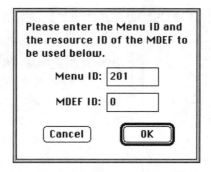

Figure 6.15 Changing a MENU ID in ResEdit's Edit Menu
& MDEF ID window.

Make sure to leave the MDEF ID set to **0**. Then click the **OK** button. That's it for resource changes. Now it's on to the source code.

Setting up the Hierarchical Menu

When you give a menu item a submenu you are, in effect, changing the item from a menu item to a menu. In Figure 6.16, the Edit menu is obviously a menu. Clicking on it displays the drop-down menu containing what appears to be three menu items: **New**, **Lesson**, and **Quit**. But the **Lesson** item is not quite as obviously a menu. Clicking on **Lesson** also displays a drop-down menu, just as did clicking on **Edit**.

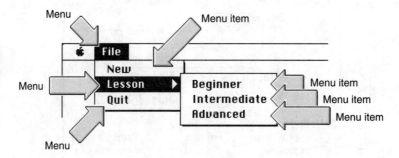

Figure 6.16 Menus and menu items.

You know that when you set up your program's menu bar with
GetNewMBar(), a menu list is created that contains a handle to each
menu in the menu bar. Your program can obtain a copy of one of these
handles by calling the Toolbox function GetMenuHandle():

```
#define      rMenuBar          128
#define      mFileMenu         129

MenuHandle  gFileMenu;

Handle  theMenuBar;

theMenuBar = GetNewMBar( rMenuBar );

gFileMenu = GetMenuHandle( mFileMenu );
```

GetNewMBar() reads in the descriptions of the menus that will appear in
the menu bar from the MENU resources listed in the MBAR resource. It also
notes the menu ID of any submenus. It does not, however, read in the
description of submenus. To read in that data, you use the Toolbox function GetMenu(). Pass this routine the ID of the MENU resource to load into
memory, and GetMenu() will do that and return a handle to the menu
data. After that, you need to insert the submenu into the menu list using
the Toolbox function InsertMenu(). Here's an example:

```
#define      mLessonSubMenu      201

MenuHandle  theSubmenu;

theSubmenu = GetMenu( mLessonSubMenu );
InsertMenu( theSubmenu, -1 );
```

The -1 parameter passed to InsertMenu() tells the Menu Manager that
this menu is a submenu.

The following snippet is a revision of the SetUpMenuBar() routine
introduced near the start of this chapter. This new version adds the code
for the insertion of a submenu into the File menu.

```
#define      rMenuBar          128
#define      mAppleMenu        128
```

```
#define     mFileMenu          129
#define     mEditMenu          130
#define     mLessonSubMenu     201

void  SetUpMenuBar( void )
{
   Handle       theMenuBar;
   MenuHandle   theSubmenu;
   Style        theItemStyle;

   theMenuBar = GetNewMBar( rMenuBar );
   if ( theMenuBar == nil )
      ExitToShell();

   SetMenuBar( theMenuBar );
   DisposeHandle( theMenuBar );

   gAppleMenu = GetMenuHandle( mAppleMenu );
   gFileMenu  = GetMenuHandle( mFileMenu );
   gEditMenu  = GetMenuHandle( mEditMenu );

   theSubmenu = GetMenu( mLessonSubMenu );
   InsertMenu( theSubmenu, -1 );

   AppendResMenu( gAppleMenu, 'DRVR' );

   DrawMenuBar();
}
```

You'll be pleased to find that once a hierarchical menu is displayed, you handle it in the same way you handle traditional menus. Begin by including the hierarchical menu's MENU resource ID in your HandleMenuChoice() routine, done as follows.

```
#define     mAppleMenu         128
#define     mFileMenu          129
#define     mEditMenu          130
#define     mLessonSubMenu     201

void  HandleMenuChoice( long  theMenuChoice )
{
   // extract menu and menu item from theMenuChoice

   switch ( theMenu )
```

```
    {
        case mAppleMenu:
            HandleAppleChoice( theMenuItem );
            break;

        case mFileMenu:
            HandleFileChoice( theMenuItem );
            break;

        case mLessonSubMenu:
            HandleLessonHierarchicalMenu( theMenuItem );
            break;

        case mEditMenu:
            HandleEditChoice( theMenuItem );
            break;
    }

    HiliteMenu( 0 );
}
```

The application-defined routine that handles a selection from your program's hierarchical menu should be centered around a switch statement, just as are the application-defined routines for handling selections
from other menus. As a simplistic example, consider the submenu shown
in Figure 6.16. If a selection of any of the three menu items (**Beginner**,
Intermediate, or **Advanced**) in the **Lessons** hierarchical menu item was
to result in the display of an alert that held some informative text, then
HandleLessonHierarchicalMenu( ) might look like this:

```
#define     iBeginnerSubMenuItem         1
#define     iIntermediateSubMenuItem     2
#define     iAdvancedSubMenuItem         3
#define     rBeginnerAlert               501
#define     rIntermediateAlert           502
#define     rAdvancedAlert               503

void  HandleLessonHierarchicalMenu( short theItem )
{
    switch ( theItem )
    {
        case iBeginnerSubMenuItem:
            Alert( rBeginnerAlert, nil );
```

```
        break;

    case iIntermediateSubMenuItem:
        Alert( rIntermediateAlert, nil );
        break;

    case iAdvancedSubMenuItem:
        Alert( rAdvancedAlert, nil );
        break;
    }
}
```

Changing Menu Characteristics

When working with various Macintosh programs, you've noticed that menu items might occasionally change during the running of a program. A menu item may have a check mark placed to the left of it, or the text of a menu item might change. The most common change in a menu item or an entire menu is being enabled or disabled—so that topic is discussed first.

Disabling and Enabling Menus and Menu Items

During the running of a program, not all menu options apply to all situations. When a menu item is not applicable, you should disable, or dim, the item to prevent the user from choosing it. The most common example of the disabling of a menu item might be the **Paste** command in the Edit menu. If the user hasn't cut or copied anything, the clipboard will be empty and there will be nothing to paste. That's when a program will disable the **Paste** menu item.

You can disable a single item within a menu or an entire menu. In either case, the user can still click on the menu name in the menu bar to drop down the menu. If the entire menu is disabled, then the name in the menu bar will dim, along with the name of every item in the menu. Figure 6.17 shows that case on the left side of the picture. Disabling a single item in the menu does just that; every other item in the menu, along with the menu name in the menu bar, appear normal. That's shown on the right side of Figure 6.17.

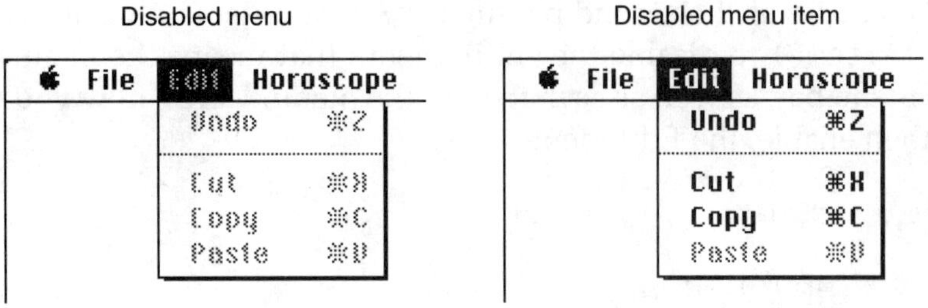

Disabled menu   Disabled menu item

Figure 6.17 A disabled menu and a disabled menu item.

To disable a single item use the `DisableItem()` Toolbox function, passing a handle to the menu in which the item appears and the number of the item. Using the Edit menu pictured in Figure 6.17, the following code disables the **Paste** item. It then goes on to use the Toolbox function `EnableItem()` to enable the same item. Remember, even though a dashed line in a menu can't be selected by the user, it still counts as a menu item.

```
#define    mEditMenu      130
#define    iUndo            1
//         —-              -
#define    iCut             3
#define    iCopy            4
#define    iPaste           5

MenuHandle  gEditMenu;

gEditMenu = GetMenuHandle( mEditMenu );

DisableItem( gEditMenu, iPaste );

// do other stuff here

EnableItem( gEditMenu, iPaste );
```

Both `DisableItem()` and `EnableItem()` accept the same parameters. The first is a MenuHandle to the menu that holds the affected item, while the second is the number of the item.

Disabling an entire menu is just as easy as disabling a single menu item. In fact, you use the same Toolbox routine. The difference is in the value you pass as the second parameter. A menu item value of zero tells `DisableItem()` to disable the entire menu; that means the menu name in the menu bar, as well as each item in the menu. Here's how you'd disable, then enable, the Edit menu.

```
#define       mEditMenu            130

MenuHandle   gEditMenu;

gEditMenu = GetMenuHandle( mEditMenu );

DisableItem( gEditMenu, 0 );

// do other stuff here

EnableItem( gEditMenu, 0 );
```

Various circumstances can lead to the disabling and enabling of menu items. Every program may be different. Rather than scattering menu setting calls all about your source code, try the commonly used technique of grouping all the calls within one function.

For an example of menu highlighting, take a look at a hypothetical program named Horoscope; its menu bar is pictured back in Figure 6.17, while the Horoscope menu itself is pictured in Figure 6.18. Assume that under certain conditions, either the **Enter Information** item or the **Show Forecast** item may be disabled. When a condition occurs that requires a change in the state of a menu item, a global_Boolean variable is appropriately set. When there is a call to the menu-setting routine these flags are checked and the state of each menu item is set accordingly.

```
#define       mHoroscope          131
#define       iEnterInfo            1
//            ─────               -
#define       iPrintSign            3
#define       iNoPrintSign          4
//            ─────               -
#define       iShowForecast         6

MenuHandle   gHoroscopeMenu
Boolean      gAllowInfoInput;
Boolean      gAllowShowForecast;
```

```
gHoroscopeMenu = GetMenuHandle( mHoroscope );

// as program runs, the two Boolean flags get set

void  EnableDisableMenuItems( void )
{
   if ( gAllowInfoInput == true )
      EnableItem( gHoroscopeMenu, iEnterInfo );
   else
      DisableItem( gHoroscopeMenu, iEnterInfo );

   if ( gAllowShowForecast == true )
      EnableItem( gHoroscopeMenu, iShowForecast );
   else
      DisableItem( gHoroscopeMenu, iShowForecast );
}
```

The only time a user sees a menu item is when he clicks the mouse in the menu bar. So that's the only time you need to worry about each menu item being in its proper state. If you've set all flag variables at the appropriate places in the program, and if you place the call to EnableDisableMenuItems() at a place in your code that corresponds to the handling of a mouse click in the menu bar, then that's the one and only time you have to make the call.

As you saw earlier in this chapter, the Toolbox routine MenuSelect() is your means to handling all menu selections. If you call your menu-setting routine right before MenuSelect(), you'll be assured of having all your menu items in the proper state.

```
void  HandleMouseDown( EventRecord theEvent )
{
   // declare variables, determine part of screen hit by click

   switch ( thePart )
   {
      case inMenuBar:
         EnableDisableMenuItems();
         theMenuChoice = MenuSelect( theEvent.where );
         HandleMenuChoice( theMenuChoice );
         break;
   }
}
```

Adding a Check Mark to a Menu Item

A menu item can have a check mark to the left of it to mark it as the current selection. Often a menu item that can be marked in this way is found in a group of two or more items. These items act as radio buttons in a dialog box—only one item in the grouping can be checked at any given time. Figure 6.18 shows a grouping of two menu items.

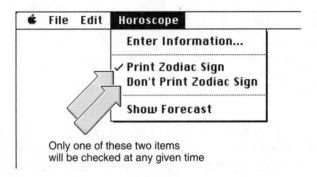

Figure 6.18 A menu item with a check mark.

Use the Toolbox routine CheckItem() to place a check mark by an item or to remove a mark by an item. Pass CheckItem() a handle to the affected menu, the number of the item to check or uncheck, and a value of true to check the item or false to uncheck it. Here's an example that places a check by the third item—the **Print Zodiac Sign** item—in the Horoscope menu.

```
#define      mHoroscope        131
#define      iEnterInfo          1
//           ———            -
#define      iPrintSign          3
#define      iNoPrintSign        4
//           ———            -
#define      iShowForecast       6

MenuHandle  gHoroscopeMenu;
Boolean     gAllowInfoInput;
Boolean     gAllowShowForecast;

gHoroscopeMenu = GetMenuHandle( mHoroscope );
```

```
CheckItem( gHoroscopeMenu, iPrintSign, true );
```

The preceding snippet shows the checking of an item. You'll also have to uncheck whichever item was checked previously. The example program in Figure 6.18 illustrates that process. A selection in any menu is handled by `HandleMenuChoice()`. From there a routine is called to handle the particular menu selected; in this case the program ends up at `HandleHoroscopeChoice()`. Here's that routine:

```
void  HandleHoroscopeChoice( short theItem )
{
    switch ( theItem )
    {
        case iEnterInfo:
            OpenInfoDialog();
            break;

        case iPrintSign:
        case iNoPrintSign:
            HandleMenuCheckedItem( theItem );
            break;

        case iShowForecast:
            OpenHoroscopeWindow();
            break;
    }
}
```

The two menu items involved in the checkmarking are both handled in the same way by `HandleMenuCheckedItem()`—as shown here:

```
Boolean  gPrintSignFlag;

void  HandleMenuCheckedItem( short theItem )
{
    if ( theItem == iPrintSign )
    {
        CheckItem( gHoroscopeMenu, iNoPrintSign, false );
        gPrintSignFlag = true;
    }
    else
    {
        CheckItem( gHoroscopeMenu, iPrintSign, false );
```

```
        gPrintSignFlag = false;
    }

    CheckItem( gHoroscopeMenu, theItem, true );
}
```

The one value passed to HandleMenuCheckedItem() is the number of the menu item selected; that is, the menu item to check. This number is first used in an if-else statement to *uncheck* the item that was on. Then the same number is used to *check* the selected item.

What if the user selects a menu item that is already checked? The preceding code shows that CheckItem() will be called to uncheck an *already* unchecked item. Using CheckItem() to uncheck an unchecked item has no effect. The same applies to using the routine to check an already checked item. That's why the technique used in HandleMenuCheckedItem() works. Figure 6.19 shows what happens if the **Print Zodiac Sign** item is already checked when it is again selected. Figure 6.20 shows the case of **Print Zodiac Sign** in an unchecked state when this menu item is selected.

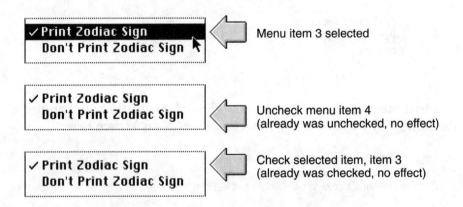

Figure 6.19 Selecting an already checked item has no ill effect.

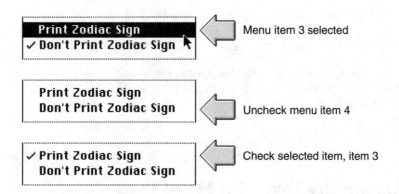

Figure 6.20 Selecting an unchecked item checks it.

Notice that in HandleMenuCheckedItem() the global Boolean variable gPrintSignFlag is set according to the selection made. This flag variable could then be used at some other point in the program, perhaps to determine whether to display the user's astrological sign on each page of his horoscope when **Show Forecast** is selected.

One last point: If you're including menu items that get checked, make sure to check one and set any pertinent flags when you first set up the menu:

```
#define       mHoroscope          131
#define       iEnterInfo            1
//            ─────             -
#define       iPrintSign            3
#define       iNoPrintSign          4
//            ─────             -
#define       iShowForecast         6

MenuHandle    gHoroscopeMenu;
Boolean       gPrintSignFlag;
```

```
void   SetUpMenuBar( void )
{
   // other menu code here

   gHoroscopeMenu = GetMenuHandle( mHoroscope );
   CheckItem( gHoroscopeMenu, iPrintSign, true );
   gPrintSignFlag = true;

   // other menu code here
}
```

Changing the Text of a Menu Item

You define the text that makes up each item in a menu in the MENU
resource of your program's resource file. If you want to change the text
of a menu item during the execution of your program, use the Toolbox
routine SetMenuItemText(). This function requires a handle to the
effected menu, the item number of the menu item to change, and a string
that represents the new text. Here's an example that changes the text of
a menu item from its resource definition of **Enter Information...** to
Supply Missing Info...:

```
#define       mHoroscope           131
#define       iEnterInfo             1

MenuHandle  gHoroscopeMenu;

gHoroscopeMenu = GetMenuHandle( mHoroscope );

SetMenuItemText( gHoroscopeMenu, iEnterInfo,
              "\pSupply Missing Info..." );
```

Figure 6.21 shows the results of executing the previous snippet. If you're
concerned about the length of the new text exceeding the width of the
drop down menu, don't be. The Menu Manager knows to set the size of
the menu according to the number of characters in the longest item string.

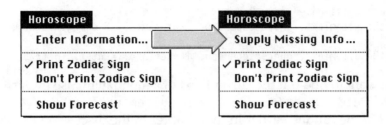

Figure 6.21 Changing the text of a menu item.

If you like the liberal use of #define directives you might want to pre-define the two titles the menu item might have:

```
#define      kEnterInfoStr        "\pEnter Information..."
#define      kMissingInfoStr      "\pSupply Missing Info..."

SetMenuItemText( gHoroscopeMenu, iEnterInfo, kMissingInfoStr );
```

N O T E If you *really* want to do things right, you'll follow Apple's recommendation of not including text strings in your source code; they make it difficult to convert your program to another language. Instead, make each of the two menu item titles STR# resources and store them in your project's resource file. What's that, you say you aren't familiar with the STR# resource? After reading Chapter 7, you will be.

Of course, you won't be changing menu item text randomly. In Figure 6.21, the decision to change the name of the menu item might be based on the amount of information the user entered in an Information dialog box. When the user closes the Information dialog box, the program can check for missing data and set the value of a global variable, gDataMissing, based on the results of this check:

```
// close Information dialog box

// check for missing user-supplied information and
// set gDataMissing accordingly
```

```
if ( gDataMissing == true )
    SetMenuItemText( gHoroscopeMenu, iEnterInfo, kMissingInfoStr );
else
    SetMenuItemText( gHoroscopeMenu, iEnterInfo, kEnterInfoStr );
```

If you want to find out the current text of a menu item, use the sister routine of SetMenuItemText(): GetMenuItemText(). You were introduced to the routine earlier in this chapter in the discussion on opening items from the Apple menu.

Changing the Style of a Menu Item

Now that you know you can change the text of a menu item, you may have guessed that you can also change the style of an item. The SetItemStyle() function is your means of doing this.

The Macintosh has a Style data type that is used to change the look of text. A variable of type Style can take on any the following Apple-defined constant values: plain, bold, italic, underline, outline, shadow, condense, and extend. You can set a variable of type Style to any one of these values or, to apply more than one style, you can add values. The following code sets a Style variable to bold and italic.

```
Style   theItemStyle;

theItemStyle = bold + italic;
```

With the style set, make a call to SetItemStyle(). Pass SetItemStyle() a MenuHandle and the item number corresponding to the menu item to change. A good time to do this is when you're setting up the menu bar. Here's an example that will outline the fourth of four menu items. Figure 6.22 shows the result.

```
#define     mHoroscope         131
#define     iEnterInfo           1
//          ————           -
#define     iPrintSign           3
#define     iNoPrintSign         4
//          ————           -
#define     iShowForecast        6
```

```
MenuHandle  gHoroscopeMenu;

Style  theItemStyle;

gHoroscopeMenu = GetMenuHandle( mHoroscope );

theItemStyle = outline;
SetItemStyle( gHoroscopeMenu, iShowForecast, theItemStyle );
```

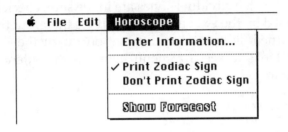

Figure 6.22 A menu item with the outline style applied to it.

Perhaps you'll want your program to allow the user to change a menu item's style. If so, you might not know just how a menu item is being displayed at any given time. In this case you can use the Toolbox routine GetItemStyle(). The parameters to this function are the same as those for SetItemStyle(), except that the last one is a pointer to a Style variable rather than a Style variable. This allows the Toolbox to change its value, and it does. It will return a number that represents the menu item's current style, or combination of styles. Here's a call to GetItemStyle():

```
Style  theCurrentItemStyle;

GetItemStyle( gHoroscopeMenu, iShowForecast, &theCurrentItemStyle );
```

Each style has a value, shown as follows. A menu item's current style is the sum of all the styles that have been applied to that item. As an example, if GetItemStyle() sets theCurrentItemStyle to a value of 35, you know that the menu item is displayed in a combination of condensed, italic, and bold styles (32 + 2 + 1).

```
plain        0
bold         1
italic       2
underline    4
outline      8
shadow      16
condense    32
extend      64
```

To determine which individual styles are in the sum, check for the largest value, as defined by the extend constant. If it's there, subtract that value from the returned style total and move on down the line. Here's an example that looks to see if a menu item has the extend or condense styles applied to it.

```
Boolean  isStyleExtend   = false;
Boolean  isStyleCondense = false;
Style    theCurrentItemStyle;

GetItemStyle( gHoroscopeMenu, iShowForecast, &theCurrentItemStyle );

if ( theCurrentItemStyle >= extend )
{
    isStyleExtend = true;
    theCurrentItemStyle -= extend;
}
if ( theCurrentItemStyle >= condense )
{
    isStyleCondense = true;
    theCurrentItemStyle -= condense;
}
// add same tests for other styles
```

EDITING TEXT IN A MODAL DIALOG BOX

Before System 7 a modal dialog box owned the screen entirely. If the dialog box appeared due to a menu selection, the menu name would invert in the menu bar, and all the menu names would dim. The user could not use the Edit menu to edit text in an edit text item. This situation is shown in the left of Figure 6.23.

System 7 adds a handy feature to the use of modal dialog boxes. If your application displays a modal dialog box with one or more editable text items, the system is now more generous. It will check to see if your program has a menu with the keyboard equivalents Command-X, Command-C, and Command-V. If your program does, the system will allow the user access to the Edit menu by enabling that menu, along with the **Cut**, **Copy**, and **Paste** items found in that menu. It will also take care of the editing, whether the user makes use of the menu or keyboard equivalents. The System 7 screen for this situation is shown on the right side of Figure 6.23

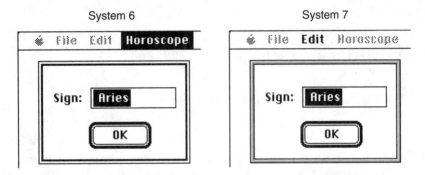

Figure 6.23 The menu while a modal dialog box is on the screen.

If you are absolutely sure that the program you're writing will never run on a preSystem 7 machine, you're all set. The system will take care of **Cut**, **Copy**, and **Paste** in a dialog box. If your program might run on a Mac equipped with pre-System 7 software, but you aren't concerned with allowing the user access to cut and paste features in a dialog box, you're again all set.

Before System 7, many programmers wrote their own code that allowed text editing in a modal dialog box. To do this, they placed the code in a filter function and then instructed the Toolbox function ModalDialog() to call that function. Now that the Mac takes care of text editing in a modal dialog box, that use of a filter function is obsolete. As you'll see on the upcoming pages, there are plenty of other reasons you might want to familiarize yourself with the filter function, though.

Modal Dialog Box Filter Function

In the previous chapter you saw that the Toolbox routine `ModalDialog()` takes care of most of the work of handling a modal dialog box. Here's a refresher:

```
// open modal dialog

while ( dialogDone == false )
{
   ModalDialog( nil, &theItem );

   switch ( theItem )
   {
      case kDialogOKButton:
         dialogDone = true;
         break;

      // handle clicks on other dialog items
   }
}
```

What Chapter 5 didn't tell you is that you can handle an event that occurs in a modal dialog box however you see fit—before `ModalDialog()` gets a crack at things. After you do process the event, you can then tell `ModalDialog()` to further handle things if you want.

The first parameter passed to `ModalDialog()` is the name of a *filter function* that does any special handling of the current event. This routine is optional. If you don't want to write one, pass in a `nil` pointer, as you've done up to now. The time to use a filter function is when you have a dialog box with special needs that `ModalDialog()` can't handle.

`ModalDialog()` handles update and activate events. It also intercepts mouse-down events and determines if an event occurred in an enabled item in the dialog box. If it did, it lets your program know which item was involved.

`ModalDialog()` will also track the user's actions in edit text boxes. It will flash the insertion bar in an edit text box, display typed characters, and invert selected text. It will also take care of any editing performed using keyboard equivalents for commands such as **Cut**, **Copy**, and **Paste**.

One thing that `ModalDialog()` won't do is handle keystrokes that aren't related to an editable text item. For instance, if you want to allow the user to type **Command-H** in order to display some help information in the dialog box, `ModalDialog()` won't be of assistance—the keystrokes will be ignored. So the recognizing and handling of keystrokes that don't pertain to editable text items is a perfect application for a filter function.

To create a filter function, you write a function that performs the chores your dialog box needs. The filter function always has three arguments: a pointer to the dialog box itself, a pointer to an `EventRecord`, and a pointer to a variable of type `short`. The return type of the function is always `Boolean`. The filter function needs to be prefaced with the `pascal` keyword. Here's a partial definition of a filter function called `DialogHelpFilter()`:

```
pascal  Boolean DialogHelpFilter( DialogPtr     theDialog,
                                  EventRecord *theEvent,
                                  short       *theItem )
{
   // check keystrokes, handle certain ones
}
```

Here's what a call to `ModalDialog()` would look like using a filter function:

```
ModalDialog( DialogHelpFilter, &theItem );
```

NOTE

Do you find it a little distressing that you can just use the name of a function as a parameter, without any parentheses or parameters? It's possible because `ModalDialog()` is expecting a pointer to a function as the first argument, not a call to a function. `ModalDialog()` uses the filter function name as a pointer to the function. It takes this pointer and uses it to go off into memory in search of your filter function.

When your program reaches a call to `ModalDialog()`, it branches off to the filter function. If the user performed some action that the filter function needs to handle, it does. It then returns a value of true to `ModalDialog()`. The question is, "Did the filter function handle the event?," and the answer is yes—or true. If the filter function handled the event, `ModalDialog()` doesn't have to. If it turns out that the user action did *not* require handling by the filter function, the function will return `false`. `ModalDialog()` knows it must then handle things itself. Figure 6.24 sums this all up.

If you're generating PowerPC code, your filter function can be written exactly as it is for a program that will run only on a 68K machine. The code that *calls* the filter function, however, will need a couple of minor, but important, changes. Those changes are described in the Chapter 8, "PowerPC Programming". It want to test the filter function code, create a 68K project for now. The Book's CD holds only a 68K version of the project for this chapter's example program, MenuMaster. Chapter 8 presents the PowerPC version of the project for this same program.

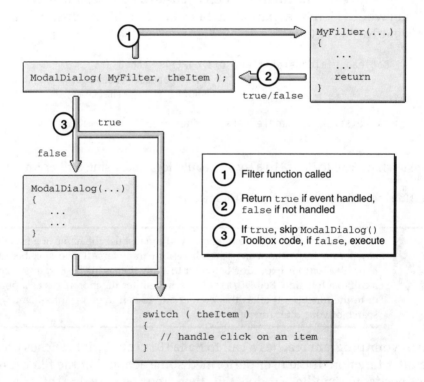

Figure 6.24 Course of action when `ModalDialog()` uses a filter function.

Enough theory—now it's time for a look at a real filter function. The `DialogHelpFilter()` shown below allows the user to type **Command-H** in order to display an alert that holds some help information.

```
#define       rHelpAlert              300
#define       kReturnKey      (char)0x0D
#define       kEnterKey       (char)0x03

pascal  Boolean DialogHelpFilter( DialogPtr     theDialog,
                                  EventRecord *theEvent,
                                  short        *theItem )
{
   char   theChar;

   if ( theEvent->what != keyDown )
      return ( false );

   theChar = theEvent->message & charCodeMask;

   if ( ( theEvent->modifiers & cmdKey ) != 0 )
   {
      switch ( theChar )
      {
         case 'h':
            Alert( rHelpAlert, nil );
            break;
      }

      return ( true );
   }

   if ( ( theChar == kReturnKey ) || ( theChar == kEnterKey ) )
   {
      *theItem = 1;
      return ( true );
   }

   return ( false );
}
```

ModalDialog() passes the filter function each and every event it sees. The filter is only interested in events that involve the **Command** key. If the event didn't involve a keystroke, the filter function will let ModalDialog() handle it. So the very first thing the filter does is check the what field of the event's EventRecord to see if the event is a keystroke. If it isn't, the filter is through. It bails out and passes back a value of false; the event was not processed.

If the event survives the first test, it's an event involving a keystroke. The next step is to determine which key was pressed. This is done in the same way as this chapter's `HandleKeyDown()` routine did it. That routine was covered in the discussion on keyboard equivalents:

```
theChar = theEvent->message & charCodeMask;
```

In `HandleKeyDown()` the above line looked like this:

```
theChar = theEvent.message & charCodeMask;
```

Remember your C? A structure member is accessed using the structure member operator, commonly called the dot:

```
EventRecord   theEvent;
```

```
theEvent.message
```

If you're working with a *pointer* to a structure, rather than the structure itself (as is the case in `DialogHelpFilter()`) you must use the structure pointer operator: a hyphen followed by the greater than symbol:

```
EventRecord   *theEvent;
```

```
theEvent->message
```

Now, you want to see if the **Command** key was pressed. This too was done back in `HandleKeyDown()`. It involves looking at the modifiers member of the current event's `EventRecord`:

```
if ( ( theEvent->modifiers & cmdKey ) != 0 )
```

If the **Command** key was pressed, the filter might actually be doing some real work! If the character key pressed along with the **Command** key is an 'h', the user wants to see the help alert displayed. The filter uses the Toolbox routine `Alert()` to take care of that. The event is handled, so the filter returns `true`.

The last test the filter makes is to see if the key that was pressed was either the **Return** key or the **Enter** key. The snippet defines two character constants that represent the two keys. The ASCII table you keep handy will tell you that the Return key has a value of 0x0D, or 13, while the Enter key has a value of 0x03, or 3. If the typed key was either of these characters, the filter treats the event as if was a mouse-click on item 1, the Done or OK button. It does this by setting the passed item variable to 1. That's why a pointer was passed in—so the filter could change its value.

WARNING

Wait! Doesn't `ModalDialog()` normally assume that a press of the **Return** or **Enter** key is the same as a click on the **OK** button? The answer is "yes...sometimes." If a dialog box doesn't have any editable text items, then pressing either of these two keys will result in the dismissal of the modal dialog box. If, on the other hand, a dialog box has an editable text item, then keystrokes are all directed at that editable text box. This includes the press of the **Return** key. The `DialogHelpFilter()` makes sure that typing either of these two keys will have the same effect as clicking on the **OK** button of the dialog box.

If none of the preceding cases applied to the event, the event wasn't handled, so the filter returns a value of `false` to let `ModalDialog()` handle things.

If that breakdown of the filter function seemed a bit wordy, then you know it's time for a figure. Figure 6.25 sums it all up.

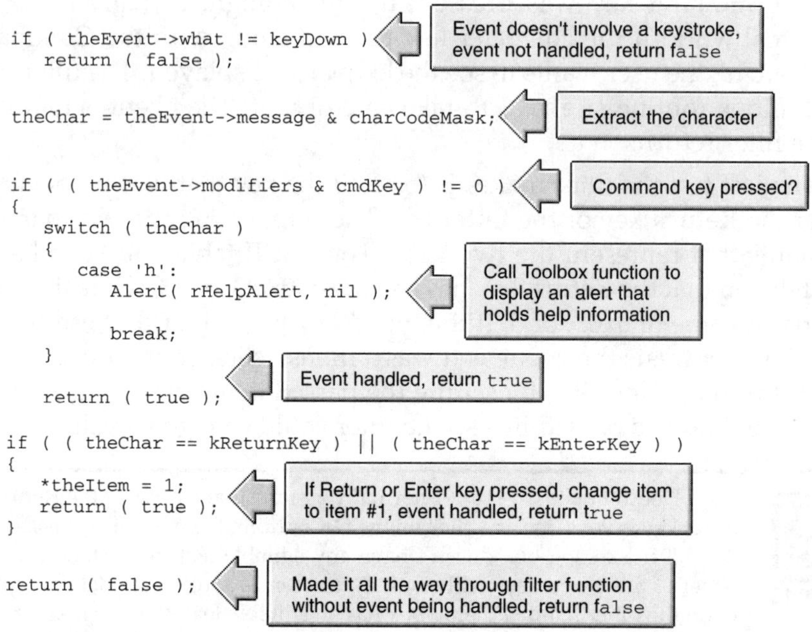

```
if ( theEvent->what != keyDown )
    return ( false );
```
Event doesn't involve a keystroke, event not handled, return `false`

```
theChar = theEvent->message & charCodeMask;
```
Extract the character

```
if ( ( theEvent->modifiers & cmdKey ) != 0 )
{
    switch ( theChar )
    {
        case 'h':
            Alert( rHelpAlert, nil );

        break;
    }
    return ( true );
```
Command key pressed?

Call Toolbox function to display an alert that holds help information

Event handled, return `true`

```
if ( ( theChar == kReturnKey ) || ( theChar == kEnterKey ) )
{
    *theItem = 1;
    return ( true );
}
```
If Return or Enter key pressed, change item to item #1, event handled, return `true`

```
return ( false );
```
Made it all the way through filter function without event being handled, return `false`

Figure 6.25 A closer look at a dialog box filter function.

Chapter Program: MenuMaster

The example program for this chapter is MenuMaster. When you run the program, you'll see a menu bar with three menus in it. Of most interest will be the File menu, shown in Figure 6.26.

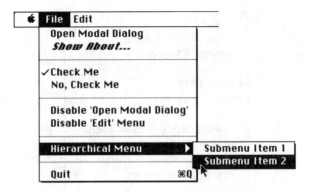

Figure 6.26 MenuMaster's file menu.

A good deal of this chapter was devoted to demonstrating various techniques for changing the look of menu items. MenuMaster shows how these techniques work. It does all of the following:

- Includes the Apple menu in the menu bar.
- Enables and disables a menu item.
- Enables and disables an entire menu.
- Places a check mark by menu items.
- Changes the text of menu items.
- Changes the style of the text of a menu item.
- Displays a hierarchical menu.
- Uses a keyboard equivalent for a menu item.

Figure 6.27 shows the File menu of MenuMaster after a few of the menu items have been changed.

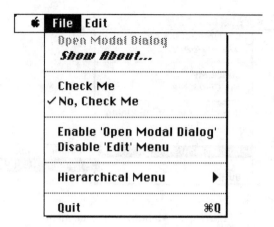

Figure 6.27 MenuMaster's File menu, with a few items changed.

Selecting the **About MenuMaster** item from the Apple menu displays an alert that tells a little (a very little) about the program. That alert is shown in Figure 6.28.

Figure 6.28 The About MenuMaster alert.

Selecting **Open Modal Dialog** from the File menu opens the modal dialog box shown in Figure 6.29. This dialog box demonstrates that the text in an editable text box can be edited without any help from your code. It also provides an example of how a filter function works. By pressing **Command-D**, the user causes the picture to disappear and in its place appears a promo for the software company that developed this sophisticated program! Figure 6.30 shows the results of pressing **Command-D**.

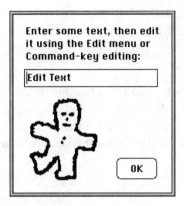

Figure 6.29 MenuMaster's modal dialog, boxes with editing capabilities.

Figure 6.30 The modal dialog box after pressing **Command-D**.

N O T E

The 'D' in **Command-D** stands for "Dancing," of course. If a "feature" such as this isn't documented in the program's user's manual, then it's referred to as an *easter egg*. Generally, an easter egg is implemented through a key combination or a click of the mouse button while the cursor is over a particular part of a dialog box. Here's an example of an easter egg, as supplied by Apple. If you have System 7.5 on your Mac, select **Stickies** from the Apple menu. In the new, *empty* note that opens, type **Antler!** and press the **Return** key to see a picture added to the note.

The **Show About** item in the File menu displays the very same alert that the **About MenuMaster** item in the Apple menu displays.

When you choose the **Check Me** or **No, Check Me!**, that item will receive a check mark by it.

The **Disable 'Open Modal Dialog'** menu item does just that. Selecting it disables the first item in the File menu. With the first menu item now disabled, it would now be more appropriate if the text of the **Disable 'Open Modal Dialog'** read **Enable 'Open Modal Dialog'**—and it does.

The **Disable 'Edit' Menu** item works in the same manner as the previous item. It, however, disables an entire menu rather than just a single menu item.

The menu item titled **Hierarchical Menu** is exactly that. It has two items in its submenu: **Submenu Item 1** and **Submenu Item 2**. Each opens an alert that displays which choice was made. The alert for the first submenu item is shown in Figure 6.31.

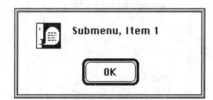

Figure 6.31 A hierarchical submenu selection displays an alert.

The last menu item in the File menu is **Quit**. You can use the keyboard equivalent **Command-Q** to quit the program.

Program Resources: MenuMaster.rsrc

MenuMaster demonstrates menus in a Macintosh program and gives you a quick review of some of the topics found in the previous chapter. The program uses two alerts and one dialog box. Figure 6.32 shows the six resource types used by the application.

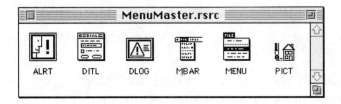

Figure 6.32 The resource file for the MenuMaster project.

The two ALRT resources have IDs of 128 and 129. So do their corresponding DITL resources. The DITL resources are shown in Figure 6.33.

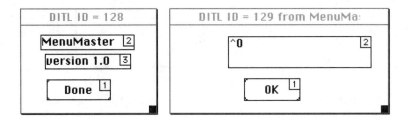

Figure 6.33 The DITL resources used by MenuMaster's two ALRT resources.

Of particular note is the strange **^0** text in item 2 in DITL 129, as shown in Figure 6.33. The alert that uses this DITL is displayed by MenuMaster when either of the two items in its hierarchical submenu is selected. But rather than displaying **^0**, the text in item 2 will be either **Submenu, Item 1** or **Submenu, Item 2**. How do you use one alert to display different strings on different occasions? The answer is simple and clever, and involves just one Toolbox call: ParamText().

You pass ParamText() four strings. Your program will retain these four strings, and may use them in any alert or dialog box that has one or more static items. How does it know which string to use in which item? The text of the static text item, defined when you create the DITL, must be one or more of the following: **^0, ^1, ^2, ^3**. Your program will substitute the four ParamText() strings for each of these **^x** strings. Here's an example:

```
#define        kDayAlert        128

ParamText("\pMonday ", "\pTuesday", "\pWednesday ", "\pThursday");
Alert( kDayAlert, nil );
```

Figure 6.34 shows a DITL resource that displays all four of the ParamText() strings. Figure 6.35 shows the alert that results from executing the preceding code. In Figure 6.35, you can see that the strings will be word-wrapped to the confines of the static text item.

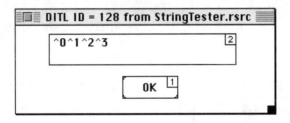

Figure 6.34 A DITL with a static text item to display four strings.

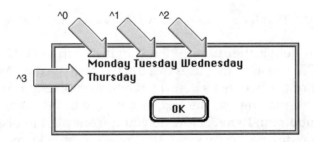

Figure 6.35 An alert that displays ParamText() strings.

Now, what would happen if your program called ParamText() again, this time substituting different strings? The same call to Alert() would result in the display of different text. Here's the code:

```
#define        kDayAlert        128

ParamText("\pMonday ", "\pTuesday", "\pWednesday ", "\pThursday");
Alert( kDayAlert, nil );
ParamText("\pFriday ", "\pSaturday ", "\pSunday ", "\p");
Alert( kDayAlert, nil );
```

When the previous snippet executes, the alert pictured in Figure 6.35 would be displayed. After clicking the **OK** button, the alert shown in Figure 6.36 would then appear. Remember, both these alerts are using the same DITL—the one pictured back in Figure 6.34.

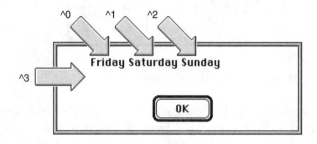

Figure 6.36 The same alert pictured in Figure 6.35, now displaying different ParamText() strings.

Notice in Figure 6.36 that only three strings seem to be displayed. The call to ParamText() defined the fourth string, the one to be displayed in the ^3 spot, as a null string—"\p".

If you look back a few pages you'll see that this whole discussion started with Figure 6.33. In that figure you saw DITL 129, which contained a static text item with the text ^0 in it. This DITL will be used in an alert that will substitute a single string in place of the ^0 text in the static text item.

The third and final DITL resource is used for the dialog box displayed when the user selects **Open Modal Dialog** from the File menu. It's pictured in Figure 6.37.

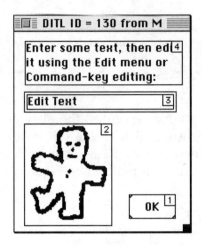

Figure 6.37 The DITL for MenuMaster's modal dialog.

Now, to the menu-related resources. MenuMaster's MBAR resource is pictured in Figure 6.38. You can tell from the figure that the program will display a menu bar that holds three menus. Figure 6.39 shows the three MENU resources used in the menu bar, and the one MENU that will serve as the hierarchical menu.

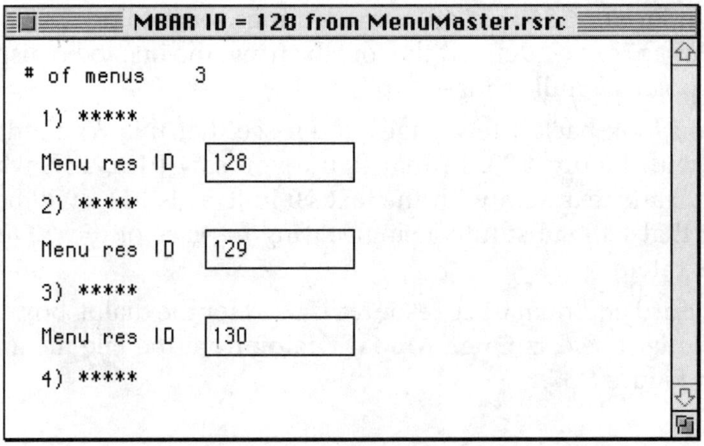

```
=|=======  MBAR ID = 128 from MenuMaster.rsrc  =======

# of menus    3

 1) *****

 Menu res ID   | 128              |

 2) *****

 Menu res ID   | 129              |

 3) *****

 Menu res ID   | 130              |

 4) *****
```

Figure 6.38 The MBAR for MenuMaster.

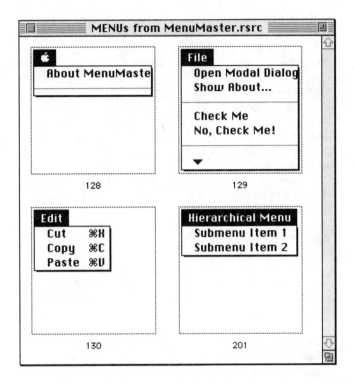

Figure 6.39 The three MENU resources for MenuMaster.

The final resource used by MenuMaster is a PICT with an ID of 128. As shown in Figure 6.37, this PICT is used by item 2 in the DITL that is associated with the program's modal dialog box.

Program listing: MenuMaster.c

The following is the complete source code listing for the MenuMaster program. As always, a walk through of the code appears after the listing.

```
//_____

#define    rAboutAlert            128
#define    rInformationAlert      129
#define    rModalDialog           130
```

```
#define        kDialogOKButton            1
#define        kManPictureItem            2

#define        rMenuBar                 128

#define        mAppleMenu               128
#define        iShowAboutApple            1

#define        mFileMenu                129
#define        iOpenDialog                1
#define        iShowAboutFile             2
//             ───────      -  item  3 is a dashed line
#define        iCheckMe                   4
#define        iNoCheckMe                 5
//             ───────      -  item  6 is a dashed line
#define        iDisableOpenDialog         7
#define        iDisableEditMenu           8
//             ───────      -  item  9 is a dashed line
//             ───────      -  item 10 is hierarchical menu
//             ───────      -  item 11 is a dashed line
#define        iQuit                     12

#define        mSubMenu                 201
#define        iSubmenuItem1              1
#define        iSubmenuItem2              2

#define        mEditMenu                130
#define        iCut                       1
#define        iCopy                      2
#define        iPaste                     3

#define        kEntireMenu                0
#define        kReturnKey         (char)0x0D
#define        kEnterKey          (char)0x03


//_____

Boolean     gAllDone = false;
MenuHandle  gAppleMenu;
MenuHandle  gFileMenu;
MenuHandle  gEditMenu;
Boolean     gCheckMeItemChecked = false;
Boolean     gOpenDialogItemDisabled = false;
Boolean     gEditMenuDisabled = false;
```

```
//_____

void   main( void )
{
   MaxApplZone();
   MoreMasters();
   MoreMasters();
   MoreMasters();

   InitializeToolbox();

   SetUpMenuBar();

   EventLoop();
}


//_____

void   SetUpMenuBar( void )
{
   Handle       theMenuBar;
   MenuHandle   theSubmenu;
   Style        theItemStyle;

   theMenuBar = GetNewMBar( rMenuBar );
   if ( theMenuBar == nil )
      ExitToShell();

   SetMenuBar( theMenuBar );
   DisposeHandle( theMenuBar );

   gAppleMenu = GetMenuHandle( mAppleMenu );
   gFileMenu  = GetMenuHandle( mFileMenu );
   gEditMenu  = GetMenuHandle( mEditMenu );

   theSubmenu = GetMenu( mSubMenu );
   InsertMenu( theSubmenu, -1 );

   theItemStyle = bold + italic;
   SetItemStyle( gFileMenu, iShowAboutFile, theItemStyle );

   CheckItem( gFileMenu, iNoCheckMe, true );

   AppendResMenu( gAppleMenu, 'DRVR' );
```

```
      DrawMenuBar();
}


//_____

void  EventLoop( void )
{
   EventRecord  theEvent;

   while ( gAllDone == false )
   {
      WaitNextEvent( everyEvent, &theEvent, 15L, nil );

      switch ( theEvent.what )
      {
         case keyDown:
            HandleKeyDown( theEvent );
            break;

         case mouseDown:
            HandleMouseDown( theEvent );
            break;
      }
   }
}


//_____

void  HandleKeyDown( EventRecord theEvent )
{
   short  theChar;
   long   theMenuChoice;

   theChar = theEvent.message & charCodeMask;

   if ( ( theEvent.modifiers & cmdKey ) != 0 )
   {
      if ( theEvent.what != autoKey )
      {
         theMenuChoice = MenuKey( theChar );
         HandleMenuChoice( theMenuChoice );
      }
   }
```

```
   }


//_____

void  HandleMouseDown( EventRecord theEvent )
{
   WindowPtr    theWindow;
   short        thePart;
   long         theMenuChoice;

   thePart = FindWindow( theEvent.where, &theWindow );

   switch ( thePart )
   {
      case inMenuBar:
         theMenuChoice = MenuSelect( theEvent.where );
         HandleMenuChoice( theMenuChoice );
         break;
   }
}


//_____

void  HandleMenuChoice( long  theMenuChoice )
{
   short  theMenu;
   short  theMenuItem;

   if ( theMenuChoice != 0 )
   {
      theMenu = HiWord( theMenuChoice );
      theMenuItem = LoWord( theMenuChoice );

      switch ( theMenu )
      {
         case mAppleMenu:
            HandleAppleChoice( theMenuItem );
            break;

         case mFileMenu:
            HandleFileChoice( theMenuItem );
            break;
```

```
        case mSubMenu:
            HandleHierarchicalMenu( theMenuItem );
            break;

        case mEditMenu:
            break;
    }

    HiliteMenu( 0 );
    }
}


//_____

void  HandleAppleChoice( short theItem )
{
    Str255  theItemName;
    short   theReference;

    switch ( theItem )
    {
        case iShowAboutApple :
            Alert( rAboutAlert, nil );
            break;

        default :
            GetMenuItemText( gAppleMenu, theItem, theItemName );
            theReference = OpenDeskAcc( theItemName );
            break;
    }
}


//_____

void  HandleFileChoice( short theItem )
{
    switch ( theItem )
    {
        case iOpenDialog:
            OpenModalDialog();
            break;

        case iShowAboutFile:
```

```
            Alert( rAboutAlert, nil );
            break;

        case iCheckMe:
        case iNoCheckMe:
            HandleMenuCheckedItem( theItem );
            break;

        case iDisableOpenDialog:
            HandleDisableOpenDialogItem();
            break;

        case iDisableEditMenu:
            HandleDisableEditItem();
            break;

        case iQuit:
            gAllDone = true;
            break;
    }
}


//_____

void  OpenModalDialog( void )
{
    DialogPtr  theDialog;
    short      theItem;
    Boolean    dialogDone = false;

    theDialog = GetNewDialog( rModalDialog, nil, (WindowPtr)-1L );
    ShowWindow( theDialog );

    while ( dialogDone == false )
    {
        ModalDialog( DialogPromoFilter, &theItem );

        switch ( theItem )
        {
            case kDialogOKButton:
                dialogDone = true;
                break;
        }
    }
```

```
        DisposeDialog( theDialog );
}


//_____

pascal  Boolean DialogPromoFilter( DialogPtr    theDialog,
                                   EventRecord *theEvent,
                                   short       *theItem )
{
    char    theChar;
    short   theType;
    Handle  theHandle;
    Rect    theRect;

    if ( theEvent->what != keyDown )
        return ( false );

    theChar = theEvent->message & charCodeMask;

    if ( ( theEvent->modifiers & cmdKey ) != 0 )
    {
        switch ( theChar )
        {
            case 'd':
                SetPort( theDialog );
                GetDialogItem( theDialog, kManPictureItem, &theType,
                               &theHandle, &theRect );
                EraseRect( &theRect );
                MoveTo( theRect.left + 5, theRect.top + 45 );
                DrawString( "\p Buy Dancing" );;
                MoveTo( theRect.left + 5, theRect.top + 60 );
                DrawString( "\pMan Software!" );
                break;
        }

        return ( true );
    }

    if ( ( theChar == kReturnKey ) || ( theChar == kEnterKey ) )
    {
        *theItem = 1;
        return ( true );
    }
```

```
    return ( false );
}


//_____

void   HandleMenuCheckedItem( short theItem )
{
    if ( theItem == iCheckMe )
    {
        CheckItem( gFileMenu, iNoCheckMe, false );
        gCheckMeItemChecked = true;
    }
    else
    {
        CheckItem( gFileMenu, iCheckMe, false );
        gCheckMeItemChecked = false;
    }

    CheckItem( gFileMenu, theItem, true );
}


//_____

void   HandleDisableOpenDialogItem( void )
{
    if ( gOpenDialogItemDisabled == true )
    {
        EnableItem( gFileMenu, iOpenDialog );
        SetMenuItemText( gFileMenu, iDisableOpenDialog,
                        "\pDisable 'Open Modal Dialog'" );
        gOpenDialogItemDisabled = false;
    }
    else
    {
        DisableItem( gFileMenu, iOpenDialog );
        SetMenuItemText( gFileMenu, iDisableOpenDialog,
                        "\pEnable 'Open Modal Dialog'" );
        gOpenDialogItemDisabled = true;
    }
}


//_____
```

```c
void  HandleDisableEditItem( void )
{
   if ( gEditMenuDisabled == true )
   {
      EnableItem( gEditMenu, kEntireMenu );
      DrawMenuBar();
      SetMenuItemText( gFileMenu, iDisableEditMenu,
                       "\pDisable 'Edit' Menu" );
      gEditMenuDisabled = false;
   }
   else
   {
      DisableItem( gEditMenu, kEntireMenu );
      DrawMenuBar();
      SetMenuItemText( gFileMenu, iDisableEditMenu,
                       "\pEnable 'Edit' Menu" );
      gEditMenuDisabled = true;
   }
}


//_____


void  HandleHierarchicalMenu( short theItem )
{
   switch ( theItem )
   {
      case iSubmenuItem1:
         ParamText("\pSubmenu, Item 1", "\p", "\p", "\p" );
         NoteAlert( rInformationAlert, nil );
         break;

      case iSubmenuItem2:
         ParamText("\pSubmenu, Item 2", "\p", "\p", "\p" );
         NoteAlert( rInformationAlert, nil );
         break;
   }
}


//_____


void  InitializeToolbox( void )
{
   InitGraf( &qd.thePort );
```

```
    InitFonts();
    InitWindows();
    InitMenus();
    TEInit();
    InitDialogs( 0L );
    FlushEvents( everyEvent, 0 );
    InitCursor();
}
```

Stepping through the Code

Once again, it's time to step through the source code to see just what's going on.

The #define Directives

All but three of the constants defined by this program are resource IDs or resource item numbers. If you want to make any changes to MenuMaster's resource file, you only have to go to one place in the source code to make changes or additions—the #define directives section.

The two ALRT resources have IDs of rAboutAlert and rInformationAlert. The modal dialog box has a DLOG ID of rModalDialog. The **OK** button in that dialog box has an item number of kDialogOKButton, while the picture item has an item number of kManPictureItem.

The MBAR has an ID of rMenuBar. This resource makes use of three MENU resources—mAppleMenu, mFileMenu, and mEditMenu. The first MENU resource has one item, iShowAboutApple. The second MENU has 12 items, but four of them are dashed lines and one is a hierarchical menu—so those five don't require constants. That leaves iOpenDialog, iShowAboutFile, iCheckMe, iNoCheckMe, iDisableOpenDialog, iDisableEditMenu, and iQuit.

The hierarchical menu that appears in the File menu has its own MENU resource to define the items in it. The two items in this menu are SubmenuItem1i and iSubmenuItem2.

The final MENU in the menu bar, the Edit menu, has three items in it. As the source code will demonstrate, you won't be using any of them directly, so they don't require constants.

Normally a call to `DisableItem()` disables a single menu item. If you pass the routine `kEntireMenu` as a parameter, though, an entire menu will be disabled.

`kReturnKey` and `kEnterKey` are the character constants for the **Return** key and the **Enter** key. The filter function for `ModalDialog()` will use them.

```
#define      rAboutAlert             128
#define      rInformationAlert       129
#define      rModalDialog            130
#define      kDialogOKButton           1
#define      kManPictureItem           2

#define      rMenuBar                128

#define      mAppleMenu              128
#define      iShowAboutApple           1

#define      mFileMenu               129
#define      iOpenDialog               1
#define      iShowAboutFile            2
#define      iCheckMe                  4
#define      iNoCheckMe                5
#define      iDisableOpenDialog        7
#define      iDisableEditMenu          8
#define      iQuit                    12

#define      mSubMenu                201
#define      iSubmenuItem1             1
#define      iSubmenuItem2             2

#define      mEditMenu               130
#define      iCut                      1
#define      iCopy                     2
#define      iPaste                    3

#define      kEntireMenu               0
#define      kReturnKey         (char)0x0D
#define      kEnterKey          (char)0x03
```

The Global Variables

Like the previous examples, MenuMaster uses gAllDone to signal the end of the program. You'll want a global MenuHandle variable for each, so that you can easily work with MenuMaster's three menus. They are gAppleMenu, gFileMenu, gEditMenu. MenuMaster will be toggling the text of some menu items. Simplistically, you'll be checking for something like this: if a selected menu item is named **A**, change its name to **B**. If its name is **B**, change it to **A**. These Boolean variables will keep track of the current state of three of the menu items: gCheckMeItemChecked, gOpenDialogItemDisabled, and gEditMenuDisabled.

```
Boolean     gAllDone = false;
MenuHandle  gAppleMenu;
MenuHandle  gFileMenu;
MenuHandle  gEditMenu;
Boolean     gCheckMeItemChecked = false;
Boolean     gOpenDialogItemDisabled = false;
Boolean     gEditMenuDisabled = false;
```

The main() Function

Earlier in this chapter, you saw that your program should put up the menu bar soon after starting. MenuMaster does just that. Right after the traditional initialization of the Toolbox and memory, the application-defined routine SetUpMenuBar() is called.

```
void  main( void )
{
    MaxApplZone();
    MoreMasters();
    MoreMasters();
    MoreMasters();

    InitializeToolbox();

    SetUpMenuBar();

    EventLoop();
}
```

Setting Up the Menu Bar

MenuMaster calls SetUpMenuBar() to put the menu bar on the screen. This routine is similar to the one by the same name developed in this chapter's *Setting Up the Hierarchical Menu* section—just a few lines are new. This version adds a Style variable named theItemStyle and these three lines:

```
theItemStyle = bold + italic;
SetItemStyle( gFileMenu, iShowAboutFile, theItemStyle );

CheckItem( gFileMenu, iNoCheckMe, true );
```

The name of the second item in the File menu, the **Show About** item, appears in the menu in bold and italic. To accomplish this, the desired styles are added together, and the result is passed to SetItemStyle(). This is the only place the style change needs to be made; the menu item text will appear in this style for the remainder of the program's execution.

MenuMaster has two items that can receive a check mark. The program starts with one of the items checked, so that's taken care of here with a call to CheckItem().

```
void   SetUpMenuBar( void )
{
    Handle        theMenuBar;
    MenuHandle    theSubmenu;
    Style         theItemStyle;

    theMenuBar = GetNewMBar( rMenuBar );
    if ( theMenuBar == nil )
        ExitToShell();

    SetMenuBar( theMenuBar );
    DisposeHandle( theMenuBar );

    gAppleMenu = GetMenuHandle( mAppleMenu );
    gFileMenu  = GetMenuHandle( mFileMenu );
    gEditMenu  = GetMenuHandle( mEditMenu );

    theSubmenu = GetMenu( mSubMenu );
    InsertMenu( theSubmenu, -1 );
```

```
    theItemStyle = bold + italic;
    SetItemStyle( gFileMenu, iShowAboutFile, theItemStyle );

    CheckItem( gFileMenu, iNoCheckMe, true );

    AppendResMenu( gAppleMenu, 'DRVR' );

    DrawMenuBar();
}
```

Handling a Keystroke

The EventLoop() routine should be old-hat by now. This program's version has just one addition—the handling of a keystroke. A case section has been added to handle a keyDown event. Under the case the application-defined HandleKeyDown() is called. This routine appears exactly as it was developed in this chapter's *Handling A Keystroke* section.

```
void  EventLoop( void )
{
    EventRecord  theEvent;

    while ( gAllDone == false )
    {
        WaitNextEvent( everyEvent, &theEvent, 15L, nil );

        switch ( theEvent.what )
        {
            case keyDown:
                HandleKeyDown( theEvent );
                break;

            case mouseDown:
                HandleMouseDown( theEvent );
                break;
        }
    }
}


void  HandleKeyDown( EventRecord theEvent )
{
    short  theChar;
```

```
long    theMenuChoice;

theChar = theEvent.message & charCodeMask;

if ( ( theEvent.modifiers & cmdKey ) != 0 )
{
    if ( theEvent.what != autoKey )
    {
        theMenuChoice = MenuKey( theChar );
        HandleMenuChoice( theMenuChoice );
    }
}
}
```

Handling a Click in the Menu Bar

A mouse click results in a call to HandleMouseDown(), which in turn calls
HandleMenuChoice(). Here's HandleMouseDown():

```
void  HandleMouseDown( EventRecord theEvent )
{
    WindowPtr   theWindow;
    short       thePart;
    long        theMenuChoice;

    thePart = FindWindow( theEvent.where, &theWindow );

    switch ( thePart )
    {
        case inMenuBar:
            theMenuChoice = MenuSelect( theEvent.where );
            HandleMenuChoice( theMenuChoice );
            break;
    }
}
```

Regardless of the program it appears in, the routine
HandleMenuChoice() has the same form: first call the Toolbox functions
HiWord() and LoWord() to determine the selected menu and menu item,
then enter a switch statement that determines which menu-handling
routine to branch to.

MenuMaster has three menus in the menu bar, yet there are four `case` sections in the `switch`. That's because MenuMaster has a hierarchical menu; don't forget to include all hierarchical menus in the body of the `switch`. Even though the user goes through the File menu to reach the hierarchical menu, it still acts as if it were a menu perched in the menu bar.

Notice that a click in the Edit menu doesn't get any attention. That's because MenuMaster only uses the Edit menu when the modal dialog box is open. When that's the case, the system will handle things.

```
void  HandleMenuChoice( long  theMenuChoice )
{
   short   theMenu;
   short   theMenuItem;

   if ( theMenuChoice != 0 )
   {
      theMenu = HiWord( theMenuChoice );
      theMenuItem = LoWord( theMenuChoice );

      switch ( theMenu )
      {
         case mAppleMenu:
            HandleAppleChoice( theMenuItem );
            break;

         case mFileMenu:
            HandleFileChoice( theMenuItem );
            break;

         case mSubMenu:
            HandleHierarchicalMenu( theMenuItem );
            break;

         case mEditMenu:
            break;
      }

      HiliteMenu( 0 );
   }
}
```

A menu selection in the Apple menu brings the program to HandleAppleChoice(). This is a typical "cut and paste" routine; it will appear, as is, in almost any program you write. What would make you change this routine? If you have more than one item in the menu, other than the user's Apple Menu Item folder contents. Figure 6.40 gives an example.

```
void  HandleAppleChoice( short theItem )
{
    Str255   theItemName;
    short    theReference;

    switch ( theItem )
    {
        case iShowAboutApple :
            Alert( rAboutAlert, nil );
            break;

        default :
            GetMenuItemText( gAppleMenu, theItem, theItemName );
            theReference = OpenDeskAcc( theItemName );
            break;
    }
}
```

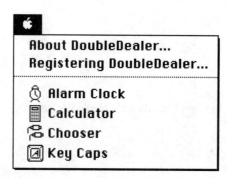

Figure 6.40 Example of a "nonstandard" Apple menu.

A selection in the File menu sends the program to HandleFileChoice(). Typical of menu-handling routines, this routine isn't much more than a branching-off point. A **Show About** selection simply puts up the same alert that was used for the Apple menu's **About MenuMaster** item. Choosing **Quit** just sets the global variable gAllDone to true. The other menu items are a bit more complicated, so they have their own application-defined routines.

```
void  HandleFileChoice( short theItem )
{
    switch ( theItem )
    {
        case iOpenDialog:
            OpenModalDialog();
            break;

        case iShowAboutFile:
            Alert( rAboutAlert, nil );
            break;

        case iCheckMe:
        case iNoCheckMe:
            HandleMenuCheckedItem( theItem );
            break;

        case iDisableOpenDialog:
            HandleDisableOpenDialogItem();
            break;

        case iDisableEditMenu:
            HandleDisableEditItem();
            break;

        case iQuit:
            gAllDone = true;
            break;
    }
}
```

The Modal Dialog Box

A menu choice of **Open Modal Dialog** takes the program to a routine called OpenModalDialog(). How's that for descriptive naming? The source code for this routine is pretty much straight out of the *Modal Dialog Source Code* section of Chapter 5.

```
void  OpenModalDialog( void )
{
    DialogPtr  theDialog;
    short      theItem;
    Boolean    dialogDone = false;

    theDialog = GetNewDialog( rModalDialog, nil, (WindowPtr)-1L );
    ShowWindow( theDialog );

    while ( dialogDone == false )
    {
        ModalDialog( DialogPromoFilter, &theItem );

        switch ( theItem )
        {
            case kDialogOKButton:
                dialogDone = true;
                break;
        }
    }

    DisposeDialog( theDialog );
}
```

The modal dialog box uses a filter function so that the user's keystrokes can be monitored. If the user presses the **Return** key or the or **Enter** key, the DialogPromoFilter() function that gets called by ModalDialog() sets theItem to a value of 1 to "trick" OpenModalDialog() into thinking that the user clicked the mouse button while the cursor was over the **OK** button. If both the **Command** key and the **D** key are pressed by the user, DialogPromoFilter() handles things by erasing the dialog box picture and replacing it with a short promotional blurb. All in all, the DialogPromoFilter() function follows the same format of the filter function discussed earlier in this chapter—the difference is in which Command-key combination is handled, and how.

```
pascal  Boolean DialogPromoFilter( DialogPtr    theDialog,
                                    EventRecord *theEvent,
                                    short       *theItem )
{
    char    theChar;
    short   theType;
    Handle  theHandle;
    Rect    theRect;
```

```
    if ( theEvent->what != keyDown )
        return ( false );

    theChar = theEvent->message & charCodeMask;

    if ( ( theEvent->modifiers & cmdKey ) != 0 )
    {
        switch ( theChar )
        {
            case 'd':
                SetPort( theDialog );
                GetDialogItem( theDialog, kManPictureItem, &theType,
                               &theHandle, &theRect );
                EraseRect( &theRect );
                MoveTo( theRect.left + 5, theRect.top + 45 );
                DrawString( "\p Buy Dancing" );;
                MoveTo( theRect.left + 5, theRect.top + 60 );
                DrawString( "\pMan Software!" );
                break;
        }

        return ( true );
    }

    if ( ( theChar == kReturnKey ) || ( theChar == kEnterKey ) )
    {
        *theItem = 1;
        return ( true );
    }

    return ( false );
}
```

Checking a Menu Item

This chapter demonstrated how to use CheckItem() to either set or clear
a check mark by a menu item. MenuMaster uses this same technique.

```
void  HandleMenuCheckedItem( short theItem )
{
    if ( theItem == iCheckMe )
    {
        CheckItem( gFileMenu, iNoCheckMe, false );
        gCheckMeItemChecked = true;
    }
```

```
    else
    {
        CheckItem( gFileMenu, iCheckMe, false );
        gCheckMeItemChecked = false;
    }

    CheckItem( gFileMenu, theItem, true );
}
```

Disabling and Enabling a Menu and Menu Item

If the user selects the File menu item **Disable 'Open Modal Dialog'**, check the global flag gOpenDialogItemDisabled to see which state this item is already in. Whatever the state, toggle it to its opposite state. The HandleDisableOpenDialogItem() routine performs two tasks. It enables or disables the first item in the File menu, and then makes a call to SetMenuItemText() to change the text of the selected item to whatever title is appropriate. Figure 6.41 shows the two possible scenarios.

```
void   HandleDisableOpenDialogItem( void )
{
    if ( gOpenDialogItemDisabled == true )
    {
        EnableItem( gFileMenu, iOpenDialog );
        SetMenuItemText( gFileMenu, iDisableOpenDialog,
                            "\pDisable 'Open Modal Dialog'" );
        gOpenDialogItemDisabled = false;
    }
    else
    {
        DisableItem( gFileMenu, iOpenDialog );
        SetMenuItemText( gFileMenu, iDisableOpenDialog,
                            "\pEnable 'Open Modal Dialog'" );
        gOpenDialogItemDisabled = true;
    }
}
```

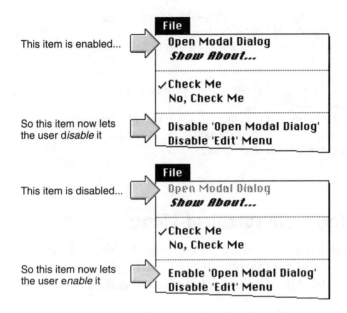

Figure 6.41 Enabling/disabling an item and changing an item's text.

`HandleDisableEditItem()` works in the same way as the previous routine. The difference is in the second parameter passed to `EnableItem()` and `DisableItem()`. By passing a value of 0 (`kEntireMenu`) to either `EnableItem()` or `DisableItem()`, MenuMaster is telling the Toolbox to enable or disable the entire Edit menu—not a particular item in it.

```
void   HandleDisableEditItem( void )
{
   if ( gEditMenuDisabled == true )
   {
      EnableItem( gEditMenu, kEntireMenu );
      DrawMenuBar();
      SetMenuItemText( gFileMenu, iDisableEditMenu,
```

```
                                "\pDisable 'Edit' Menu" );
        gEditMenuDisabled = false;
    }
    else
    {
        DisableItem( gEditMenu, kEntireMenu );
        DrawMenuBar();
        SetMenuItemText( gFileMenu, iDisableEditMenu,
                            "\pEnable 'Edit' Menu" );
        gEditMenuDisabled = true;
    }
}
```

Handling a Hierarchical Menu

MenuMaster displays an alert if either of the hierarchical submenu items are selected. To display two different strings in the same alert the program uses the ParamText() trick discussed earlier.

```
void    HandleHierarchicalMenu( short theItem )
{
    switch ( theItem )
    {
        case iSubmenuItem1:
            ParamText("\pSubmenu, Item 1", "\p", "\p", "\p" );
            NoteAlert( rInformationAlert, nil );
            break;

        case iSubmenuItem2:
            ParamText("\pSubmenu, Item 2", "\p", "\p", "\p" );
            NoteAlert( rInformationAlert, nil );
            break;
    }
}
```

Chapter Summary

To display a menu bar in your Macintosh program you use MENU resources and a single MBAR resource. Each MENU resource defines the menu items that appear in a single pull-down menu. The MBAR resource packages the individual MENU resources into single menu bar.

Several Toolbox routines are involved in setting up an application's menu bar. GetNewMBar() creates a menu list that holds a handle to each menu in the menu bar. SetMenuBar() installs the individual menus within the menu bar. AppendResMenu() fills the Apple menu with the names of the items in the Apple Menu Items folder in the user's System Folder. Finally, the menu bar is displayed on the screen with a call to DrawMenuBar().

To get access to a handle to an individual menu—a MenuHandle— call GetMenuHandle(). You'll then use this handle in subsequent calls to Toolbox routines that change the characteristics of the menu or items in it. Some of the changes you can make are: enabling and disabling a menu item, changing the name of a menu item, and displaying a check mark by an item.

When the user clicks the mouse button, you'll want to check to see if the click took place in the menu bar area of the screen. A call to FindWindow() determines that. If the mouse down event did occur in the menu bar, you'll call the powerful Toolbox routine MenuSelect() to track the mouse in the menu bar, dropping down menus as the user moves the mouse over them.

If the user makes a selection from a menu, call MenuSelect() to determine what item was selected. You'll use the Toolbox routines HiWord() and LoWord() to extract both the menu and the menu item from the single value that MenuSelect() returns.

You can make things easier for the user by creating keyboard equivalents for commonly-used menu selections. You'll include the keyboard equivalent in the MENU resource, then write a HandleKeyDown() routine that keeps watch for this keystroke combination.

You can expand the amount of information in a menu by changing a menu item into a hierarchical menu. By marking a menu as such in the MENU resource you'll add a pull-down menu to a menu item. You make your program aware of a hierarchical menu when you set up the program's menu bar. At that time you call GetMenu() and InsertMenu() for each hierarchical menu your program has.

To change menu characteristics you'll again rely on the Toolbox. EnableItem() and DisableItem() enable and disable a single menu item or an entire menu. Depending on the parameters you pass to it, the CheckItem() routine adds or takes away a checkmark from alongside a menu item. You can use `SetItemStyle()` to change the look of a menu item. You can give a menu item text characteristics such as bold or outline.

You can use a special filter function to give the user access to special commands available only through Command-equivalents. Your program will call this filter function every time it calls the Toolbox routine `ModalDialog()`.

Chapter 7

Text and Strings

The distinction between text and graphics is blurred in a graphical user interface environment like the Macintosh operating system. Text, like graphics, gets *drawn* to a window or dialog box. Because your program can treat text like it would graphics, your program can display text in a rich variety of formats. In this chapter, you'll learn how to use a number of Toolbox routines to change the font, size, style, and transfer mode (how text interacts with its background) of the strings your program draws.

While you no doubt program in C or C++, the Macintosh is most comfortable with strings that are in a Pascal format. In this chapter, you'll see the difference between C-formatted strings and Pascal-formatted strings. Knowing the format of Macintosh strings will also provide you with an understanding of how to convert a user-entered string into the floating-point number—a task that can't be handled by a single Toolbox function.

STRING DATA TYPES

While you no doubt program the Mac using either C or C++, when it comes to working with text you'll be using Pascal-style strings. When the Macintosh came into existence just over a decade ago, Pascal was the high-level language of choice. A holdover from those times is that many Toolbox functions that expect a string as a parameter expect that string to be in the form of a Pascal string.

The Str255 Data Type

In C, a string is an array of characters. To designate the end of the string, the last character in the array must be the null character, \0. Because an array element must be reserved for this string terminator escape sequence, the number of elements in a string array must be at least one greater than the number of characters in the text of the string. For example, the five characters in the string "Hello" require a string declaration as follows:

```
char  theString[5] = "Hello";
```

The first element in a C array always has an index of 0, so the array theString consists of six elements (numbered 0 through 5). As shown in Figure 7.1, the compiler automatically adds the null character to the end of the string.

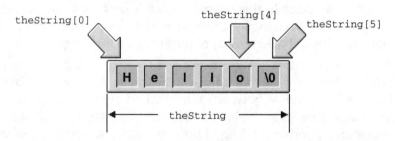

Figure 7.1 A C-formatted string in memory.

Like a C-formatted string, a Pascal-formatted string is an array of characters. And again like a string in C, a string in Pascal requires that one element be used to denote the end of the string. A Pascal string always uses the first element for this purpose. This first element defines the number of bytes in the text of the string. Thus the "Hello" string in Pascal would have a memory representation, as shown in Figure 7.2.

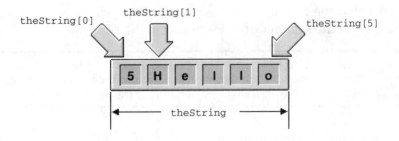

Figure 7.2 A Pascal-formatted string in memory.

In Macintosh programming, the Str255 is the data type that is typically used to hold the text that makes up a single string. As shown below, this data type is nothing more than an array of 256 characters, meaning the text that makes up a single string of type Str255 can have up to 255 characters, along with the first character that holds the length of string.

```
typedef unsigned char  Str255[256];
```

N O T E

A char can be either signed (meaning it can take on both positive and negative values) or it can be unsigned (meaning it can have only positive values). While both types can hold up to 256 different values, the range of values each type can support differs. A signed char has a range of -128 to +127, while an unsigned char has a range of 0 to 255. The conventional ASCII character set defines character codes in the range of 0 to 128 (0x00 to 0x7F). The Macintosh supports the Standard Roman character set, which adds additional characters to the conventional ASCII character set. These additional characters have codes from 129 to 255 (0x80 to 0xFF). Because any one character in a string can thus represent a character with a code in the range of 0 to 255, each character in the string must be declared to be of type unsigned char—as is the case with the definition of the Str255 type.

When programming the Macintosh in C or C++, the declaration of the "Hello" string would look like this:

```
Str255  theString = "\pHello";
```

The "\p" that starts off the string is an escape sequence that tells the compiler to expect a string in Pascal format rather than C format. Among other things, specifying that the string is in Pascal format will tell the compiler that the first byte of the string isn't a printable character, but instead holds the number of bytes of text in the string.

NOTE

While unusual looking, including the \p sequence in a string is no different than any other C escape sequence. For example, to denote that a string should end with the newline character, you include the \n escape sequence, as in:

```
char   theString[6] = "Hello\n";
```

Toolbox routines that expect a string as one parameter usually expect that string to be in the form of a `Str255` variable, as in this call to the Toolbox routine `DrawString()`:

```
Str255  theString = "\pQuickTime is not installed";
MoveTo( 20, 50 );
DrawString( theString );
```

Optionally, you can pass a string directly—provided that you specify that the string is in Pascal format. The following snippet produces the same results as the previous one:

```
MoveTo( 20, 50 );
DrawString( "\pQuickTime is not installed" );
```

Other String Data Types

A variable of type `Str255` *always* occupies 256 bytes, no matter how many characters of text actually are in the string. In the following snippet, the compiler would reserve 256 bytes for each of the two strings:

```
Str255  theRightString = "\pThat answer is correct!";
Str255  theWrongString = "\pWrong!";
```

If you *know* that the string or strings you'll be working with will be considerably shorter, you can use one of the other five string data types defined by Apple. The `Str63` type is used for strings up to 63 characters in length, while the shortest string type, the `Str15` type, is used for strings up to 15 characters in length. Here are the definitions of the half-dozen string types:

```
typedef unsigned char   Str255[256];
typedef unsigned char   Str63[64];
typedef unsigned char   Str32[33];
typedef unsigned char   Str31[32];
typedef unsigned char   Str27[28];
typedef unsigned char   Str15[16];
```

N O T E

In general, you'll be best off "wasting" a few bytes and declaring your string to be of type `Str255`—that's the data type most Toolbox routines are looking for.

You will use two other string-related data types—the `StringPtr` and the `StringHandle`—whose definitions appear below. In the next section, you'll see that the `StringHandle` data type is used when working with some strings that are stored as resources.

```
typedef unsigned char *StringPtr, **StringHandle;
```

Assigning a `Str255` **Variable a Value**

Except during initialization, the C language does not allow the assignment of an array of characters to be made in "one shot." That is, while the assignment of `theBeginMonth` is valid, the assignment of `theEndMonth` is not:

```
Str255  theBeginMonth = "\pMarch";     // valid assignment
Str255  theEndMonth;

theEndMonth = "\pMay";                  // invalid assignment!!
```

Like any array type, a `Str255` can be assigned a value character-by-character:

```
Str255  theEndMonth;

theEndMonth[1] = 'M';
theEndMonth[2] = 'a';
theEndMonth[3] = 'y';
theEndMonth[0] =  5;        // specify number of characters
```

While the preceding method does work, you can see that it is somewhat awkward—especially for lengthy strings. To easily assign a string a value, you can use instead the general-purpose memory-copying routine `BlockMoveData()`. This routine is used to copy a sequence of bytes from one memory location to another. After `BlockMoveData()` executes, both the string `theDestStr` and the string `theSourceStr` will have the same value. Using either as the parameter in a call to `DrawString()` will result in **My test string** being drawn to a window.

```
Str255    theSourceStr = "\pMy test string.";
Str255    theDestStr;
Size      theNumBytes;

theNumBytes = theSourceStr[0] + 1;
BlockMoveData( theSourceStr, theDestStr, theNumBytes );
```

The first parameter in `BlockMoveData()` is a pointer to the data to copy—the source data. The second parameter is a pointer to the area in memory that is to receive the data—what will become the destination data. The final parameter tells `BlockMoveData()` how many bytes to copy from the source to the destination. The value of this parameter should be the number of characters in the string (`theSourceStr[0]` yields that number) plus one byte for the first byte in the string (`theSourceStr[0]` itself). The `Size` data type is nothing more than a `long`—it exists to provide a little descriptive flair. Because C allows an array name to be used as a pointer, and because a `Str255` variable is nothing more than an array, `BlockMoveData()` will accept a `Str255` variable as either the first or second parameter—that's what's happening in the preceding snippet.

Strings and Resources

A major advantage of a program that relies heavily on resources, as all Macintosh programs do, is that you can make many changes to a program even after compiling it. Apple recommends that programmers store all displayable text as resources. Then, if you want to make a version of your program usable by non-English speaking people, you can edit the text within the program's resources. Depending on other factors in your program, you might not even have to change any source code or recompile your program. This, of course, is easier said than done; in practice, *internationalizing*, or *localizing*, an application is more involved. But resource editing provides a very good start.

If your program includes just a couple of strings, you might want to store each in a separate string resource—a STR resource. If your program uses several strings, then you can group the strings together into a single string list resource—a STR# resource. Both resource types are covered on the following pages.

The STR **Resource**

To create a STR resource in ResEdit, select **Create New Resource** from the Resource menu. Type **STR** in the editable text box found in the Select New Type window, then click the **OK** button. Note that like all resource types, the STR resource name consists of four characters. Here, the fourth character is a space.

In the string editor, click in the editable text box labeled **The String** and type up to 255 characters. As shown in Figure 7.3, that's all there is to creating a STR resource.

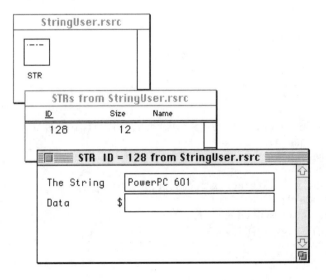

Figure 7.3 A Pascal-formatted string in memory.

Using a String in a Program

To load a string from a STR resource to memory, use the Toolbox function GetString(). Pass this routine the ID of a STR resource and GetString() will load the string into memory and return a handle to the start of the block of memory that holds the string. Here's an example that loads the STR resource pictured in Figure 7.3:

```
#define         kProcessorTypeStringRes        128

StringHandle  theStringHand;

theStringHand = GetString( kProcessorTypeStringRes );
```

A handle to a string is of limited value when working with the Toolbox—Toolbox functions look for a pointer to a string as a parameter. A variable of the array data type Str255 serves as a pointer, as does a variable of the StringPtr data type. So too does a string handle that's been dereferenced once. The following snippet opens a window based on WIND resource 200, then loads to memory the string resource shown in Figure 7.3. The StringHandle variable returned by GetString() is dereferenced once when used as a parameter to the Toolbox function DrawString(). Figure 7.4 shows the result of running the following code.

```
#define         rDisplayWindow                 200
#define         kProcessorTypeStringRes        128

WindowPtr       theWindow;
StringHandle  theStringHand;

theWindow = GetNewWindow( rDisplayWindow, nil, (WindowPtr)-1L );
ShowWindow( theWindow );
SetPort( theWindow );

theStringHand = GetString( kProcessorTypeStringRes );
MoveTo( 10, 20 );
DrawString( "\pTested on a " );
DrawString( *theStringHand );
```

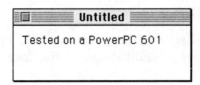

Figure 7.4 The result of using a STR resource in a call to DrawString().

A string that has been loaded from a STR resource can be used by your program just as it would use any Str255 variable. In the following snippet, a window is opened and, before the window is displayed on the screen, its title is set to the string PowerPC 601. Once again the STR resource pictured back in Figure 7.3 is used. Figure 7.5 shows the result.

```
#define       rDisplayWindow              200
#define       rProcessorTypeStringRes     128

WindowPtr      theWindow;
StringHandle   theStringHand;

theWindow = GetNewWindow( rDisplayWindow, nil, (WindowPtr)-1L );

theStringHand = GetString( rProcessorTypeStringRes );
SetWTitle( theWindow, *theStringHand );

ShowWindow( theWindow );
SetPort( theWindow );
```

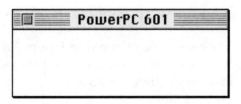

Figure 7.5 The result of using a STR resource in a call to SetWTitle().

The STR Resource

A STR# resource is a list of strings, each up to 255 characters in length. Figure 7.6 shows how ResEdit displays the four strings in a typical STR# resource.

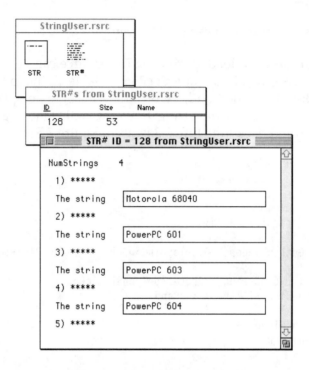

Figure 7.6 A STR# resource that holds four strings.

The strings in the STR# resource pictured in Figure 7.6 could be instead stored in four separate STR resources. It makes more sense to use a single STR# resource instead, though; here's why:

- It's easier to edit and view the strings in a single STR# resource than it is to do so in separate STR resources.

- It makes for a logical grouping of strings. For instance, one STR# resource could be devoted to storing processor name strings, as shown in Figure 7.6, while another STR# resource could be devoted to holding, say, monitor screen size strings.

- The system reads strings from a list more efficiently than it does strings stored individually.

To create the STR# resource, select **Create New Resource** from the Resource menu in ResEdit. You'll then see the Select New Type window. Scroll to the STR# type in the window's list and click on it, or type in the type yourself. Then click the **OK** button.

To add a new string to the STR#, first click the **mouse button** on the row of asterisks in the string lists editor. Next, select **Insert New Field(s)** from the Resource menu. ResEdit will respond by adding an editable text box in which you can type your new string.

Using a String in a Program

To use a string stored in string list resource, your code must first load it into memory with a call to the Toolbox routine GetIndString(). Because a STR# contains more than one string, you must specify which string in the list you want. This is done by including an index to the string. The first string in the STR# has an index of 1, the second an index of 2, and so forth.

Unlike GetString(), which results in your program having access to a handle to a string, GetIndString() provides your program with a Str255 variable. The first parameter in GetIndString() should be a Str255 variable that will be used to hold the returned string. The second parameter is the ID of the STR# resource that holds the string, while the third parameter is the index of the string.

As shown in the following snippet, you'll typically define a constant that holds the ID of a STR# resource, along with a constant for each string in the string list resource. If you refer to Figure 7.6 you'll see that after executing the following code variable theString will hold the string **PowerPC 601**—the second string of the string list resource with ID 128.

```
#define     rProcessorStringList     128
#define     kM68040Index             1
#define     kPPC601Index             2
#define     kPPC603Index             3
#define     kPPC604Index             4

Str255  theString;

GetIndString( theString, rProcessorStringList, kPPC601Index );
```

Earlier you saw how to use the string from a STR resource to change a window's title, and how to write that string to a window. You can do the same with strings obtained from a STR# resource. Because each call to GetIndString() returns a string as a Str255 variable rather than a handle, there's now no need to worry about dereferencing—simply use the returned string as a parameter to a Toolbox call. The following snippet loads both the third and fourth of the four strings from STR# 128. The third string is used for the window's title, and the fourth string is drawn to the window's content area. Figure 7.7 shows the result.

```
#define      rDisplayWindow             200
#define      rProcessorStringList       128
#define      kM68040Index                 1
#define      kPPC601Index                 2
#define      kPPC603Index                 3
#define      kPPC604Index                 4

WindowPtr   theWindow;
Str255      theString;

theWindow = GetNewWindow( rDisplayWindow, nil, (WindowPtr)-1L );

GetIndString( theString, rProcessorStringList, kPPC603Index );
SetWTitle( theWindow, theString );

ShowWindow( theWindow );
SetPort( theWindow );
GetIndString( theString, rProcessorStringList, kPPC604Index );
MoveTo( 10, 20 );
DrawString( "\pTested on a " );
DrawString( theString );
```

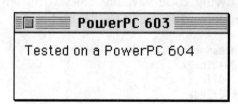

Figure 7.7 The result of using two strings from a single STR# resource.

TEXT CHARACTERISTICS

The Macintosh Toolbox offers a host of functions that make it easy for your program to change the look of the text it draws to the screen.

Text Font

To change the font that's used by `DrawString()`, call the Toolbox routine `TextFont()`. This function requires a single parameter—a short that holds an identifying number for the font that is to be used. You can pass `TextFont()` any of the Apple-defined constants shown here:

```
systemFont
applFont
newYork
geneva
monaco
venice
london
athens
sanFran
toronto
cairo
losAngeles
times
helvetica
courier
symbol
mobile
```

Once the font has been changed, the new font remains in effect until another call to `TextFont()` is made. The following snippet draws three lines of text to a window—each line using a different font. The results are shown in Figure 7.8.

```
TextFont( newYork );
MoveTo( 10, 20 );
DrawString( "\pNew York" );

TextFont( systemFont );
```

```
MoveTo( 10, 40 );
DrawString( "\pChicago" );

TextFont( sanFran );
MoveTo( 10, 60 );
DrawString( "\pSan Francisco" );
```

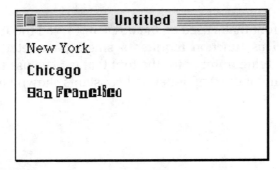

Figure 7.8 Changing the font using TextFont().

Text Size

To change the size of text drawn with calls to DrawString(), use the Toolbox function TextSize(). Pass TextSize() the new size, in points, to be used for drawn text. Once called, the text drawn by all subsequent calls to DrawString() will be affected.

The following snippet sets the font to **New York**, then draws two lines of text in 24 point size and a third line in 14 point size. The result is shown in Figure 7.9.

```
TextFont( newYork );

TextSize( 24 );
MoveTo( 10, 30 );
DrawString( "\pQuickTime" );
MoveTo( 10, 55 );
DrawString( "\pMusical Instruments" );

TextSize( 14 );
```

```
MoveTo( 10, 75 );
DrawString( "\pAdding music to your applications" );
```

Figure 7.9 Changing the font size using TextSize().

Text Style

Chapter 6 introduced you to the idea that a font's style can be easily altered. In that chapter, the text of a menu item was changed using a call to TextFace(). Recall from Chapter 6 that you pass TextFace() an Apple-defined constant—or a combination of constants—that describe the look you wish subsequently drawn text to have. Here's the list of Apple-defined text styles, or faces:

```
normal
bold
italic
underline
outline
shadow
condense
extend
```

A call to TextFace() changes the look of all text drawn using DrawString(). To combine two or more different styles, add the appropriate Apple-defined constants. To return text to a normal, or plain, look, use the Apple-defined normal constant as the parameter in TextFace(). The following snippet draws five lines of text in a variety of styles. Refer to Figure 7.10 to see the output generated by each pair of calls to TextFace() and DrawString().

```
TextFont( times );
TextSize( 14 );

TextFace( bold );
MoveTo( 10, 20 );
DrawString( "\pBold style" );

TextFace( underline );
MoveTo( 10, 40 );
DrawString( "\pUnderline style" );

TextFace( shadow );
MoveTo( 10, 60 );
DrawString( "\pShadow style" );

TextFace( bold + underline );
MoveTo( 10, 80 );
DrawString( "\pBold and underline style" );

TextFace( normal );
MoveTo( 10, 100 );
DrawString( "\pPlain style" );
```

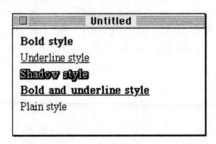

Figure 7.10 Changing the font style using `TextFace()`.

Rather than pass a constant directly to `TextFace()`, you can use a `Style` variable as the parameter:

```
Style   theStyle;

theStyle = shadow + condense;
TextFace( theStyle );
```

```
MoveTo( 10, 20 );
DrawString( "\pShadow and condense style" );
```

Transfer Mode

When a string is drawn using `DrawString()`, the text is drawn using the foreground color—typically black. Text is also typically drawn without regard for the values of the pixels that are being drawn over. That is, black text will be drawn over a white, black, or colored background. Figure 7.11 illustrates. In this figure the same string is drawn twice: one over an all white background, once over a white and black background.

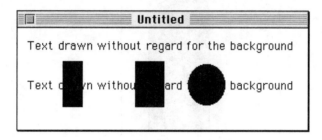

Figure 7.11 Text is typically drawn in black, regardless of what
is being drawn over.

Your program can change the *transfer mode* of text—the way text interacts with the pixels it is being drawn against. The Toolbox function `TextMode()` allows you to do this. Pass `TextMode()` one of the eight Apple-defined text transfer mode constants shown as follows, and the way strings drawn by subsequent calls to `DrawString()` appear in a window will be altered.

```
srcCopy
srcOr
srcXor
srcBic
notSrcCopy
notSrcOr
notSrcXor
notSrcBic
```

When a window opens, its graphics port is set to draw text in srcOr transfer mode. That produces the effect shown in Figure 7.11. If you'd like to change the way characters appear against the bit image over which they are drawn, change the mode. Once finished, you'll most likely want to return the mode to srcOr so that text drawn later on appears in the mode users are familiar with. Figure 7.12 draws the same string eight times to demonstrate how a text drawn against both a white and black background looks in each transfer mode. The top view shows the window before drawing takes place, the bottom view shows the window afterward.

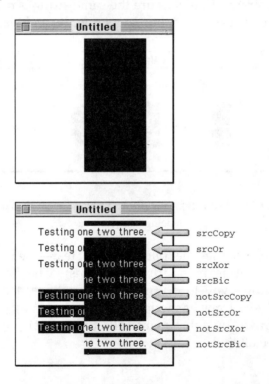

Figure 7.12 Changing the font mode using TextMode().

The following snippet changes the text transfer mode to notSrcCopy. The string that is then drawn will appear in white text on a black background—regardless of what is already drawn in the window at the time of the call to DrawString(). After drawing a single string, the snippet returns the transfer mode to the default setting of srcOr:

```
TextMode( notSrcCopy );
MoveTo( 30, 20 );
DrawString( "\pThis text will be white on black" );
TextMode( srcOr );
```

Besides the eight transfer mode constants already mentioned, Apple defines another text transfer mode that is of limited use, but still quite handy. If you want to draw text that matches the look of the text of a disabled menu item or dialog box item, use the grayishTextOr mode. The following snippet provides an example. Note that this mode works best for the system, or Chicago, font—other fonts may appear unreadable. Figure 7.13 shows the results of executing the following code:

```
TextFont( systemFont );
TextSize( 12 );

TextMode( grayishTextOr );
MoveTo( 20, 40 );
DrawString( "\pThis mode works best with the system font" );
TextMode( srcOr );
```

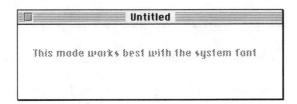

Figure 7.13 Changing the font mode to a gray, or dimmed, look.

CHAPTER PROGRAM: STRINGHANDLER

This chapter's example program demonstrates how to read strings from STR and STR# resources, and how to then use those strings in a program. It also illustrates how a string that represents a floating-point value can be converted to a float variable—a very handy feature that you'll find useful in many other programs you write. StringHandler also provides an example of changing the font, size, and style of text draw to a dialog box using DrawString(). Finally, StringHandler is, of all things, actually quite useful! The program shows how easy it is to display a picture and then scale the picture to a size of the user's choosing. Figure 7.14 shows how your screen will look when you run StringHandler.

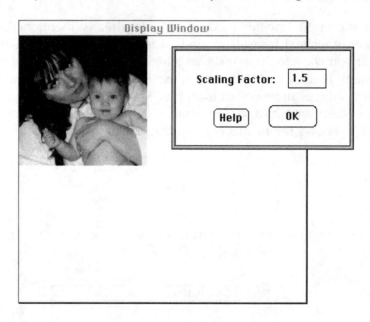

Figure 7.14 StringHandler's display window and Scaling dialog box.

StringHandler begins by opening a window and displaying a picture in the window. It then posts a modal dialog box that allows the user to scale the picture to a smaller or larger size. As shown in Figure 7.15, pressing the **Help** button enlarges the dialog box (a simple but useful feature in itself) and draws a few lines of instructions to the new area in the dialog box. The instructions are drawn in a variety of fonts and styles. It's not a very visually appealing look, but it provides for a demonstration of how the various characteristics of text can be altered.

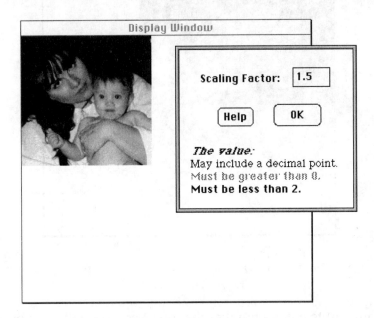

Figure 7.15 The Scaling dialog box after it has been enlarged to accommodate additional text.

When the **OK** button is clicked the dialog box is dismissed and the picture is redrawn at its new size—a size based on the scaling value entered in the modal dialog box editable text item. Figure 7.16 shows the picture redrawn at one and a half times its original size.

Figure 7.16 StringHandler's display window after its picture has been
resized and redrawn.

If you attempt to enter a number that is either too small (zero or less) or
too large (greater than 2), StringHandler will respond by displaying an
alert and ignoring your request to resize the picture. The alert message
for a scaling factor that is too large is shown in Figure 7.17. In all cases,
once the dialog box is dismissed the program ends at the next click of the
mouse button.

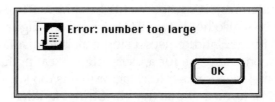

Figure 7.17 StringHandler posts an alert if the user-entered scaling value is out of range.

Program Resources: StringHandler.rsrc

StringHandler uses a variety of resources—you can see the seven different types in Figure 7.18. Only the STR and STR# resource types are new to this chapter.

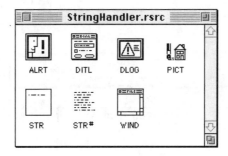

Figure 7.18 The resource types found in the StringHandler project's resource file.

The StringHandler project's resource file has one ALRT resource and one DLOG resource, so it also holds two DITL resources. Figure 7.19 shows all four resources. StringHandler uses a single alert to display two different error messages: one message for a user-entered scaling factor that is too small, another message for a scaling-factor that is too large. The ^0 string in the alert's DITL resource hints that the StringHandler source code will be calling the Toolbox function ParamText().

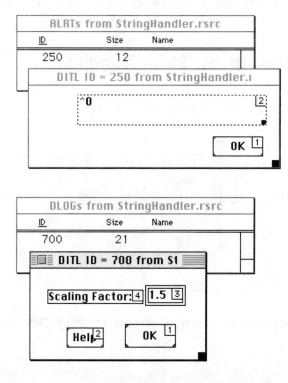

Figure 7.19 The ALRT, DLOG and two DITL resources found in the StringHandler project's resource file.

StringHandler keeps a STR resource that holds a string that will be used in the title bar of its one window. As shown in Figure 7.20 its ID is 300. There's also a STR# resource with an ID of 400. This string list holds a descriptive string of each of the errors StringHandler is aware of. While the list holds only two strings, this technique of storing error strings in a resource could be expanded easily to handle any number of error messages.

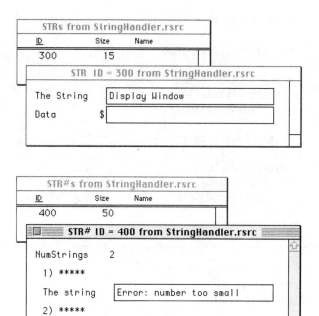

Figure 7.20 The STR and STR# resources found in the StringHandler project's resource file.

The remaining two resources used by StringHandler are a PICT resource and a WIND resource—types you've become quite familiar with already.

Program Listing: StringHandler.c

Once again, the chapter closes with a complete source code listing for the chapter example, then a source code walkthrough.

```
//_____

#define      rDisplayWindow                200
#define      rErrorAlert                   250
#define      rScalingDialog                700
#define      kOKButton                       1
#define      kHelpButton                     2
```

```
#define          kScalingEditTextBox              3

#define          rWindowTitleStringRes          300

#define          rErrorMessageStringList        400
#define          kErrorNumTooSmallIndex           1
#define          kErrorNumTooBigIndex             2

#define          rMomAndBabyPicture             500

#define          kDialogNormalWidth             230
#define          kDialogNormalHeight            100
#define          kDialogExpandHeight            180


//_____

Boolean     gAllDone = false;
PicHandle   gCurrentPicture;
Rect        gPictureRectangle;


//_____

void   main( void )
{
    MaxApplZone();
    MoreMasters();
    MoreMasters();
    MoreMasters();

    InitializeToolbox();

    OpenDisplayWindow();

    LoadPicture();

    OpenScalingDialog();

    EventLoop();
}


//_____
```

```
void   OpenDisplayWindow( void )
{
    WindowPtr      theWindow;
    StringHandle   theStringHand;

    theWindow = GetNewWindow( rDisplayWindow, nil, (WindowPtr)-1L );

    theStringHand = GetString( rWindowTitleStringRes );
    SetWTitle( theWindow, *theStringHand );

    ShowWindow( theWindow );
    SetPort( theWindow );
}



//_____


void   LoadPicture( void )
{
    gCurrentPicture = GetPicture( rMomAndBabyPicture );

    gPictureRectangle = (**gCurrentPicture).picFrame;
    OffsetRect( &gPictureRectangle, -gPictureRectangle.left,
                -gPictureRectangle.top );

    DrawPicture( gCurrentPicture, &gPictureRectangle );
}



//_____


void   OpenScalingDialog( void )
{
    DialogPtr  theDialog;
    short      theItem;
    Boolean    dialogDone = false;

    theDialog = GetNewDialog( rScalingDialog, nil, (WindowPtr)-1L );
    ShowWindow( theDialog );

    while ( dialogDone == false )
    {
        ModalDialog( nil, &theItem );

        switch ( theItem )
```

```
      {
         case kHelpButton:
            SetPort( theDialog );
            SizeWindow( theDialog, kDialogNormalWidth,
                        kDialogExpandHeight, true );

            TextFont( newYork );
            TextSize( 12 );
            TextFace( bold + italic );
            MoveTo( 10, 120 );
            DrawString( "\pThe value:" );

            TextFace( normal );
            MoveTo( 10, 135 );
            DrawString( "\pMay include a decimal point." );

            TextFont( systemFont );
            TextMode( grayishTextOr );
            MoveTo( 10, 150 );
            DrawString( "\pMust be greater than 0." );

            TextMode( srcOr );
            MoveTo( 10, 165 );
            DrawString( "\pMust be less than 2." );
            break;

         case kOKButton:
            RecalculatePictureSize( theDialog );
            dialogDone = true;
            break;
      }
   }

   DisposeDialog( theDialog );
}


//_____

void  RecalculatePictureSize( DialogPtr theDialog )
{
   short    theType;
   Handle   theHandle;
   Rect     theRect;
   Str255   theString;
```

```
    float    theFloat;

    GetDialogItem( theDialog, kScalingEditTextBox,
                    &theType, &theHandle, &theRect );
    GetDialogItemText( theHandle, theString );

    theFloat = ConvertStringToFloat( theString );

    if ( theFloat < 0.1 )
    {
        GetIndString( theString, rErrorMessageStringList,
                    kErrorNumTooSmallIndex );
        ParamText( theString, "\p", "\p", "\p" );
        NoteAlert( rErrorAlert, nil );
    }
    else if ( theFloat > 2.0 )
    {
        GetIndString( theString, rErrorMessageStringList,
                    kErrorNumTooBigIndex );
        ParamText( theString, "\p", "\p", "\p" );
        NoteAlert( rErrorAlert, nil );
    }
    else
    {
        gPictureRectangle.right  *= theFloat;
        gPictureRectangle.bottom *= theFloat;
    }
}


//_____

float  ConvertStringToFloat( Str255 theString )
{
    short    theLength;
    short    thePlaces = 0;
    long     theLong;
    float    theDivisor = 1;
    float    theFloat;
    Boolean  isFloat = false;
    int      i;

    theLength = theString[0];

    for ( i = theLength; i > 0; i- )
```

```
   {
      if ( theString[i] == '.' )
      {
         i = 0;
         isFloat = true;
      }
      else
      {
         thePlaces++;
      }
   }

   if ( isFloat == false )
   {
      StringToNum( theString, &theLong );
      theFloat = theLong * 1.0;

      return ( theFloat );
   }

   for ( i = theLength - thePlaces; i < theLength; i++ )
   {
      theString[i] = theString[i + 1];
   }

   theString[0] = theLength - 1;

   StringToNum( theString, &theLong );

   for ( i = 1; i <= thePlaces; i++ )
      theDivisor *= 10.0;

   theFloat = theLong / theDivisor;

   return ( theFloat );
}


//_____

void  HandleUpdate( EventRecord theEvent )
{
   GrafPtr    theSavePort;
   WindowPtr  theWindow;
```

```
        theWindow = (WindowPtr)theEvent.message;

        GetPort( &theSavePort );
        SetPort( theWindow );

        BeginUpdate( theWindow );
            EraseRgn( theWindow->visRgn );
            DrawPicture( gCurrentPicture, &gPictureRectangle );
        EndUpdate( theWindow );

        SetPort( theSavePort );
}


//_____

void  EventLoop( void )
{
    EventRecord  theEvent;

    while ( gAllDone == false )
    {
        WaitNextEvent( everyEvent, &theEvent, 15L, nil );

        switch ( theEvent.what )
        {
            case updateEvt:
                HandleUpdate( theEvent );
                break;

            case mouseDown:
                gAllDone = true;
                break;
        }
    }
}


//_____

void  InitializeToolbox( void )
{
    InitGraf( &qd.thePort );
    InitFonts();
```

```
    InitWindows();
    InitMenus();
    TEInit();
    InitDialogs( OL );
    FlushEvents( everyEvent, 0 );
    InitCursor();
}
```

The #define **Directives**

As usual, most of the listing's constants are resource related. The WIND resource has an ID of rDisplayWindow, while the ALRT resource has an ID of rErrorAlert. The DLOG resource has an ID of rScalingDialog. The **OK** button in the dialog box has an item number of kOKButton and the **Help** button has an item number of kHelpButton. The editable text item used to hold the scaling factor has an item number of kScalingEditTextBox.

The single STR resource has an ID of rWindowTitleStringRes. The list of strings, the STR# resource, has an ID of rErrorMessageStringList. Each string in the list is given its own constant. To make it easy to reference a particular string, each string constant has a descriptive name: kErrorNumTooSmallIndex and kErrorNumTooBigIndex.

The picture displayed in the program's window is stored as a PICT resource with an ID of rMomAndBabyPicture. Of course you're free to replace the supplied PICT with one of your own.

When the program expands the dialog box in response to a user's mouse click on the **Help** button, the dimensions of the dialog box need to be known to the program. The constants kDialogNormalWidth, kDialogNormalHeight, and kDialogExpandHeight hold that information. The unexpanded height of the dialog box, kDialogNormalHeight, goes unused by the program, but will be of use if you add a feature to the program that returns the dialog box to its original size.

NOTE Many of the resources in previous examples have each had an ID of 128—the default ID ResEdit gives to the first resource of most resource types. Just to emphasize that there's nothing magic about the number 128, the StringHandler resources have a variety of different IDs. Remember, to use ResEdit to change the ID of a resource you first click on its name or number of the resource, then select **Get Resource Info** from the Resource menu.

```
#define        rDisplayWindow              200
#define        rErrorAlert                 250
#define        rScalingDialog              700
#define        kOKButton                     1
#define        kHelpButton                   2
#define        kScalingEditTextBox           3

#define        rWindowTitleStringRes       300

#define        rErrorMessageStringList     400
#define        kErrorNumTooSmallIndex        1
#define        kErrorNumTooBigIndex          2

#define        rMomAndBabyPicture          500

#define        kDialogNormalWidth          230
#define        kDialogNormalHeight         100
#define        kDialogExpandHeight         180
```

The Global Variables

As is true of all the book example's, StringHandler uses `gAllDone` to keep track of when it should terminate. To allow easy updating of the display picture, a handle to it is kept in the global `PicHandle` variable `gCurrentPicture`. The same applies to the boundaries of the picture. The rectangle coordinates that define where the picture will be drawn in the window are stored in the global variable `gPictureRectangle`. These coordinates will change when the user enters a scaling factor and clicks the dialog box **OK** button to redraw the picture.

```
Boolean    gAllDone = false;
PicHandle  gCurrentPicture;
Rect       gPictureRectangle;
```

The main( ) Function

StringHandler starts with the usual initializations, then opens a window, loads a picture, and displays that picture in the window. The program then opens the Scaling dialog box to allow user input. A real-world Mac application could implement the opening of the window and dialog box via menu selections, as discussed in Chapter 6.

```
void  main( void )
{
   MaxApplZone();
   MoreMasters();
   MoreMasters();
   MoreMasters();

   InitializeToolbox();

   OpenDisplayWindow();

   LoadPicture();

   OpenScalingDialog();

   EventLoop();
}
```

Using a String from a STR Resource

A STR resource is loaded into memory by calling the Toolbox function GetString(). After dereferencing once, the StringHandle that is returned by this function can be used just like any Str255 variable. In StringHandler the STR resource is used in a call to the Toolbox function SetWTitle() to change the window's title from **Untitled** to **Display Window**.

```
void  OpenDisplayWindow( void )
{
   WindowPtr     theWindow;
   StringHandle  theStringHand;
```

```
theWindow = GetNewWindow( rDisplayWindow, nil, (WindowPtr)-1L );

theStringHand = GetString( rWindowTitleStringRes );
SetWTitle( theWindow, *theStringHand );

ShowWindow( theWindow );
SetPort( theWindow );
}
```

Loading and Displaying a Picture

From Chapter 3 you already know how to load a PICT resource—call the Toolbox function GetPicture(). The application-defined LoadPicture() routine does that, then saves the returned PicHandle to the global variable gCurrentPicture. It also offsets the picture to guarantee that it gets positioned in the upper-left corner of the window and saves the picture's frame in the global Rect variable gPictureRectangle. You'll see both of these global variables again when the window gets updated in the application-defined HandleUpdate() function. LoadPicture() ends by drawing the picture to the window using the Toolbox function DrawPicture().

```
void  LoadPicture( void )
{
   gCurrentPicture = GetPicture( rMomAndBabyPicture );

   gPictureRectangle = (**gCurrentPicture).picFrame;
   OffsetRect( &gPictureRectangle, -gPictureRectangle.left, -
   gPictureRectangle.top );

   DrawPicture( gCurrentPicture, &gPictureRectangle );
}
```

NOTE In most instances, it wouldn't be necessary to call DrawPicture() here. As you look over the code, you'll see that DrawPicture() is called when an update event that involves the window occurs. When the window is opened, an update event is generated—so normally the picture would get drawn by the update routine. In StringHandler, however, the window is opened, then the modal dialog box is opened—before EventLoop() is ever called. Thus the dialog box appears on the screen—and owns the screen—before the program enters its event loop. So the update event generated by the opening of the window doesn't get processed until after the modal dialog box is dismissed.

The Modal Dialog Box

The application-defined OpenScalingDialog() function is responsible for opening and handling the program's modal dialog box. If you need a refresher on the details of working with modal dialog boxes, refer to Chapter 6.

A mouse click on the dialog box **Help** button results in the dialog box changing size. This is a simple trick performed through the use of the Toolbox routine SizeWindow(). Recall that a Toolbox routine that expects a WindowPtr as a parameter will also accept a DialogPtr. The width of the dialog box remains the same, so the constant kDialogNormalWidth is used as the second parameter. The value of this constant was obtained from looking at the DLOG resource in ResEdit. The height of the dialog box does change—it gets larger. The value of kDialogExpandHeight was selected after estimating how much space the four lines of about-to-be-drawn help instructions would need.

After expanding the dialog box, four lines of text are drawn in it. While a single font, size, and style would make for easier reading, each line is given a different look in order to demonstrate the use of the Toolbox functions TextFont(), TextSize(), TextFace(), and TextMode().

```
case kHelpButton:
   SetPort( theDialog );
   SizeWindow( theDialog, kDialogNormalWidth,
               kDialogExpandHeight, true );

   TextFont( newYork );
   TextSize( 12 );
   TextFace( bold + italic );
   MoveTo( 10, 120 );
   DrawString( "\pThe value:" );

   TextFace( normal );
   MoveTo( 10, 135 );
   DrawString( "\pMay include a decimal point." );

   TextFont( systemFont );
   TextMode( grayishTextOr );
   MoveTo( 10, 150 );
   DrawString( "\pMust be greater than 0." );

   TextMode( srcOr );
```

```
MoveTo( 10, 165 );
DrawString( "\pMust be less than 2." );
break;
```

If the **OK** button is clicked, an application-defined function named `RecalculatePictureSize()` is called to determine the new size of the picture—based on the user-entered scaling factor. After that, the dialog box is dismissed.

```
case kOKButton:
    RecalculatePictureSize( theDialog );
    dialogDone = true;
    break;
```

Recalculating a Picture's Size

After the user enters a scaling factor and clicks the **OK** button, the application-defined `RecalculatePictureSize()` function is called. This routine relies on the Toolbox routines `GetDialogItem()` and `GetDialogItemText()` to obtain the number the user entered in the dialog box scaling factor editable text item. Both of these routines are described in detail in Chapter 5.

```
short    theType;
Handle   theHandle;
Rect     theRect;
Str255   theString;

GetDialogItem( theDialog, kScalingEditTextBox,
               &theType, &theHandle, &theRect );
GetDialogItemText( theHandle, theString );
```

The number that the user enters is retrieved as a string. To be of use to the StringHandler program, this string must be converted to a number. If the program restricted the user to integer input only, this would be a simple case of calling the Toolbox function `StringToNum()`. Integers won't due here, though. StringHandler wants to give the user great freedom in resizing the picture, so it allows fractional scaling values. Once the string is retrieved, the application-defined function `ConvertStringToFloat()` is called. This routine, discussed in the next section, converts the user-entered string to a floating-point value and returns that number to the caller—`RecalculatePictureSize()` in this case.

```
theFloat = ConvertStringToFloat( theString );
```

After ConvertStringToFloat() returns the scaling factor, RecalculatePictureSize() performs a series of tests to see if the user-entered number is valid. StringHandler expects the number to be greater than 0 (so that the redrawn picture is visible) and less than or equal to 2.0 (much bigger and it would exceed the content area of the display window). If either of these conditions isn't met, an alert is displayed. The same ALRT resource is used in either case, but the text displayed in the static text item of the ALRT differs. The text that is displayed in either alert comes from the STR# resource pictured in Figure 7.20—the Toolbox function GetIndString() is used to load the appropriate string. Calls to the Toolbox function ParamText() enable the same ALRT to be used for either error type. ParamText() is described in detail in Chapter 6. If no error is encountered, the size of the picture's bounding rectangle is changed. The left and top values, which were both offset to 0 when the picture was loaded in the application-defined LoadPicture() routine, are left constant, while the right and bottom values are multiplied by the scaling factor.

```
if ( theFloat < 0.1 )
{
    GetIndString( theString, rErrorMessageStringList,
                  kErrorNumTooSmallIndex );
    ParamText( theString, "\p", "\p", "\p" );
    NoteAlert( rErrorAlert, nil );
}
else if ( theFloat > 2.0 )
{
    GetIndString( theString, rErrorMessageStringList,
                  kErrorNumTooBigIndex );
    ParamText( theString, "\p", "\p", "\p" );
    NoteAlert( rErrorAlert, nil );
}
else
{
    gPictureRectangle.right  *= theFloat;
    gPictureRectangle.bottom *= theFloat;
}
```

Because the dialog box overlaps the display window, the dismissal of the dialog box triggers an update event. When the display window gets updated, the picture will be redrawn using the new picture boundaries.

```
void   RecalculatePictureSize( DialogPtr theDialog )
{
    short    theType;
    Handle   theHandle;
    Rect     theRect;
    Str255   theString;
    float    theFloat;

    GetDialogItem( theDialog, kScalingEditTextBox,
                    &theType, &theHandle, &theRect );
    GetDialogItemText( theHandle, theString );

    theFloat = ConvertStringToFloat( theString );

    if ( theFloat < 0.1 )
    {
        GetIndString( theString, rErrorMessageStringList,
                        kErrorNumTooSmallIndex );
        ParamText( theString, "\p", "\p", "\p" );
        NoteAlert( rErrorAlert, nil );
    }
    else if ( theFloat > 2.0 )
    {
        GetIndString( theString, rErrorMessageStringList,
                        kErrorNumTooBigIndex );
        ParamText( theString, "\p", "\p", "\p" );
        NoteAlert( rErrorAlert, nil );
    }
    else
    {
        gPictureRectangle.right  *= theFloat;
        gPictureRectangle.bottom *= theFloat;
    }
}
```

Converting aString to a Floating-Point Number

Converting a string to an integral value (a number without a decimal point) is easy—just pass the string to the Toolbox routine `StringToNum()`. The Toolbox will do the conversion work and return the result in a parameter of type `long`. Converting a string to a floating-point value requires a little extra work on your part.

N O T E

There are several approaches to tackling the problem of converting a string to a floating point number. The most sophisticated approach is to use *number format specification strings*, an involved topic described in the *Text* volume of the *Inside Macintosh* series of books. If you're familiar with ANSI C standard functions and libraries, then the `sscanf()` function is another tool you can use in string conversions. As you're about to see, this book uses a third approach.

The StringHandler program uses an application-defined function named `ConvertStringToFloat()` to perform the conversion of a numerical string stored in a `Str255` variable to a floating-point number stored in a `float` variable. Here's an overview of how `ConvertStringToFloat()` performs this task:

1. Convert the floating-point string to an integral string by removing the decimal point from the string.
2. Use the Toolbox function `StringToNum()` to convert the string to a long integer.
3. Divide the resulting long number by the appropriate value (10, 100, 1000, etc.) to turn the integer into a floating-point value.

`ConvertStringToFloat()` begins by getting the length of `theString`—the string to convert:

```
Str255    theString;
short     theLength;

theLength = theString[0];
```

Next, a for loop is entered. The purpose of the loop is to start at the last character in the string and, working toward the front of the string, to examine each character to see if it is a decimal point. Once the decimal point is found, the number of digits to the right of the decimal point is known—variable thePlaces holds that information. If the string **1.54** is used as an example, then the length of the string is four and the value of thePlaces is 2, as shown in Figure 7.21.

```
short    thePlaces = 0;
Boolean  isFloat = false;
int      i;

for ( i = theLength; i > 0; i- )
{
    if ( theString[i] == '.' )
    {
        i = 0;              // decimal found, exit the loop
        isFloat = true;     // yes, the string represents a float
    }
    else
    {
        thePlaces++;        // decimal not found, increment
    }
}
```

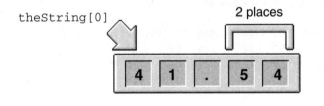

```
theLength = theString[0] = 4
thePlaces = digits to right of decimal = 2
```

Figure 7.21 Determining the length of a string and the number of digits to the right of the string's decimal point.

If no decimal point is encountered, the string represents an integral value—and the Boolean variable isFloat will still have its initial value of false. Because the numerical string represents an integer, it can be converted by simply using the Toolbox function StringToNum(). The return type of ConvertStringToFloat() is float, so the long variable returned by StringToNum() is multiplied by 1.0 to convert it to a floating-point value. ConvertStringToFloat() has completed its task, so it ends by returning the following converted number:

```
long   theLong;

if ( isFloat == false )
{
    StringToNum( theString, &theLong );
    theFloat = theLong * 1.0;

    return ( theFloat );
}
```

If the numerical string contains a decimal point, it's time to strip out the decimal point. A simple for loop takes care of that by shifting each character that is currently to the right of the decimal point one element to the left. Figure 7.22 shows how this step works for the string **1.54**. Using this example string, theLength would have a value of **4** and thePlaces would have a value of **2**. The top part of the figure shows the string after the first of two passes through the for loop, while the bottom part of the figure shows the string after the second pass.

```
for ( i = theLength - thePlaces; i < theLength; i++ )
{
    theString[i] = theString[i + 1];
}
```

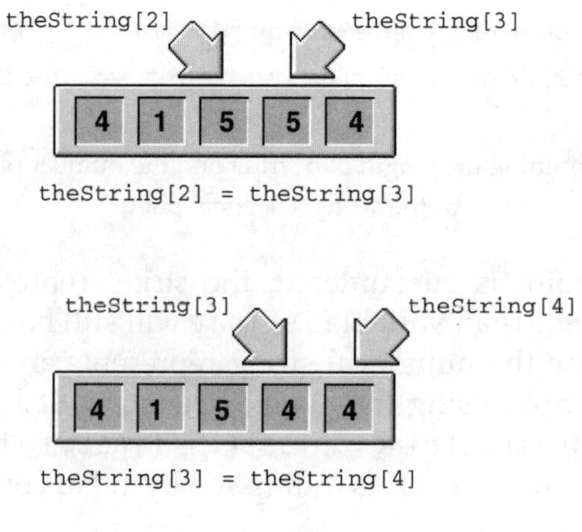

theString[2]   theString[3]

| 4 | 1 | 5 | 5 | 4 |

theString[2] = theString[3]

theString[3]   theString[4]

| 4 | 1 | 5 | 4 | 4 |

theString[3] = theString[4]

Figure 7.22 Removing the decimal point from a string.

After removing the decimal point, the string is one character shorter. The following assignment makes the necessary adjustment. Figure 7.23 shows that the **1.54** example string is now **154**.

```
theString[0] = theLength - 1;
```

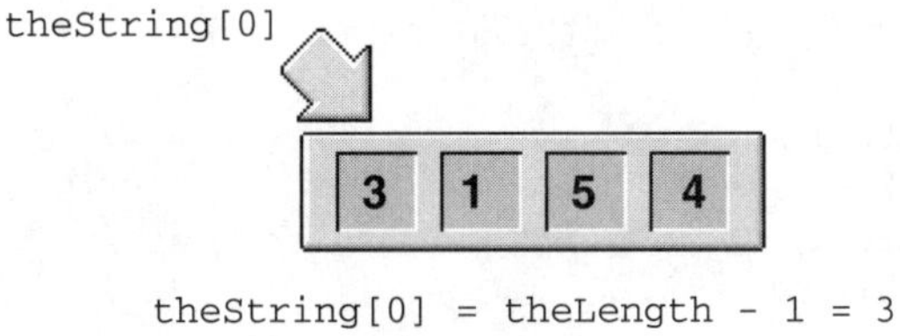

Figure 7.23 Resetting the string's length after removing the decimal point.

Now that the string has been converted to an integral value, the Toolbox routine `StringToNum()` can be called:

```
StringToNum( theString, &theLong );
```

At this point, the program has a number to work with (in this example, the number 154), rather than a string. All that's left to do is divide the integer by an appropriate power of 10 to convert it to a floating-point value. Continuing with the example, the number 154 needs to be divided by 100 to result in a value of 1.54. Regardless of the numerical value of the initial string, the number to divide by can be determined from the number of digits to the right of the decimal point—information calculated earlier and saved to the variable `thePlaces`:

```
float   theDivisor = 1;

for ( i = 1; i <= thePlaces; i++ )
    theDivisor *= 10.0;
```

For the number 154, which started out as the string 1.54, `thePlaces` has a value of **2**. That means the `for` loop executes twice, and `theDivisor` ends up with a value of **100**. To turn the integral value held in `theLong` to a floating-point value, divide `theLong` by `theDivisor`:

```
theFloat = theLong / theDivisor;
```

Finally, return the resulting floating-point value to the calling function:

```
return ( theFloat );
```

Here's a look at the completed ConvertStringToFloat() function—each line has been just discussed above.

```
float   ConvertStringToFloat( Str255 theString )
{
    short    theLength;
    short    thePlaces = 0;
    long     theLong;
    float    theDivisor = 1;
    float    theFloat;
    Boolean  isFloat = false;
    int      i;

    theLength = theString[0];

    for ( i = theLength; i > 0; i- )
    {
        if ( theString[i] == '.' )
        {
            i = 0;
            isFloat = true;
        }
        else
        {
            thePlaces++;
        }
    }

    if ( isFloat == false )
    {
        StringToNum( theString, &theLong );
        theFloat = theLong * 1.0;

        return ( theFloat );
    }

    for ( i = theLength - thePlaces; i < theLength; i++ )
    {
        theString[i] = theString[i + 1];
    }
```

```
    theString[0] = theLength - 1;

    StringToNum( theString, &theLong );

    for ( i = 1; i <= thePlaces; i++ )
        theDivisor *= 10.0;

    theFloat = theLong / theDivisor;

    return ( theFloat );
}
```

Checking for Valid Typed Input

The ConvertStringToFloat() function works just fine, assuming the user entered a number of some sort in the dialog box editable text box. You shouldn't, however, assume that the user will always do so. For instance, if the user types **1.a**, the StringHandler program will still attempt to convert this string to a floating-point value. You already know the solution to limiting the user's input—take a moment to think about the problem before reading on!

Times up. To check each key as it's typed, have ModalDialog() call a modal dialog box filter function, as described in Chapter 6. In the filter function, make a check to ensure that only one of the ten digit keys or the period key was pressed. The following example is just such a filter function.

```
#define      kPeriodKey      (char)0x2E
#define      kZeroKey        (char)0x30
#define      kNineKey        (char)0x39

pascal  Boolean DialogNumberOnlyFilter( DialogPtr     theDialog,
                                        EventRecord  *theEvent,
                                        short        *theItem )
{
    char   theChar;

    if ( theEvent->what != keyDown )
        return ( false );

    theChar = theEvent->message & charCodeMask;
```

```
if ( ( theChar >= kZeroKey ) && ( theChar <= kNineKey ) )
    return ( false );
else if ( theChar == kPeriodKey )
    return ( false );
else
{
    SysBeep( 1 );
    return ( true );
}
}
```

DialogNumberOnlyFilter() first checks to see if the event was a key press. If it wasn't, the event isn't handled by the filter—so false is immediately returned to ModalDialog(). If the event *was* a key press, the typed character is determined and then the check for a valid character begins.

If the value of the typed character is in the range of 0x30 (ASCII 48) to 0x39 (ASCII 57), then the character was in the range of 0 to 9—a valid keystroke. The filter *doesn't* handle valid characters, it lets ModalDialog() do that. ModalDialog() handles a valid character as it always does—it echoes the character to the editable text box. The same applies to the next test. If the character is a period, then assume the user is entering a decimal point for a floating-point number. Again, let ModalDialog() handle this valid character.

If the keystroke is any other character, let the filter function handle it and return true. DialogNumberOnlyFilter() handles an invalid character by sounding the system alert. By then returning a value of true, the character doesn't get echoed to the editable text box. ModalDialog() has been told that the event was suitably handled, so it doesn't take the liberty of working with the event—it won't echo the character to the dialog box.

Updating the Display Window

When the dialog box is dismissed, an update event occurs. The display window, which was partially obscured by the dialog box, is the focus of this event. The application-defined HandleUpdate() function—called from the EventLoop() routine—takes care of updating the window. In StringHandler, this is a simple task: erase the current contents of the window with a call to the Toolbox function EraseRgn(), and then redraw the picture by calling the Toolbox function `DrawPicture()`. As described in Chapter 5, window updating takes place between calls to the Toolbox functions `BeginUpdate()` and `EndUpdate()`.

```
void  HandleUpdate( EventRecord theEvent )
{
    GrafPtr     theSavePort;
    WindowPtr   theWindow;

    theWindow = (WindowPtr)theEvent.message;

    GetPort( &theSavePort );
    SetPort( theWindow );

    BeginUpdate( theWindow );
        EraseRgn( theWindow->visRgn );
        DrawPicture( gCurrentPicture, &gPictureRectangle );
    EndUpdate( theWindow );

    SetPort( theSavePort );
}
```

CHAPTER SUMMARY

A Macintosh Toolbox function that expects a string as a parameter generally requires that the string be of type `Str255`. The `Str255` data type is an array of 256 characters and holds a single string in Pascal format. The first byte of a Pascal string holds the length of the string. That is, it holds a number that tells how many of the remaining 255 bytes are occupied by the characters that make up the string.

A variable of type `Str255` can be assigned a string value at declaration, but not later in the program. Rather, use the Toolbox function `BlockMoveData()` to copy a hard-coded string or the contents of another string to a `Str255` variable.

To create strings that can be edited without altering or recompiling source code, use one of the two string resource types. Strings can be held in resources of type `STR` or `STR#`. The `STR` resource holds a single string, while the `STR#` is a string list that holds a number of strings. To load a string from a `STR` resource, use the Toolbox function `GetString()`. To load one of the strings from a STR# resource, call the Toolbox routine GetIndString().

Because the Macintosh treats text as it does other graphic entities, changing the characteristics of a string is easy. The Toolbox holds several routines that can be used to change the look of a string that is to be drawn with DrawString(). To change the font, call TextFont(). To change the size of drawn text, call TextSize(). The style of text can be altered by using TextFace(). Finally, the transfer mode—how text interacts with the bits it is drawn against—can be changed with a call to TextMode().

Chapter 8

Power Mac Programming

Porting older source code that was created for the 68K-based Macs so that it compiles and runs on the newer Power Macs is often trivial. For the smallest of programs, such as most of the examples in this book, the same source code file can be used when compiling with either a 68K compiler or a PowerPC compiler. *No* changes are necessary. More involved programs, however, may require some source code modification. Fortunately, any necessary changes usually involve a single programming topic—the universal procedure pointer, or UPP. This type of pointer is new to Macintosh programming—there was no need for it before the Power Macs came into existence. In this chapter you'll learn about the UPP and how it may effect your code.

A program that is built using a 68K compiler runs on both Macintosh and Power Macintosh computers, but when running on a Power Mac it doesn't take advantage of the speed inherent in the PowerPC chip. A program that is built using a PowerPC compiler will run fast on a Power Mac, but it won't run at all on a 68Kbased Mac. The solution to this dilemma is to merge two versions of the same program into one application. The resulting program will run on both types of Mac, and will take advantage of the power of the PowerPC chip when running on a

Power Mac. As you'll see in this chapter, you can build this fat binary application after you've modified your source code such that it compiles and executes on both 68Kbased Macs and Power Macs.

Universal Procedure Pointers (UPPs)

Even though a Macintosh and a Power Mac have microprocessors that come from different families, and thus work with different instruction sets, the PowerPC-based Macintosh computer is capable of running code that was generated for the 68Kbased Mac. For reasons of both necessity and user support, Apple went to great lengths to ensure that this was so.

A Power Mac excels when it runs *native code*—when it is processing instructions that are from the PowerPC instruction set. While the ideal scenario would be for a Power Mac to execute only native code, this is almost never the case. That's because while much of the Macintosh Toolbox has been ported and recompiled to native code, some of it has not. So even a program that was built using a PowerPC compiler will be at times executing instructions from the 68K instruction set.

A Toolbox that isn't completely native is one reason the Power Mac must be able to work with 68K-based code. A second reason is user-support. Many owners of Power Mac computers have a substantial investment in older Mac software—programs developed before the advent of the Power Macs. So as not to force these users to lose out on their possibly large software investments, Apple made sure that older programs ran on newer computers.

Apple achieved backwards compatibility through the inclusion of emulation software and the Mixed Mode Manager. The emulator is software that translates instructions from the 68K instruction set to the PowerPC instruction set. As a Power Mac executes a program that isn't 100% native (which is almost always the case), the mode of the Power Mac is constantly switching. One moment a native instruction is being executed directly by the PowerPC microprocessor, and the next moment a 68K instruction is being passed to the emulator and then onto the PowerPC chip. Keeping track of this perpetual mode switching is the job of the code that is a part of the Mixed Mode Manager.

For the user, the emulator and the Mixed Mode Manager take all of the worry out of code compatibility—a Mac user never considers what mode his or her computer is currently in. For the Mac programmer, the emulator and the Mixed Mode Manager take most of the worry out of code compatibility—there are a couple of areas where the programmer most make a programming effort to ensure code will run properly on a PowerPC-based Mac. The use of procedure pointers, or ProcPtrs, is the area of compatibility of most interest to you, the Mac programmer.

Procedure Pointers (ProcPtrs) and Universal Procedure Pointers (UPPs)

In Chapter 6, you were introduced to the `ProcPtr` data type, though you might not have been aware of it. There you saw that the first parameter to the Toolbox routine `ModalDialog()` could be the name of a filter function, as in this snippet:

```
ModalDialog( DialogPromoFilter, &theItem );
```

`DialogPromoFilter` is the name of an application-defined filter function. In the preceding code `DialogPromoFilter` serves as a pointer to the `DialogPromoFilter()` routine. Before the arrival of the Power Macs, a parameter that was a pointer to a routine was a *procedure pointer*, and had a data type of `ProcPtr`.

When storing executable code and loading executable code into memory, Power Macs follow a different set of rules than 68K-based Macs. A Power Mac keeps code in a code fragment, which may or may not be a part of the application that uses the code. Because of this and other complexities, each function that is in the memory of a Power Mac has a *routine descriptor* data structure to hold information about the function. One piece of information in a routine descriptor is a `ProcPtr`. On a Power Mac, a `ProcPtr` isn't quite the same as it is on a 68K-based Mac. On a Power Mac, a `ProcPtr` points to still another data structure—a transition vector, or TVector. The TVector consists of two pointers, one of which is the address of the start of the function's executable code. Figure 8.1 shows the differences between a `ProcPtr` on a 68K-based Mac and on a Power Mac.

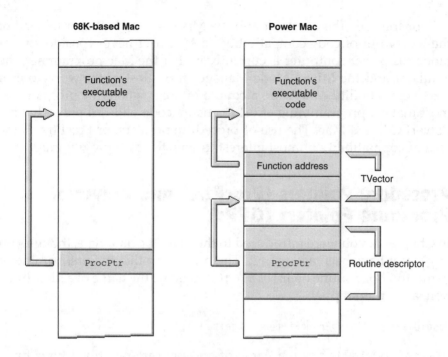

Figure 8.1 How the system accesses a user-defined function on both a 68K-based and PowerPC-based Mac.

If it sounds like things are getting a bit confusing, you'll enjoy this next sentence. As a programmer, you won't have to keep track of routine descriptors, TVectors, or `ProcPtrs`. In fact, you won't have to even fully understand what they exist for. Instead, you'll just have to know about the universal procedure pointer, or UPP. The UPP, represented by the `UniversalProcPtr` data type, indirectly leads to the starting address of a function. As shown in Figure 8.2, a UPP holds the address of a function's routine descriptor. The routine descriptor in turn contains a `ProcPtr` that holds the address of a TVector, which in turn holds a pointer to a function's executable code.

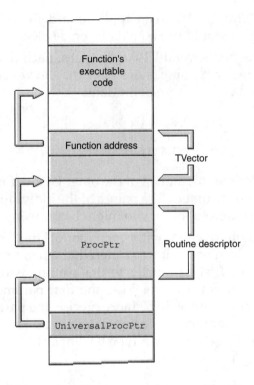

Figure 8.2 How the system uses a universal procedure pointer to access a user-defined function.

 If you're a glutton for punishment, you can obtain more details about routine descriptors, TVectors, and other PowerPC-related data structures by picking up *Programming the PowerPC* by M&T Books or the *PowerPC System Software* volume from the *Inside Macintosh* series.

N O T E

Using a `UniversalProcPtr` is easy—almost as easy as using a `ProcPtr` when programming for a 68K-based Macintosh. First, declare a universal procedure pointer variable. Then use one of several Toolbox functions to associate the UPP with an application-defined function. Finally, use the UPP as you would use a `ProcPtr` on a 68K-based machine.

Apple has defined several UPP data types. Each data type is identical—they're all really nothing more than the `UniversalProcPtr` type renamed. Here's a few of those definitions:

```
typedef UniversalProcPtr   ModalFilterUPP;
typedef UniversalProcPtr   UserItemUPP;
typedef UniversalProcPtr   FileFilterUPP;
```

The preceding definitions, and all of the other UPP definitions, exist as a convenience to programmers. The names of the individual types provide some extra description to those who might be perusing your code.

This discussion opened with mention of the Toolbox function `ModalDialog()`. In specific, it was stated that when programming for a 68K-based Mac the first parameter to this routine is of type `ProcPtr`. When programming for a Power Mac, the first parameter is instead a universal procedure pointer. To be more precise, the parameter is of type `ModalFilterUPP`. From the preceding snippet you know that this parameter is really nothing more than type `UniversalProcPtr`. Here's how Apple defines `ModalDialog()`:

```
void ModalDialog( ModalFilterUPP modalFilter, short *itemHit )
```

When programming for a 68K-based Mac, here's how `ModalDialog()` would be called when using a filter function named `DialogPromoFilter()`:

```
ModalDialog( DialogPromoFilter, &theItem );
```

When programming for a PowerPC-based Mac, here's how things are done:

```
ModalFilterUPP   theFilterUPP;

theFilterUPP = NewModalFilterProc( DialogPromoFilter );

// open dialog box, then enter ModalDialog() loop

ModalDialog( theFilterUPP, &theItem );
```

The above snippet declares a variable of type ModalFilterUPP. It then calls the Toolbox function NewModalFilterProc() to associate the application-defined DialogPromoFilter() function with the UPP. Once the dialog box is opened, ModalDialog() is called with the UPP as the first parameter.

Chapter Program: MenuMaster (revisited)

The Chapter 6 example program was named MenuMaster. Selecting **Open Modal Dialog** from the program's File menu displayed the modal dialog box pictured in Figure 8.3.

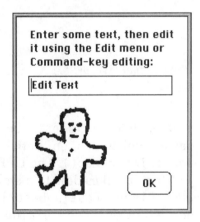

Figure 8.3 The modal dialog box displayed by the MenuMaster program.

The MenuMaster program includes a function named OpenModalDialog(). Below is that same function, modified so that it compiles using a PowerPC compiler. Lines that differ from the Chapter 6 version of the function are shown in italic type.

```
void  OpenModalDialog( void )
{
    DialogPtr       theDialog;
    short           theItem;
    Boolean         dialogDone = false;
    ModalFilterUPP  theFilterUPP;
```

```
    theFilterUPP = NewModalFilterProc( DialogPromoFilter );

    theDialog = GetNewDialog( rModalDialog, nil, (WindowPtr)-1L );
    ShowWindow( theDialog );

    while ( dialogDone == false )
    {
        ModalDialog( theFilterUPP, &theItem );

        switch ( theItem )
        {
            case kDialogOKButton:
                dialogDone = true;
                break;
        }
    }

    DisposeRoutineDescriptor( theFilterUPP );
    DisposeDialog( theDialog );
}
```

The previous version of OpenModalDialog() begins by declaring a ModalFilterUPP variable, which is then initialized by calling the Toolbox function NewModalFilterProc(). The UPP is then used in the call to ModalDialog(). When it comes time to dismiss the modal dialog box, the Toolbox function DisposeRoutineDescriptor() is called to release the memory allocated by OpenModalDialog().

WARNING

Any time you're writing code that (a) will be compiled with a PowerPC compiler and (b) uses a filter function with ModalDialog(), you *must* take the steps shown in the above example: declare a variable of type ModalFilterUPP, call NewModalFilterProc(), then pass the ModalFilterUPP variable to ModalDialog(). Omitting any of these steps will result in a compile-time error. Omitting the last step, the calling of DisposeRoutineDescriptor() to dispose of the allocated data structures, is considered good housekeeping—though your code will still compile and run without this Toolbox function call.

The remainder of the PowerPC version of the MenuMaster code is *identical* to that found in the 68K version presented in Chapter 6. If your development system includes both a 68K compiler and a PowerPC compiler, try compiling and running both versions. Whether you own a Metrowerks or Symantec IDE, you'll find projects for each in the Chapter 6 and Chapter 8 folders on this book's CD.

NOTE A reminder: A program built using a PowerPC compiler is a PowerPC-only application. Attempting to run the resulting application on a 68K-based Mac won't work—the system will display a -192 error alert upon your attempt to launch the app. Later in this chapter you'll see how to make a fat app—an application compiled using a PowerPC compiler, but able to run on any Mac.

Universal Procedure Pointers and User Items

Using a filter function with `ModalDialog()` is one instance of when a UPP is necessary. Another is when your program makes use of a user item. Recall from Chapter 5 that when a dialog box includes a user item, your program must pair the user item with an application-defined routine that updates that item. The means to making this association is the Toolbox function `SetDialogItem()`. The fourth parameter to this function is the name of the user item updating function—typecast to a Handle. The following snippet is from the Chapter 5 version of the `DialogPlus` program. In that program the user item drawing function is named `DoUserItem()`.

```
#define      kManUserItem       6

short        theType;
Handle       theHandle;
Rect         theRect;
DialogPtr    theDialog;

// open dialog box

GetDialogItem( theDialog, kManUserItem, &theType,
               &theHandle, &theRect );
SetDialogItem( theDialog, kManUserItem, theType,
               (Handle)DoUserItem, &theRect );
```

Just when do you use a universal procedure pointer? Here's the UPP rule of thumb. If your code passes a function name as a parameter in a call to another function, and you're compiling with a PowerPC compiler, you need to use universal procedure pointers.

N O T E

The fact that in this program `SetDialogItem()` requires a routine name as a parameter is the give away that a `ProcPtr` is involved—a function name as a parameter serves as a pointer to that function. If this code is to be compiled with a PowerPC compiler, it will have to be modified such that the `ProcPtr` is replaced with a universal procedure pointer.

Take heed of this note—it's important. Normally, when you compile code that requires a universal procedure pointer, and you haven't used one, your PowerPC compiler will choke—it won't compile the code and will return an error message. Not so with calls to `SetDialogItem()`. That's because the fourth parameter to `SetDialogItem()`—the parameter that must be a UPP when working with a user item—gets typecast to type Handle. That means your PowerPC compiler will be looking for a handle as the fourth parameter. The compiler won't be able to tell if the thing you're typecasting is a UPP, or a `ProcPtr`, or anything else for that matter—so it won't issue any error message if you forget to port your code. However, when you attempt to run the program it will fail. You can avoid this hard-to-detect bug by searching your source code for `SetDialogItem` and `SetDItem` (the older, now obsolete name for this function) and then confirming that you've made the necessary changes.

N O T E

Using a UPP with `SetDialogItem()` is similar to using one with `ModalDialog()`: declare a UPP variable, call a Toolbox routine to associate that variable with the application-defined function, then use the UPP as a parameter to the Toolbox routine that requires it. Here's a specific example that assumes the user item update function is named `DoUserItem()`:

```
UserItemUPP  theUserUPP;

theUserUPP = NewUserItemProc( DoUserItem );

// open dialog box

GetDialogItem( theDialog, kManUserItem, &theType,
               &theHandle, &theRect );
SetDialogItem( theDialog, kManUserItem, theType,
               (Handle)theUserUPP, &theRect );
```

Just as the `ModalDialog()` example declared a universal procedure pointer variable, so to does the `SetDialogItem()` example. For the `ModalDialog()` example, the variable was of type `ModalFilterUPP`. For this example, the variable is of type `UserItemUPP`. Recall that both data types are equivalent to the `UniversalProcPtr` data type.

After the UPP variable is declared, it needs to be associated with an application-defined routine. Again, as was the case in the `ModalDialog()` example, a Toolbox function handles this task. Here the `NewUserItemProc()` routine is used. After that, the UPP is passed to `SetDialogItem()`. Because this fourth parameter is defined to be of type **Handle**, the UPP must be typecast.

Chapter Program: DialogPlus (revisited)

The Chapter 5 example program DialogPlus displays a modeless dialog box that includes two user items. Figure 8.4 serves as a reminder of what the user sees when DialogPlus is running.

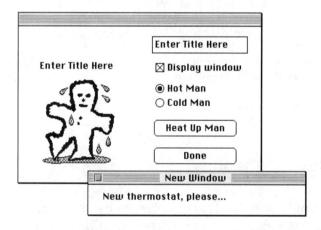

Figure 8.4 The modeless dialog box displayed by the DialogPlus program.

For the PowerPC version of the DialogPlus program, a UPP will be needed. The `OpenTemperatureDialog()` function, which calls `SetDialogItem()` twice to associate the application-define `DoUserItem()` function with each user item, is the only routine that needs to be altered. Lines that differ from the Chapter 5 version of the function are shown in italic type.

```
void  OpenTemperatureDialog( void )
{
    short       theType;
    Handle      theHandle;
    Rect        theRect;
    DialogPtr   theDialog;
    UserItemUPP theUserUPP;

    theUserUPP = NewUserItemProc( DoUserItem );

    theDialog = GetNewDialog( rTemperatureDialog,
                              gDlogStorage, (WindowPtr)-1L );
    if ( theDialog == nil )
        ExitToShell();

    GetDialogItem( theDialog, kManUserItem, &theType,
                    &theHandle, &theRect );
    SetDialogItem( theDialog, kManUserItem, theType,
                    (Handle)theUserUPP, &theRect );

    GetDialogItem( theDialog, kTitleUserItem, &theType,
                    &theHandle, &theRect );
    SetDialogItem( theDialog, kTitleUserItem, theType,
                    (Handle)theUserUPP, &theRect );

    gCurrentPict  = rManHotPicture;
    gOldButtonNum = kHotRadioButton;

    GetDialogItem( theDialog, gOldButtonNum, &theType,
                    &theHandle, &theRect);
    SetControlValue( (ControlHandle)theHandle, kControlOn );

    ShowWindow( theDialog );
}
```

This version of OpenModalDialog() begins by declaring a UserItemUPP variable. That variable is then initialized by calling the Toolbox function NewUserItemProc(). The universal procedure pointer is then used in the two calls to SetDialogItem().

Notice that unlike the first UPP example in this chapter—the one that used a UPP with a call to ModalDialog()—this example *doesn't* call DisposeRoutineDescriptor(). Though both examples in this chapter use a universal procedure pointer with a dialog box, the UPP used in each example must be treated differently. In the Menu Manager example, the dialog box was modal. When the application-defined `OpenModalDialog()` function ended, the dialog box was dismissed with a call to the Toolbox routine `DisposeDialog()`. In this DialogPlus example, the dialog box is modeless. It *doesn't* get dismissed at the end of the `OpenTemperatureDialog()` function—it remains open for the duration of the program. While the UPP variable `theUserUPP` won't be used after the `OpenTemperatureDialog()` function ends, the information it provides to the system will be used. The two calls to `SetDialogItem()` have associated the user items with the `DoUserItem()` update function, and the system will use the routine descriptor allocated by the call to `NewUserItemProc()` to access the `DoUserItem()` code.

NOTE
If you experiment with the source code and add a call to `DisposeRoutineDescriptor()` at the end of the `OpenTemperatureDialog()` function, you'll find that the program terminates almost immediately after you try running it. The program will fail the first time the system tries to update the user items—which will be upon opening the dialog box. That's because the system won't be able to find the executable code for the `DoUserItem()` routine.

Fat Applications

Macintosh computers and Power Mac computers have different microprocessors, and thus have different instruction sets. The instructions that make up a program designed to run on one machine aren't understood by the other machine. Yet you know from experience that many Mac applications can in fact run on either type of machine. There are two ways to create a single program capable of performing this feat, but only one method takes advantage of the speed of the PowerPC chip.

68K, PowerPC-Only, and fat Applications

Most programs that were developed long before the Power Macintosh came into existence will run flawlessly on a Power Mac. As mentioned, Apple made this possible by including emulation software in each Power Mac computer. When a program compiled for a 68K-based

Macintosh runs on a PowerPC-based Mac, the instructions that make up that program are sent through the emulation software and converted to PowerPC instructions. The advantage to this scheme is that it is possible to run a 68K program on a Power Mac. The disadvantage is that emulation slows processing, and the program won't take advantage of the speed of the PowerPC microprocessor.

A program that was developed with the purpose of running on Power Macs *can't* run on a 68K-based Macintosh. While a Power Mac is capable of translating 68K instructions to PowerPC instructions, the reverse isn't true—a 68K-based Mac won't recognize PowerPC instructions. The advantage to developing a PowerPC application is that the program will be made up of native PowerPC code; its instructions will execute without the need to pass through the emulator. The disadvantage is that owners of 68K-based Macs will be unable to run the program.

To capture the best of both worlds—a program that runs on a 68K-based Macintosh and runs quickly on a Power Mac—a developer creates a *fat binary application*, or *fat app*. A fat app is nothing more than the combination of two versions of the same program into a single application.

Creating the fat Application

Both the Metrowerks and Symantec development environments are capable of easily creating fat applications. Regardless of the development environment you use, the process is similar. A little later in this chapter, you'll see a specific example of creating a fat application. For now, here's an overview of how this task is accomplished:

1. Create a 68K project.
2. Compile and build a 68K application from the 68K project.
3. Create a PowerPC project.
4. Add the 68K *application* to the PowerPC project.
5. Compile and build a PowerPC application from the PowerPC project.

Including the 68K application itself in the PowerPC project causes your IDE to embed the 68K program within the PowerPC program. The result is two versions of the same program within a single file. The resulting application will have a single icon and will appear to the user as a single program. The only indication the user might have is in the size of the fat app. Because it holds two versions of the same program, it will occupy more disk space than either the 68K or PowerPC version alone.

Once you've built the fat binary application, there are two ways you can verify that it is indeed a fat app. One way is to run the program on both a 68K-based Mac and on a Power Macintosh. Since you'll have built the fat app from a PowerPC project, this will tell you that the app is in fact fat—an application built from a PowerPC project that doesn't include a merged 68K application won't run on a 68K-based Mac. A second way to verify that your application is fat is to run ResEdit and open the fat application. Don't open the project resource file, open the application itself. If the application's resource fork contains both a `cfrg` resource and `CODE` resources, it's a fat app.

The fat App and the `cfrg` Resource

Each and every PowerPC application contains a `cfrg` resource—a resource type which was created with the advent of the Power Mac. You're not responsible for creating a `cfrg` resource for your application—one will be added to the resource fork of your program by your IDE at the time the application is built.

The `cfrg` resource tells the system where to find the executable code that makes up a program. While 68K applications store executable code in `CODE` resources in the application's resource fork, PowerPC applications generally keep executable code in the data fork of the application. When a 68K application gets launched, the system knows exactly where the executable code is—in the `CODE` resources in the application's resource fork. When a PowerPC application gets launched, the system needs some help in determining where the executable code is—the code may not be at the very start of the data fork. The `cfrg` resource holds this information.

A fat app holds two sets of executable code. The code for the 68K version exists in `CODE` resources in the resource fork of the fat app. The code for the PowerPC version exists in the data fork of the fat app. When the user double-clicks on the icon of a fat app, only one set of code will end up in memory. The proper code gets loaded into memory thanks to the presence of the fat app's cfrg resource.

A resource of type cfrg is recognized by a Power Mac, but ignored by a 68K-based Macintosh. If a fat application resides on the drive of a Power Mac, double-clicking on its icon will cause the system to look at the application's cfrg resource. That leads the system to the fat app's data fork, where the PowerPC version of the executable code resides. If the same fat app is copied to the drive of a 68K-based Mac, double-clicking on the program icon will have a different result. The 68K system software is unaware of cfrg resources, so the system won't attempt to examine the fat app's cfrg resource. Instead, the system will simply load the executable code found in the CODE resources in the resource fork of the fat app.

Metrowerks CodeWarrior and the DialogPlus fat app

If you use the CodeWarrior IDE, read this section to see an example of creating a fat application from the DialogPlus program described in Chapter 5 and in this chapter. If you're a Symantec IDE owner, skip to the next section—the information you need lies there.

To create a fat binary version of the DialogPlus application, you'll make use of both the 68K DialogPlus and the PowerPC DialogPlus project so if you haven't already built a 68K version of DialogPlus, use the Chapter 5 DialogPlus.µ project to do that now. Then, copy the DialogPlus68K application to a new folder. Next, copy the source code file and PowerPC project file for this chapter's version of the DialogPlus program to the same folder (Figure 8.5).

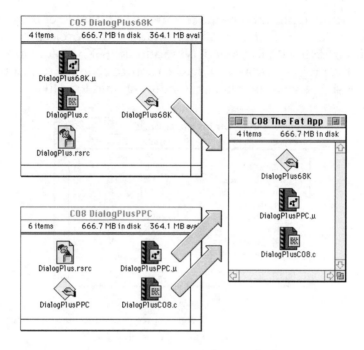

Figure 8.5 Creating a new folder that holds the files to be used for a fat application built using the CodeWarrior IDE.

You'll create the fat application from the new version of the PowerPC project—that's shown in the C08 The Fat App folder in Figure 8.5. From within the CodeWarrior IDE, open this project. Then click once on the name of the resource file, *DialogPlus.rsrc,* in the project window. Select **Remove Files** from the Project menu to remove the resource file from the project. The fat application needs resources, but it will get them all from the 68K application that your about to add to the project. Next, select **Add Files** from the Project menu. Now add the 68K version of the application to the project, just as you'd add a source code file or resource file. Figure 8.6 shows what the project window should look like.

File	Code	Data 🐾		
▽ **Sources**	2K	250	•	▽
DialogPlus.c	2848	250	•	▶
▽ **Mac Libraries**	6K	1K		▽
InterfaceLib	0	0		▶
MathLib	0	0		▶
MWCRuntime.Lib	6608	1318		▶
▷ **ANSI Libraries**	121K	19K		▽
▽ **68K Application**	0	0		▽
DialogPlus68K	n/a	n/a		▶
8 file(s)	130K	21K		

DialogPlusPPC.µ

Figure 8.6 The CodeWarrior PowerPC project used to build a fat app version of the DialogPlus program.

NOTE You can add the 68K application to any group, of course. If you'd like to place it in its own group for organizational purposes, as shown in Figure 8.6, drag the file below the last group in the project window. That will create a new group. To rename this group, double-click on the group's name and type in a new name, such as **68K Application** as was done in Figure 8.6.

Before building the new application, select **Preferences** from the Edit menu. Click once on the **PPC Project** icon in the icon list found on the left side of the Preferences dialog box. In the **Project** panel, enter the name you'd like the fat application to have. For this example, DialogPlusFat seems quite appropriate (seeFigure 8.7). Click the **OK** button to dismiss the Preferences dialog box.

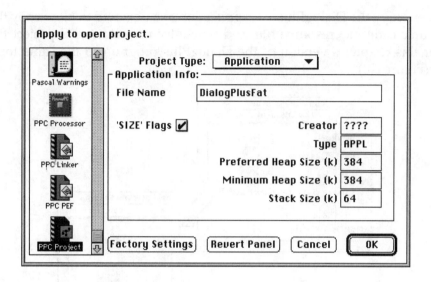

Figure 8.7 Supplying the CodeWarrior IDE with the name that it should use when building the fat application version of DialogPlus.

To create the fat app, select **Make** from the Project menu. When you return to the desktop you'll find the fat application DialogPlusFat—all ready for you to test.

Symantec and the DialogPlus fat app

If you're a CodeWarrior IDE owner, skip this section—you now have the information you need in order to create a fat application. Symantec owners, read on.

To create a fat app version of DialogPlus, you'll make use of both the 68K DialogPlus project and the PowerPC DialogPlus project. If you haven't already done so, use the Chapter 5 DialogPlus.π project and your THINK C compiler to build a 68K version of the DialogPlus program.

Then, copy the DialogPlus68K application to a new folder. Now copy the source code file, resource file, and Symantec C++ PowerPC project file for this chapter's version of the DialogPlus program to the same folder(Figure 8.8).

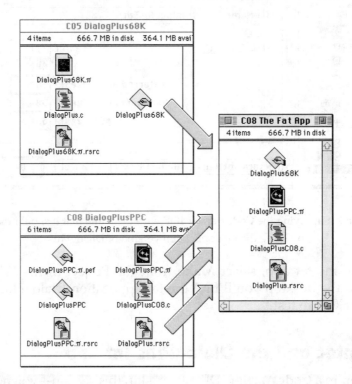

Figure 8.8 Creating a new folder that holds the files to be used for a fat application built using the Symantec IDE.

NOTE

Symantec's next IDE, which may be available as you read this will be truly integrated. You won't need to use THINK C to create a 68K application and Symantec C++ to create a PowerPC application. Instead, the process will be much like that used by Metrowerks CodeWarrior owners: A single IDE will be able to generate both 68K and PowerPC apps.

You'll create the fat application from the new version of the PowerPC project—the one shown in the C08 The Fat App folder in Figure 8.8. From within the Symantec Project Manager, open this project. Then select **Options** from the Project menu. Click on the **Project Type** icon in the column of icons on the left side of the Project Options dialog box.

The Project Type page of the Project Options dialog box allows you to set a variety of project options. Figure 8.9 shows how you can use this page to set the name of the fat application when it gets built later on. First, click the **Set destination** button. In the dialog box that opens, type in a name for the program. After dismissing the dialog box, the entered name will appear in the Project Type page—to the right of the **Set destination** button.

The second, and most important, task to perform on the Project Type page is the setting of the **Merge** feature. Click on the **Merge 680x0 Application** checkbox to check it. Then click the **Select application** button. When you that, a dialog box like the one shown in Figure 8.10 opens. From this dialog box, you select an application to merge with the PowerPC application during the build process. For this example, select the 68K version of the DialogPlus application, as is being done in Figure 8.10. After you dismiss the dialog box, the name of the selected application will appear in the Project Type page, just to the right of the **Select application** button. Now click the **Save** button to dismiss the Project Options dialog box.

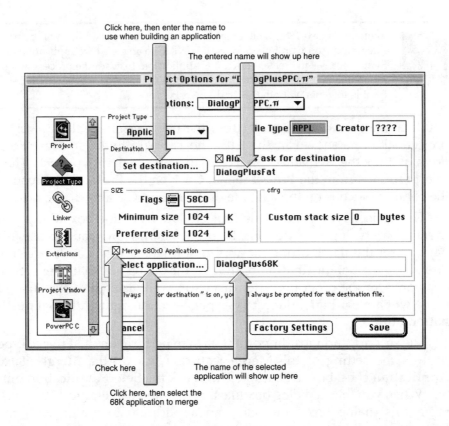

Figure 8.9 Supplying the Symantec IDE with the name of the 68K program to merge with, and the name to use for the fat app.

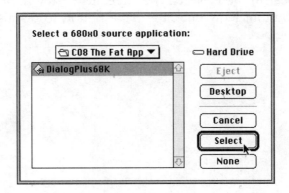

Figure 8.10 Selecting the 68K program that will be merged with the PowerPC program.

As shown in Figure 8.11, the project window won't appear any different than it did before the merge; it still appears to hold just the source code file, resource file, and libraries used to build the PowerPC version of DialogPlus. Don't worry, though. After performing the build, you will in fact have a fat application.

✓	⇕Name	🦟	Code
◇ 🖼	DialogPlus.rsrc		N/A
◇ 📄	DialogPlusC08.c	◆	2792
▷ ◇ 🗀	**Libraries**		**2128**
	Totals 5 (0 ✓)		**4920**

✓ DialogPlusPPC.π

Figure 8.11 The Symantec PowerPC project used to build a fat app version of the DialogPlus program.

To create the fat app, select **Build Application** from the Build menu. Because you set the destination in the Project Options dialog box (see Figure 8.9), the application name will already appear in the editable text box of the dialog box that opens, as shown in Figure 8.12. Simply click the **Save** button to build the fat application. After the program builds, return to the desktop to find the icon for the fat application DialogPlusFat. If you have access to both a 68K-based Mac and a Power Mac, execute the program on each machine so that you're satisfied that the program is indeed a fat binary.

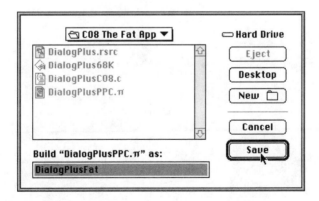

Figure 8.12 Supplying CodeWarrior with the name that it should use when building the fat application version of DialogPlus.

Chapter Summary

Porting older source code that was created for the 68K-based Macs so that it compiles and runs on the newer Power Macs often involves working with universal procedure pointers, or UPPs. This pointer type, which is new to the Power Mac, replaces the procedure pointer, or `ProcPtr`, used by programs that run on 68K machines. The use of a UPP is straightforward. First, declare a UPP variable. Then call a Toolbox routine that creates the data structures the system will need in order to access the function the UPP will point to. Finally, in place of a `ProcPtr` use the now-initialized UPP as a parameter to a Toolbox function.

When developing a program, you'll derive the greatest marketability from it if you turn it into a fat binary application, or fat app. A fat app is a single program that actually contains two versions of executable code. One version is created using a 68K compiler, and its code is stored in `CODE` resources in the resource fork of the fat app. The second version is created using a PowerPC compiler, and its code is stored in the data fork of the fat app. Both versions share the same resources, which are stored in the fat application's resource fork. When a user launches a fat app only one set of executable code gets loaded into memory—the set appropriate for the machine the user is working on. Both the Metrowerks and Symantec development environments support the creation of fat applications.

Chapter 9

The Varying Mac

When the Macintosh was introduced a decade ago, there was just a single model. Now there are numerous models, each with a slightly different configuration. A user further complicates the picture by customizing a machine with a floating-point coprocessor, extra RAM, or a large-screen color monitor. The system software that drives the Macintosh has also evolved over the years.

While every Mac owner would like to have the most current, feature-laden model, the truth is that millions of Macintosh owners are running programs on older machines. As a service to this varied audience, and to ensure that your program has the widest distribution and usage as possible, you will want to write applications that execute on as many Macintosh models as possible.

Writing code that is guaranteed to run on several different models requires a little extra work on your part, but the effort will be worth it. This chapter describes the programming tricks necessary to ensure that anyone using a Macintosh will also be able to use your applications easily.

THE FEATURES OF A MACINTOSH

The different members of the Macintosh family of computers differ in their hardware features. They can also differ in the version of System software they run. To make matters worse (for you, the compatibility-minded programmer), users can make a host of changes to both the hardware and software once they get their computers home or to the office.

There will be times when you want to know if the computer your program is running on has a particular hardware or software feature. One way to get some of this information is by making a call to the Toolbox routine SysEnvirons(). Here's a typical call:

```
SysEnvRec  theMacInfo;
SysEnvirons( curSysEnvVers, &theMacInfo );
```

As Macintosh features have evolved, so has SysEnvirons()—there is more than one version available. To make use of SysEnvirons(), you pass it the version you'll be using. Always pass curSysEnvVers as the version number. You needn't worry about the value of this Apple-defined constant—it's listed in the universal header files that accompanied your compiler.

The second parameter to pass to SysEnvirons() is a pointer to a variable of type SysEnvRec. After making the call, the several members of the SysEnvRec data structure will yield useful information such as the CPU the machine has and the version of the System software currently running. The SysEnvRec structure follows:

```
struct SysEnvRec
{
    short     environsVersion;
    short     machineType;
    short     systemVersion;
    short     processor;
    Boolean   hasFPU;
    Boolean   hasColorQD;
    short     keyBoardType;
    short     atDrvrVersNum;
    short     sysVRefNum;
};
```

As this section ends, you'll notice that I haven't provided you with an in-depth example of `SysEnvirons()`. The next section tells you why.

The Gestalt() function

Starting with the 1989 release of System 6.0.4, the use of `SysEnvirons()` became virtually obsolete. After reading the material in the last section, you're probably wondering why this fact wasn't mentioned a little sooner!

System 6.0.4 introduced a new Toolbox routine, `Gestalt()`. This function is capable of returning all of the same information that `SysEnvirons()` returns, and much more. When it comes to determining the various features on a Macintosh, `SysEnvirons()` pales in comparison to `Gestalt()`. Figure 9.1 sums this up.

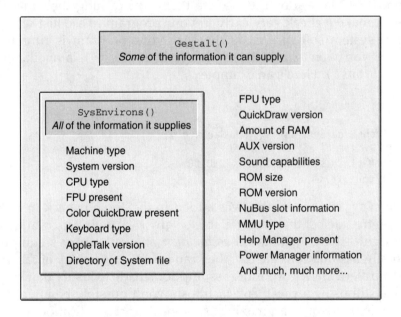

Figure 9.1 The advantages of `Gestalt()`.

Now that you know about the existence of the amazing `Gestalt()` function, why would you ever bother with `SysEnvirons()`? Because there's a catch to Gestalt(); it's not available on Macs running an older version of the system software. If it is available, you'll want to use it; if not, you'll have to use the older SysEnvirons() routine.

Checking for the availability of Gestalt()

The Gestalt() function is available on Macs running System 6.0.4 and later, including any version of System 7. Since System 6.0.4 was released in 1989, most Mac owners have a version at least that new on their Macs. That means there's a very good chance that any Mac your application runs on will support Gestalt(). But you, of course, can't make that assumption.

Life is hard enough for those unfortunate enough to still be working on pre-1989 Macs—don't aggravate them by crashing their machines! Instead, make a check very early in your program to see just what version of system software is on the Mac your program is running on. Because you won't immediately know if Gestalt() is available, use SysEnvirons(). Here's an example:

```
SysEnvRec   theMacInfo;

SysEnvirons( curSysEnvVers, &theMacInfo );

if ( theMacInfo.systemVersion < 0x0700 )
   ExitToShell();
```

The SysEnvirons() routine was added to the Toolbox back in 1986, so it's a pretty safe bet that it's available on any Mac your program will see. Your right—that's making an *assumption* about the user's equipment. Normally, assumptions are *bad*; they can lead to the display of the dreaded bomb alert. Here's one more assumption, made to justify that last one: anyone still using a pre-1986 Macintosh won't possibly be interested in paying money for the amazing, state-of-the-art application you'll be writing anyway!

Now, back to work. When Apple released System 7, a host of new features were added to the system software. Many programs support some of these features and aren't designed to run on Macs that use a version of System 6. With Copland (System 8) on the horizon (or possibly available as you read this), you might consider following suit.

N O T E If you're using Metrowerks CodeWarrior to compile your code, then you're using a program that requires System 7. Page through any Mac mail-order catalog and you'll find several others. Adobe Photoshop, Microsoft Office, and Symantec Norton Utilities are a few examples of applications that now require System 7.

If you want to require users to have a version of System 7 or later as their operating system, check to see if the systemVersion field of the SysEnvRec has a value of at least 0x0700. After making the call to SysEnviron() your program can examine any of the members of the SysEnvRec structure. Typically, your application will check the systemVersion member. This hexadecimal value holds the system version in its last three digits. For example, a value of 0x0607 represents System 6.0.7, a value of 0x0701 represents System 7.0.1, and a value of 0x0752 represents system software version 7.5.2.

You'll be using Gestalt() to check for some Mac features, so you want to establish that the Mac contains a System with the Gestalt() function. If it doesn't, use a call to the Toolbox function ExitToShell() to terminate your program.

It's a good idea to exit a program in a more graceful manner than shown in the preceding example. Before you ever abnormally terminate a program, you will want to give the user some information as to why he or she is being whisked back to the Finder. This information can come in the form of an alert that displays an descriptive message. Here the previous example has been rewritten to include the display such an alert. This chapter's example program does the same. Figure 9.2 shows a typical alert that could be used here.

```
#define      rSysIncompatibleAlert      128

SysEnvRec   theMacInfo;

SysEnvirons( curSysEnvVers, &theMacInfo );

if ( theMacInfo.systemVersion < 0x0700 )
```

```
{
    StopAlert( rSysIncompatibleAlert, nil );
    ExitToShell();
}
```

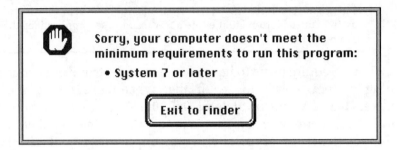

Figure 9.2 Letting the user know what needs to be done in order
to run your program.

Once you've made it past this check, you know that your application is
running on a Macintosh that supports Gestalt(). That means that you
can freely use Gestalt() anywhere in your program.

Determining Machine Features Using Gestalt()

To use Gestalt(), you pass it a *selector code* that tells Gestalt() what hardware or software feature you want to examine. In exchange for the selector
code, Gestalt() fills the second parameter, the *response parameter*, with
information pertinent to the request. The response parameter then holds the
answer to the question you posed in the selector code. Here's an example
that checks for the version of QuickDraw present on the user's Mac:

```
OSErr   theError;
long    theResponse;

theError = Gestalt( gestaltQuickdrawVersion, &theResponse );
```

In this example, gestaltQuickdrawVersion is the Apple-defined selector code, and theResponse is the response parameter. This call asks
Gestalt() to return the version of QuickDraw present on the machine

the program is currently executing on. After the call to Gestalt() is complete, the response will have one of the following values:

```
gestaltOriginalQD
gestalt8BitQD
gestalt32BitQD
gestalt32BitQD11
gestalt32BitQD12
gestalt32BitQD13
```

You can use the above as constants because your compiler recognizes them from their definitions in the Gestalt.h universal header file. Here are the actual values from part of that enum:

```
gestaltOriginalQD    = 0x000,    // original 1-bit QD
gestalt8BitQD        = 0x100,    // 8-bit color QD
gestalt32BitQD       = 0x200,    // 32-bit color QD
gestalt32BitQD11     = 0x210,    // 32-bit color QDv1.1
gestalt32BitQD12     = 0x220,    // 32-bit color QDv1.2
gestalt32BitQD13     = 0x230,    // 32-bit color QDv1.3
```

The constant gestaltQuickdrawVersion, along with numerous other selector codes, is also defined in the Gestalt.h header file. Appendix C shows many of the selector codes and responses included in this file.

Gestalt() gives you verification that it was able to return the requested information in the form of a *result code* of type OSErr. After a call to Gestalt(), always compare the result code to the Apple-defined constant noErr. Apple defines noErr to have a value of zero.

If Gestalt() returns a result code of 0, the call was successful. If it's any other value, you should not base the code that follows on the response that Gestalt() returned. The following example shows a call to Gestalt() and a test of the returned result code:

```
OSErr   theError;
long    theResponse;

theError = Gestalt( gestaltQuickdrawVersion, &theResponse );

if ( theError == noErr )
{
   if ( theResponse == gestaltOriginalQD )
```

```
      DrawString("\pYou have the original version of QuickDraw.");
}
else
    DrawString("\pGestalt error: QuickDraw version unknown.");
```

Figure 9.3 sums up what goes on in a typical call to Gestalt().

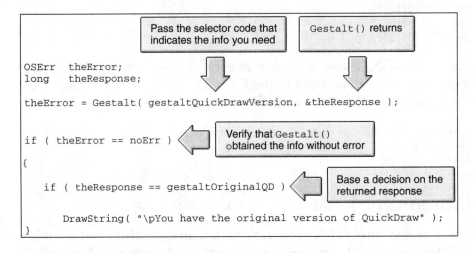

Figure 9.3 Using Gestalt().

Now that you know just how to use Gestalt(), what can you use it for? The following sections cover a few of the Macintosh features you can determine with Gestalt(). Appendix C covers several more.

Determining the QuickDraw Version

The drawing routines that make up QuickDraw have been improved and increased over the years. The original version did not support color; subsequent versions do.

If you're working with color, the Mac your program runs on must have a version of QuickDraw that supports color. Use the selector gestaltQuickdrawVersion to determine the version of QuickDraw that is present on the user's Mac.

Selector code:

```
gestaltQuickdrawVersion        // QuickDraw version
```

Response parameters:

```
gestaltOriginalQD              // original 1-bit QD
gestalt8BitQD                  // 8-bit color QD
gestalt32BitQD                 // 32-bit color QD
gestalt32BitQD11               // 32-bit color QD v1.1
gestalt32BitQD12               // 32-bit color QD v1.2
gestalt32BitQD13               // 32-bit color QD v1.3
```

Example:

```
Boolean   usersMacHasColor = false;
OSErr     theError;
long      theResponse;

theError = Gestalt( gestaltQuickdrawVersion, &theResponse );

if ( theError == noErr )
{
    if ( theResponse == gestaltOriginalQD )
        usersMacHasColor = false;
    else
        usersMacHasColor = true;
}
else
    DrawString( "\pGestalt error: QuickDraw version unknown" );
```

NOTE Notice that the preceding snippet initializes the `Boolean` value. If for some odd reason the call to `Gestalt()` fails, then `usersMacHasColor` will have the "safer" of the two values—false. That way the program won't attempt to work with color on what may not be a color system.

Determining the CPU Type

All Macintoshes use a CPU (central processing unit) from either the Motorola 680x0 family or the PowerPC family. You can determine which family the user's processor is from by passing the `gestaltSysArchitecture` selector code to `Gestalt()`.

Selector code:

```
gestaltSysArchitecture      // system architecture
```

Response parameters:

```
gestalt68k                    // Motorola MC68k architecture
gestaltPowerPC                // IBM PowerPC architecture
```

Example:

```
Boolean   usersMacIsPowerMac = false;
OSErr     theError;
long      theResponse;

theError = Gestalt( gestaltSysArchitecture, &theResponse );

if ( theError == noErr )
{
   if ( theResponse == gestaltPowerPC )
      usersMacIsPowerMac = true;
   else
      usersMacIsPowerMac = false;
}
else
   DrawString( "\pGestalt error: CPU family unknown" );
```

Gestalt() allows you not only to determine the family the user's processor belongs to, but to determine the specific type of chip within a family. To get this more detailed information, use the gestaltNativeCPUtype selector code.

Selector code:

```
gestaltNativeCPUtype          // central processor type
```

Response parameters:

```
gestaltCPU68000               // Motorola 68000
gestaltCPU68010               // Motorola 68000
gestaltCPU68020               // Motorola 68000
gestaltCPU68030               // Motorola 68000
gestaltCPU68040               // Motorola 68000
gestaltCPU601                 // IBM PowerPC 601
gestaltCPU603                 // IBM PowerPC 603
gestaltCPU604                 // IBM PowerPC 604
```

Example:

```
OSErr   theError;
long    theResponse;

theError = Gestalt( gestaltNativeCPUtype, &theResponse );

if ( theError == noErr )
{
    if ( theResponse == gestaltCPU68000 )
        DrawString( "\pSorry, that feature requires a faster Mac" );
}
else
    DrawString( "\pGestalt error: CPU type unknown" );
```

Determining the Amount of Physical RAM

In the last few years, RAM prices have dropped considerably. Consequently, many Macs have plenty of RAM. You may be fortunate enough to have a Mac loaded with RAM, but compatibility concerns dictate that you keep in mind the less fortunate! Millions of Macs with 4 MB of RAM were sold, and many are still in daily use. Much of that 4 MB is taken up by the Mac OS, leaving precious little left over for applications.

If you want to check for the amount of RAM a machine has, use the gestaltPhysicalRAMSize selector in a call to Gestalt(). The response will be the number of bytes of physical RAM. It will be up to your program to convert that value to megabytes, if that value is necessary.

Selector code:

```
gestaltPhysicalRAMSize        // physical RAM size
```

Response parameters:

```
// long value that holds the number of bytes of RAM
```

Example:

```
#define     kBytesInOneKB       1024L

long    theNumKB = -99;
```

```
long    theNumMB = -99;
OSErr   theError;
long    theResponse;

theError = Gestalt( gestaltPhysicalRAMSize, &theResponse );

if ( theError == noErr )
{
    theNumKB = theResponse / kBytesInOneKB;
    theNumMB = theResponse / ( kBytesInOneKB * kBytesInOneKB );
}
else
    DrawString( "\pGestalt error: Amount of RAM unknown" );
```

NOTE Because the preceding snippet initializes theNumKB and theNumMB to "impossible" RAM amounts, these two variables will have predictable values should the call to Gestalt() fail. Later in the program—when either of these variables is used—a check can be made to verify that they hold valid, positive values.

NOTE If you're compiling your code on a 68K-based Mac, include the above snippet in a test program. Change the value of kBytesInOneKB, which is defined to be 1024L, to 1024—then compile the test code. Depending on what environment you're using, either your compiler responded by posting a compile-time error message or the source compiled and started to run, but quit when the code that uses kBytesInOneKB was executed. This occurs because the #define directive doesn't explicitly state that kBytesInOneKB should be interpreted as a long value. Later in the snippet kBytesInOneKB is multiplied by itself. The result, which is a value greater than one million, needs to be stored in a long. Unless you explicitly tell the compiler the byte size of kBytesInOneKB, it won't know how many bytes to use to store the multiplication result. When you create a #define, and you want to force your compiler to recognize the defined value as a long, add an uppercase L character to the value.

Determining the Macintosh Machine Type

You can determine the type of Macintosh, or machine, your application is running on by passing the gestaltMachineType selector to Gestalt(). But be aware that two Macs of the same type may be running different systems, have different amounts of memory, or differ in other ways. Because they may differ in many respects, you should not use the machine type to assume certain features do or don't exist on the user's computer.

Selector code:

```
gestaltMachineType                        // machine type
```

Response parameters:

```
gestaltClassic
gestaltMacXL
gestaltMac512KE
gestaltMacPlus
gestaltMacSE
gestaltMacII
gestaltMacIIx
gestaltMacIIcx
gestaltMacSE030
gestaltPortable
gestaltMacIIci
gestaltMacIIfx
gestaltMacClassic
gestaltMacIIsi
gestaltMacLC
gestaltQuadra900
gestaltPowerBook170
gestaltQuadra700
gestaltClassicII
gestaltPowerBook100
gestaltPowerBook140
gestaltQuadra950
gestaltMacLCIII
gestaltPerforma450
gestaltPowerBookDuo210
gestaltMacCentris650
gestaltPowerBookDuo230
gestaltPowerBook180
gestaltPowerBook160
gestaltMacQuadra800
gestaltMacQuadra650
gestaltMacLCII
gestaltPowerBookDuo250
gestaltAWS9150_80
gestaltPowerMac8100_110
gestaltAWS8150_110
```

```
gestaltMacIIvi
gestaltMacIIvm
gestaltPerforma600
gestaltPowerMac7100_80
gestaltMacIIvx
gestaltMacColorClassic
gestaltPerforma250
gestaltPowerBook165c
gestaltMacCentris610
gestaltMacQuadra610
gestaltPowerBook145
gestaltPowerMac8100_100
gestaltMacLC520
gestaltAWS9150_120
gestaltMacCentris660AV
gestaltPerforma46x
gestaltPowerMac8100_80
gestaltAWS8150_80
gestaltPowerBook180c
gestaltPowerMac6100_60
gestaltAWS6150_60
gestaltPowerBookDuo270c
gestaltMacQuadra840AV
gestaltPerforma550
gestaltPowerBook165
gestaltMacTV
gestaltMacLC475
gestaltPerforma47x
gestaltMacLC575
gestaltMacQuadra605
gestaltQuadra630
gestaltPowerMac6100_66
gestaltAWS6150_66g
gestaltPowerBookDuo280
gestaltPowerBookDuo280c
gestaltPowerMac7100_66
gestaltPowerBook150
```

Example:

```
OSErr   theError;
long    theResponse;

theError = Gestalt( gestaltMachineType, &theResponse );
```

```
if ( theError == noErr )
{
   switch ( theResponse )
   {
      case gestaltPowerMac6100_60:
      case gestaltPowerMac7100_66:
      case gestaltPowerMac8100_80:
         DrawString( "\pYou have one of the original Power Macs!" );
         break;
   }
}
else
   DrawString( "\pGestalt error: Mac model type unknown" );
```

Determining the Operating System Version

The operating system version number can be determined by using the gestaltSystemVersion selector. Like the machine type, knowledge of the operating system version may not lend enough information to make programming decisions regarding the features of a particular Macintosh model.

The response that Gestalt() returns is a hexadecimal representation of the system version. For example, if the system is version 6.0.4, the parameter theResponse will have a value of 0x0604. If the system version is 7.1.0, theResponse will have a value of 0x0710.

Selector code:

```
gestaltSystemVersion                    // operating system version
```

Response parameters:

```
// hexadecimal value that holds the version number of the OS
```

Example:

```
OSErr  theError;
long   theResponse;

theError = Gestalt( gestaltSystemVersion, &theResponse );

if ( theError == noErr )
```

```
{
    if ( theResponse < 0x0701 )
    {
        DrawString( "\pThis program requires System 7.0.1 or later" );
        ExitToShell();
    }
}
else
    DrawString( "\pGestalt error: system version unknown" );
```

CHECKING FOR TRAPS

The machine instructions for routines that you write exist, of course, within your compiled source code. The machine instructions for Toolbox routines, such as `DrawString()`, exist outside your compiled source code. This Toolbox machine code is housed in ROM, or occasionally, in RAM. A Toolbox routine is also called a *trap*. The technique for placing shared system code outside your compiled application is sometimes called *dynamic linking* or *shared libraries*. This is different from the ANSI library routines such as `strcpy()` that are compiled and linked together with your application code so that every application has its own copy of the compiled code.

NOTE

If you are a Windows programmer, the Toolbox routines are similar to routines found in Windows DLLs (Dynamic Link Libraries).

Toolbox Routines are Traps

A Toolbox routine is usually located in ROM, though the System may on occasion load a routine in RAM. Where, exactly, is any particular routine located in memory? The memory location of the routine is determined from the routine's *trap number*. Each trap (each Toolbox routine) has a unique trap number. The trap number is used by the system when the code that makes up a Toolbox routine needs to be executed. If your application makes a call to DrawString(), the execution of your application will be interrupted while the processor makes use of the DrawString() trap number to locate the code for the DrawString() routine.

N O T E

Chapter 1 stated that Toolbox routines are in ROM. Why renege here in Chapter 9 by saying that some may be in RAM? For any given Macintosh, the contents of ROM are fixed. A new and improved ROM with additional routines may be included with the newer Macs. Can an older, existing model, with its older ROM, ever get these newer routines? Yes, when Apple provides a new system software. The new system software may contain patches—code that loads routines from the System file into RAM. Such a routine can be found in the ROM of a newer Mac and, via the patch, be placed in the RAM of an older Mac.

Trap *numbers* are stored in a *dispatch table* in RAM. Each trap number serves as an index to an entry in the dispatch table. Each entry is an address. An address to? Yes, finally—an address to the code that makes up a trap, or Toolbox routine.

Figure 9.4 shows how a call to a hypothetical Toolbox routine called RoutineB() results in the system first going to a trap number in RAM—Trap 2 in this simplified example. The address associated with Trap 2 is the address of the executable code for RoutineB()—address 0x00400500. This address is the memory address of RoutineB(). From there, the processor goes to address 0x00400500 to find and execute the code for the function RoutineB(). Whether this address is a RAM or ROM address is unimportant to you, the programmer.

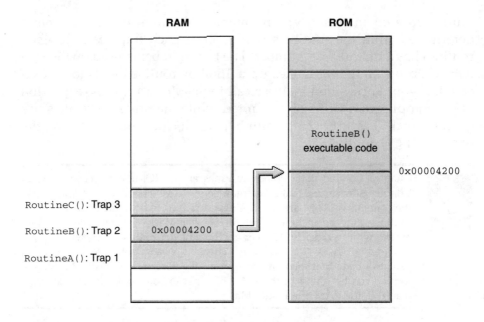

Figure 9.4 A trap number leads to a Toolbox routine.

Figure 9.5 summarizes what's been covered up to this point. This figure shows what happens when your application makes a call to the Toolbox routine `DrawString()`.

As mentioned, while the executable code for most of the Toolbox routines exists in ROM, some does exist in RAM—it gets loaded there from the System file each time your Mac boots up.

NOTE

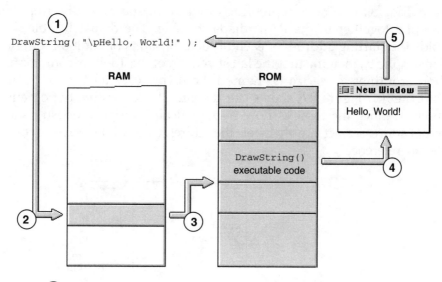

① A call to `DrawString()`.

② Using the `DrawString()` trap number, check in RAM to find the address

③ Using the address from RAM, find the `DrawString()` code in ROM.

④ Execute the code that makes up the `DrawString()` function.

⑤ After execution of `DrawString()` is complete, return to the application code.

Figure 9.5 Sequence of events in a call to `DrawString()`.

Each Toolbox routine is represented by a trap, and all of the traps are grouped together in the RAM dispatch table. The dispatch table thus holds the starting address of each of the thousands of Toolbox routines. For simplicity, imagine that the latest version of the Toolbox contains just three routines generically named RoutineA(), RoutineB(), and RoutineC(). Figure 9.6 shows the dispatch table for this hypothetical Toolbox. Since the topic is now hypothetical, the figure doesn't show actual addresses—it simply labels the addresses as address1, address2, etc. for reference.

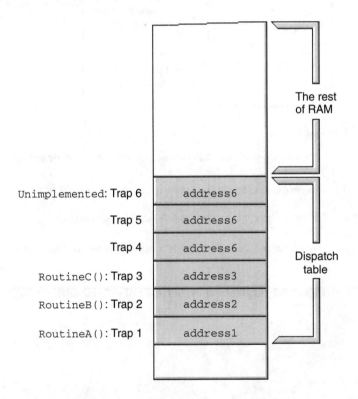

Figure 9.6 A hypothetical dispatch table in RAM.

Figure 9.6 serves as a reminder that a trap represents a Toolbox routine, and has both a trap number and an address associated with it. Notice further that there are traps that don't represent any function; in this hypothetical example those traps are Trap 4 and Trap 5. Notice further that these two empty traps both have the same address—address6. This is the same address as the dispatch table entry labeled Unimplemented. Take careful note of this point; it will serve as the basis for determining whether a Toolbox routine exists in the Toolbox of the computer your application is running on.

The unimplemented trap exists not only in the hypothetical Macintosh—it exists in every real Macintosh computer as well. And Apple guarantees that it will *never* change its trap number and will *never* use it to house the address of a Toolbox routine. You'll see the relevance of this just ahead.

A dispatch table is not full. As you saw in Figure 9.6, it has empty entries. As Apple releases new versions of the system software, some of these previously empty entries will contain valid addresses that direct the processor to the code of new Toolbox routines. Figure 9.7 illustrates this.

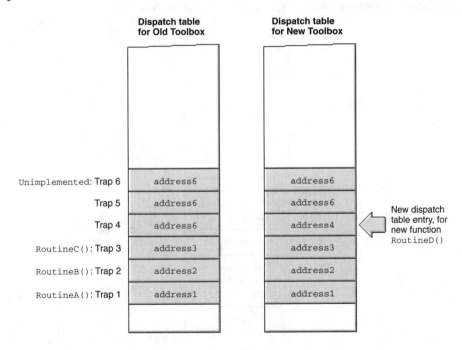

Figure 9.7 The dispatch table for an old and a new Toolbox.

In Figure 9.7, the new dispatch table and the old dispatch table differ by just one entry. For the new Toolbox, Trap 4 now holds the address of a new Toolbox routine, RoutineD().

Now, after that very lengthy introduction to traps, it's time to cover the topic that is really of interest to you. Namely, if different Macs contain different versions of the Toolbox, how can you be sure that a Toolbox call you'd like to include in your source code is present on the Macintosh that will be running your application?

Why all the fuss about traps and their availability? Quite simply, if you attempt to make a call to a nonpresent Toolbox routine, your application will crash.

N O T E

The answer to the preceding question lies in the fact that dispatch table entries that are empty all contain the identical address: the one found in the unimplemented trap. Figure 9.8 illustrates this.

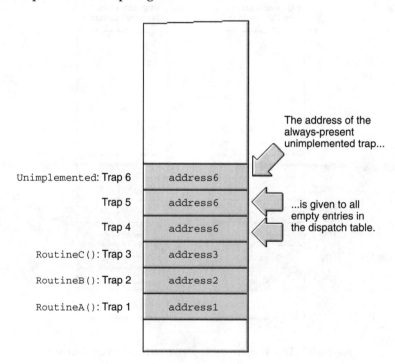

Figure 9.8 Addresses in empty entries of the dispatch table.

To determine if a Toolbox routine is present, you compare its address to the address of the unimplemented trap. In doing so, you'll rely on the trap numbers to supply your program with the addresses. Remember, empty dispatch table entries have been assigned the same address as that placed in the unimplemented trap. That means that if your comparison results in two identical addresses, the routine is *not* present in the version of the Toolbox you are checking. Figure 9.9 illustrates this, again using the hypothetical Toolbox.

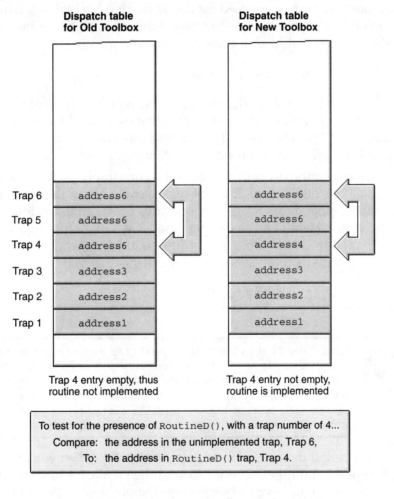

Figure 9.9 Testing for routine Toolbox implementation.

Now that you know the theory behind checking for implemented Toolbox routines, it's time to move on to the real thing: the code to include in your application to perform this check.

Determining If a Toolbox routine is Implemented

In the previous section, you saw that each Toolbox routine has a trap number by which the code for the routine is accessed. In that section generic names and numbers were used for the traps. Here's a look at a real C definition of a real trap number—the trap number for GetNewCWindow(), the Toolbox routine that loads a color window into memory:

```
#define     _GetNewCWindow    0xAA46
```

The Traps.h universal header file included with the Symantec IDE and the Metrowerks IDE takes care of definitions such as the above. You can include _GetNewCWindow and other traps in your program, and your IDE will compile your source code without complaint.

To refer to a trap in your source code, you simply preface the routine name with an underscore; it is not necessary to know the trap number. The trap number exists for the processor to use as an index into the dispatch table. Here's an example that uses the Toolbox function NGetTrapAddress() to get the memory address of the GetNewCWindow() code, as found in the dispatch table:

```
UniversalProcPtr  theCWindTrapAddr;
theCWindTrapAddr = NGetTrapAddress( _GetNewCWindow, ToolTrap );
```

NOTE In pre-PowerPC days NGetTrapAddress() was defined such that it returned a long value. The four bytes of a long were perfect for holding the 4-byte address of a Toolbox routine's code. As shown in the above snippet, newer versions of Apple's Traps.h universal header file define the return value of NGetTrapAddress() as type UniversalProcPtr. Whether you're compiling with a 68K compiler or PowerPC compiler, the above code will work.

The preceding code by itself is not very useful. But when you also get the address of the unimplemented trap, and then make a comparison of the two addresses, you have the solution to the problem of determining if a routine is present in the Toolbox. Below is a snippet that can be used to check to see if the GetNewCWindow() function is in the Toolbox of the user's machine:

```
UniversalProcPtr   theCWindTrapAddr;
UniversalProcPtr   theUnimplementedAddr;

theCWindTrapAddr = NGetTrapAddress( _GetNewCWindow, ToolTrap );
theUnimplementedAddr = NGetTrapAddress( _Unimplemented, ToolTrap );

if ( theCWindTrapAddr == theUnimplementedAddr )
{
    // the GetNewCWindow() function is not available
}
else
{
    // the GetNewCWindow() function is available
}
```

The second parameter in the call to NGetTrapAddress()—ToolTrap—may have caught your eye. There is one final point to make about traps. There are actually two separate dispatch tables in RAM. One holds the traps for Operating System routines, while the other holds the traps for Toolbox routines. In general, Operating System routines are functions that perform low-level tasks. An example of an Operating System routine is Eject(), which, not surprisingly, ejects a disk from the disk drive. Examples of Toolbox routines are MoveWindow(), which moves a window, and the numerous drawing routines, such as FrameRect() and PaintOval().

To allow you to distinguish between the Operating System traps and the Toolbox traps, Apple has created the Macintosh C enumerated type TrapType. There are two members to this type: OSTrap and ToolTrap.

In the previous code fragment, how would you know that GetNewCWindow() was a Toolbox trap and not an Operating System trap? One method is to look up the routine name in Apple's Inside Macintosh series of books. All trap numbers begin with $A. If the next digit in the trap number is between 0 and 7, then the trap is in the OS dispatch table and is of the OSTrap type. If the digit is instead between 8 and F, then the trap is in the Toolbox dispatch table and is a ToolTrap type. You know that GetNewCWindow() is a ToolTrap type because the digit following the $A (it too just happens to be an A) falls in the range of 8 and F. Figure 9.10 shows a listing of a few Toolbox trap numbers.

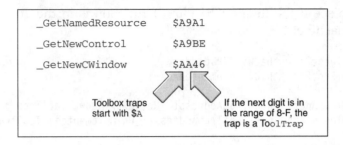

Figure 9.10 Determining the type of trap.

If you don't have a reference book handy, there is a second method to determine a trap's type. It's done by writing a couple of routines of your own, and it's a little tricky. By now you probably already know more about traps than you ever hoped you would. For that reason, those application-defined functions have been thrown into an appendix. If you're brave, or perhaps masochistic, refer to Appendix B.

So that you can fully understand what was transpiring, the previous snippet was intentionally made a little wordy. Now that you are a trap master, that code can be tightened up a little:

```
Boolean   colorWindAvail;

colorWindAvail = ( NGetTrapAddress( _GetNewCWindow, ToolTrap )
                   != ( NGetTrapAddress( _Unimplemented, ToolTrap ) );

if ( colorWindAvail == true )
{
    // call GetNewCWindow() to open a color window
}
else
{
    // the GetNewWindow() to open a regular window
}
```

A general approach is to make your Boolean variable global and perform the trap check near the start of your code. Then you can use the Boolean every time you have to check for the presence of this one Toolbox routine.

MONITOR-AWARE

The original Ford Model T car came in a choice of colors: black, or black. Like the car, the original Macintosh model came with your choice of monitor: built-in 9-inch diagonal black and white or . . . you get the point. No choice of size, no choice of color display. Things have changed in ten years, and so have the tricks you'll need to use to make sure the programs you write are compatible with both color and monochrome monitors, with monitors of different sizes, and with Mac systems with more than one monitor. The topic of multiple monitors is covered first.

Dealing with Multiple Monitors

Though most users have just a single monitor, don't assume this is so. If you don't allow the user to drag windows across monitors, or a window comes up centered between two monitors, the user will quickly become frustrated with your program.

Setting the Window Drag Region

In Chapter 4 the boundaries of the screen were used to set the boundaries for dragging a window. That method works just fine for a system that has a single monitor. If you don't want to make that assumption (and you shouldn't), you'll need to use a reference other than the screen boundaries.

For a system with multiple monitors, it is important that you properly set the boundaries for window dragging. The size of this drag boundary rectangle is dependent on the size of the monitor. More correctly, it is dependent on the area that makes up the desktop. Because the desktop is usually gray, this area is known as the gray region. Formally, it consists of a region that is the union of any active screen devices (monitors) minus the menu bar. Figure 9.11 shows the gray region for a dual-monitor system that is made up of a Mac with a built-in monitor and an additional 15" display.

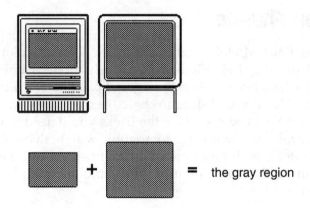

Figure 9.11 The gray region of a dual-monitor system.

If you want to give the user the ability to drag windows created by your application across monitors, you need to set up your drag boundary rectangle so that it encompasses the entire gray region. Luckily, a routine you call during initialization does much of the work for you. When your initialization routine calls InitWindows() it calculates this region and saves it to a global rgnHandle variable called GrayRgn. To get the value of this variable, call the Toolbox routine LMGetGrayRgn(), as shown here:

```
RgnHandle  theGrayRegion;
theGrayRegion = LMGetGrayRgn();
```

The following application-defined function is a replacement for the SetWindowDragBoundaries() routine created in Chapter 4. This new version creates a rectangle independent of the number of monitors running—a drag rectangle set to the size of the gray region. The rest of the routine is the same as the old version. Recall that the constant kDragEdge is used to inset the drag rectangle a few pixels so that the drag area is not quite as big as the gray region, thus preventing the user from dragging windows off the screen. Here's the new routine:

```
#define    kDragEdge    10

Rect   gDragRect;

void   SetWindowDragBoundaries( void )
```

```
{
   RgnHandle  theGrayRegion;

   theGrayRegion = LMGetGrayRgn();

   gDragRect = (**theGrayRegion).rgnBBox;
   gDragRect.left   += kDragEdge;
   gDragRect.right  -= kDragEdge;
   gDragRect.bottom -= kDragEdge;
}
```

After getting the value of the desktop area, the region handle is derefer-enced twice in order to access the `rgnBBox` field of the `Region` data struc-ture. The `rgnBBox` member holds the boundaries of the region.

Accessing System Global Variables

Before moving on to the next monitor-related topic, this section provides a few words regarding system global variables—a topic just introduced with the new version of the application-defined function `SetWindowDragBoundaries()`.

The discussion of the gray region brought up mention of the system global variable `GrayRgn`. In the past, Mac programmers often included variables such as `GrayRgn` in their code. Because a system global variable is defined system-wide, any application can use it without first declaring it. In the preceding section, though, `GrayRgn` wasn't used directly, as in:

```
gDragRect = (**GrayRgn).rgnBBox;
```

Instead, a Toolbox function was used to obtain the value of `GrayRgn` and to then return this value to your program:

```
RgnHandle  theGrayRegion;

theGrayRegion = LMGetGrayRgn();
```

System global variables are stored in the very bottom of the system par-tition—that's why they're also called *low-memory global variables*. While programmers have included low-memory global variables in their code, Apple states that the best approach to using these variables is to do so through Toolbox *accessor functions*. Letting an accessor function find the global variable and return its value provides Apple the freedom to relocate these variables in the future—something that may or may not be necessary. If your code relies directly on a system global variable, it will "break" at a later date should that variable be moved to a different memory location.

You'll find numerous accessor functions in the LowMem.h universal header file. You've already seen one such function—LMGetGrayRgn().

Setting the Center Point for Windows

As a programmer writing an application that may run on a dual-monitor system, you should be concerned with the centering of windows and dialog boxes. If you're still excited about your introduction to the gray region, and why wouldn't you be, your first thought may be just to center windows according to the value of the global GrayRgn variable. It's a good thought, but you should reconsider.

Centering a window by the GrayRgn works fine for a single-monitor system. For a dual-monitor Mac it would place the window between the two monitors, something that the user would find less than desirable. Figure 9.12 illustrates the results of window centering using GrayRgn.

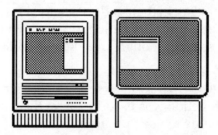

Figure 9.12 An improper window centering on a dual-monitor system.

Instead of using the entire desktop for centering, as you do for window dragging, you can use just the main screen: the screen that displays the menu bar. The window or dialog box you're going to bring to the screen and center is no doubt a result of the user choosing a menu option. So it is most likely that's where the user is focused—on the monitor with the menu bar.

If your program is designed so that it requires System 7 or later, you can use your resource editor to set window centering for a window. In ResEdit, open the WIND resource that will be used for the window that is to be centered. Then select **Auto Position** from the WIND menu. Using the pop-up menu found on the left of the dialog box that opens, mark the WIND as one that will be used to open windows that are centered on the user's screen main screen, as is being done in Figure 9.13.

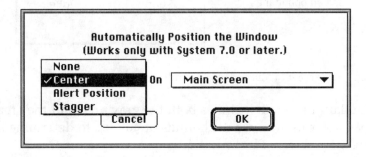

Figure 9.13 Using ResEdit to mark a WIND resource for automatic centering.

As stated in the ResEdit Auto Position window, marking the WIND resource for centering only works for programs running under System 7 or later. If you'll be allowing users with System 6 to run your program, you can't rely on the ResEdit trick. Instead, you'll have to perform window centering from within your application's source code.

To center the window, you need to get the gray area of that one monitor. You can accomplish this with a call to the Toolbox routine GetMainDevice().

A monitor is a graphic display device. When the Mac starts up it checks its expansion slots for display devices. The Mac stores the information it obtains for a device in a device structure—a GDevice data structure to be exact. It then stores these structures in a device list. You'll learn more about devices later in this chapter when color issues are discussed. For now, your only interest will be in getting a handle to the main display device; that is, the device that displays the menu bar. That's exactly what GetMainDevice() does.

One of the members of a GDevice structure is gdRect. This rectangle is the boundary rectangle of the device's display. Figure 9.14 shows the relationship between GDHandle and GDevice. For simplicity, just a couple of the members of the GDevice structure are shown.

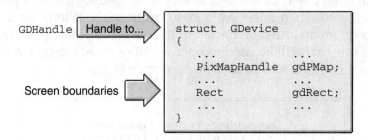

Figure 9.14 GDHandle is a handle to a GDevice structure.

The boundary rectangle includes both the gray area and the area of the menu bar. You can thus use the bounds of gdRect to determine the center of the main screen. Here's how:

```
Point    gScreenCenter;

void  DetermineScreenCenter( void )
{
    short       theMBarHeight;
    GDHandle    theMainDevice;
    Rect        theBoundsRect;

    theMBarHeight = LMGetMBarHeight();
    theMainDevice = LMGetMainDevice();

    theBoundsRect = (**theMainDevice).gdRect;

    gScreenCenter.h = ( theBoundsRect.right /2 );
    gScreenCenter.v = ( theBoundsRect.bottom/2 ) + ( theMBarHeight/2 );
}
```

The DetermineScreenCenter() routine begins by calling the accessor function LMGetMBarHeight() to determine the height of the menu bar—that value will need to get factored into calculation of the screen's center. Next, another accessor function is called. The Toolbox routine LMGetMainDevice() returns a handle to the display device holding the main screen. Dereference the handle so that you can look at this screen's boundary rectangle, gdRect. Make the Point variable that holds the center point, gScreenCenter, global so that you can use it throughout your program for centering any windows, dialog boxes, or alerts.

Data structures and routines that Apple introduced to support the use of graphics devices are a part of Color QuickDraw. If the user doesn't have Color QuickDraw, your program can't use them.

N O T E

A second method for centering a window on the main screen is to use the screenBits field of the global variable qd. The screenBits field is a structure that represents a bitmap of the main screen. The bounds member is a Rect that defines the boundaries of the screen of the main display. Here, in its entirety, is a means to determine the center of the main screen without using graphics device structures:

```
short   theMBarHeight;

theMBarHeight = LMGetMBarHeight();

gScreenCenter.h = qd.screenBits.bounds.right/2;
gScreenCenter.v = ( qd.screenBits.bounds.bottom/2 ) +
                  ( theMBarHeight/2 );
```

Easy, huh? So why were you forced to go through the much longer explanation using the GDHandle? Because you'll need all of this information on graphics devices for the upcoming discussion about working with color. Determining the screen center from the GDHandle provides you with a sound explanation of device theory.

N O T E

Once you know the center of the screen it's simple math to center a window or dialog box. The following snippet uses a call to GetNewWindow() to demonstrate how to center a window using the gScreenCenter point.

```
#define    rDisplayWindow     128
#define    kWindowWidth       350   // obtain from ResEdit
#define    kWindowHeight      200   // obtain from ResEdit

Point  gScreenCenter;
```

```
void  OpenAndCenterWindow( void )
{
    WindowPtr   theWindow;
    short       theTop;
    short       theLeft;

    theWindow = GetNewWindow( rDisplayWindow, OL, (WindowPtr)-1L );

    if ( theWindow == nil )
        ExitToShell();

    theLeft = gScreenCenter.h - ( kWindowWidth /2 );
    theTop  = gScreenCenter.v - ( kWindowHeight/2 );

    MoveWindow( theWindow, theLeft, theTop, true );

    ShowWindow( theWindow );
}
```

After `GetNewWindow()` loads a window into memory, use the `Point` variable `gScreenCenter` to establish the top left corner of the window. You set the width and height of the window when you create the `WIND` resource in ResEdit. Use `MoveWindow()` to move the window to the center of the screen.

If the `WIND` resource that defines this window made the window invisible, then the centering of the window took place behind the scenes—as desired. Now it's time to display it with a call to `ShowWindow()`.

Dealing with Different Sized Monitors

In the previous section, you saw how to use the accessor function `LMGetGrayRgn()` to determine the boundaries of the desktop for a system that has more than one monitor. You then learned how to make a call to another accessor function—`LMGetMainDevice()`—to help determine the center of the screen that holds the menu bar. Both of these techniques, which are used to avoid problems should multiple monitors be present, work for a single monitor system regardless of the screen size of the monitor.

You should use the last section's `SetWindowDragBoundaries()` routine in all of your applications; it works for single- or dual-monitor systems, regardless of the size of the monitor or monitors. The same is true for the `DetermineScreenCenter()` routine and the window centering technique used in the `OpenAndCenterWindow()` example.

Color Aware

The way in which your program behaves may be dependent on the monitor on which it is displayed. To make your program truly compatible with the variety of Macintosh systems on the market, you'll want it to be able to display color on a color Macintosh while still being able to run on a monochrome or grayscale system.

Color Representation

A monochrome monitor represents a single pixel on the screen using a single bit of memory. A bit has two possible values, 0 and 1, so any pixel on the screen of a monochrome monitor can have two possible values: white or black.

To allow a pixel to be capable of displaying more than two colors, that pixel must be represented by more than a single bit of memory. If 2 bits are used per pixel, then a pixel can take on any one of four colors. Four bits per pixel yields 16 colors, while 8 bits gives 256 colors. Using 8 bits (a byte) of memory per pixel is common. After 8 bits comes 16-bit and 24-bit color representation. Systems that use 16-bit color are becoming more common, but 24-bit color is still usually reserved for high-end, expensive systems.

The number of bits that represent a single pixel is the monitor's *pixel depth*, or pixel value. Determining a monitor's pixel depth will be the primary focus of this section.

Knowing the pixel depth of the monitor that is displaying your program is important because your program may make decisions based on the level of color the monitor can display. Here's a typical decision your program might make:

```
if machine has color, and monitor is set to display color
    draw color text
```

```
otherwise
    draw black and white text
```

Another example is the displaying of pictures. If your program is to display a picture in a window, you might want to have two or three separate ones to pick from. The picture the program displays will depend on the amount of color the user's Macintosh can display. When a black and white Mac shows a color picture, the computer translates the colors to black and white. A monochrome Mac displays similar shades of a dark color as black. If these colors are adjacent, the areas that should be separate and distinct will blend into one. Figure 9.15 shows the display of the same picture on a 16-color, four-color, and monochrome monitor. Note that the monochrome monitor can't make the distinction between shades and produces an undesirable display of the picture.

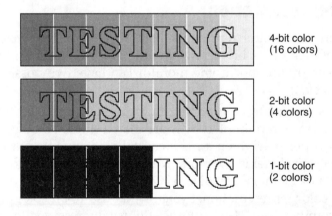

Figure 9.15 The same picture viewed at 4-, 2-, and 1-bit color.

Getting the Pixel Depth of a Monitor

In this chapter's discussion of how to determine the center of a monitor, the concepts of graphics devices and the device list arose. A monitor is a graphics device. More technically, a video card or built-in video interface is a graphics device. The RAM memory that holds the value of each display pixel is located on the video card, not the RAM in the Macintosh. Information about a graphics device is stored in a GDevice structure, which is in turn placed in a device list. Recall that a GDHandle is a handle to a GDevice structure.

NOTE Video devices such as a plug-in video card or a built-in video interface are actually just one of three types of graphics devices. Offscreen graphics worlds (used to store an image in memory) and printing graphics ports (used to send graphics and text to a printer) are the second and third types of graphics devices. The M&T publication *Graphics and Sound Programming Techniques for the Mac* covers offscreen graphics worlds in detail. The book *More Mac Programming Techniques*, also by M&T Books, describes printing from within Macintosh applications.

You obtain a handle to the first device in the device list by calling the Toolbox routine GetDeviceList(). Once you have the handle, pass it to an application-defined routine that determines the pixel depth of the display:

```
GDHandle    theCurrentDevice;
short       thePixelDepth;

theCurrentDevice = GetDeviceList();
thePixelDepth = GetPixelDepth( theCurrentDevice );
```

Before you look at GetPixelDepth(), a little background information is necessary. A graphics device has a pixel map that is represented by a PixMap data structure. A PixMap is a structure that holds such information as the starting address of the device's video RAM and the depth of each pixel in the map. What you're after is the pixel depth; that is, the pixelSize member of the PixMap structure.

One member of the GDevice structure, gdPMap, is a handle to the pixel map of the screen—a PixMapHandle. Once you have the handle to the screen's pixel map, look at the pixelSize member of the PixMap. This gives you the pixel depth of the display. Figure 9.16 shows the path to the pixel depth.

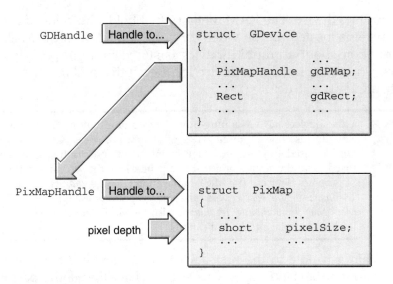

Figure 9.16 The path from `GDHandle` to `pixelSize`.

Now that you have background information on `PixMaps`, `GetPixelDepth()` should make sense to you. Here it is:

```
short  GetPixelDepth( GDHandle theDevice )
{
   PixMapHandle  screenPMapH;
   short         thePixelDepth;

   screenPMapH = (**theDevice).gdPMap;
   thePixelDepth = (**screenPMapH).pixelSize;
   return ( thePixelDepth );
}
```

`GetPixelDepth()` first takes the passed in `GDHandle` variable and dereferences it get to the `GDevice` structure. There you get `gdPMap`, a `PixMap` handle to the screen of the device being examined. Because you have a handle, not the actual pixel map itself, you have to dereference it to get to the `pixelSize` member of the `PixMap`.

Now that you have the pixel depth of a monitor, how do you use it? One use is for displaying pictures to a window. Your technique might be to store two pictures in a resource file—one designed for monochrome systems and one for color systems, as shown in Figure 9.17. Which picture gets drawn to the window is dependent on the current pixel depth of the user's monitor.

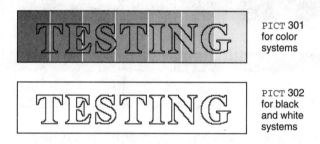

PICT 301
for color
systems

PICT 302
for black
and white
systems

Figure 9.17 Two similar `PICT` resources: one for color, one for monochrome systems.

Multiple Monitors and Pixel Depth

What about a system that has more than one monitor? If there is more than one display device, your interest will be in determining the pixel depth of each monitor and saving the minimum depth. Why? If one monitor is black and white, and a second is color, you'll want to display program features in monochrome so that they are properly viewed on both monitors. If you displayed `PICT` 301 from Figure 9.17 in a window that spanned both monochrome and color monitors, the result would be undesirable, as demonstrated in Figure 9.18.

Black and white monitor   Color monitor

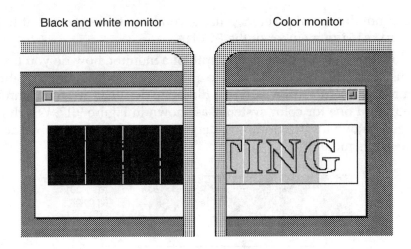

Figure 9.18 A color picture displayed across two monitors.

To avoid the problem shown in Figure 9.18, you'd display the picture designed for the monitor with the lower pixel depth, PICT 302, as shown in Figure 9.19. The same discussion holds true for a system that has two color monitors; your program should execute as if it were running on a system of the smaller depth.

Black and white monitor   Color monitor

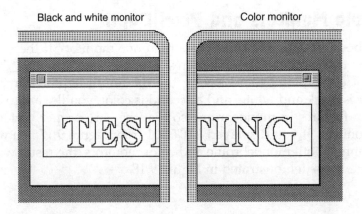

Figure 9.19 A monochrome picture displayed across two monitors.

This discussion brings up another point. The GetPixelDepth() routine determines and returns the pixel depth of a single device. Since your application may be running on a dual-monitor system, shouldn't you check each device? Good point. You'll want to check the pixel depth of each device and set a global variable to keep track of the smallest (shallowest?) depth.

Instead of directly calling GetPixelDepth(), call an application-defined routine that loops through each graphics device, checking the pixel depth of each and adjusting a global variable as it finds a device of a smaller depth.

If there is more than one device, there will be more than one item in the device list. So the device list is what you'll loop through. As before, use the Toolbox function GetDeviceList() to return the first device in the list. Use the Toolbox routine GetNextDevice() to return the following entry in the device list. When GetNextDevice() returns a value of nil, you know you've reached the end of the list.

Begin by setting the local variable theMinimumDepth to the largest value you're likely to encounter—most likely 24-bit color. Then get a handle to the first device in the device list. Enter a loop and check the pixel depth. If the pixel depth is smaller than the previous low value, reset the theMinimumDepth to this new lower value. Call GetNextDevice() in the loop to get a handle to the next device.

What happens if the system has just one monitor? At the first call to GetNextDevice() you'll get a value of nil. When you go to the top of the while loop the test will fail and the loop will end. In that case, theMinimumDepth will hold the pixel depth of the one monitor. Here's the code, along with a reprint of GetPixelDepth():

```
#define     kPixelDepthBW        1     // 1 bit = 2 colors
#define     kPixelDepth2Bit      2     // 2 bits = 4 colors
#define     kPixelDepth4Bit      4     // 4 bits = 16 colors
#define     kPixelDepth8Bit      8     // 8 bits = 256 colors
#define     kPixelDepth16Bit     16    // 16 bits=thousands of colors
#define     kPixelDepth24Bit     24    // 24 bits=millions of colors

short  GetMinPixelDepth( void )
{
    GDHandle    theCurrentDevice;
    short       thePixelDepth;
    short       theMinimumDepth;

    theMinimumDepth = kPixelDepth24Bit;
```

```
    theCurrentDevice = GetDeviceList();
    while ( theCurrentDevice != nil )
    {
        thePixelDepth = GetPixelDepth( theCurrentDevice );
        if ( thePixelDepth < theMinimumDepth )
            theMinimumDepth = thePixelDepth;
        theCurrentDevice = GetNextDevice( theCurrentDevice );
    }
    return  theMinimumDepth;
}

short  GetPixelDepth( GDHandle theDevice )
{
    PixMapHandle  screenPMapH;
    short         thePixelDepth;

    screenPMapH = (**theDevice).gdPMap;
    thePixelDepth = (**screenPMapH).pixelSize;
    return  ( thePixelDepth );
}
```

Note that the previous snippet defines several constants, one for each possible values theMinimumDepth might have. Though they aren't used here, you might use them later on in various tests. Here's an example from a program that runs best on a machine displaying 256 colors. It calls the GetMinPixelDepth() routine to set a global variable, theMinimumDepth, to the lowest pixel depth.

```
short  gMinPixelDepth;

gMinPixelDepth = GetMinPixelDepth();

switch ( gMinPixelDepth )
{
    case kPixelDepthBW:
        DrawString( "\pThis program looks better in color!" );
        break;

    case kPixelDepth2Bit:
    case kPixelDepth4Bit:
        DrawString( "\pSet your monitor(s) to 256 color if available.");
        break;

    case kPixelDepth8Bit:
```

```
         DrawString( "\pLeave monitor settings as they are now." );
         break;

      default:
         DrawString( "\pThis program displays only 256 colors." );
         break;
}
```

When to Call the Pixel Depth Routines

Your program can test for the availability of Color QuickDraw shortly after it launches. If your program requires color and the user has a mono-chrome system, exit—or post a descriptive alert and then exit:

```
#define      rNoColorAlert             128
#define      rFailedGestaltAlert       129

OSErr   theError;
long    theResponse;

theError = Gestalt( gestaltQuickdrawVersion, &theResponse );

if ( theError == noErr )
{
   if ( theResponse == gestaltOriginalQD )
   {
      Alert( rNoColorAlert, nil );
      ExitToShell();
   }
}
else
{
   Alert( rFailedGestaltAlert, nil );
   ExitToShell();

}
```

If your program prefers color, but will run on a monochrome system, you can set a global flag variable based on the value returned by the call to Gestalt():

```
Boolean   gColorQDPresent;
```

```
OSErr   theError;
long    theResponse;

theError = Gestalt( gestaltQuickdrawVersion, &theResponse );

if ( theError == noErr )
{
    if ( theResponse == gestaltOriginalQD )
        gColorQDPresent = true;
    else
        gColorQDPresent = false;
}
else
{
    Alert( rFailedGestaltAlert, nil );   // don't quit, just play it
    gColorQDPresent = false;             // safe and assume monochrome
}
```

If the user's machine has color QuickDraw, determine the lowest color level setting of the attached monitors. If Color QuickDraw isn't present you can, of course, safely assume a pixel depth of 1 bit:

```
#define    kPixelDepthBW          1    // 1 bit = black and white

short  gMinPixelDepth;

if ( gColorQDPresent == true )
    gMinPixelDepth = GetMinPixelDepth();
else
    gMinPixelDepth = kPixelDepthBW;
```

The Macintosh is a computer with flexible features; there are Macintosh models designed to please all types of users. One of the features that can be varied is the level of colors the monitor will display. As a convenience to the user, Apple lets users change the color level at any time, even during the running of your application. This can be accomplished from the Monitors Control Panel or the Control Strip (depending on the Mac the user has), or from third-party utilities such as Ambrosia Software's ColorSwitch. All three of these color-setting solutions are pictured in Figure 9.20. Your program should be aware of the fact that the user can change the color depth during the running of your program, and it should thus not assume that the level of color at the onset of execution will be the color level throughout the program's entire execution.

If the color level can be changed at any time, how can you possibly know when to check to see if the user has made a change? If the user selects the Monitor's control panel (or any other color-changing utility) while your program is running, an update event will occur. Your program, ever watchful for the occurrence of an event, will be aware of this update event. When an update event occurs, it's your cue to check if the color level changed.

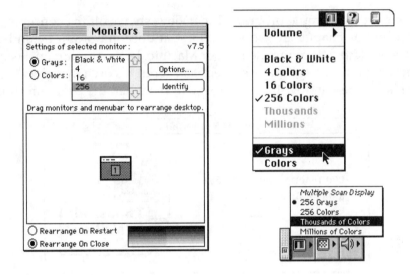

Figure 9.20 The Monitors Control Panel, ColorSwitch, and the Control Strip.

If your program makes use of color, place a call to `GetMinPixelDepth()` within the `updateEvt` case of the `switch` statement in your program's event loop. Then, every time an update event occurs, your program will recalculate `gMinPixelDepth` in case the update event was generated due to a change in the color level. Here's the affected section of the event loop:

```
switch ( theEvent.what )
{
    case mouseDown:
        HandleMouseDown();
        break;

    // other event types here
```

```
case updateEvt:
    gMinPixelDepth = GetMinPixelDepth();
    HandleUpdateEvent();
    break;
}
```

Chapter Program: InnerView

This chapter's example program, InnerView, shows off the concepts presented in this chapter in two ways. First, it does important behind-the-scenes work to determine the type of Macintosh it's running on. Second, it shows you how to give a user feedback about his own machine. Figure 9.21 shows the window that the user will see when the program runs.

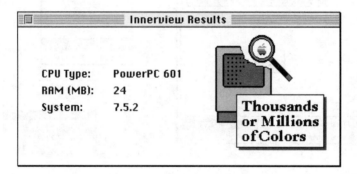

Figure 9.21 InnerView program in action.

Before jumping right into the display of information, Innerview follows this chapter's recommendation to make sure that the user's machine has what it takes to run the program. Innerview demonstrates how to use the Gestalt() function to verify that the user has System 7 or later on his or her machine—a common requirement of many of today's Macintosh programs. If the user is running a version of System 6, the alert shown in Figure 9.22 is displayed. When the alert is dismissed, Innerview quits.

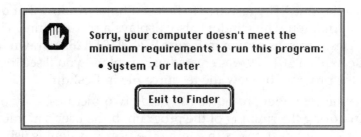

Figure 9.22 InnerView requires that the user's Mac have System 7 or later.

Program Resources: InnerView.rsrc

The InnerView program has one `ALRT` and one `DITL` resource for displaying the alert that appears should the user be running a machine that doesn't have System 7 or later. Figure 9.23 shows the `DITL`, along with a look at the four types of resources used by Innerview.

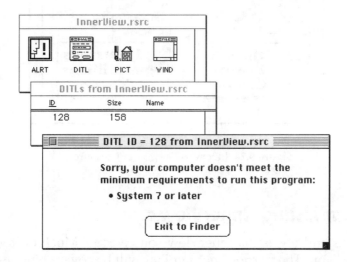

Figure 9.23 The `DITL` used in the Innerview alert.

InnerView has one WIND resource to be used for a window that displays system information. The window also displays a picture. InnerView has two PICT resources, as shown in Figure 9.24. PICT 128 is drawn in black and white, while PICT 129 was created using color—you'll see that when you run the program or view the resource file in ResEdit.

While the Innerview resource file holds two pictures, only one will be shown during the running of the program. If the user's monitor is set to display 256 or fewer colors (meaning the user's system is using 8 bits or less to keep track of any one color), InnerView will display PICT 128. If the user's monitor is set to display 16-bit or greater color, the program will put up PICT 129. Since the bits-per-color information may not be meaningful to nonprogrammers running Innerview, the picture displays the number of colors the user's machine is capable of displaying at the time the program is running.

Figure 9.24 InnerView's two PICT resources.

Program Listing: InnerView.c

Here, in its entirety, is the InnerView source code. Much of it will look familiar to you. The portions not familiar will be covered in the sections that follow.

```
//_____

#define    rResultsWindow          128
```

```
#define     kWindowTitleString        "\pInnerview Results"
#define     rSysIncompatibleAlert              128
#define     r8BitOrLessPicture                 128
#define     rGreaterThan8BitPicture            129
#define     kPixelDepth8Bit                      8
#define     kPixelDepth24Bit                    24
#define     kPictureLeft                       240
#define     kPictureTop                          5
#define     kInfoNameX                          30
#define     kInfoMacX                          120
#define     kInfoStartY                         60
#define     kLineSpacing                        20
#define     kInfoProcessorY       kInfoStartY + (0 * kLineSpacing )
#define     kInfoMemoryY          kInfoStartY + (1 * kLineSpacing )
#define     kInfoSystemY          kInfoStartY + (2 * kLineSpacing )
#define     kDragEdge                           20
#define     kASCIIzero               (char)0x030
#define     kASCIIperiod             (char)0x02E
#define     kBytesInOneKB               1024L


//_____

Boolean   gAllDone = false;
Rect      gDragRect;
Boolean   gCPUisPowerPC;
short     gMinPixelDepth;



//_____

void main( void )
{
    MaxApplZone();
    MoreMasters();
    MoreMasters();
    MoreMasters();

    InitializeToolbox();
    CheckSystem();
    SetWindowDragBoundaries();

    OpenInnerViewWindow();

    EventLoop();
```

```
}


//_____

void  CheckSystem( void )
{
   SysEnvRec   theMacInfo;
   OSErr       theError;
   long        theResponse;

   SysEnvirons( curSysEnvVers, &theMacInfo );

   if ( theMacInfo.systemVersion < 0x0700 )
   {
      StopAlert( rSysIncompatibleAlert, nil );
      ExitToShell();
   }

   theError = Gestalt( gestaltSysArchitecture, &theResponse );
   if ( theResponse == gestaltPowerPC )
      gCPUisPowerPC = true;
   else
      gCPUisPowerPC = false;

   gMinPixelDepth = GetMinPixelDepth();
}


//_____

short  GetMinPixelDepth( void )
{
   GDHandle   theCurrentDevice;
   short      thePixelDepth;
   short      theMinimumDepth;

   theMinimumDepth = kPixelDepth24Bit;
   theCurrentDevice = GetDeviceList();
   while ( theCurrentDevice != nil )
   {
      thePixelDepth = GetPixelDepth( theCurrentDevice );
      if ( thePixelDepth < theMinimumDepth )
         theMinimumDepth = thePixelDepth;
      theCurrentDevice = GetNextDevice( theCurrentDevice );
```

```
   }
   return  theMinimumDepth;
}
```

//_____

```
short  GetPixelDepth( GDHandle theDevice )
{
   PixMapHandle  screenPMapH;
   short         thePixelDepth;

   screenPMapH = (**theDevice).gdPMap;
   thePixelDepth = (**screenPMapH).pixelSize;
   return  ( thePixelDepth );
}
```

//_____

```
void  SetWindowDragBoundaries( void )
{
   RgnHandle  theGrayRegion;

   theGrayRegion = LMGetGrayRgn();

   gDragRect = (**theGrayRegion).rgnBBox;
   gDragRect.left   += kDragEdge;
   gDragRect.right  -= kDragEdge;
   gDragRect.bottom -= kDragEdge;
}
```

//_____

```
void  OpenInnerViewWindow( void )
{
   WindowPtr  theWindow;

   theWindow = GetNewCWindow( rResultsWindow, nil, (WindowPtr)-1L );

   if ( theWindow == nil )
      ExitToShell();

   SetWTitle( theWindow, kWindowTitleString );
```

```
    ShowWindow( theWindow );
}


//_____

void  EventLoop( void )
{
    EventRecord  theEvent;

    while ( gAllDone == false )
    {
        WaitNextEvent( everyEvent, &theEvent, 15L, nil );

        switch ( theEvent.what )
        {
            case mouseDown:
                HandleMouseDown( theEvent );
                break;

            case updateEvt:
                gMinPixelDepth = GetMinPixelDepth();
                HandleUpdate( theEvent);
                break;
        }
    }
}


//_____

void  HandleMouseDown( EventRecord theEvent )
{
    WindowPtr  theWindow;
    short      thePart;

    thePart = FindWindow( theEvent.where, &theWindow );

    switch ( thePart )
    {
        case inDrag:
            DragWindow( theWindow, theEvent.where, &gDragRect );
            break;

        case inGoAway:
```

```
           if ( TrackGoAway( theWindow, theEvent.where ) )
               gAllDone = true;
           break;

       case inContent:
           if ( theWindow != FrontWindow() )
               SelectWindow( theWindow );
           break;
   }
}



//_____

void  HandleUpdate( EventRecord theEvent )
{
   WindowPtr   theWindow;
   GrafPtr     theSavePort;

   theWindow = (WindowPtr)theEvent.message;

   GetPort( &theSavePort );
   SetPort( theWindow );

   TextFont( systemFont );
   TextSize( 12 );

   BeginUpdate( theWindow );
       DrawMacPicture();
       DrawSystemInfoHeadings();
       GetSystemInfo();
   EndUpdate( theWindow );

   SetPort( theSavePort );
}



//_____

void  DrawMacPicture( void )
{
   PicHandle   thePicture;
   Rect        theRect;
   short       theWidth;
   short       theHeight;
```

```
    short       thePictureID;

    if ( gMinPixelDepth > kPixelDepth8Bit )
        thePictureID = rGreaterThan8BitPicture;
    else
        thePictureID = r8BitOrLessPicture;

    thePicture = GetPicture( thePictureID );

    theRect = (**thePicture).picFrame;
    theWidth  = theRect.right - theRect.left;
    theHeight = theRect.bottom - theRect.top;
    SetRect( &theRect, kPictureLeft, kPictureTop,
             kPictureLeft + theWidth, kPictureTop + theHeight );

    DrawPicture( thePicture, &theRect );
}


//_____

void  DrawSystemInfoHeadings( void )
{
    MoveTo( kInfoNameX, kInfoProcessorY );
    DrawString( "\pCPU Type:");
    MoveTo( kInfoNameX, kInfoMemoryY );
    DrawString( "\pRAM (MB):");
    MoveTo( kInfoNameX, kInfoSystemY );
    DrawString( "\pSystem:");
}


//_____

void  GetSystemInfo( void )
{
    GetUsersProcessorType();
    GetUsersAmountOfRam();
    GetUsersSystemVersion();
}


//_____

void  GetUsersProcessorType( void )
```

```
{
    OSErr    theError;
    long     theResponse;

    theError = Gestalt( gestaltNativeCPUtype, &theResponse );
    if ( theError == noErr )
    {
        MoveTo( kInfoMacX, kInfoProcessorY );

        switch ( theResponse )
        {
            case gestaltCPU68000:
                DrawString( "\p68000" );
                break;
            case gestaltCPU68010:
                DrawString( "\p68010" );
                break;
            case gestaltCPU68020:
                DrawString( "\p68020" );
                break;
            case gestaltCPU68030:
                DrawString( "\p68030" );
                break;
            case gestaltCPU68040:
                DrawString( "\p68040" );
                break;
            case gestaltCPU601:
                DrawString( "\pPowerPC 601" );
                break;
            case gestaltCPU603:
                DrawString( "\pPowerPC 603" );
                break;
            case gestaltCPU604:
                DrawString( "\pPowerPC 604" );
                break;
            default:
                DrawString( "\pType unknown" );
                break;
        }
    }
}


//_____
```

```
void  GetUsersAmountOfRam( void )
{
    OSErr   theError;
    long    theResponse;
    long    theNumMB;
    Str255  theMegabyteString;

    theError = Gestalt( gestaltPhysicalRAMSize, &theResponse );
    if ( theError == noErr )
    {
        theNumMB = theResponse/( kBytesInOneKB * kBytesInOneKB );
        NumToString( theNumMB, theMegabyteString );

        MoveTo( kInfoMacX, kInfoMemoryY );
        DrawString( theMegabyteString );
    }
}


//_____

void  GetUsersSystemVersion( void )
{
    OSErr   theError;
    long    theResponse;
    long    theTemp;
    short   theDigit;
    Str255  theVersionString;

    theError = Gestalt( gestaltSystemVersion, &theResponse );
    if ( theError == noErr )
    {
        theTemp = theResponse;
        theDigit = ( theTemp &= 0x0F00 ) / 0x0100;
        theVersionString[1] = theDigit + kASCIIzero;
        theVersionString[2] = kASCIIperiod;

        theTemp = theResponse;
        theDigit = ( theTemp &= 0x00F0 ) / 0x0010;
        theVersionString[3] = theDigit + kASCIIzero;
        theVersionString[4] = kASCIIperiod;

        theTemp = theResponse;
        theDigit = ( theTemp &= 0x000F ) / 0x0001;
        theVersionString[5] = theDigit + kASCIIzero;
```

```
        theVersionString[0] = 5;
    }

    MoveTo( kInfoMacX, kInfoSystemY );
    DrawString( theVersionString );
}


//_____

void  InitializeToolbox( void )
{
    InitGraf( &qd.thePort );
    InitFonts();
    InitWindows();
    InitMenus();
    TEInit();
    InitDialogs( OL );
    FlushEvents( everyEvent, 0 );
    InitCursor();
}
```

Stepping Through the Code

Once again it's time to take a journey through the example's source code, emphasizing on the new material.

The #define directives

InnerView has a slew of #define directives. Ready? rResultsWindow is the resource ID of the program's window. The title for the window is held in the string kWindowTitleString.

rSysIncompatibleAlert is the ID of the ALRT resource for the alert displayed if the user's machine isn't up to snuff.

The program has two PICT resources—r8BitOrLessPicture is a black and white picture, and rGreaterThan8BitPicture has color. That's it for the resources. kPixelDepth8Bit and kPixelDepth24Bit will be used in the determination of the pixel depth of the user's monitor.

InnerView draws text and a picture in its one window. All of the following constants are used to help evenly space things: kPictureLeft, kPictureTop, kInfoNameX, kInfoMacX, kInfoStartY, kLineSpacing, kInfoProcessorY, kInfoMemoryY, and kInfoSystemY. By relying on these constants, you can easily make changes to the layout of the window—just go to the #define section of the source code listing and change the pixel values of some of the constants. If you want to make Innerview more useful by giving it the ability to provide more feedback to the user, you'll want to add more information names (headings) and resulting Macintosh information (the returned values about the user's machine). Again, the use of constants will make this task easy. Figure 9.25 shows just how the above-mentioned constants are used.

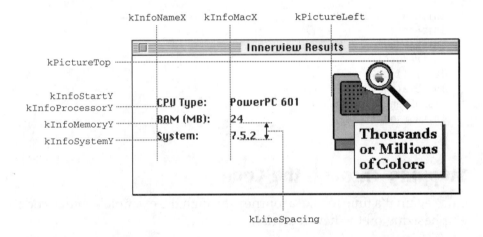

Figure 9.25 The constants used to place graphics and text in the Innerview window.

The constant kDragEdge is used to limit window dragging. kASCIIzero and kASCIIperiod are used when creating a string from a hexadecimal variable that holds the version number of the user's system. Finally, kBytesInOneKB is used in converting bytes to megabytes.

```
#define    rResultsWindow                128
#define    kWindowTitleString            "\pInnerview Results"
#define    rSysIncompatibleAlert         128
#define    r8BitOrLessPicture            128
#define    rGreaterThan8BitPicture       129
#define    kPixelDepth8Bit                 8
#define    kPixelDepth24Bit               24
```

```
#define    kPictureLeft                  240
#define    kPictureTop                     5
#define    kInfoNameX                     30
#define    kInfoMacX                     120
#define    kInfoStartY                    60
#define    kLineSpacing                   20
#define    kInfoProcessorY    kInfoStartY + (0 * kLineSpacing )
#define    kInfoMemoryY       kInfoStartY + (1 * kLineSpacing )
#define    kInfoSystemY       kInfoStartY + (2 * kLineSpacing )
#define    kDragEdge                      20
#define    kASCIIzero            (char)0x030
#define    kASCIIperiod          (char)0x02E
#define    kBytesInOneKB               1024L
```

The Global Variables

InnerView uses global variable gAllDone to signal the end of the program. The variable gDragRect is used for window dragging. The Boolean variable gCPUisPowerPC takes on a value of true if the program is running on a PowerPC-based Mac, false if the program is running on a 68K-based computer. For keeping track of the color setting of the user's monitor, gMinPixelDepth is used.

```
Boolean   gAllDone = false;
Rect      gDragRect;
Boolean   gCPUisPowerPC;
short     gMinPixelDepth;
```

The main() Function

InnerView's main() function should look familiar; it's much like the main() of previous examples. It starts with program initializations and, as always, ends with the event-handling routine EventLoop().

```
void main( void )
{
   MaxApplZone();
   MoreMasters();
   MoreMasters();
   MoreMasters();

   InitializeToolbox();
```

```
CheckSystem();
SetWindowDragBoundaries();

OpenInnerViewWindow();

EventLoop();
}
```

Checking the System

Because the Macintosh scene is constantly changing, you can never be sure on just what kind of Macintosh a program you write will be running. You've got to cover all bases. That's what this chapter is all about. The application-defined routine `CheckSystem()` demonstrates a few of the topics discussed in this chapter. This function first calls the Toolbox function `SysEnvirons()` and checks the returned information to verify that the user's Mac is running System 7 or later. If it is, the routine carries on by checking to see if the Mac is PowerPC based or 68K based. This information will be written to the program's window later. If your own program finds this information useful, it should save it in a global `Boolean` variable, as done in `CheckSystem()`. `CheckSystem()` ends by calling the application-defined routine `GetMinPixelDepth()` to determine the color level of the user's Mac. All your Mac programs should have a routine similar to InnerView's `CheckSystem()` routine and the utility routines it calls.

```
void  CheckSystem( void )
{
    SysEnvRec   theMacInfo;
    OSErr       theError;
    long        theResponse;

    SysEnvirons( curSysEnvVers, &theMacInfo );

    if ( theMacInfo.systemVersion < 0x0700 )
    {
        StopAlert( rSysIncompatibleAlert, nil );
        ExitToShell();
    }

    theError = Gestalt( gestaltSysArchitecture, &theResponse );
    if ( theResponse == gestaltPowerPC )
```

```
        gCPUisPowerPC = true;
    else
        gCPUisPowerPC = false;

    gMinPixelDepth = GetMinPixelDepth();
}
```

After `CheckSystem()` are several utility functions. These are functions that will appear in many or all of your programs, with little or no modification. `GetMinPixelDepth()` determines the minimum color level of all monitors connected to the Macintosh. It appears just as it was developed earlier in this chapter. `GetMinPixelDepth()` calls `GetPixelDepth()`, also covered in this chapter.

```
short   GetMinPixelDepth( void )
{
    GDHandle   theCurrentDevice;
    short      thePixelDepth;
    short      theMinimumDepth;

    theMinimumDepth = kPixelDepth24Bit;
    theCurrentDevice = GetDeviceList();
    while ( theCurrentDevice != nil )
    {
        thePixelDepth = GetPixelDepth( theCurrentDevice );
        if ( thePixelDepth < theMinimumDepth )
            theMinimumDepth = thePixelDepth;
        theCurrentDevice = GetNextDevice( theCurrentDevice );
    }
    return   theMinimumDepth;
}

short   GetPixelDepth( GDHandle theDevice )
{
    PixMapHandle   screenPMapH;
    short          thePixelDepth;

    screenPMapH = (**theDevice).gdPMap;
    thePixelDepth = (**screenPMapH).pixelSize;
    return ( thePixelDepth );
}
```

`SetWindowDragBoundaries()` sets the limits that a window can be dragged, based on the desktop area of the Macintosh monitor or monitors. Note the use of the accessor function `LMGetGrayRgn()`, as described in this chapter.

```
void   SetWindowDragBoundaries( void )
{
    RgnHandle   theGrayRegion;

    theGrayRegion = LMGetGrayRgn();

    gDragRect = (**theGrayRegion).rgnBBox;
    gDragRect.left    += kDragEdge;
    gDragRect.right   -= kDragEdge;
    gDragRect.bottom -= kDragEdge;
}
```

This chapter showed a few methods of determining the center of the main screen—the screen that holds the menu bar. One method used a call to `GetMainDevice()` to return a `GDHandle`. Since graphics device routines are part of Color QuickDraw, this method won't work for monochrome systems. Another method simply uses the QuickDraw global variable `screenBits`. This method works on any system. Finally, programs that run only on Macs equipped with System 7 can use a `WIND` that is marked to automatically open centered on the user's screen. Since Innerview requires System 7 or later, this final approach is the one the program uses.

Opening a Window

`OpenInnerViewWindow()` opens and display a color window by calling `GetNewCWindow()`. Since Innerview requires System 7, and System 7 includes Color QuickDraw, you know this is safe. If your program may be running on older machines and under older versions of the Mac OS, your program should call `Gestalt()` to ensure that Color QuickDraw is available. If it isn't, and you wish to go ahead and allow your program to execute anyway, your program should set a global flag variable indicating that the user doesn't have color. This is a technique described in this chapter's *When to call the pixel depth routines* section. If color isn't available, call `GetNewWindow()` rather than `GetNewCWindow()`.

After opening the window, OpenInnerViewWindow() goes on to set the window's title and then display the window, as described in Chapter 4.

```
void  OpenInnerViewWindow( void )
{
    WindowPtr  theWindow;

    theWindow = GetNewCWindow( rResultsWindow, nil, (WindowPtr)-1L );

    if ( theWindow == nil )
       ExitToShell();

    SetWTitle( theWindow, kWindowTitleString );

    ShowWindow( theWindow );
}
```

Event Handling

InnerView looks for two event types: updateEvt and mouseDown. This program's version of EventLoop() is similar to previous versions, with one new addition. As mentioned earlier in this chapter, the occurrence of an update event is used as a signal to check for the pixel depth. Why? If the user selects the Monitors control panel and changes the color setting of his monitor (or uses some other utility to perform this task), it will trigger an update event. How do you know that a particular update event was caused by selecting Monitors and not by some other situation? You don't, so you run the pixel depth check with every update—just in case.

```
void  EventLoop( void )
{
    EventRecord  theEvent;

    while ( gAllDone == false )
    {
        WaitNextEvent( everyEvent, &theEvent, 15L, nil );

        switch ( theEvent.what )
        {
```

```
        case mouseDown:
           HandleMouseDown( theEvent );
           break;

        case updateEvt:
           gMinPixelDepth = GetMinPixelDepth();
           HandleUpdate( theEvent);
           break;
     }
   }
}
```

A click of the mouse is handled by `HandleMouseDown()`. This function allows the user to drag the window. A click in the window's **Close** box ends the program. Nothing new here; everything you see in this routine has been covered in earlier chapters.

After a mouse down event, the second event type handled is an update event. After saving and setting the port, the `HandleUpdate()` function makes a couple of calls to Toolbox routines to set the text to the system font in a 12 point size. The program nests three routines between calls to `BeginUpdate()` and `EndUpdate()`. These three routines are described next.

```
void  HandleUpdate( EventRecord theEvent )
{
    WindowPtr  theWindow;
    GrafPtr    theSavePort;

    theWindow = (WindowPtr)theEvent.message;

    GetPort( &theSavePort );
    SetPort( theWindow );

    TextFont( systemFont );
    TextSize( 12 );

    BeginUpdate( theWindow );
        DrawMacPicture();
        DrawSystemInfoHeadings();
        GetSystemInfo();
    EndUpdate( theWindow );

    SetPort( theSavePort );
}
```

NOTE

With only one window, why bother setting the port? Because there are other ports on the screen, including the screen itself! Always keep track of ports, as is done here. Remember, the screen, or desktop, is a port. If you don't set the port there's a good chance that any drawing you do will end up on the desktop, not in your window. You can see for yourself by commenting out the SetPort() line in InnerView.c, and then recompiling and rerunning the program.

DrawMacPicture() draws a picture in the InnerView window. If the user's system currently has color set to 256 or fewer colors, DrawMacPicture() will load into memory and then draw PICT 128—the black and white picture. The results are shown in the top window of Figure 9.26. If the color level is greater, PICT 129 will instead be loaded and drawn—that's shown in the bottom window of the same figure.

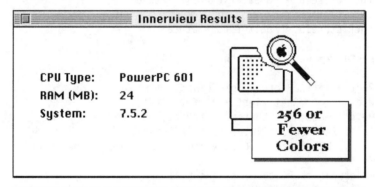

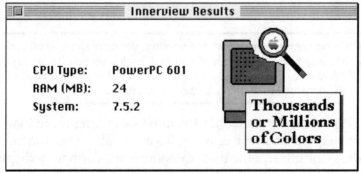

Figure 9.26 InnerView is capable of displaying two different pictures.

If you have a color monitor and a system capable of displaying more than 256 colors, try running InnerView with the color level set at 256 colors or less. At that color level Innerview will display the monochrome picture. Then, with InnerView still running, use the color-setting utility on your Mac to change the color level to thousands or millions of colors. When you do that, Innerview will update its window to display the color picture.

```
void  DrawMacPicture( void )
{
    PicHandle   thePicture;
    Rect        theRect;
    short       theWidth;
    short       theHeight;
    short       thePictureID;

    if ( gMinPixelDepth > kPixelDepth8Bit )
        thePictureID = rGreaterThan8BitPicture;
    else
        thePictureID = r8BitOrLessPicture;

    thePicture = GetPicture( thePictureID );

    theRect = (**thePicture).picFrame;
    theWidth  = theRect.right - theRect.left;
    theHeight = theRect.bottom - theRect.top;
    SetRect( &theRect, kPictureLeft, kPictureTop,
            kPictureLeft + theWidth, kPictureTop + theHeight );

    DrawPicture( thePicture, &theRect );
}
```

NOTE DrawMacPicture() draws to a window, yet it doesn't lead off with port-saving and port-setting calls. If you look back a bit you'll see that this task is taken care of in HandleUpdate(). The HandleUpdate() function makes consecutive calls to three application-drawing routines.

The DrawSystemInfoHeadings() routine is nothing more than a series of pen movement and text drawing Toolbox calls. This function draws the headings, or titles, of the three categories of information displayed by Innerview. If you'd like to enhance the Innerview program, you might consider moving the strings that make up the heading into a string list STR# resource.

```
void  DrawSystemInfoHeadings( void )
{
   MoveTo( kInfoNameX, kInfoProcessorY );
   DrawString( "\pCPU Type:");
   MoveTo( kInfoNameX, kInfoMemoryY );
   DrawString( "\pRAM (MB):");
   MoveTo( kInfoNameX, kInfoSystemY );
   DrawString( "\pSystem:");
}
```

Now it's time to obtain the information from the user's Mac. To do this, GetSystemInfo() relies on three application-defined functions. Each routine calls Gestalt() to get one piece of information. Once you understand how one routine works, you can easily add more of your own.

```
void  GetSystemInfo( void )
{
   GetUsersProcessorType();
   GetUsersAmountOfRam();
   GetUsersSystemVersion();
}
```

GetUsersProcessorType() calls Gestalt() with a selector code of gestaltNativeCPUtype. Each possible response has its own case label in the routine's switch section.

GetUsersAmountOfRam() passes a selector code of gestaltPhysicalRAMSize to Gestalt(). The returned value is the number of bytes of RAM memory installed in the user's Mac. This value is divided by the number of bytes in one megabyte (1024*1024) to get the number of megabytes—a more informative number for the user.

GetUsersSystemVersion() calls Gestalt() with a selector code of gestaltSystemVersion. The rest of the routine is devoted to individually converting to characters each of the three system digits from theResponse, and then merging these characters into one string. Here's a look at how the first digit is converted:

```
#define     kASCIIzero      (char)0x030    // decimal 48
#define     kASCIIperiod    (char)0x02E    // decimal 46

long    theResponse;
long    theTemp;
short   theDigit;
```

```
Str255   theVersionString;

theTemp = theResponse;
theDigit = ( theTemp &= 0x0F00 ) / 0x0100;
theVersionString[1] = theDigit + kASCIIzero;
theVersionString[2] = kASCIIperiod;
```

If the user has, say, System 7.5.2 on his machine, theResponse will have a value of 0x0752. This value is first saved in theTemp. Then, theTemp is ANDed with 0x0F00. That serves to extract the 7 from 0x0752. If you know your Boolean logic operations, you know that an AND operation is performed bit-by-bit on a pair of binary numbers. You also know that an AND operation on a pair of bits results in a binary 1 only when both values that are ANDed are each a 1. If either value is a binary 0, the result is a 0. With that in mind, here's how the AND operation for the given example looks:

```
0000   0111  0101  0010      // binary of 0x0752
0000   1111  0000  0000      // binary of 0x0F00
─────────────
0000   0111  0000  0000      // binary of 0x0700
```

Because the &= operator is used, the result of the AND operation is stored back in theTemp:

```
//   theTemp &= 0x0F00 is the same as: theTemp = theTemp & 0x0F00
```

Dividing theTemp by 0x0100 results in a value of 7:

```
//   0x0700/0x0100 = 7
```

This single digit is then converted to a character by adding 48 (kASCIIzero) to it. You can check your ASCII chart to confirm that ASCII 55 is the character that represents the number 7. This character is then stored in element 1 of a Str255 variable:

```
theVersionString[1] = theDigit + kASCIIzero;
```

Next, element 2 of the same string is assigned to be a period, or decimal point:

```
theVersionString[2] = kASCIIperiod;
```

The preceding steps are repeated until the Response has been converted to a string. Then the length of the string is set to **5**—the three digits found in a system version, plus the two decimal points that appear between the digits, as in 7.5.2—the version used in this example.

```
void   GetUsersSystemVersion( void )
{
    OSErr     theError;
    long      theResponse;
    long      theTemp;
    short     theDigit;
    Str255    theVersionString;

    theError = Gestalt( gestaltSystemVersion, &theResponse );
    if ( theError == noErr )
    {
        theTemp = theResponse;
        theDigit = ( theTemp &= 0x0F00 ) / 0x0100;
        theVersionString[1] = theDigit + kASCIIzero;
        theVersionString[2] = kASCIIperiod;

        theTemp = theResponse;
        theDigit = ( theTemp &= 0x00F0 ) / 0x0010;
        theVersionString[3] = theDigit + kASCIIzero;
        theVersionString[4] = kASCIIperiod;

        theTemp = theResponse;
        theDigit = ( theTemp &= 0x000F ) / 0x0001;
        theVersionString[5] = theDigit + kASCIIzero;
        theVersionString[0] = 5;
    }

    MoveTo( kInfoMacX, kInfoSystemY );
    DrawString( theVersionString );
}
```

Chapter Summary

Thousands of Toolbox routines exist in the ROM chips of each Macintosh. A Toolbox routine is also called a trap, and each trap has a trap number. When you include a call to a Toolbox routine in your code, the trap number for that routine tells the processor where in memory it will find the code that makes up that routine.

As Macintosh computers are improved, so is the ROM. New versions of ROM contain new Toolbox calls, and thus new trap numbers. Many of the Toolbox functions you call will have been present in the ROM of the first Macintosh computer, and in every Macintosh since. Some routines you'll want to use, however, only reside in more recent versions of ROM. If a user has an older ROM set but a recent version of system software, then that user may have most or all of the available Toolbox routines on his or her machine. That's because the system software also contains versions of many of the Toolbox routines. It's up to you to determine if the computer your program is running on supports the calls you're going to make.

The `NGetTrapAddress()` routine is a powerful means of determining the availability of a Toolbox function. By passing it the name of a routine, preceded by an underscore, you can see if that routine exists on any given Macintosh. If it doesn't, you'll want to either use a substitute routine or exit the program and return to the Finder.

The `Gestalt()` function is used to determine many different hardware and software features of the machine your program is running on. By passing `Gestalt()` different selector codes, you can find out whether a Macintosh supports color, what version of the system is installed, the amount of RAM in the computer, and a host of other environmental factors.

Chapter 10

Applications and the Finder

Anyone who uses a Macintosh is constantly using the Finder application—though that person might not be aware of it. The Finder is the "middleman" between the user and the Macintosh desktop. One the primary tasks the Finder is responsible for is keeping track of, and displaying, application icons. In this chapter you'll see how to provide your application with a distinct icon of its own. You'll also see how to make the Finder aware of this unique icon.

Through the use of a high level event type named the Apple event, the Macintosh makes it possible for programs to communicate with one another. One of the primary uses of the Apple event is to facilitate communication between an application and the Finder. In this chapter you'll learn how to add Apple event support to your own applications so that the Finder will be able to quit your application in response to a user's request to shut down the Mac.

GIVING A PROGRAM AN ICON

When you use a Macintosh compiler to build, or create, your application it ends up with the generic icon displayed in Figure 10.1. If you want your application to display its own custom icon on the desktop, you'll need to create a BNDL resource in the program's resource file before building the program.

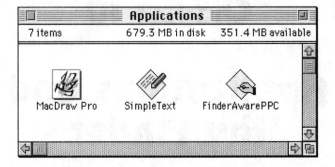

Figure 10.1 Typical program icons on the desktop

The Finder is responsible for displaying an icon for each program and program file that appears on the desktop. To keep track of what file gets what icon, the Finder makes use of a file's type and creator identifiers. The following paragraphs cover the essential background information you'll need before working with a BNDL resource.

The Finder and icons

Every program has an icon, a type identifier, and a *creator* identifier. The Finder looks to a program's identifiers to see what icon it should display on the desktop to represent that program. All applications have a type of 'APPL'. Each application should have a four letter creator code that is unique to that application.

You can give your application any combination of four upper- and lowercase letters for it to use as its creator code. At the end of this chapter is a sample program called FinderAware. When you read about this program you'll see that it has a creator name of 'Fawr', though any one of countless combinations of letters would have worked equally as well.

For any one program you develop, you will specify the creator name at two times: when you create a BNDL resource for the program and when you build your program.

Creating the BNDL resource

In ResEdit, selecting **Create New Resource** from the Resource menu allows you to create a BNDL resource. You'll be presented with the Select New Type dialog box. There, scroll to the BNDL type and double click on it. When you do, you'll see the BNDL editor shown in Figure 10.2.

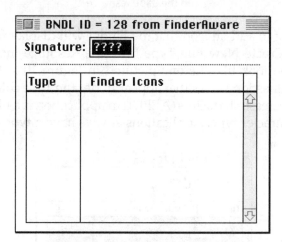

Figure 10.2 The BNDL resource in ResEdit

In this editor you'll type in your program's *signature*, which is simply another name for the creator (the creator is also referred to as the creator signature). This chapter's FinderAware program uses a signature of 'Fawr'—as shown in Figure 10.3.

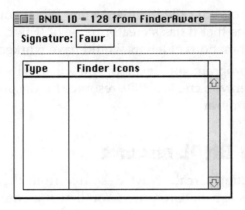

Figure 10.3 The program's signature, or creator, gets typed
into the BNDL resource

Next, you want to add an icon that the Finder will display for your application. Select **Create New File Type** from the Resource menu. The BNDL editor will then look like the one pictured in Figure 10.4. Then click the mouse on the question marks that appear under the Type column and type in the four uppercase characters 'APPL'. An application is a file, and all files have a four character type. Applications always have a type of 'APPL'.

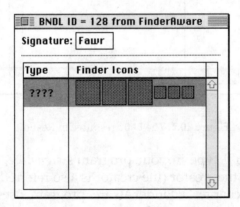

Figure 10.4 Adding a new file type to the BNDL resource

Creating the icons that make up the BNDL resource

The bundle resource is used to bundle, or associate, a few icons with an application. Figure 10.4 shows that up to six icons can be associated with the application.

To create the icons, double-click on any of the six gray boxes in the Finder Icons column of the BNDL. You'll see a dialog box like that in Figure 10.5. You're creating the icons from scratch, so click the **New** button.

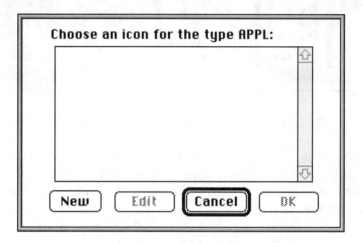

Figure 10.5 Click the New button to open the icon family editor

Now you'll be in the icon family editor. Here you can select a tool, such as the pencil, from the tool palette and then draw your own icon. The FinderAware program demonstrates how a program communicates with the Finder via Apple Events. This is symbolized in the example icon in Figure 10.6 by drawing a small versions of a Macintosh and application icon, then adding arrows.

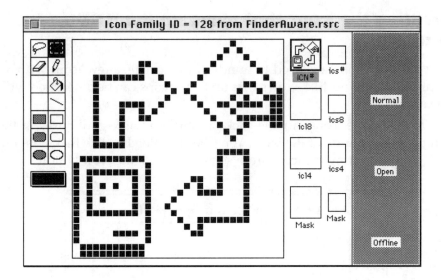

Figure 10.6 Editing an icon using the icon family editor

After creating the icon, look back at the BNDL resource window. You'll see that one of the six boxes is no longer gray—it now displays the icon you just created (see Figure 10.7). As you create other icons, they'll appear in the BNDL window as well.

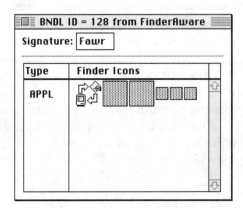

Figure 10.7 Editing an icon using the icon family editor

As you draw the icon you'll see it displayed in actual size in the right side of the icon family editor. You may be wondering why there are so many blank icons shown there. If you want to fully accommodate users of System 7 you can create several versions of each icon—a *family* of icons. Here's a summary of what the different versions are for:

ICN#   The original icon resource that has been used for years and years. The Finder will use this version to display a black and white icon.

ic14   The Finder will display the icon that is here if the user has a 4-bit, or 16-color system.

ic18   If the user has an 8-bit (256-color) or greater system, the user will see this icon.

ics#   The Finder sometimes displays a small icon for a program. When it does, it uses an ics# icon for black and white.

ics4   A small 4-bit (16 color) color icon.

ics8   A small 8-bit (256 color) color icon.

NOTE   You can get a jump start on your icon by using ResEdit to open other files. Double-click on various icon resources to see how different icons are drawn. The icon pictured in Figure 10.6 was created with the help of two ics# resources found in the System file.

The minimum requirement for a custom program icon is that you create the ICN# version. Then, no matter what color level the user's system has, the Finder will display this black and white icon.

You can reduce the work in creating new versions of an icon by first creating the black and white ICN#, then clicking the mouse on the small picture of it in the icon editor. While holding the mouse button down, drag to any of the other small boxes in the area of the small view of the ICN#. This will copy the existing icon to the new version. Figure 10.8 shows an ICN# being dragged down to the ic18 icon rectangle. When you start editing the icon, you'll be working on this new ic18 version.

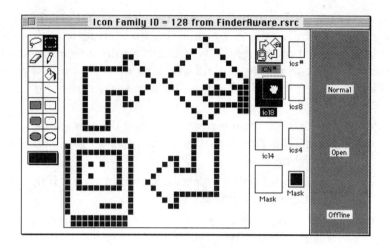

Figure 10.8 Creating an ic18 icon from an ICN# icon

If you're working with any of the color icons, you can of course add color to them. Click on the small rectangle found in the lower-left of the icon editor to display a color palette—as shown in Figure 10.9. Selecting a color from the palette effects the tools in the tool palette of the icon editor. Figure 10.10 shows the ic18 icon after color has been added.

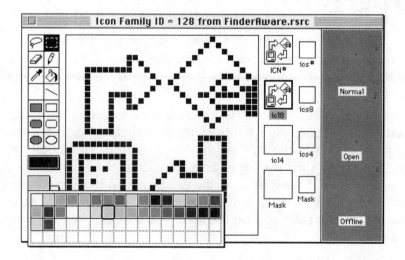

Figure 10.9 Adding color to an icon using the color palette

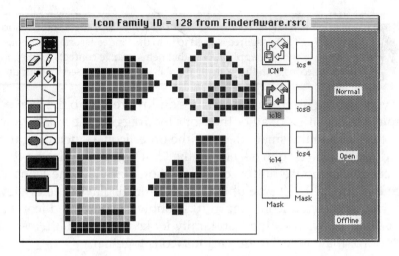

Figure 10.10 An ic18 icon with color added to it

When you look at the main window of the resource file you'll notice that there are several new resource types, as shown in Figure 10.11. Creating a BNDL resource will automatically add an FREF resource to the file. Depending on what icons types you created in the icon editor, ResEdit will also add the various icon resource types to the file. Each icon you create through the BNDL resource is represented by its own icon resource type. On the previous pages you saw ICN# and ic18 icons being created in the icon editor opened from the BNDL resource. Thus the resource file now contains ICN# and ic18 resources. ResEdit also adds a resource with the signature, or creator, name. In Figure 10.11 you can see that a resource of type Fawr has been added to the file.

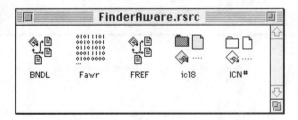

Figure 10.11 A resource file gains new resources after a BNDL resource is added

NOTE You won't need to be concerned with the contents of the resources added by ResEdit. The FREF resource is used to help the Finder associate the icons in the resource file with the application—that helps resolve conflicts if other applications have icons with the same ID numbers as the ones used by your program.

After viewing the resource file's main window, return to the icon editor. Complete the creation of all of the icons by dragging the small view of a completed icon to the small views of the other icons—including the one labeled **Mask**. The icon mask effects the "hot" area of an icon—the area that recognizes mouse button clicks. As you complete the icons you'll notice that the far-right side of the icon editor displays several views of the currently selected icon. Figure 10.12 shows a completed icon family. Figure 10.13 shows how the icon family looks from the BNDL resource— the resource that "links" these various icons together.

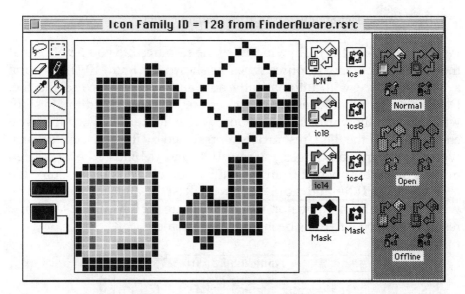

Figure 10.12 A completed icon family

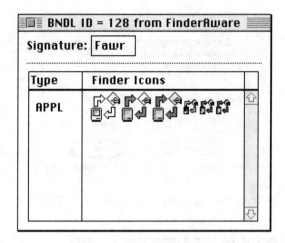

Figure 10.13 A completed icon family, as viewed from the BNDL resource

Setting the creator in the compiler

Once your BNDL resource is complete you'll want to let your project in on things. You do this by telling your IDE the four character signature, or creator, you used in the BNDL resource. As you're about to see, accomplishing this task varies depending on the IDE you use.

Setting the creator in the THINK C IDE

In the THINK C environment you enter the creator by selecting **Set Project Type** from the Project menu. That results in the display of the dialog box shown in Figure 10.14. There you enter a four-letter creator name in place of the four question marks that the IDE supplies as a default creator value.

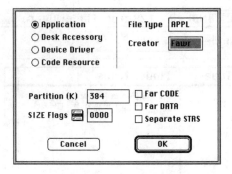

Figure 10.14 Setting a project's creator in the THINK C IDE

Setting the creator in the Symantec C++ IDE

In the Symantec C++ IDE you enter the creator by first selecting **Options** from the Project menu. Then bring up the Project Type page by clicking on the **Project Type** icon in the options dialog box—as shown in Figure 10.15. In the **Creator** field, enter the four-letter creator name in place of the four question marks that the Symantec IDE uses as the default creator value.

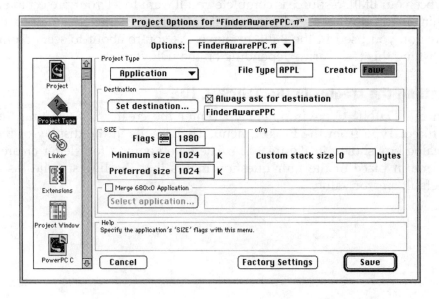

Figure 10.15 Setting a project's creator in the Symantec C++ IDE

Setting the creator in the Metrowerks CodeWarrior IDE

If you're working with CodeWarrior, select **Preferences** from the Edit menu. Then click on the **68K Project** or **PPC Project** icon to bring up the Project panel. Replace the four question marks in the **Creator** field by typing the four characters used as the BNDL resource signature—as shown in Figure 10.16.

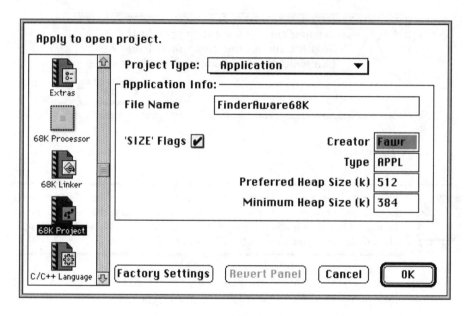

Figure 10.16 Setting a project's creator in the Metrowerks CodeWarrior IDE

Making the Finder aware of the icon

After your project's resource file has a BNDL resource and your project has the creator set to match the BNDL signature, you're all set to perform a build, or make, of the project. After you do that, you'll have a new icon in your project's folder. It might, however, appear as nothing more than the generic icon you're used to seeing after you create a stand-alone application. If that's the case, there is one more step you need to take to see your application's custom icon on the desktop: you must *rebuild* the desktop.

The Finder stores icons in a file called the Desktop file. To get the Finder to notice a new icon you'll need to rebuild the desktop. This scary-sounding practice is really quite simple—you simply restart the Macintosh, holding down the **Command** and **Option** keys as the Mac starts up. If you keep these keys pressed, in a little while you'll see an alert like that shown in Figure 10.17. Press the **OK** button to continue.

Figure 10.17 A last chance to back out of the desktop rebuild

If you have one or more external hard drives attached to your Mac, you'll see the above alert more than once. You only need to rebuild the desktop file for the hard drive that holds the project file. After that, click the **Cancel** button when the alert appears for each additional hard drive.

Giving your program its own unique icon, rather than the generic one issued to new programs that don't have a BNDL resource, is an easy way to add polish to your final application.

APPLE EVENTS

Apple events are high-level events that allow programs to communicate with the Finder. While Apple defines numerous Apple events, this chapter will focus on just one type—the Quit Application Apple event.

If you've ever selected **Restart** or **Shut Down** from the Special menu of the desktop, you've noticed that your Mac doesn't immediately turn itself off. Instead, it brings each running application to the front, one at a time. Each time it brings an application to the front, it quits that program. When all the running applications have been quit, only then does your computer turn off. This *graceful* shutdown is accomplished through the use of the Quit Application Apple event.

If an application doesn't implement the Quit Application Apple event, it can't be a part of the shutdown process. Though the system will bring that application to the front, it won't have adequate means of communicating with the program. Instead, after a brief pause you'll see the alert shown in Figure 10.18. After dismissing the alert, the shutdown process will end without your Mac being turned off. You can verify that this is indeed what happens by running last chapter's Innerview program, which doesn't use Apple events. With the program running, click on the desktop. Then select **Restart** from the Special menu.

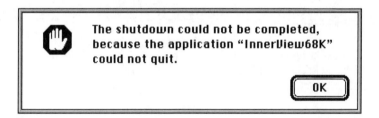

Figure 10.18 A shutdown foiled by an application that doesn't
use Apple events

In the next section you'll see how easy it is to add the Quit Application Apple event to any of your programs.

Making your application Apple event-aware

You'll need to do two things to make sure your program recognizes Apple events when they occur. One of these things is to add a case label to the switch statement in your program's event loop. Then, when your EventLoop() routine checks events returned by WaitNextEvent(), it will look for Apple events as well as the standard event types such as mouseDown, updateEvt, and keyDown. The Apple-defined constant used to denote an event as an Apple event is kHighLevelEvent. If your event loop's call to WaitNextEvent() does return an event of this type, you're application should call the Apple Event Manager function AEProcessAppleEvent(). This Toolbox routine expects a pointer to an EventRecord as its only parameter. Here's a look at a version of `EventLoop()` that is capable of handling mouse down events and Apple events:

```
void  EventLoop( void )
{
   EventRecord  theEvent;

   while ( gAllDone == false )
   {
      WaitNextEvent( everyEvent, &theEvent, 15L, nil );

      switch ( theEvent.what )
      {
         case mouseDown:
            HandleMouseDown( theEvent );
            break;

         case kHighLevelEvent:
            AEProcessAppleEvent( &theEvent );
            break;
      }
   }
}
```

The second step to making sure your application is Apple event-aware is to ensure that the project is high level-event aware. The process for doing this is straightforward, but varies depending on the development environment you're using.

 This step is important! If you fail to make the following change to your project, your program won't recognize the Quit Application Apple event—even if you add all the correct code to your project's source code file. Look over the following sections to find the one that pertains to the IDE you're using.

NOTE

Making your THINK C project Apple event-aware

In the THINK C environment you make your project high level event-aware by selecting **Set Project Type** from the Project menu. In the dialog box that appears, click on the small menu icon labeled **SIZE Flags**. Select **HighLevelEvent-Aware** from the pop-up menu.

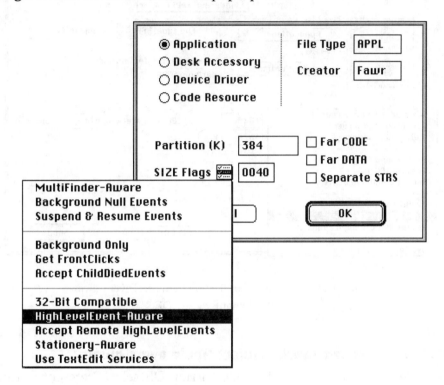

Figure 10.19 Making an application high level event-aware in the THINK C IDE

Making your Symantec C   project Apple event-aware

To make your Symantec C++ project high level event-aware, begin by selecting **Options** from the Project menu. Then bring up the Project Type page by clicking on the **Project Type** icon in the options dialog box. Next, click on the small menu icon labeled Flags. When you do that, a pop-up menu will appear. If the **HighLevelEvent-Aware** item isn't already checked, select it now—as is being done in Figure 10.20.

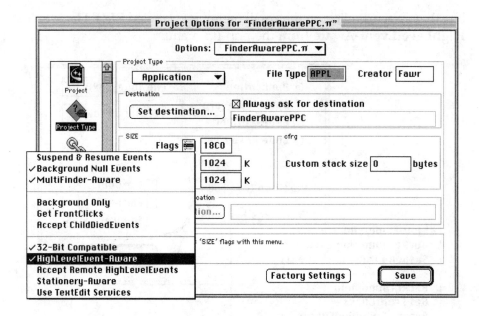

Figure 10.20 Making an application high level event-aware
in the Symantec C++ IDE

Making your Metrowerks project Apple event-aware

If you're using the Metrowerks CodeWarrior IDE, select **Preferences** from
the Edit menu. Then click on the **68K Project** or **PPC Project** icon to display the Project panel. Click on the small checkmark icon labeled **'SIZE'**
Flags. A pop-up menu will then appear. If the **isHighLevelEventAware**
item isn't already checked, select it now—as shown in Figure 10.21.

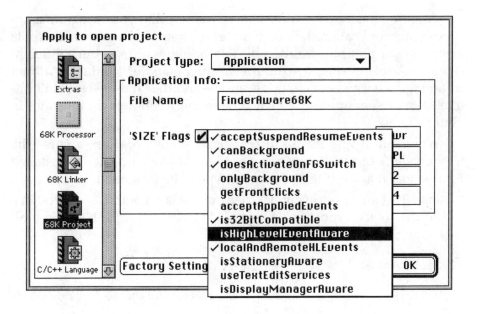

Figure 10.21 Making an application high level event-aware
in the Metrowerks CodeWarrior IDE

Installing an Apple event handler

Each Apple event that your application is capable of recognizing requires an Apple event *handler* routine. This application-defined function specifies exactly how a particular Apple event should be handled by your program. In the next section you'll see the *two* lines of code that make up a typical Quit Application Apple event handler. Here, you'll see how a handler routine is *installed*.

Installing a handler routine is necessary so that your program associates your application-defined handler routine with a particular Apple event. If your program was capable of working with, say, three different types of Apple events, it would have three handler routines. Without installing each routine, your application—and the Finder—wouldn't differentiate these routines from any other application-defined functions in your program.

When an Apple Event that affects your program occurs, the EventLoop() call to AEProcessAppleEvent() will invoke the installed routine that matches the Apple event type to be processed.

Installing an Apple event handler routine is accomplished through a call to the Toolbox function AEInstallEventHandler(). Here's a typical call to this routine:

```
AEInstallEventHandler( kCoreEventClass,
                kAEQuitApplication,
                NewAEEventHandlerProc( AEHandleQuit ),
                0,
                false );
```

AEInstallEventHandler() requires five parameters. The first is the *event class* of the event to be handled. The Quit Application Apple event is a *core event*, so the installer routine is passed the Apple-defined constant kCoreEventClass.

The second parameter in AEInstallEventHandler() is an event ID used to specify which particular Apple event is to be processed by the application-defined event handler routine that is being installed. For the Quit Application Apple events, this ID is the Apple-defined constant kAEQuitApplication.

The third parameter is a pointer to the application-defined function that will handle this one Apple event. Regardless of the Apple event that is to be handled, pass the Toolbox function NewAEEventHandlerProc() as this parameter. Use the name of the application-defined handler function as the parameter in NewAEEventHandlerProc(). In the above snippet the application-defined handler routine is named AEHandleQuit(). You're free to use any name of your own choosing.

The fourth parameter `AEInstallEventHandler()` is a reference value that the Apple Event Manager will use each time it invokes the event handler function. Simply pass a value of 0 for this parameter. The final parameter to is a `Boolean` value that specifies in which Apple event *dispatch table* the handler should be added. This table creates a correlation between an Apple event and your application-defined event handler routine. A value of `false` provides the Apple Event Manager with the information it needs to fill in the correct table.

As you'll see in this chapter's example program, an event handler routine should be installed early in your program—typically just after Toolbox initialization.

The Quit Application Apple event handler

Many Apple event handlers require information about an Apple event in order to properly handle the event. Some Apple event handlers return information to the event. All Apple event handlers return an error result to let the event know if the event was handled successfully.

While the internals of application-defined Apple event handler routines will vary, they will all have a similar look. Each event handler routine starts with the `pascal` keyword, and has a return type of `OSErr`. An event handler always has three parameters. The first is a pointer to the Apple event to handle. The second parameter is a pointer to a structure that is capable of holding information that gets returned to the Apple event. The last parameter is a reference value that your application can typically ignore. Here's the format of an Apple event handler:

```
pascal OSErr RoutineName( AEDescList *theAppleEvent,
                          AEDescList *theReply,
                          long        theRefCon )
{
    // handle the Apple event

    // return an OSErr value
}
```

Now, here's an actual application-defined routine that's used to handle a Quit Application Apple event:

```
pascal OSErr AEHandleQuit( AEDescList *theAppleEvent,
                           AEDescList *theReply,
                           long        theRefCon )
{
    All_Done = true;
    return noErr;
}
```

All a Quit Application event handler usually needs to do to process a Quit Application Apple event is set the application's global variable gAllDone to true. In a trivial routine such as this you can assume that the assignment of a Boolean value to a variable won't generate an operating system error. With that in mind, return the Apple-defined constant noErr.

NOTE The event handler routine can also invoke other application-defined functions. If your program gives the user the opportunity to save user-entered data, then you'll want to call the same application-defined function that would get called when the user selects **Save** or **Save As** from the File menu of your program.

Chapter Program: FinderAware

This chapter's example program, FinderAware, demonstrates how to make an application Apple event-aware, and how to provide an application with its own icon on the desktop. As a bonus (and to give the program something to do), FinderAware provides you with the simple technique for playing a sound from your Mac's speakers.

If you look in this chapter's project folder you'll see that the FinderAware application has its own icon. Figure 10.22 shows that the icon is the same one used in this chapter's *Giving a Program an Icon* section.

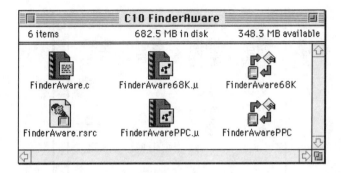

Figure 10.22 The FinderAware application has its own distinct icon

When you run FinderAware, you'll see a window like the one pictured in Figure 10.23. You'll also hear a sound playing for a few seconds. When the sound completes, the words in the window will disappear. To quit the program, simply press any key.

Figure 10.23 The FinderAware window as it appears when a sound is playing

Program resources: FinderAware.rsrc

As Figure 10.24 shows, the FinderAware project file holds resources of eleven different types. All but two of the resources are related to the icons used by the application. Those two resources are of type WIND and snd.

FinderAware.rsrc
BNDL
Fawr
FREF
icl4
icl8
ICN#
ics#
ics4
ics8
snd
WIND

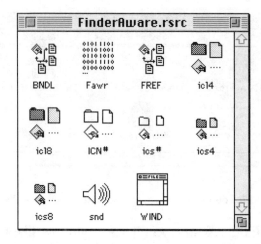

Figure 10.24 The resources used by the FinderAware project

You're already quite familiar with the `WIND` resource type. In this book you haven't, however, encountered the `snd` resource. As it's name implies, a snd resource holds data that represents a sound. As you'll see later in this chapter, your program can easily load to memory the data from a sound resource, then play that data as a sound from the Mac's speakers. Figure 10.25 shows that the sound resource used by the FinderAware program has an ID of 9000 and contains about 45 KB of data. To view the sound data in ResEdit you can double-click on the sound's ID—just as you do for a resource of any type. Be forewarned, though, that double-clicking on the sound resource will result in the hexadecimal display of the sound data—information that you won't find meaningful.

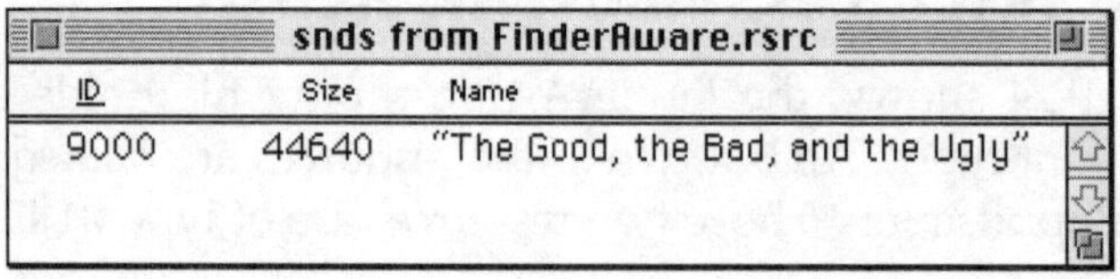

snds from FinderAware.rsrc
ID
Size
Name
9000
44640
"The Good, the Bad, and the Ugly"

Figure 10.25 A snd resource in the FinderAware resource file

Sound resources are available from a variety of sources. Mail order companies sell CD-ROMs that contain hundreds or thousands of digitized sounds. You can also download public domain sound from the libraries of online services such as America Online and CompuServe. You can also use your Mac's microphone to record your own sounds. The M&T Books text *Graphics and Sound Programming Techniques for the Mac* provides more details.

N O T E

Program listing: FinderAware.c

The following is the complete listing for this book's last example program. Following the listing is the usual source code walkthrough.

```
//_____

#include <Sound.h>


//_____

void    InitializeToolbox( void );
void    OpenWindowAndPlaySound( void );
void    EventLoop( void );

pascal OSErr AEHandleQuit( AEDescList *, AEDescList *, long );


//_____

#define        rSoundPlayingWindow        128
#define        rGoodBadUglySound          9000


//_____

Boolean gAllDone = false;


//_____
```

```
void main( void )
{
    MaxApplZone();
    MoreMasters();
    MoreMasters();
    MoreMasters();

    InitializeToolbox();

    AEInstallEventHandler( kCoreEventClass, kAEQuitApplication,
                           NewAEEventHandlerProc(AEHandleQuit),
                           0, false );

    OpenWindowAndPlaySound();

    EventLoop();
}


//_____


pascal OSErr AEHandleQuit( AEDescList *theAppleEvent,
                           AEDescList *theReply,
                           long       theRefCon )
{
    gAllDone = true;
    return noErr;
}


//_____


void  OpenWindowAndPlaySound( void )
{
    WindowPtr   theWindow;
    Handle      theSound;
    OSErr       theError;
    Rect        theRect;

    theWindow = GetNewWindow( rSoundPlayingWindow, nil, (WindowPtr)-1L );
    ShowWindow( theWindow );
    SetPort( theWindow );

    MoveTo( 20, 20 );
    DrawString( "\pPlaying sound..." );
```

```
    theSound = GetResource( 'snd ', rGoodBadUglySound );
    if ( theSound == nil )
       ExitToShell();

    theError = SndPlay( nil, (SndListHandle)theSound, true );
    if ( theError != noErr )
       ExitToShell();

    SetRect( &theRect, 5, 5, 125, 25 );
    EraseRect( &theRect );
}


//_____

void  EventLoop( void )
{
    EventRecord   theEvent;

    while ( gAllDone == false )
    {
       WaitNextEvent( everyEvent, &theEvent, 15L, nil );

       switch ( theEvent.what )
       {
          case keyDown:
             gAllDone = true;
             break;

          case kHighLevelEvent:
             AEProcessAppleEvent( &theEvent );
             break;
       }
    }
}


//_____

void  InitializeToolbox( void )
{
    InitGraf( &qd.thePort );
    InitFonts();
    InitWindows();
    InitMenus();
```

```
    TEInit();
    InitDialogs( 0L );
    FlushEvents( everyEvent, 0 );
    InitCursor();
}
```

Stepping through the code

One last time: it's time to walk through the example program's source code listing.

The #include files

Your IDE automatically includes many of the Apple universal header files in each project you compile. But it doesn't include all of the one hundred plus header files. One of the headers it doesn't include is Sound.h. Normally that doesn't present a problem—if your project doesn't make any calls to sound-related Toolbox functions, there's no need for your compiler to know the definitions for these routines. FinderAware does, however, call a sound-related Toolbox routine. So you'll need to include Sound.h at the top of your source code listing.

```
#include <Sound.h>
```

The #define directives

FinderAware makes use of just two application-defined constants. The first is rSoundPlayingWindow, which defines the ID of the WIND resource. The second is rGoodBadUglySound, which defines the ID of the snd resource.

```
#define     rSoundPlayingWindow     128
#define     rGoodBadUglySound       9000
```

N O T E

A snd , like any resource, has an ID. Apple has reserved ID numbers 0 to 8191 for its own use. You can change the ID of a snd by selecting the resource and the choosing **Get Resource Info** from ResEdit's Resource menu. Then type in a new ID. Taking into consideration the reserved numbers, FinderAware uses 9000 as the ID of its one sound resource.

The global variables

FinderAware needs only a single global variable—the `Boolean` variable `gAllDone`.

```
Boolean  gAllDone = false;
```

The main() function

FinderAware's `main()` function starts with program initializations and ends with the event-handling routine EventLoop(). In between the program's one Apple event handler is installed, a window is opened, and a sound is played.

```
void main( void )
{
   MaxApplZone();
   MoreMasters();
   MoreMasters();
   MoreMasters();

   InitializeToolbox();

   AEInstallEventHandler( kCoreEventClass, kAEQuitApplication,
                          NewAEEventHandlerProc(AEHandleQuit),
                          0, false );

   OpenWindowAndPlaySound();

   EventLoop();
}
```

The Quit Application Apple Event Handler

Apple event handler routines should be installed right near the start of a program. FinderAware does this by installing the Quit Application Apple event handler routine `AEHandleQuit()` just after the Toolbox is initialized.

```
AEInstallEventHandler( kCoreEventClass, kAEQuitApplication,
                       NewAEEventHandlerProc(AEHandleQuit),
                       0, false );
```

Like any Apple event handler, the Quit Application Apple event handler found in the FinderAware program is an application-defined routine. It follows the format outlined in this chapter:

```
pascal OSErr AEHandleQuit( AEDescList *theAppleEvent,
                           AEDescList *theReply,
                           long       theRefCon )
{
    gAllDone = true;
    return noErr;
}
```

Playing a sound from a sound resource

Playing a sound from a sound resource is a simple process. Begin by calling the Toolbox function GetResource() to load the sound resource data into memory. The GetResource() function can be used to load the data of various resource types, so you need to specify the resource type in the first parameter. Notice that the fourth character in the four-character resource name is a space. The name of every resource type consists of four characters, and the sound resource is no exception. When naming the resource type in the first parameter to GetResource(), enclose the four characters in single quotations. The second parameter to GetResource() is the resource ID of the resource to load. In the following snippet, snd resource 9000 is being loaded into memory:

```
#define      rGoodBadUglySound          9000

Handle   theSound;
OSErr    theError;

theSound = GetResource( 'snd ', rGoodBadUglySound );

theError = SndPlay( nil, (SndListHandle)theSound, true );
```

After loading the sound resource data, play the sound by calling the Toolbox function SndPlay(). The first parameter to SndPlay() specifies the *sound channel* to use. If you pass a nil pointer, as done here, then the Sound Manager takes care of opening and closing a sound channel for you. The second parameter is a handle to the sound resource data that was previously loaded into memory. The third parameter tells the Sound Manager whether the sound is to be played *asynchronously*—that is, whether this is the only sound playing (asynchronous) or if more than one sound will be playing at the same time (synchronous). You will just be playing one sound at a time, so set this parameter to `true`.

N O T E As of this writing the THINK C and Symantec C++ compilers don't require typecasting of the second parameter to `SndPlay()`—so the FinderAware.c file found in the THINK C and Symantec C++ folders on the included CD pass a `Handle` rather than a `SndListHandle`. Whether this parameter gets typecast depends on the version of the universal header files included with your IDE. If you're using one of these two compilers, and you get a compile-time error at this line of code, add the typecasting as shown in the above snippet.

FinderAware plays its sound from the `OpenWindowAndPlaySound()` routine. That function begins by opening and displaying a small window. Just before the sound is played a call to `DrawString()` is made to inform the user that the sound is playing. This note will come in handy for users who have the volume set to 0—without the notice they might not realize what the program is doing. When `SndPlay()` completes the playing of the sound, the note is erased using a call to the Toolbox function `EraseRect()`.

Event handling

FinderAware looks for two event types: `keyDown` and `kHighLevelEvent`. In response to a press of a key, the program ends. In response to an Apple event, the Toolbox function `AEProcessAppleEvent()` is called. This is the function that is responsible for invoking the application-defined Quit Application Apple event handler routine `AEHandleQuit()`:

```
void  EventLoop( void )
{
   EventRecord  theEvent;

   while ( gAllDone == false )
   {
      WaitNextEvent( everyEvent, &theEvent, 15L, nil );

      switch ( theEvent.what )
      {
```

```
        case keyDown:
            gAllDone = true;
            break;

        case kHighLevelEvent:
            AEProcessAppleEvent( &theEvent );
            break;
    }
  }
}
```

Chapter Summary

Giving a program its own icon to be displayed in the Finder is the finishing touch that makes your program look professional. The BNDL resource allows you to create your own icon and associate it with a program you write.

When the user elects to shut down his or her Macintosh, the Finder will attempt to quit all applications that are currently running. The Finder will be successful only if each currently running program supports the Quit Application Apple event. You can add Apple event support to your own program by writing a simple application-defined Quit Application Apple event handler routine and installing that routine in your program.

Appendix A

Macintosh Data Types

ANSI C data types, such as int, float, and char, all exist in the Macintosh programming world. But to meet the special GUI needs of the Macintosh, Apple has created several new data types. These types allow access to the Toolbox, provide you with a means to create and work with the graphical user interface, and give you the resources to work within Apple's memory addressing scheme. Many of these data types are defined alphabetically in this appendix.

CGrafPort

The color version of a GrafPort. *See* GrafPort.

ControlHandle

The push buttons, radio buttons, and check boxes found in dialog boxes are controls. To work with them, Toolbox routines use handles called ControlHandles.

Cursor

The data type that represents a 16-by-16 bit image that defines a cursor. The on-screen cursor is set to the arrow cursor by a call to

InitCursor(). To access the other four system-defined cursors, use the constants iBeamCursor, crossCursor, plusCursor, and watchCursor.

CursHandle

Cursors are stored as CURS resources and are accessed by Toolbox routines that return, and expect as a parameter, the cursor handle CursHandle.

DialogPtr

A pointer to another Macintosh data type, the DialogRecord. The DialogRecord holds information about a dialog box. You access this information via Toolbox calls that require a DialogPtr rather than the DialogRecord itself. Many Toolbox routines that work with WindowPtrs also work with a DialogPtr as the parameter.

DialogRecord

A structure that holds information about a single dialog box—descriptive information needed by the Dialog Manager. You seldom need to work directly with a DialogRecord. Instead, you access information indirectly through Toolbox routines that use a DialogPtr, a pointer to a DialogRecord.

EventRecord

An EventRecord holds information about a single event. An EventRecord is created for every event that occurs. These EventRecords are held in an event queue. Unlike some Macintosh data types, that you deal with through the use of pointers or handles, you work with events directly through the record itself.

GrafPort

A graphics port is a drawing environment that defines how text and shapes will be drawn. So that it can display unique text or shape styles, each window has its own graphics port. A GrafPort is the Macintosh data type that holds this information about a graphics port. To access information within a graphics port you use a pointer to a `GrafPort`, rather than the `GrafPort` itself.

GrafPtr

A pointer to a `GrafPort`. A `GrafPort` is the data structure that holds information about a graphics port. *See* `GrafPort`.

Handle

A pointer to a master pointer. A master pointer keeps track of the location of a relocatable block in the application's heap. Some Toolbox functions return a Handle to your program. To make use of this generic `Handle` in future Toolbox calls, you may have to typecast it to a specific type of handle, such as a `ControlHandle`.

MenuHandle

A handle to a menu record. A menu record holds information about a single menu—descriptive information needed by the Menu Manager. Toolbox routines that work with menus use `MenuHandles` rather than the menu record itself.

PatHandle

A data type. `Patterns` can be created and stored in `PAT` resources. Toolbox routines that work with `Patterns` obtained from a resource file use the `PatHandle` data type.

Pattern

An 8-by-8 bit image that defines a design that can be repeated to fill an area of any given size. There are five system `Patterns` defined by the constants `white`, `ltGray`, `gray`, `dkGray`, and `black`.

PicHandle

A handle type. Pictures, or `PICT` resource types, are accessed through a handle of type `PicHandle`. Toolbox routines that work with pictures will expect a `PicHandle` as a parameter.

Point

Any pixel on the Macintosh screen can be referred to by a pair of coordinates. That data type `Point` holds one such pair.

Rect

A rectangle. It is the Macintosh data type that is used as a basis for drawing rectangles, ovals, and round rectangles. The coordinates that make up a rectangle's upper-left corner and the two that make up its lower-right corner define a rectangle. The Macintosh data type that holds this information is the `Rect`.

WindowPtr

A pointer to another Macintosh data type, the `WindowRecord`. The `WindowRecord` holds information about a window. You'll access this information via Toolbox calls that require a `WindowPtr` rather than the `WindowRecord` itself.

WindowRecord

A structure that holds information about a single window—descriptive information needed by the Window Manager. You seldom need to work directly with a `WindowRecord`. Instead, you access information indirectly through Toolbox routines that use a `WindowPtr`, a pointer to a `WindowRecord`.

Appendix B

Determining a Trap's Type

Chapter 9, The Varying Mac, thoroughly covered the concept of traps. For you trap fanatics, here's a little more.

If your program is running on a computer that has System 6.0.4 or later, you can use the Gestalt() function to determine the availability of a trap quickly and easily. The Gestalt() routine is discussed in Chapter 9. If you're on a machine that is pre-1989, you have to use the NGetTrapAddress() function in place of Gestalt().

If you're using NGetTrapAddress(), and you know the trap you are looking for is a Toolbox trap (as opposed to an Operating System trap), you can simply make the comparison to the Unimplemented trap. Here's the example used in Chapter 9:

```
Boolean  colorWindAvail;

colorWindAvail = ( NGetTrapAddress( _GetNewCWindow, ToolTrap )
            != ( NGetTrapAddress( _Unimplemented, ToolTrap ) );
```

If, however, you're writing a program that is to run on a pre-1989 Macintosh, and you don't know the type of the trap, ToolTrap or

OSTrap, you'll need to include extra code in your program. Below is the necessary code. The routine TrapIsPresent() and the two routines that it calls are summarized here.

GetTrapType()

The setting of one bit of a trap—bit 11—determines whether the trap is a Toolbox trap (ToolTrap) or an Operating System trap (OSTrap). This routine performs an & operation on this one bit to determine if it is set or not.

NumToolTraps()

Macintosh models may have one of two different sized trap tables. This routine uses the trap for the InitGraf() routine, present on all Macs, to determine if the Toolbox has 512 (0x200) Toolbox traps or 1024 (0x400) Toolbox traps.

TrapIsPresent()

This routine makes use of the GetTrapType() and NumToolTraps() routines and the Toolbox routine NGetTrapAddress() to determine if the trap you've passed in is present.

Now, the code. For in-depth trap-checking, copy the following three routines to your source code—even if you don't fully understand them! Then, to check for the availability of a trap, simply call TrapIsPresent(), passing in the trap to check for. Following the routines is an example of a call to TrapIsPresent().

```
Boolean    TrapIsPresent( short );
TrapType   GetTrapType( short );
short      NumToolTraps( void );

Boolean    TrapIsPresent( short theTrap )
{
```

```
    TrapType    theType;
    Boolean     isPresent;

    theType = GetTrapType( theTrap );

    if ( ( theType == ToolTrap ) &&
         ( ( theTrap &= 0x07FF ) >= NumToolTraps() ) )
        isPresent = false;
    else
        isPresent = ( NGetTrapAddress( _Unimplemented, ToolTrap ) !=
                      NGetTrapAddress( theTrap, theType ) );

    return isPresent;
}


TrapType  GetTrapType( short theTrap )
{
    if ( ( theTrap & 0x0800 ) == 0 )
        return ( OSTrap );
    else
        return ( ToolTrap );
}


short  NumToolTraps( void )
{
    if ( NGetTrapAddress( 0xA86E, ToolTrap ) ==
         NGetTrapAddress( 0xAA6E, ToolTrap ) )
        return ( 0x200 );
    else
        return ( 0x400 );
}
```

Here's an example that checks for the presence of `WaitNextEvent()`. If its not available, an alert will be posted.

```
#define    rWNEnotHereAlert    128

if ( TrapIsPresent(_WaitNextEvent) == false )
    Alert( rWNEnotHereAlert, nil );
```

Appendix C

Gestalt Definitions

Chapter 9 gave several examples for obtaining information about a Macintosh using the Gestalt() function. Here are several more selector codes that yield system software and hardware information. If you plan on expanding Chapter 8's InnerView example program into a more useful utility, you'll want to add Gestalt() calls that include many of these selector codes.

Use any of the selector codes as shown in Chapter 9. Here's an example:

```
OSErr   theError;
long    theResponse;

theError = Gestalt( gestaltQuickdrawVersion, &theResponse );

if ( theError == noErr )
{
   if ( theResponse == gestaltOriginalQD )
      DrawString("\pYou have the original version of QuickDraw.");
}
```

Addressing Mode Attributes

Selector code

```
gestaltAddressingModeAttr
```

Response parameter

```
gestalt32BitAddressing = 0    /* using 32-bit addressing mode  */
gestalt32BitSysZone    = 1    /* 32-bit compatible system zone */
gestalt32BitCapable    = 2    /* 32-bit capable machine        */
```

Apple Events Attributes

Selector code

```
gestaltAppleEventsAttr
```

Response parameter

```
gestaltAppleEventsPresent = 0    /* true if Apple Events present */
gestaltScriptingSupport   = 1
gestaltOSLInSystem        = 2
```

AppleTalk Version

Selector code

```
gestaltAppleTalkVersion
```

Response parameter

Returns version number of installed AppleTalk driver.
A/UX Version

Selector code

gestaltAUXVersion

Response parameter

Returns version number of A/UX if it is currently executing.

Easy Access Attributes

Selector code

gestaltEasyAccessAttr

Response parameter

```
gestaltEasyAccessOff    = 0   /* Easy Access present, but off */
gestaltEasyAccessOn     = 1   /* Easy Access On              */
gestaltEasyAccessSticky = 2   /* Easy Access Sticky      */
gestaltEasyAccessLocked = 3   /* Easy Access Locked      */
```

Floating-Point Unit Type

Selector code

gestaltFPUType

Response parameter

```
gestaltNoFPU     = 0        /* no FPU             */
gestalt68881     = 1        /* 68881 FPU          */
gestalt68882     = 2        /* 68882 FPU          */
gestalt68040FPU  = 3        /* 68040 built-in FPU */
```

Gestalt Version

Selector code

```
gestaltVersion
```

Response parameter

Returns the current version. As of this writing the current version is 6, returned as $0006.

Hardware Attributes

Selector code

```
gestaltHardwareAttr
```

Response parameter

```
gestaltHasVIA1          = 0      /* VIA1 exists            */
gestaltHasVIA2          = 1      /* VIA2 exists            */
gestaltHasASC           = 3      /* Apple Sound Chip exists */
gestaltHasSCC           = 4      /* SCC exists             */
gestaltHasSCSI          = 7      /* SCSI exists            */
gestaltHasSoftPowerOff  = 19     /* has software power off */
```

```
gestaltHasSCSI961      = 21     /* 53C96 SCSI controller internal bus  */
gestaltHasSCSI962      = 22     /* 53C96 SCSI controller external bus   */
gestaltHasUniversalROM = 24     /* has a Universal ROM    */
gestaltHasEnhancedLtalk = 30    /* has a Enhanced LocalTalk    */
```

HELP MANAGER ATTRIBUTES

Selector code

gestaltHelpMgrAttr

Response parameter

```
gestaltHelpMgrPresent    = 0   /* true if help mgr is present */
gestaltHelpMgrExtensions = 1   /* true if help mgr extensions are
    installed */
```

KEYBOARD TYPE

Selector code

gestaltKeyboardType

Response parameter

```
gestaltMacKbd          = 1     /* Mac keyboard            */
gestaltMacAndPad       = 2     /* Mac keyboard w/pad      */
gestaltMacPlusKbd      = 3     /* MacPlus keyboard        */
gestaltExtADBKbd       = 4     /* extended ADB keyboard   */
gestaltStdADBKbd       = 5     /* standard ADB keyboard   */
gestaltPrtblADBKbd     = 6     /* portable ADB keyboard   */
gestaltPrtblISOKbd     = 7     /* portable ISO keyboard   */
```

```
gestaltStdISOADBKbd        = 8    /* standard ISO ADB keyboard  */
gestaltExtISOADBKbd        = 9    /* extended ISO ADB keyboard  */
gestaltADBKbdII            = 10   /* ADB keyboard II            */
gestaltADBISOKbdII         = 11   /* ADB ISO keyboard II        */
gestaltPwrBookADBKbd       = 12   /* Powerbook ADB keyboard     */
gestaltPwrBookISOADBKbd    = 13   /* Powerbook ISO ADB keyboard */
gestaltAppleAdjustKeypad   = 14
gestaltAppleAdjustADBKbd   = 15
gestaltAppleAdjustISOKbd   = 16
gestaltJapanAdjustADBKbd   = 17   /* Japan Adjustable Keyboard */
gestaltPwrBkExtISOKbd      = 20   /* PowerBook Extd International */
gestaltPwrBkExtJISKbd      = 21   /* PowerBook Extended Japanese  */
gestaltPwrBkExtADBKbd      = 24   /* PowerBook Extended Domestic */
```

LOGICAL RAM SIZE

Selector code

```
gestaltLogicalRAMSize       /* logical ram size */
```

Response parameter

Returns the amount of logical memory available, in bytes.

LOW MEMORY AREA

Selector code

```
gestaltLowMemorySize        /* size of low memory area */
```

Response parameter

Returns the size, in bytes, of the low-memory area. This area is used for vectors, global variables, and dispatch tables.

Memory Management Unit Type

Selector code

gestaltMMUType

Response parameter

```
gestaltNoMMU     = 0        /* no MMU                   */
gestaltAMU       = 1        /* address management unit */
gestalt68851     = 2        /* 68851 PMMU              */
gestalt68030MMU  = 3        /* 68030 built-in MMU      */
gestalt68040MMU  = 4        /* 68040 built-in MMU      */
gestaltEMMU1     = 5        /* Emulated MMU type 1  */
```

QuickDraw Version

Selector code

gestaltQuickdrawVersion

Response parameter

```
gestaltOriginalQD = 0x000    /* original 1-bit QuickDraw    */
gestalt8BitQD     = 0x100    /* 8-bit color QuickDraw       */
gestalt32BitQD    = 0x200    /* 32-bit color QuickDraw      */
gestalt32BitQD11  = 0x210    /* 32-bit color QuickDraw v1.1 */
gestalt32BitQD12  = 0x220    /* 32-bit color QuickDraw v1.2 */
gestalt32BitQD13  = 0x230    /* 32-bit color QuickDraw v1.3 */
```

Physical RAM Size

Selector code

gestaltPhysicalRAMSize

Response parameter

Returns the number of bytes of physical RAM currently installed.

ROM Size

Selector code

gestaltROMSize

Response parameter

Returns the size of the installed ROM.

ROM Version

Selector code

gestaltROMVersion

Response parameter

Returns the version number of the installed ROM.

Sound Attributes

Selector code

gestaltSoundAttr

Response parameter

```
gestaltStereoCapability    = 0  /* stereo compatabile hardware     */
gestaltStereoMixing        = 1  /* external speaker stereo mixing  */
gestaltSoundIOMgrPresent   = 3  /* Sound I/O Manager is present    */
gestaltBuiltInSoundInput   = 4  /* built-in Sound Input hardware   */
gestaltHasSoundInputDevice = 5  /* Sound Input device available    */
gestaltPlayAndRecord       = 6  /* built-in simul. play/record     */
gestalt16BitSoundIO        = 7  /* play and record 16-bit samples  */
gestaltStereoInput         = 8  /* record stereo                   */
gestaltLineLevelInput      = 9  /* sound input requires line level */
/* the following bits are not defined prior to Sound Mgr 3.0       */
gestaltSndPlayDoubleBuffer = 10 /* SndPlayDoubleBuffer available   */
gestaltMultiChannels       = 11 /* multiple channel support        */
gestalt16BitAudioSupport   = 12 /* 16 bit audio data supported     */
```

SYSTEM VERSION

Selector code

```
gestaltSystemVersion
```

Response parameter

Returns the version number of the active System file.

VIRTUAL MEMORY ATTRIBUTES

Selector code

```
gestaltVMAttr
```

Response parameter

```
gestaltVMPresent = 0    /* true if virtual memory is present */
```

Macintosh Programming Techniques, 2E

Appendix D

Toolbox Routine Summary

This appendix summarizes the Toolbox calls used throughout this book. The calls are divided into the following eight sections:

- QuickDraw
- Events
- Windows
- Dialogs
- Menus
- Memory
- Utilities
- Sound

QuickDraw

This section describes many of the important QuickDraw routines found in the Toolbox.

Constants

```
#define     systemFont      0
#define     applFont        1
#define     newYork         2
#define     geneva          3
#define     monaco          4
#define     venice          5
#define     london          6
#define     athens          7
#define     sanFran         8
#define     toronto         9
#define     cairo          11
#define     losAngeles     12
#define     times          20
#define     helvetica      21
#define     courier        22
#define     symbol         23
#define     mobile         24
```

TextFont() changes the font that subsequent calls to DrawString() uses. Pass TextFont() any of the above constants to set drawing to that font.

```
#define     normal          0
#define     bold            1
#define     italic          2
#define     underline       4
#define     outline         8
#define     shadow       0x10
#define     condense     0x20
#define     extend       0x40
```

TextStyle() sets the style of text drawn by DrawString(). Pass TextStyle() any of the above values or add any number of Styles together for a combined effect.

Global Variables

```
Pattern   dkGray;
Pattern   ltGray;
Pattern   gray;
Pattern   black;
Pattern   white;
```

The system defines five Patterns for your use in calls such as PenPat()
or FillRect(). You can use any of the five variables without declaring
them in your program. When using one of the above constants, preface
its name with qd, and include the dot operator—as in qd.ltGray.

Data Structures

```
struct GrafPort
{
    short       device;
    BitMap      portBits;
    Rect        portRect;
    RgnHandle   visRgn;
    RgnHandle   clipRgn;
    Pattern     bkPat;
    Pattern     fillPat;
    Point       pnLoc;
    Point       pnSize;
    short       pnMode;
    Pattern     pnPat;
    short       pnVis;
    short       txFont;
    Style       txFace;
    char        filler;
    short       txMode;
    short       txSize;
    Fixed       spExtra;
    long        fgColor;
    long        bkColor;
    short       colrBit;
    short       patStretch;
    Handle      picSave;
    Handle      rgnSave;
```

```
    Handle     polySave;
    QDProcsPtr grafProcs;
};

typedef  struct  GrafPort  GrafPort;
typedef  GrafPort  *GrafPtr;
```

A GrafPort is the drawing environment of a window. Each window has its own GrafPort. The fields within a GrafPort are changed through the use of Toolbox calls rather than direct manipulation.

Graphic Ports

SetPort() makes the graphics port pointed to by thePort the current port. Subsequent drawing operations will be performed in this port. Call SetPort() before first drawing to a port to ensure that graphics operations are drawn to the proper window. Before calling SetPort(), call GetPort() to save the current port so that it can be restored later.

```
void  SetPort( GrafPtr  thePort );
void  GetPort( GrafPtr  *thePort );
```

GetPort() gets the current port and saves a pointer to it in thePort. Before drawing to a port, call GetPort() to save the current port, then call SetPort() to set the port to the new port.

Graphics Pen

```
void  GetPenState( PenState  *thePenState );
```

GetPenState() gets the current state of the pen and stores it in thePenState. After making location, size, or pattern changes to the pen, you can restore the previous pen state with a call to SetPenState().

```
void  SetPenState( PenState  *thePenState );
```

Before making changes to the state of the graphics pen you can call GetPenState() to save the current state in thePenState. Then, after drawing is complete, call SetPenState(). Pass the same thePenState to restore the pen to its previous condition.

```
void  PenPat( Pattern thePattern );
```

PenPat() sets the pattern used by the graphics pen to thePattern. All subsequent drawing operations performed in the current graphics port will use this pattern until PenPat() is again called. Use GetPattern() to load a PAT resource for use by PenPat(), or use one of the standard Patterns defined as global variables and listed under the Global Variables heading of this section.

```
void  PenPixPat( PixPatHandle thePatHandle );
```

PenPixPat() sets the pattern used by the graphics pen to the pattern accessed through thePatHandle. All subsequent drawing operations performed in the current graphics port will use this pattern until PenPixPat() is again called. Call GetPixPat() to load a color ppat resource for use by PenPixPat().

```
void  PenSize( short  theWidth,
              short  theHeight );
```

Set the width and height of the graphics pen with a call to PenSize(). The parameters theWidth and theHeight are the pixel dimensions the pen will acquire. All subsequent lines drawn with the pen will be drawn in this size.

```
void  PenNormal( void );
```

To restore the pen to its default settings, call PenNormal(). PenNormal() sets the pen's size to (1,1) and its pattern to black.

```
void  MoveTo( short  theHoriz,
             short  theVert );
```

MoveTo() moves the pen to the horizontal pixel coordinate theHoriz and the theVert pixel coordinate vert. The origin is the left top corner of the current port. No drawing is performed.

```
void  Move( short  theHoriz,
           short  theVert );
```

Move() moves the pen theHoriz pixels in the horizontal direction and theVert pixels in the vertical position from the pen's current position. A negative theHoriz value moves the pen to the left. A negative theVert value moves the pen up. No drawing is performed.

```
void  LineTo( short  theHoriz,
              short  theVert );
```

LineTo() draws a line to the horizontal pixel coordinate theHoriz and the theVert pixel coordinate vert. The origin is the left top corner of the current port.

```
void  Line( short  theHoriz,
            short  theVert );
```

Line() draws a line theHoriz pixels in the horizontal direction and theVert pixels in the vertical position from the pen's current position. A negative theHoriz value draws a line to the left. A negative theVert value draws a line up.

Drawing Text

```
void  GetIndString( Str255  theStr,
                    short   theStrListID,
                    short   theIndex );
```

GetIndString() loads a string into theStr from the STR# list with an ID of theStrListID. From this list GetIndString() selects the theIndex string in the list; e.g. if theIndex = 2, the second string in the list will be loaded. Once loaded, theStr can be used as any other Str255 variable.

```
void  TextFont( short  theFontNum );
```

TextFont() sets the font to the font number theFontNum. All subsequent text will be drawn in this font. Many fonts are defined by constants given under the Constants heading of this section.

```
void  TextFace( Style  theFace );
```

`TextFace()` sets the style of text to `theFace`. The style can be one `Style` or a combination of `Styles`. All subsequent text will be drawn in this style. See the Constants heading in this section for a listing of the available `Styles`.

```
void  TextSize( short  theSize );
```

Set the size of text with a call to `TextSize()`. The size is given in points, where approximately 72 points equals one inch. All subsequent text will be drawn in this size.

```
void  DrawChar( short  theChar );
```

`DrawChar()` draws a single character `theChar` to the current port. The current font, style, and size are used. The starting location of the character is the current position of the graphics pen.

```
void  DrawString( Str255  theStr );
```

`DrawString()` draws string `theStr` to the current port. The current font, style, and size are used. The starting location of the character is the current position of the graphics pen.

Patterns

```
PatHandle  GetPattern( short  thePatternID );
```

`GetPattern()` returns a `PatHandle` to the `PAT` resource with the ID of `thePatternID`. Once you've obtained a `PatHandle`, dereference it twice and then use it as a `Pattern` type in QuickDraw calls, such as `PenPat()`.

```
PixPatHandle  GetPixPat( short  theppatID );
```

`GetPixPat()` works like `GetPattern()`. `GetPixPat()` returns a `PixPatHandle` to the ppat resource with the ID of `theppatID`. Once you've obtained a `PixPatHandle`, use it in QuickDraw calls, such as

PenPixPat(). Color QuickDraw routines that work with color patterns accept handles to them—you do not have to dereference it.

Drawing Shapes

```
void  SetRect( Rect  *theRect,
               short  theLeft,
               short  theTop,
               short  theRight,
               short  theBottom );
```

SetRect() sets the boundaries of rectangle theRect. The coordinates of the rectangle use the current graphics port's left top corner as the origin.

Always use SetRect() to establish a rectangle before performing shape-drawing operations involving a rectangle, oval, or round rectangle. SetRect() does not display a rectangle.

```
void  FrameRect( Rect  *theRect );
```

FrameRect() frames rectangle theRect. Before framing, establish the boundaries of theRect with a call to SetRect(). FrameRect() does not fill in the rectangle, it merely outlines it with a frame.

```
void  PaintRect( Rect  *theRect );
```

PaintRect() fills the rectangle theRect with the current pen pattern. Call SetRect() to establish the boundaries of theRect.

```
void  FillRect( Rect     *theRect,
                Pattern   thePat );
```

FillRect() fills the rectangle theRect with the pattern thePat. The current pen pattern is unaffected by the call to FillRect(). Call SetRect() to establish the boundaries of theRect.

```
void  EraseRect( Rect  *theRect );
```

EraseRect() fills rectangle theRect with the background pattern, which is usually white. Call SetRect() to establish the boundaries of theRect.

```
void  InvertRect( Rect  *theRect );
```

InvertRect() changes the state of each pixel in rectangle theRect. All white pixels become black; all black pixels become white.

```
void  FrameOval( Rect  *theRect);

void  PaintOval( Rect  *theRect);

void  FillOval( Rect      *theRect,
                Pattern   thePat );

void  EraseOval( Rect  *theRect);

void  InvertOval( Rect  *theRect);
```

Each of the previous five routines that perform operations on rectangles have an analogous Toolbox routine that performs the same operation on an oval. For each oval routine, the oval is drawn within the rectangle theRect.

```
void  FrameRoundRect( Rect  *theRect,
                      short   theWidth,
                      short   theHeight );

void  PaintRoundRect( Rect  *theRect,
                      short   theWidth,
                      short   theHeight );

void  FillRoundRect( Rect      *theRect,
                     short      theWidth,
                     short      theHeight,
                     Pattern   thePat );

void  EraseRoundRect( Rect  *theRect,
                      short   theWidth,
                      short   theHeight );

void  InvertRoundRect( Rect  *theRect,
                       short   theWidth,
                       short   theHeight );
```

Each of the five routines that perform operations on rectangles have an analogous Toolbox routine that performs the same operation on a round rectangle. The amount of rounding to the corner of a round rectangle is determined by width and height.

```
void  FillCRect( Rect         *theRect,
                 PixPatHandle  theppatHandle );
```

To fill a rectangle with a colored pattern, use `FillCRect()`.
`FillCRect()` fills rectangle `theRect` with the `PixPat` accessed through
`theppatHandle`. The window that is being drawn to should be a color
window created with a call to `GetNewCWindow()`.

```
void  FillCOval( Rect         *theRect,
                 PixPatHandle  theppatHandle );
```

To fill an oval with a colored pattern, use `FillCOval()`. This routine fills
the oval inscribed into `theRect` with the `PixPat` accessed through
`theppatHandle`. The window that is being drawn to should be a color
window created with a call to `GetNewCWindow()`.

```
void  FillCRoundRect( Rect          *theRect,
                      short          theWidth,
                      short          theHeight,
                      PixPatHandle  theppatHandle );
```

To fill a round rectangle with a colored pattern, use `FillCRoundRect()`.
This routine fills the round rectangle described by `theRect` with the
PixPat accessed through `theppatHandle`. The window that is being
drawn to should be a color window created with a call to
`GetNewCWindow()`.

EVENTS

This section describes the important Event Manager routines found in
the Toolbox.

Constants

```
#define    nullEvent    0
#define    mouseDown    1
#define    mouseUp      2
#define    keyDown      3
#define    keyUp        4
```

```
#define    autoKey       5
#define    updateEvt     6
#define    diskEvt       7
#define    activateEvt   8
#define    osEvt        15
```

After a call to `WaitNextEvent()`, the what field of the returned `EventRecord` will contain one of the above constants.

```
#define    mDownMask               2
#define    mUpMask                 4
#define    keyDownMask             8
#define    keyUpMask              16
#define    autoKeyMask            32
#define    updateMask            64
#define    diskMask             128
#define    activMask            256
#define    highLevelEventMask   1024
#define    osMask             -32768
#define    everyEvent             -1
```

`WaitNextEvent()` is passed a mask that tells them which events to watch for. Most applications will use `everyEvent` as this mask. The occurrance of any type of event will be reported to your program, and the logic of your program can then determine which event types to respond to.

```
#define    charCodeMask       0x000000FF
#define    keyCodeMask        0x0000FF00
#define    adbAddrMask        0x00FF0000
#define    osEvtMessageMask   0xFF000000
```

To determine which character is the result of a keystroke, perform an & operation on the `message` field of the most recent event and the `charCodeMask`.

Data Structures

```
struct EventRecord
{
    short   what;
    long    message;
```

```
    long    when;
    Point   where;
    short   modifiers;
};
```

```
typedef struct EventRecord EventRecord;
```

Unlike some record data structures, you'll access the fields of the
EventRecord directly, without using a pointer or handle.

The what field holds the type of an event, such as mouseDown or
updateEvt.

The message field holds information that varies from one event type
to the next.

The when field gives the time on the system clock when the event
occurred.

The where field holds the location of the cursor at the time the event
occurred.

The modifiers field holds the modifier keys that were pressed at the
time of the event. The **Command** and **Option** keys are examples of modifier keys.

Event Reporting

```
Boolean  WaitNextEvent( short           theEventMask,
                        EventRecord    *theEvent,
                        unsigned long   theSleep,
                        RgnHandle       theMouseRgn );
```

WaitNextEvent() sets theEvent to the next available event of the type
or types specified by theEventMask. To receive events of all types, set
theEventMask equal to the constant everyEvent. After
WaitNextEvent() receives the information that makes up theEvent, it
will remove it from the event queue in anticipation of handling the next
event. WaitNextEvent() will return a value of true if the event is of a
type your program is looking for, as defined by theEventMask.
Otherwise it returns a value of false. The theSleep parameter tells the
system the maximum number of ticks that your program is willing to
relinquish between events. A single tick is one sixtieth of a second. A
theSleep value of zero requests that the system return control to your

program as soon as possible. The `theMouseRgn` parameter is used to aid in cursor display. If your program changes the look of the cursor at different screen locations, you'll want to give `theMouseRgn` a value other than `nil`, or `0L`.

Mouse Reporting

```
void  GetMouse( Point  *theMouseLoc );
```

`GetMouse()` returns the location of the mouse at the time the call is made. The location will be given in local coordinates—that is, `theMouseLoc` will be described in terms of the coordinates of the current `GrafPort`.

```
Boolean  Button( void );
```

`Button()` will return a value of true if the mouse button is down at the time of the call.

Windows

This section details the most commonly used routines that involve the Window Manager.

Constants

```
#define    inDesk        0
#define    inMenuBar     1
#define    inSysWindow   2
#define    inContent     3
#define    inDrag        4
#define    inGrow        5
#define    inGoAway      6
#define    inZoomIn      7
#define    inZoomOut     8
```

`FindWindow()` returns the part of the window in which a mouse-down event occurred.

Data Structures

```
struct  WindowRecord
{
    GrafPort               port;
    short                  windowKind;
    Boolean                visible;
    Boolean                hilited;
    Boolean                goAwayFlag;
    Boolean                spareFlag;
    RgnHandle              strucRgn;
    RgnHandle              contRgn;
    RgnHandle              updateRgn;
    Handle                 windowDefProc;
    Handle                 dataHandle;
    StringHandle           titleHandle;
    short                  titleWidth;
    ControlHandle          controlList;
    struct WindowRecord *nextWindow;
    PicHandle              windowPic;
    long                   refCon;
};

typedef  struct  WindowRecord  WindowRecord;
typedef  WindowRecord  *WindowPeek;

typedef  GrafPtr  WindowPtr;
```

You'll seldom have cause to directly access any of the fields of a
WindowRecord other than the port member, the GrafPort. Instead,
you'll indirectly access the fields using Toolbox calls. For the times you
need direct access, use a pointer to the entire WindowRecord—a
WindowPeek.

A WindowPtr points to the first field of the WindowRecord by the following definitions:

```
struct GrafPort
{
    [ GrafPort members ]
};

typedef  struct  GrafPort  GrafPort;
```

```
typedef  GrafPort  *GrafPtr;

typedef  GrafPtr  WindowPtr;
```

The above states that a `WindowPtr` is the same as a `GrafPtr`. A `GrafPtr` is a pointer to a `GrafPort`. A `WindowPtr` is a `GrafPtr`, and points to a `GrafPort`-the first member of the `WindowRecord` structure. See the QuickDraw section of this appendix for the complete definition of a `GrafPort`.

Window Allocation

```
WindowPtr  GetNewWindow( short       theWindID,
                         Ptr         theStorage,
                         WindowPtr   theBehind );
```

`GetNewWindow()` loads a window into memory using a `WIND` resource. The description of the window is read in from the `WIND` resource with ID `theWindID`. Pass a `nil` pointer, `0L`, for the `theStorage` if you want the Window Manager to choose the memory location for the window. A behind value of `(WindowPtr)-1L` places the window in front of all other windows, a value of `nil`, `0L`, places it behind.

```
WindowPtr  GetNewCWindow( short       theWindID,
                          Ptr         theStorage,
                          WindowPtr   theBehind );
```

`GetNewCWindow()` loads a color window into memory using a `WIND` resource. If color attributes have been defined in the `WIND` resource with ID `theWindID`, they will appear in the window when it is displayed. The last two parameters are the same as for `GetNewWindow()`. Note that both `GetNewCWindow()` and `GetNewWindow()` return a `WindowPtr`. This pointer can be used in any Toolbox routines that require a `WindowPtr` as a parameter.

```
void  CloseWindow( WindowPtr  theWindow );
```

`CloseWindow()` erases theWindow and removes it from the list of open windows. It does not release the memory used by the window's `WindowRecord`. Use this routine only if you supplied the window storage in your call to GetNewWindow( ) or GetNewCWindow( ). To free the memory associated with the WindowRecord, call DisposePtr((Ptr)the_window) after CloseWindow( ).

```
void  DisposeWindow( WindowPtr  theWindow );
```

DisposeWindow( ) erases theWindow and removes it from the list of open windows. It also frees the memory used for theWindow's WindowRecord. Use DisposeWindow( ) if you passed a nil pointer, 0L, as the window storage in your call to GetNewWindow( ) or GetNewCWindow( ).

Window Display

```
void  SetWTitle( WindowPtr  theWindow,
                 Str255     theTitle );
```

SetWTitle( ) sets the title of theWindow to the text that makes up the Str255 variable title.

```
void  GetWTitle( WindowPtr  theWindow,
                 Str255     theTitle );
```

GetWTitle( ) reads the current title of theWindow and sets the Str255 variable title to that value.

```
WindowPtr  FrontWindow( void );
```

FrontWindow( ) returns a WindowPtr to the active window that is, the window that is currently frontmost on the screen. If the screen is empty of windows, FrontWindow( ) will return a nil pointer—0L.

```
void  SelectWindow( WindowPtr  the_window );
```

SelectWindow( ) activates theWindow. The previously active window is unhighlighted, theWindow is placed in front of all others, theWindow is properly highlighted, and an activate event is generated.

```
void  HideWindow( WindowPtr  theWindow );
```

HideWindow() makes theWindow invisible. It does not dispose of it. If the_window is already invisible, HideWindow() has no effect. If any other windows exist, the one that is behind theWindow becomes the active window. To make the hidden window again visible, use ShowWindow().

```
void  ShowWindow( WindowPtr  theWindow );
```

ShowWindow() makes the_window visible. If theWindow is already visible, ShowWindow() has no effect. ShowWindow() highlights theWindow but does not change the front-to-back ordering of windows. To show a hidden window and bring it to the front, use SelectWindow() in conjunction with ShowWindow(). To make the shown window again hidden, use HideWindow().

```
void  MoveWindow( WindowPtr  theWindow,
                  short      theHoriz,
                  short      theVert,
                  Boolean    theFront );
```

MoveWindow() moves theWindow to the screen location specified by the second and third arguments. The top left corner of the window will be placed at the screen point defined by horizontal and vertical. The size of theWindow will be unaffected. If the value of front is true, then theWindow will become the active window.

```
void  DragWindow( WindowPtr  theWindow,
                  Point      theStartPt,
                  Rect       *theDragRect );
```

DragWindow() should be called in response to a mouseDown event in theWindow drag region. The theStartPt should be set to the location of the cursor when the mouse was pressed, as given in the where field of the EventRecord. Window movement will be restricted to the boundaries of the rectangle defined by theDragRect.

Windows and the Mouse

```
short  FindWindow( Point      thePoint,
                   WindowPtr *theWindow );
```

A call to FindWindow() yields both the window (theWindow) and the part of the window (the short return value) in which a mouseDown event occurred. The returned short value will be one of the constants listed above in the Constants section, such as inDrag or inGrow. Set thePoint to the location of the cursor when the event occurred. This can be obtained from the where field of the EventRecord.

Updating

```
void   EraseRgn( RgnHandle   theUpdateRgn );
```

```
void   BeginUpdate( WindowPtr   theWindow );
```

Call BeginUpdate() in response to an updateEvt for theWindow. After calling BeginUpdate(), call EraseRgn(), passing EraseRgn() the visRgn of theWindow, as in: EraseRgn(&theWindow->visRgn). Then perform all the drawing necessary to draw the entire contents of the window. The EraseRgn() call will restrict the actual updating to only the area needed updating. After drawing to the window, call EndUpdate().

```
void   EndUpdate( WindowPtr   the_window );
```

EndUpdate() restores the visRgn of theWindow. This region was altered during BeginUpdate().

DIALOGS

This section describes many of the Toolbox routines that involve the Dialog Manager.

Data Structures

```
struct DialogRecord
{
    WindowRecord    window;
    Handle          items;
    TEHandle        textH;
```

```
    short        editField;
    short        editOpen;
    short        aDefItem;
};

typedef  struct  DialogRecord  DialogRecord;
typedef  DialogRecord  *DialogPeek;

typedef  WindowPtr  DialogPtr;
```

As with a `WindowRecord`, you'll seldom need direct access to any of the fields of a `DialogRecord`. You will instead use a `DialogPtr`. The first member of the `DialogRecord` is a `WindowRecord`. The first member of a `WindowRecord` is the port—the `GrafPort`. A `DialogPtr`, like a `WindowPtr`, points to a `GrafPort`. A `DialogPtr` can thus be used in Toolbox calls expecting a `WindowPtr` as an argument. See the Constants section of the Windows heading of this appendix for more information.

For the few times you need direct access to fields other than the port, use a pointer to the entire `DialogRecord`—a `DialogPeek`.

Dialog Allocation

```
DialogPtr  GetNewDialog( short        theDialogID,
                         Ptr          theStorage,
                         WindowPtr    theBehind );
```

`GetNewDialog()` loads a dialog into memory using a `DLOG` resource. The description of the dialog is read in from the `DLOG` resource with ID `theDialogID`. Pass a `nil` pointer, `0L`, for the `theStorage` if you want the Dialog Manager to choose the memory location for the dialog. A behind value of `(WindowPtr)-1L` places the dialog in front of all other windows, a value of `nil`, `0L`, places it behind.

There is no separate call to create a color dialog as there is for creating a color window. Instead, you use ResEdit to add color to any element—such as the frame or title bar—of the dialog's `DLOG` resource. That will create a `dctb` resource. Existence of the `dctb` resource tells `GetNewDialog()` to base the new dialog on a color graphics port.

```
void  CloseDialog(DialogPtr theDialog);
```

`CloseDialog()` erases `theDialog` and removes its window from the list of open windows. It does not release the memory used by the dialog's `DialogRecord` or by the dialog's item list. Use this routine only if you supplied the dialog storage in your call to GetNewDialog(). To free the memory associated with the `DialogRecord`, call `DisposePtr((Ptr)theDialog)` after `CloseDialog()`.

```
void  DisposeDialog( DialogPtr  theDialog );
```

`DisposeDialog()` erases `theDialog` and removes its window from the list of open windows. It also frees the memory used for `theDialog`'s `DialogRecord` and item list. Use `DisposeDialog()` if you passed a `nil` pointer, `0L`, as the dialog storage in your call to `GetNewDialog()`.

Dialog Events

```
void  ModalDialog( ModalFilterUPP  FilterFunction,
                   short           *theItem );
```

`ModalDialog()` performs event handling for a modal dialog box. When an event involves an enabled item, the item number of that item is returned to the program as `theItem`.

`ModalDialog()` optionally accepts a pointer to a filter function. If this value is `nil`, `0L`, `ModalDialog()` is responsible for all handling of the event. If a pointer to a filter function is included in the call, the filter function will handle some or all of the events. The filter function name, without parentheses, serves as the `ModalFilterUPP`. The filter function is application defined. Its format is given below.

```
pascal  Boolean  FilterFunction( DialogPtr    theDialog,
                                 EventRecord *theEvent,
                                 short        *theItem );
```

`FilterFunction()` is an application-defined function that should be written to perform any dialog-related tasks not performed by `ModalDialog()`. The function can have any name, but it must have the three arguments listed. The first is a pointer to the active dialog. The EventRecord should be the event currently being handled. The theItem parameter will be the item selected by the user. See Chapter 8 for a discussion of filter functions as they pertain universal procedure pointers (UPPs) and to PowerPC compilers.

```
Boolean  IsDialogEvent( EventRecord *the_event );
```

IsDialogEvent() determines if, at the time of the current event, the frontmost window was a dialog box. If a dialog box wasn't in the forefront the event is not dialog related, and IsDialogEvent() returns a value of false to the calling routine.

```
Boolean  DialogSelect( EventRecord *theEvent,
                       DialogPtr   *theDialog,
                       short       *theItem );
```

DialogSelect() does all the work for you if a dialog needs updating or activating. Call it after IsDialogEvent() has returned a value of true.

If the event was dialog related but wasn't an update or activate event, DialogSelect() doesn't handle it. Instead, DialogSelect() returns a pointer to the dialog and the item number of the clicked-on item for further processing by your program.

```
void  DlgCut( DialogPtr  theDialog );
```

DlgCut() handles the **Cut** command for text within a dialog's edit text item.

```
void  DlgPaste( DialogPtr  theDialog );
```

DlgPaste() handles the **Paste** command for text within a dialog's edit text item.

```
void  DlgCopy( DialogPtr  theDialog );
```

DlgCopy() handles the **Copy** command for text within a dialog's edit text item.

Alerts

```
short  Alert( short            theAlertID,
               ModalFilterUPP  FilterFunction );
```

Alert() loads, displays, and handles and alert defined by an ALRT resource with an ID of theAlertID. It displays no icon, as the other three forms of the Alert() function do. The ModalFilterUPP argument is a pointer to an optional filter function that handles each event before processing by the Alert() function. See ModalDialog() for more information on filter functions. Alert() returns a value of type short that contains the item number selected by the user.

```
short  StopAlert( short            theAlertID,
                   ModalFilterUPP  FilterFunction );
```

StopAlert() is identical to Alert() except that it displays a stop-sign icon in the alert's top left corner.

```
short  NoteAlert( short            theAlertID,
                   ModalFilterUPP  FilterFunction );
```

NoteAlert() is identical to Alert() except that it displays a message icon in the alert's top left corner.

```
short  CautionAlert( short            theAlertID,
                      ModalFilterUPP  FilterFunction );
```

CautionAlert() is identical to Alert() except that it displays a cautionary icon in the alert's top left corner.

Dialog and Alert Items

```
void  ParamText( Str255  str0,
                 Str255  str1,
                 Str255  str2,
                 Str255  str3 );
```

ParamText() allows up to four strings to be substituted in an alert or dialog. If a static text item contains the string "^0", the text that comprises str0 will be substituted for "^0". In addition str1 will replace "^1", str2 will replace "^2", and str3 will replace "^3". Less than four strings can be defined in ParamText() by using one or more empty strings ("\p").

```
void  GetDialogItem( DialogPtr  theDialog,
                     short       theItem,
                     short      *theType,
                     Handle     *theHandle,
                     Rect       *theRect );
```

To obtain information about a dialog item, pass GetDialogItem() a pointer to the dialog and the item number of the item in question. The item number for any item can be found in the dialog's DITL resource. After GetDialogItem() has executed, theType will contain the item's type, theHandle will hold a handle to the item, and theRect will hold the display rectangle that holds the item.

```
void  SetDialogItem( DialogPtr  theDialog,
                     short       theItem,
                     short       theType,
                     Handle      theHandle,
                     Rect       *theRect );
```

The description of an item can be changed using SetDialogItem(). All parameters are the same as they are for GetDialogItem().

```
void  GetDialogItemText( Handle  theItem,
                         Str255  theStr );
```

GetDialogItemText() returns the text from a text item in a dialog. Parameter theItem is a handle to the item. This handle can be obtained by first calling GetDialogItem(). After the call to GetDialogItemText(), theStr will hold the contents of the text item.

```
void  SetDialogItemText(Handle  theItem,
                        Str255  theStr );
```

SetDialogItemText() changes the text in a dialog text item. Parameter theItem is a handle to the item and can be obtained by first calling GetDialogItem(). The Str255 parameter theStr is the text to set the item to.

```
void  SetControlTitle( ControlHandle  theControl,
                       Str255          title );
```

SetControlTitle() sets the title of theControl to the text in title. You can get a Handle to the control by first calling GetDialogItem(). The returned handle should be typecast to the proper type when calling SetControlTitle(). Assuming the_handle is of type Handle and was returned by GetDialogItem(), a call to SetControlTitle() would look like the following: SetControlTitle((ControlHandle)the_handle, title);

```
void  GetControlTitle( ControlHandle  theControl,
                       Str255          theTitle );
```

GetControlTitle() returns the current title of the item pointed to by theControl. See SetControlTitle() for information on obtaining this ControlHandle.

```
void  SetControlValue( ControlHandle  theControl,
                       short          theValue );
```

SetControlValue() sets the value of the item pointed to by theControl. See SetControlTitle() for information on obtaining this ControlHandle. Parameter theValue should be either a 1 or 0. A value of 1 turns the control on; a value of 0 turns it off.

```
short  GetControlValue( ControlHandle  theControl );
```

GetControlValue() returns the value of the item pointed to by theControl. See SetControlTitle() for information on obtaining this ControlHandle. The returned short type will be either 1 or 0. A value of 1 means the control is on; a value of 0 means that it is off.

MENUS

This section describes the important Menu Manager routines found in the Toolbox.

Constants

```
#define    normal       0
#define    bold         1
#define    italic       2
#define    underline    4
#define    outline      8
#define    shadow       0x10
#define    condense     0x20
#define    extend       0x40
```

The style of the text of a menu item can be changed with a call to SetItemStyle(). Pass in one or a combination of the above Style constants.

Data Structures

```
typedef  unsigned  char  Style;
```

A call to SetItemStyle() changes the text style of a menu item. Use the Style constants defined above. To combine Styles, declare a variable of type Style, then add the constants that will yield the desired combination:

```
Style  item_style;
item_style = bold + italic + shadow;

struct MenuInfo
{
    short    menuID;
    short    menuWidth;
    short    menuHeight;
    Handle   menuProc;
    long     enableFlags;
    Str255   menuData;
};

typedef  struct  MenuInfo  MenuInfo;
typedef  MenuInfo  *MenuPtr,  **MenuHandle;
```

As with a `WindowRecords` and `DialogRecords`, you'll seldom need direct access to any of the fields of a `MenuInfo`. You will instead use a `MenuHandle`.

Menu Allocation and Display

```
Handle  GetNewMBar( short  theMenuBarID );
```

`GetNewMBar()` creates a menu list, using the individual `MENU`'s specified in the `MBAR` resource with an ID of `theMenuBarID`. The list contains a handle to each individual menu that will appear in the menu bar. `GetNewMBar()` does not install the individual menus or display the menu bar.

```
void  SetMenuBar( Handle  theMenuList );
```

`SetMenuBar()` installs the individual menus in the menu bar specified by `theMenuList`. This handle should be the one returned by `GetNewMBar()`. The effect of `SetMenuBar()` is to make `theMenuList` the current menu list; a resource file can have more than one `MBAR` resource.

```
MenuHandle  GetMenuHandle( short  theMenuID );
```

`GetMenuHandle()` returns a handle to the `MENU` with a resource ID of `theMenuID`. You'll then be able to change characteristics of this menu and items in it using other Toolbox routines.

```
void  AppendResMenu( MenuHandle  theMenu,
                     ResType     theType );
```

`AppendResMenu()` locates all items of type `theType` and appends them to `theMenu`. For the Apple menu, `theType` should be `DRVR`. `AppendResMenu()` adds all the desk accessories in the user's system to the Apple menu. Under System 7, `AppendResMenu()` will also append all items located in the Apple Menu Items folder in the System Folder. The `MenuHandle theMenu` should be obtained with a call to `GetMenuHandle()`.

```
void  DrawMenuBar( void );
```

None of the preceding calls actually displays the menu bar on the screen. After a menu setup has been performed, call `DrawMenuBar()` to draw it.

Menu Selections

```
long  MenuSelect( Point theStartPt );
```

When an event is of `mouseDown` type, and it is further determined that the location of the mouse down was `inMenuBar`, call `MenuSelect()`. Pass the where field of the event as the `theStartPt`. `MenuSelect()` handles the dropping and displaying of menus as the user moves the mouse over the menu bar. Both the user-selected menu and menu item will be determined by `MenuSelect()` and saved in the returned `long` type.

```
long  MenuKey( short chr );
```

If a `keyDown` event occurs, and the **Command** key was pressed simultaneously, call `MenuKey()`. Given the typed character chr, `MenuKey()` will determine which menu and menu item this keystroke combination is equivalent to, and return it in the `long` type. The value returned by `MenuKey()` will be identical to that which `MenuSelect()` would return if the menu choice had been made with the mouse rather than with a Command-key equivalent.

Hierarchical Menus

```
MenuHandle  GetMenu( short  theMenuID );
```

When `GetNewMBar()` reads in the `MENU` descriptions of the menu that will appear in the menu bar, it takes note of submenu IDs but does not read in their descriptions. `GetMenu()` does this. The `theMenuID` is the ID of the `MENU` that represents the submenu of the hierarchical menu. Call `InsertMenu()` after calling `GetMenu()`.

```
void  InsertMenu( MenuHandle  theMenu,
                  short        theBeforeID );
```

After reading in the description of a submenu using GetMenu(), call InsertMenu() to insert the submenu into the menu list. The parameter theMenu should be the MenuHandle returned by GetMenu(). Assign theBeforeID a value of -1 to let the Menu Manager know this is a submenu rather than a menu in the menu bar.

Changing Menu Characteristics

```
void  SetMenuItemText( MenuHandle  theMenu,
                       short        theItem,
                       Str255       theStr );
```

SetMenuItemText() changes the text of menu item theItem in theMenu. The new text that will appear in the menu will be that of theStr. Use GetMenuHandle() to get a handle to the menu.

```
void  GetMenuItemText( MenuHandle  theMenu,
                       short        theItem,
                       Str255       theStr );
```

GetMenuItemText() gets the text of menu item theItem in theMenu and places it in the Str255 variable theStr. Use GetMenuHandle() to get a handle to the menu.

```
void  DisableItem( MenuHandle  theMenu,
                   short        theItem );
```

DisableItem() disables the menu item theItem in theMenu by dimming it and ignoring user attempts to select it. If theItem is given a value of zero, the entire menu will be disabled. The menu name in the menu bar, and all menu items in the menu, will become dim. Use GetMenuHandle() to get a handle to the menu. Use EnableItem() to enable a disabled menu or menu item.

```
void  EnableItem( MenuHandle  theMenu,
              short       theItem );
```

EnableItem( ) enables the menu item theItem in theMenu by highlighting the dimmed item. If theItem is given a value of zero, the entire menu will be enabled. The menu name in the menu bar and all menu items in the menu will be highlighted. Use GetMenuHandle( ) to get a handle to the menu. Use DisableItem( ) to disable an enabled menu or menu item.

```
void  CheckItem( MenuHandle  theMenu,
              short       theItem,
              Boolean     isChecked );
```

CheckItem( ) places a checkmark to the left of the text in theItem in theMenu, if isChecked is true. If isChecked is false, the checkmark will be removed from the left of that item. Attempting to check an already checked item has no effect. The same is true for an attempt to uncheck a menu item that has no checkmark by it. Use DisableItem( ) to disable an enabled menu or menu item. Use GetMenuHandle( ) to get a handle to the menu.

```
void  SetItemStyle( MenuHandle  theMenu,
                short       theItem,
                Style       theStyle );
```

The text of a menu item does not have to appear in its default style of plain. SetItemStyle( ) changes the style of the text of theItem in theMenu to that given by theStyle. The style can be one or any combination of Styles from the set listed in the Constants heading of this section. Use GetMenuHandle( ) to get a handle to the menu.

```
void  GetItemStyle( MenuHandle  theMenu,
                short       theItem,
                Style       *theStyle );
```

GetItemStyle( ) returns the Style of the text in theItem in theMenu. Use GetMenuHandle( ) to get a handle to the menu.

MEMORY

This section describes the important Toolbox routines that work with memory.

Memory Allocation

```
void  MaxApplZone( void );
```

At program startup the application's heap is set to a small size. If left in that state, it will grow as objects are loaded into it. For more efficient heap management, call MaxApplZone() at program startup to immediately increase the heap to its maximum size.

```
void  MoreMasters( void );
```

Master pointers are allocated in blocks. When your program starts up, the Memory Manager gives you one block. If, during the course of program execution, your program runs out of master pointers, the Memory Manager will place another block in memory. This can lead to fragmentation. Call MoreMasters() four or five times at the very start of your program to ensure that the Memory Manager doesn't do so later on.

```
Handle  NewHandle( Size  theNumBytes );
```

NewHandle() returns a handle to a relocatable block of memory. The size of the block is theNumBytes bytes.

```
void  DisposeHandle( Handle  theHandle );
```

DisposeHandle() frees the memory occuppied by the block accessed by theHandle. Once disposed of, any other existing handles that access this same block become invalid.

```
Ptr  NewPtr( Size  theNumBytes );
```

NewPtr() returns a pointer to a nonrelocatable block of memory. The size of the block is theNumBytes bytes.

```
void  DisposePtr( Ptr  thePtr );
```

`DisposePtr()` frees the memory occupied by the block accessed by `thePtr`. Any other existing pointers that point to this same block become invalid Once the memory is disposed of.

`void ExitToShell( void );`

Always check the result of a memory allocation. If the allocation fails, it will return a value of nil. To avoid a crash, call `ExitToShell()` at that point. A call to `ExitToShell()` prevents a frozen screen and allows your application to exit gracefully by releasing the application heap and returning the user to the Finder.

UTILITIES

This section describes the important general-purpose functions found in the Toolbox.

Constants

`#define    curSysEnvVers    2`

The `SysEnvirons()` routine returns information about the system of the machine on which your program is running. Use the constant `curSysEnvVers` in calls to `SysEnvirons()`. Should Apple update the `SysEnvirons()` over time, the `curSysEnvVers` value will be changed and your calls can remain unchanged.

```
#define    envMac            -1
#define    envXL             -2
#define    envMachUnknown    0
#define    env512KE          1
#define    envMacPlus        2
#define    envSE             3
#define    envMacII          4
#define    envMacIIx         5
#define    envMacIIcx        6
#define    envSE30           7
```

```
#define    envPortable      8
#define    envMacIIci       9
#define    envMacIIfx      11
```

SysEnvirons() fills the fields of a SysEnvRec. Those fields are given below in the SysEnvRec structure listing. You may find the machineType field the most important. You can check the value of that field at program start up. If the returned value indicates that your program is running on a machine that is too old (as determined by you), you may wish to exit the program. Information from all of the other fields can be better obtained by a call to Gestalt(), which is described later in this section and throughout this book.

```
#define    iBeamCursor      1
#define    crossCursor      2
#define    plusCursor       3
#define    watchCursor      4
```

The standard arrow-shaped cursor can be changed to any one of four system-defined cursors using calls to GetCursor() and SetCursor(). Use one of the above constants in the call to GetCursor().

Data Structures

```
struct SysEnvRec
{
    short    environsVersion;
    short    machineType;
    short    systemVersion;
    short    processor;
    Boolean  hasFPU;
    Boolean  hasColorQD;
    short    keyBoardType;
    short    atDrvrVersNum;
    short    sysVRefNum;
};

typedef struct SysEnvRec SysEnvRec;
```

A call to SysEnvirons() fills a SysEnvRec with system information about the Macintosh on which your program is currently running. In most cases, you'll want to use the newer Gestalt() Toolbox function, which provides more information. On Macintoshes running older system software, however, Gestalt() may not be available.

```
struct Cursor
{
    Bits16 data;
    Bits16 mask;
    Point hotSpot;
};

typedef  struct  Cursor  Cursor;
typedef  Cursor  *CursPtr,  **CursHandle;
```

The system defines five cursors. You won't have to access fields of the Cursor structure itself. Instead, you use GetCursor() to receive a CursHandle with which to work.

System Features

```
OSErr  SysEnvirons( short        theVersion,
                    SysEnvRec *theSysEnvRec );
```

A call to SysEnvirons() fills the SysEnvRec theSysEnvRec with system information about the machine currently running your program. Set version equal to the constant curSysEnvVers. You can then examine fields of the SysEnvRec. The SysEnvRec structure is given under the Data Structures heading of this section.

```
OSErr  Gestalt( OSType  theSelector,
                long    *theResponse );
```

```
long  NGetTrapAddress( short      theTrapNum,
                       TrapType  theTrapType );
```

When passed trap number trap_num and the type of trap, trap_type, NGetTrapAddress() returns the address of the trap, or routine. To test for the availability of a Toolbox routine, call NGetTrapAddress() twice. On the first call, set theTrapNum to the trap number of the routine in question. On the second call, set theTrapNum to the unimplemented trap number. If the returned results of both calls are not equal, the trap exists and it is safe to call that routine.

Extracting Information From Long Ints

```
short  HiWord( long theLongNum );
```

HiWord( ) returns the high-order 16 bits of the 32-bit theLongNum.

```
short  LoWord( long theLongNum );
```

LoWord( ) returns the low-order 16 bits of the 32-bit theLongNum.

Causing a Delay

```
void  Delay( long  theNumTicks,
             long *theTotalTicks );
```

Delay( ) pauses your program for theNumTicks ticks. A single tick is one sixtieth of a second. When the pause is completed, theTotalTicks will be filled in with the number of ticks from system startup to the end of the delay.

Don't attempt to use a loop, as in:

```
for ( i=0; i<10000; i++ )
    ; /* do nothing, just killing time */
```

Rather, use the Delay( ) routine. A loop is processor dependent; That is, a loop will execute more quickly on a faster processor. The Delay( ) routine is processor independent its delay effect is the same on all CPUs.

Cursors

```
CursHandle  GetCursor( short  theCursorID );
```

GetCursor( ) loads the CURS resource specified by theCursorID into memory and returns a CursHandle to it. It does not display the cursor. Use SetCursor( ) for that.

```
void  SetCursor( Cursor  *theCursorHandle );
```

SetCursor() changes the shape of the cursor to that specified by the cursor. First call GetCursor() to get theCursorHandle. Dereference that handle once to get a pointer to a cursor, as required by SetCursor().

```
void  InitCursor( void );
```

InitCursor() sets the cursor to the familiar arrow shape. You do not have to call GetCursor() first.

Loading Resources

```
Handle  GetResource( ResType  theType,
                      short    theID );
```

GetResource() returns a generic handle to the resource with a resource ID of theID. The parameter theType can be any resource type. Include single quotes around the type, as in this call that loads a sound resource with an ID of 9000:

```
GetResource( 'snd ', 9000 );
```

Sound

This section describes the Sound Manager routines covered in this book.

```
#include <Sound.h>
```

Playing a Sound

```
OSErr  SndPlay( SndChannelPtr  theChannel,
                Handle         theHandle,
                Boolean        async );
```

SndPlay() plays a snd resource that has been loaded into memory. First call GetResource() using 'snd ' as the first parameter and the resource ID of the snd as the second parameter. GetResource() will return a handle to the sound; use this as theHandle. Depending on what version of compiler you're using, you may have to typecast this second parameter to a SndListHandle—as in (SndListHandle)theHandle. Pass a value of true for async if this is the only sound that will be playing (asynchronous) or false if there will be multiple sounds playing at the same time (synchronous). See the Utilities section of this appendix for information on GetResource().

Note that your snd resource should have a resource ID greater than 8192 so that it won't conflict with Apple's reserved 'snd ' resource numbering 0 to 8191.

MACINTOSH PROGRAMMING TECHNIQUES, 2E

Index

B

BeginUpdate() Toolbox function, 187-189, 234, 522, 596
bitmapped graphics
    defined, 4
    text-based, vs., 4
BNDL resource
    creating, 531-532
    defined, 19, 530
Borland Resource Workshop resource editor, 13
Button(), 591

C

Calande, John J., 148
Canvas graphics program, 137
CautionAlert() Toolbox function, 246, 600
CDEF resource, 100
CheckItem() Toolbox function, 336-338, 607
CGrafPort data type, 114, 561
CloseDialog(), 597-598
CloseWindow() Toolbox function, 238, 593
CODE resource,
    defined, 19
    loading, 93-94
    PowerPC applications and, 449
color, pixel representation, 493-494
Control Strip software, 502
ControlHandle data type, 258, 303, 561
ColorSwitch utility, 502
crossCursor Apple-defined constant, 154
CurHandle data type, 154, 562
CURS resource
    arrow cursor, 154-155
    crossCursor Apple-defined constant, 154
    CurHandle data type, 154
    defined, 154
    GetCursor() Toolbox function, 154
    iBeamCursor Apple-defined constant, 154
    loading, 154
    plusCursor Apple-defined constant, 154

SetCursor() Toolbox function, 154, 155-157
    watchCursor Apple-defined constant, 154-155
Cursor data type, 561
cursor *see* CURS resource

D

debuggers, 94, 218-225
decimal numbers, converting, 226
Delay() Toolbox function, 147, 612
desktop, rebuilding, 541-542
dialog boxes
    checkboxes, 258
    defined, 241
    DialogPtr data type, 261-262
    DialogRecord data type, 260-262
    DialogSelect() Toolbox function, 267-269
    editable text boxes, 256-258
    enabling items in, 251
    FrontWindow() Toolbox function, 267
    GetControlValue() Toolbox function, 258
    GetDialogItem() Toolbox function, 255-256, 258
    GetDialogItemText() Toolbox function, 256-257
    GetNewDialog() Toolbox function, 255, 262, 265
    icons in, 252-254
    IsDialogEvent() Toolbox function, 267-268
    item information, 255-256
    items in, 244, 247-249
    loading to memory, 255
    memory, reserving, 265-266
    modal, 246, 260-265, 344-352
    ModalDialog() Toolbox function, 263-265, 346-352
    modeless, 246, 265-269
    pictures in, 249-252
    radio buttons, 259-260
    resources, 247-255
    SetControlValue() Toolbox function, 258, 259
    StringToNum() Toolbox function, 257

About This CD

The CD-ROM included with this book contains several folders. To copy the contents of any folder to your hard drive, simply select the folder on the CD and drag it to your hard drive's icon on the desktop of your Mac.

The first of the folders, Book Examples Projects, itself contains three folders. One holds Metrowerks CodeWarrior versions of each of the example projects discussed in the book. A second folder has Symantec C++ versions of each example, while the third folder contains THINK C versions. You'll only need to make use of one of these three folders—the one that holds the projects that are for your compiler. Make sure to copy the one appropriate folder to your hard drive—your compiler won't be able to work with the projects properly if they are on the CD. You won't need the other two project folders—you can save space on your hard drive by not copying these folders.

The next three folders, the Utilities folder, contains a handful of useful programming utility programs such as Swatch, the memory-watching program. Swatch displays the contents of memory for every program that is running on your Mac—including programs you write.

A third folder on the CD contains a tutorial program named In Action! Mac Techniques. Through the use of text, graphics, and animations, this program demonstrates many of the programming techniques discussed in the Macintosh Programming Techniques book. To use In Action! Mac Techniques, copy the entire In Action! Tutorial folder to your Mac's hard drive.

Also on the CD is a limited version of the Power Mac compiler for Symantec C++ for the Macintosh. While you cannot create new projects with this compiler, you can use it to compile and play with existing projects. Symantec C++ is the leading compiler for the Macintosh, and we hope you enjoy a chance to experiment with version 8 before you buy it.